VIZ GRAPHIC NOVEL

OGRE SLAYER ™
LOVE'S BITTER FRUIT

This volume contains the OGRE SLAYER installments from MANGA VIZION Vol. 2, No. 6, 7, 10, and 11 and Vol. 3, No. 4, 5, and 8 in their entirety.

STORY AND ART BY KEI KUSUNOKI

English Adaptation/Fred Burke & Shuko Shikata
Touch-Up Art & Lettering/Bill Spicer
Cover Design/Hidemi Sahara
Editor/Annette Roman

Managing Editor/Hyoe Narita
Editor-in-Chief/Satoru Fujii
Publisher/Seiji Horibuchi

Printed in Canada

Published by Viz Communications, Inc.
P.O. Box 77010 • San Francisco, CA 94107

10 9 8 7 6 5 4 3 2 1
First printing, February 1998

Vizit us at our World Wide Web site at **www.viz.com** and our new Internet magazine, **j-pop.com**, at **www.j-pop.com**!

OGRE SLAYER GRAPHIC NOVELS TO DATE
OGRE SLAYER
LOVE'S BITTER FRUIT

VIZ GRAPHIC NOVEL

OGRE SLAYER ™
LOVE'S BITTER FRUIT

STORY AND ART BY
KEI KUSUNOKI

CONTENTS

HUNT ONE
THE WAY OF WISDOM

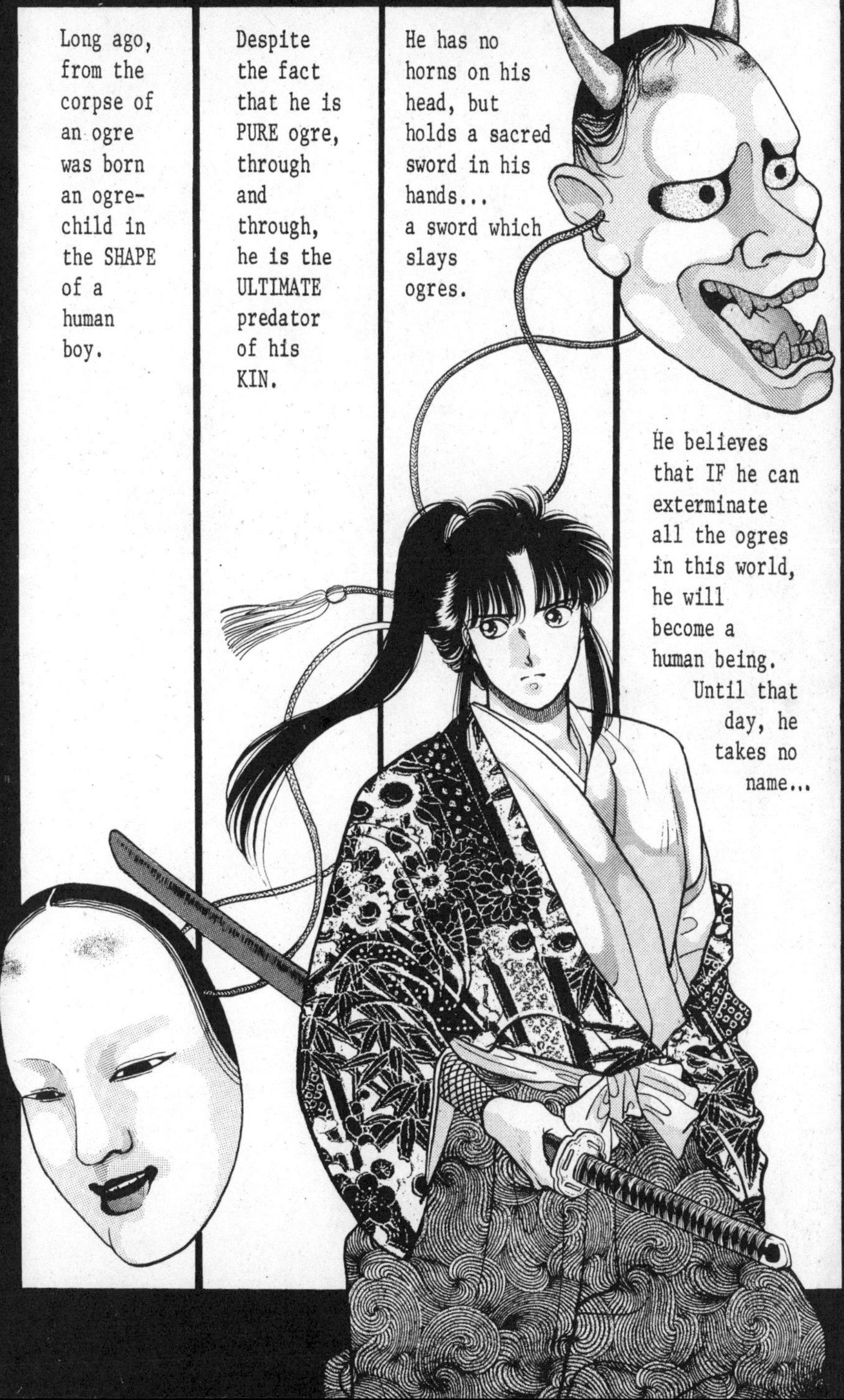
Long ago, from the corpse of an ogre was born an ogre-child in the SHAPE of a human boy.
Despite the fact that he is PURE ogre, through and through, he is the ULTIMATE predator of his KIN.
He has no horns on his head, but holds a sacred sword in his hands... a sword which slays ogres.
He believes that IF he can exterminate all the ogres in this world, he will become a human being.
Until that day, he takes no name...

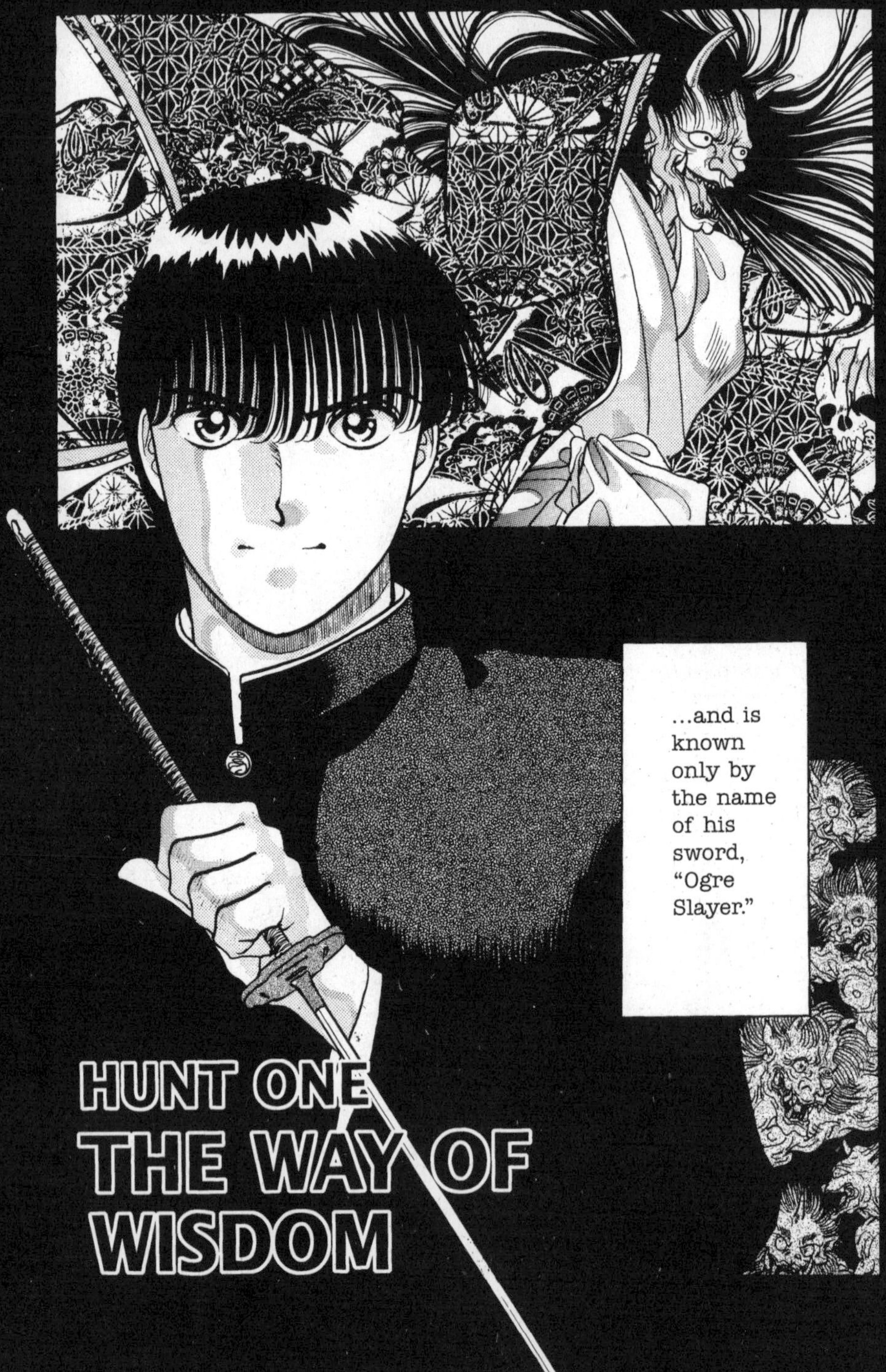
...and is known only by the name of his sword, "Ogre Slayer."
HUNT ONE
THE WAY OF WISDOM

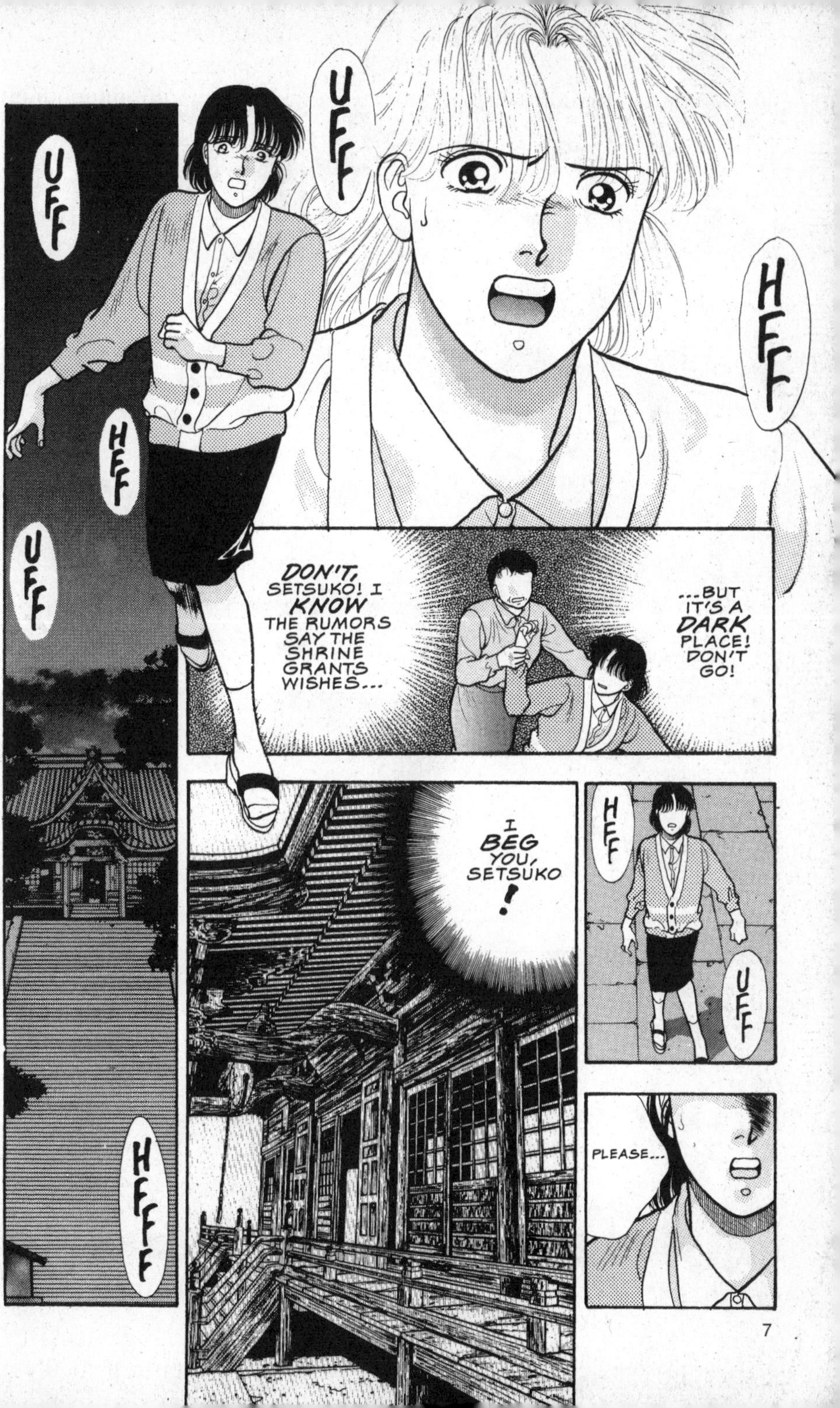
UFF
HFF
UFF
HFFF
UFF
HFF
DON'T, SETSUKO! I KNOW THE RUMORS SAY THE SHRINE GRANTS WISHES...
...BUT IT'S A DARK PLACE! DON'T GO!
I BEG YOU, SETSUKO!
HFF
UFF
PLEASE...

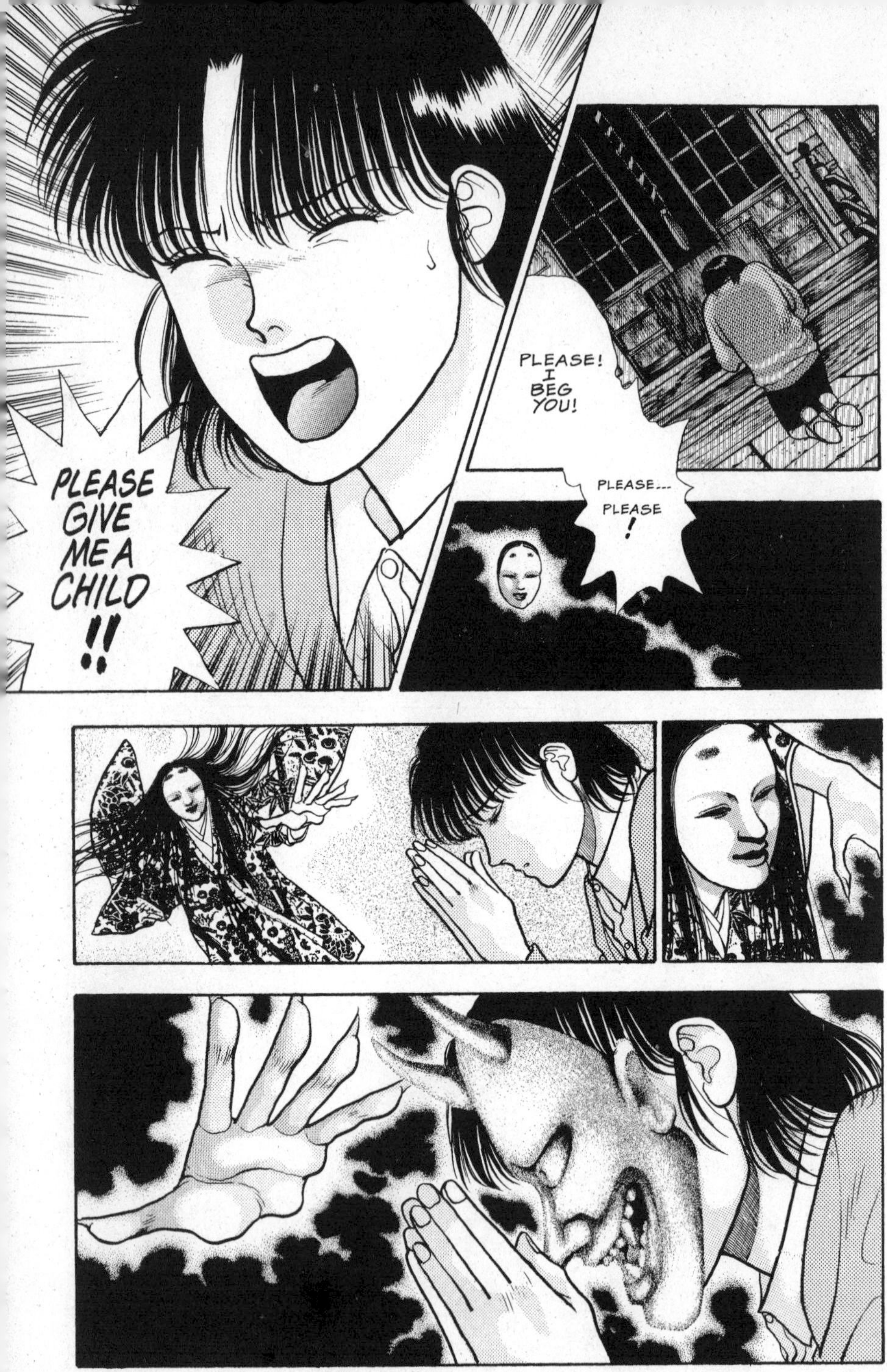
PLEASE GIVE ME A CHILD !!
PLEASE! I BEG YOU!
PLEASE... PLEASE!

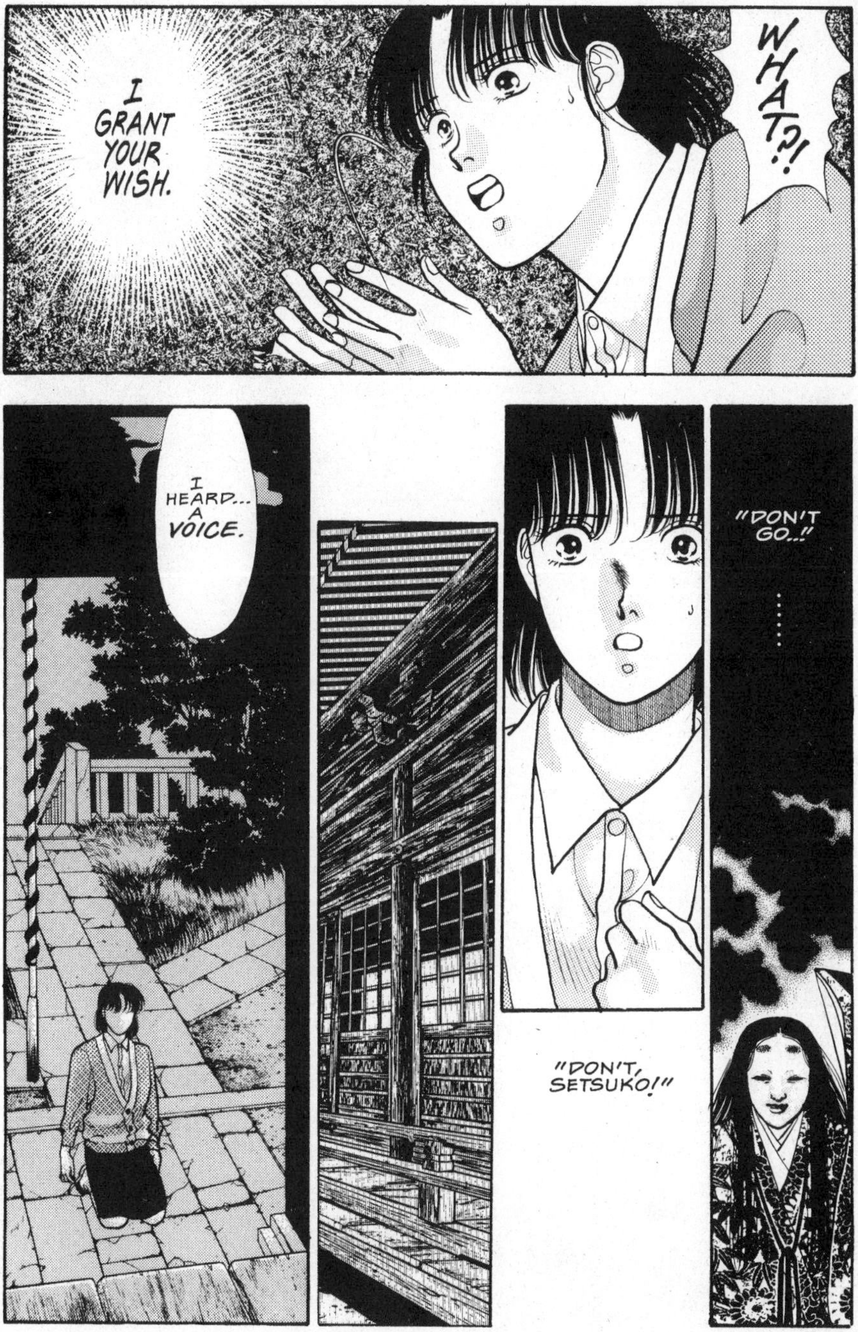
I GRANT YOUR WISH.
WHAT?!
I HEARD... A VOICE.
"DON'T, SETSUKO!"
"DON'T GO..!"
......

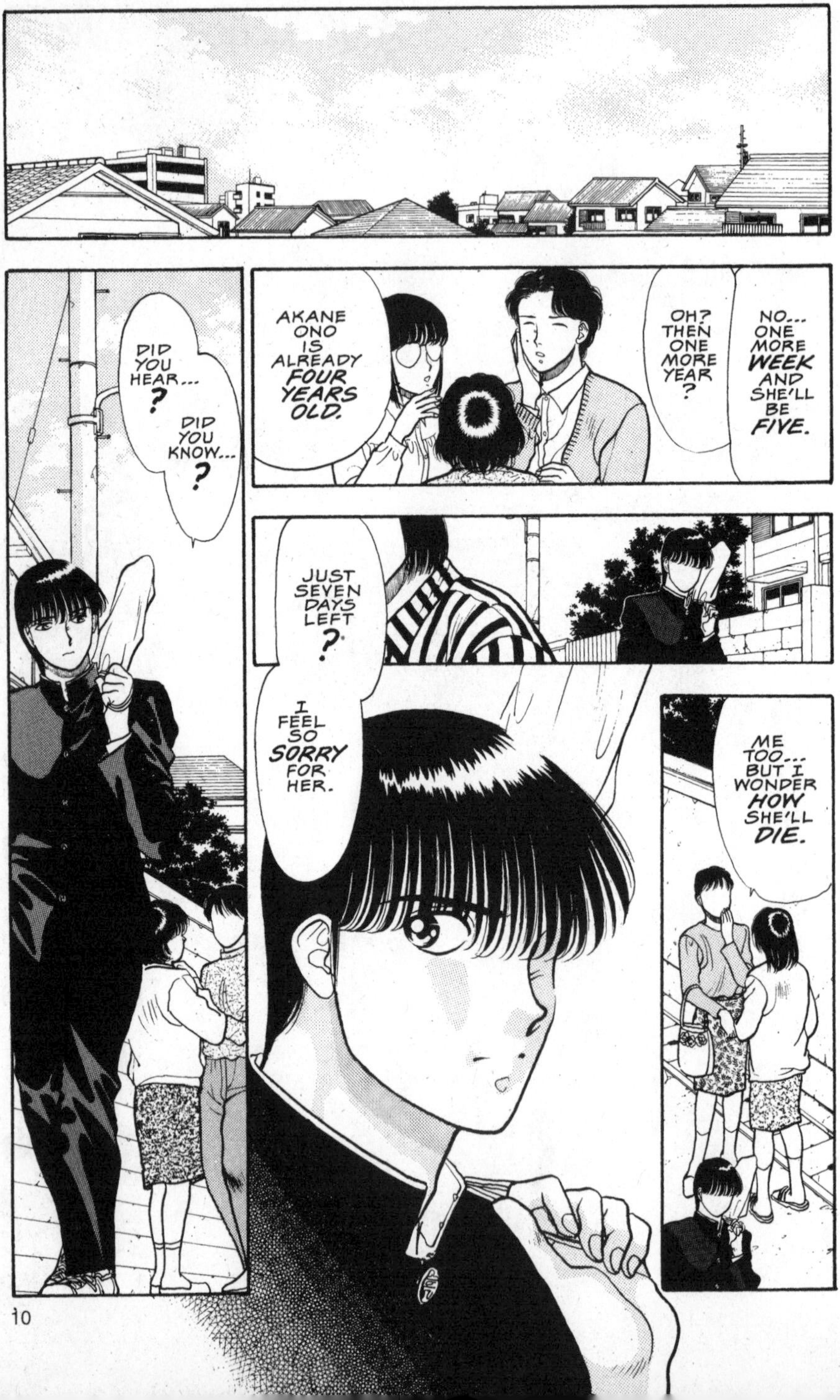
DID YOU HEAR...?
DID YOU KNOW...?
AKANE ONO IS ALREADY FOUR YEARS OLD.
OH? THEN ONE MORE YEAR?
NO... ONE MORE WEEK AND SHE'LL BE FIVE.
JUST SEVEN DAYS LEFT?
I FEEL SO SORRY FOR HER.
ME TOO... BUT I WONDER HOW SHE'LL DIE.

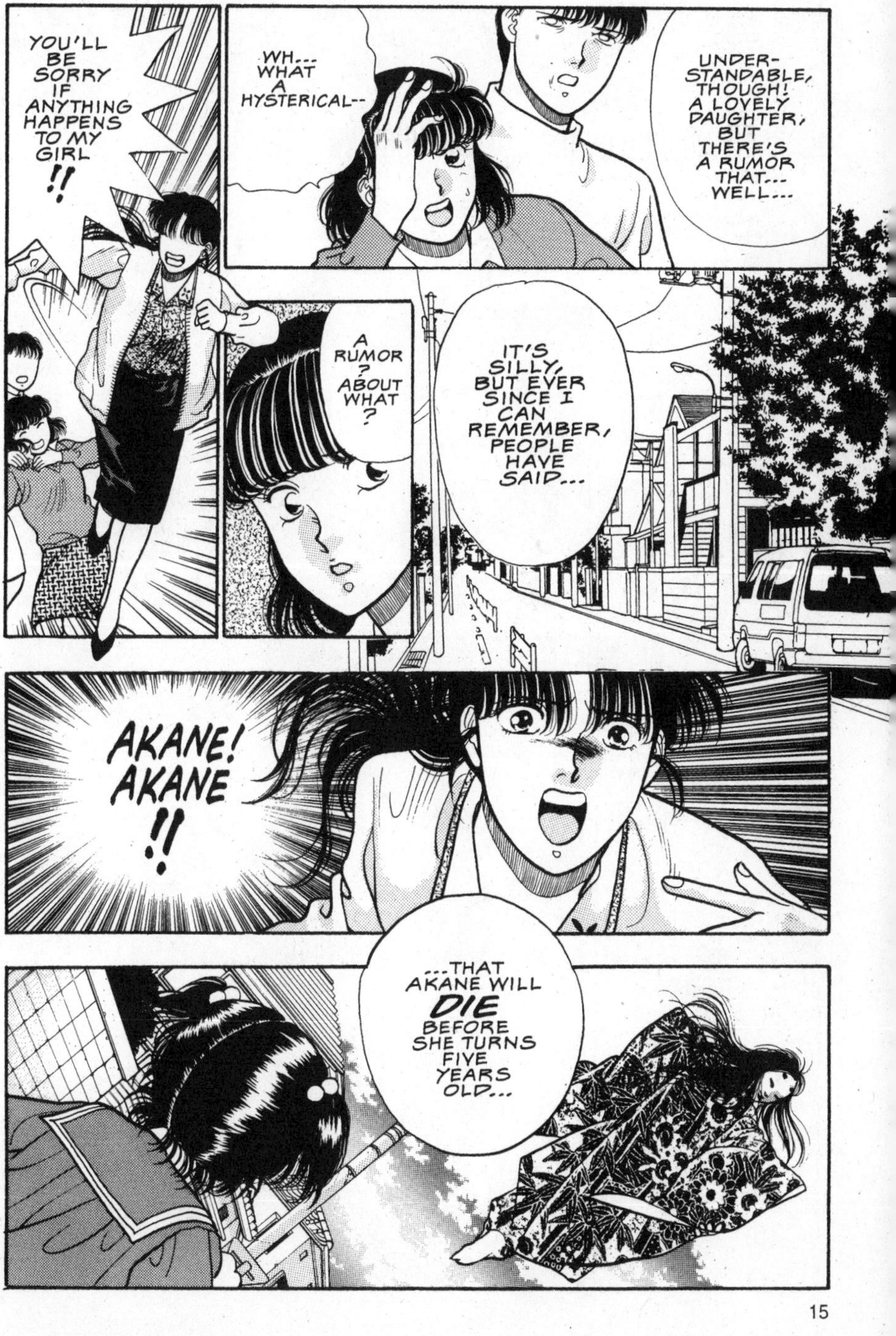

YOU'LL BE SORRY IF ANYTHING HAPPENS TO MY GIRL !!
WH... WHAT A HYSTERICAL--
UNDER-STANDABLE, THOUGH! A LOVELY DAUGHTER, BUT THERE'S A RUMOR THAT... WELL...
A RUMOR? ABOUT WHAT?
IT'S SILLY, BUT EVER SINCE I CAN REMEMBER, PEOPLE HAVE SAID...
AKANE! AKANE !!
...THAT AKANE WILL DIE BEFORE SHE TURNS FIVE YEARS OLD...

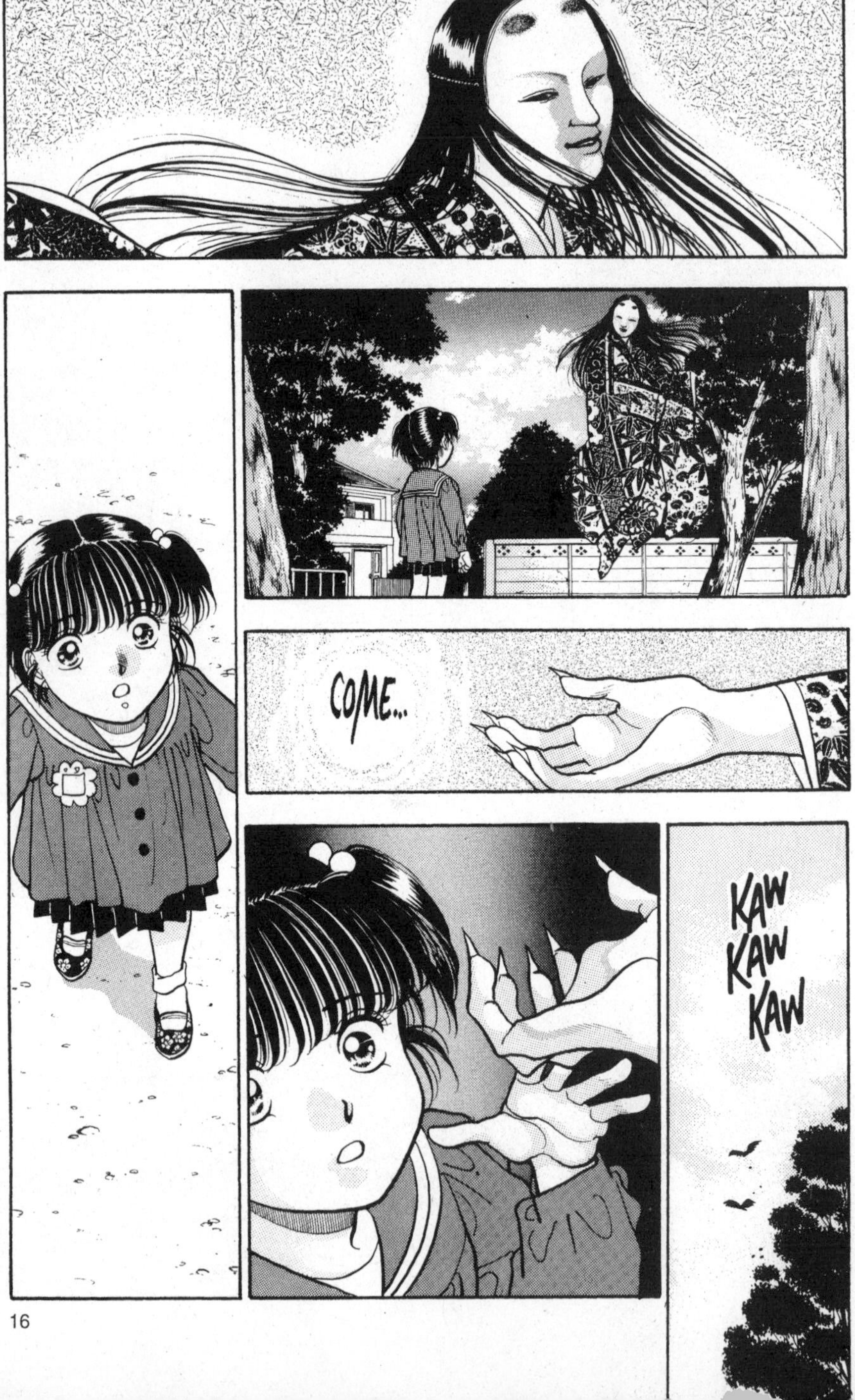
COME...
KAW
KAW
KAW

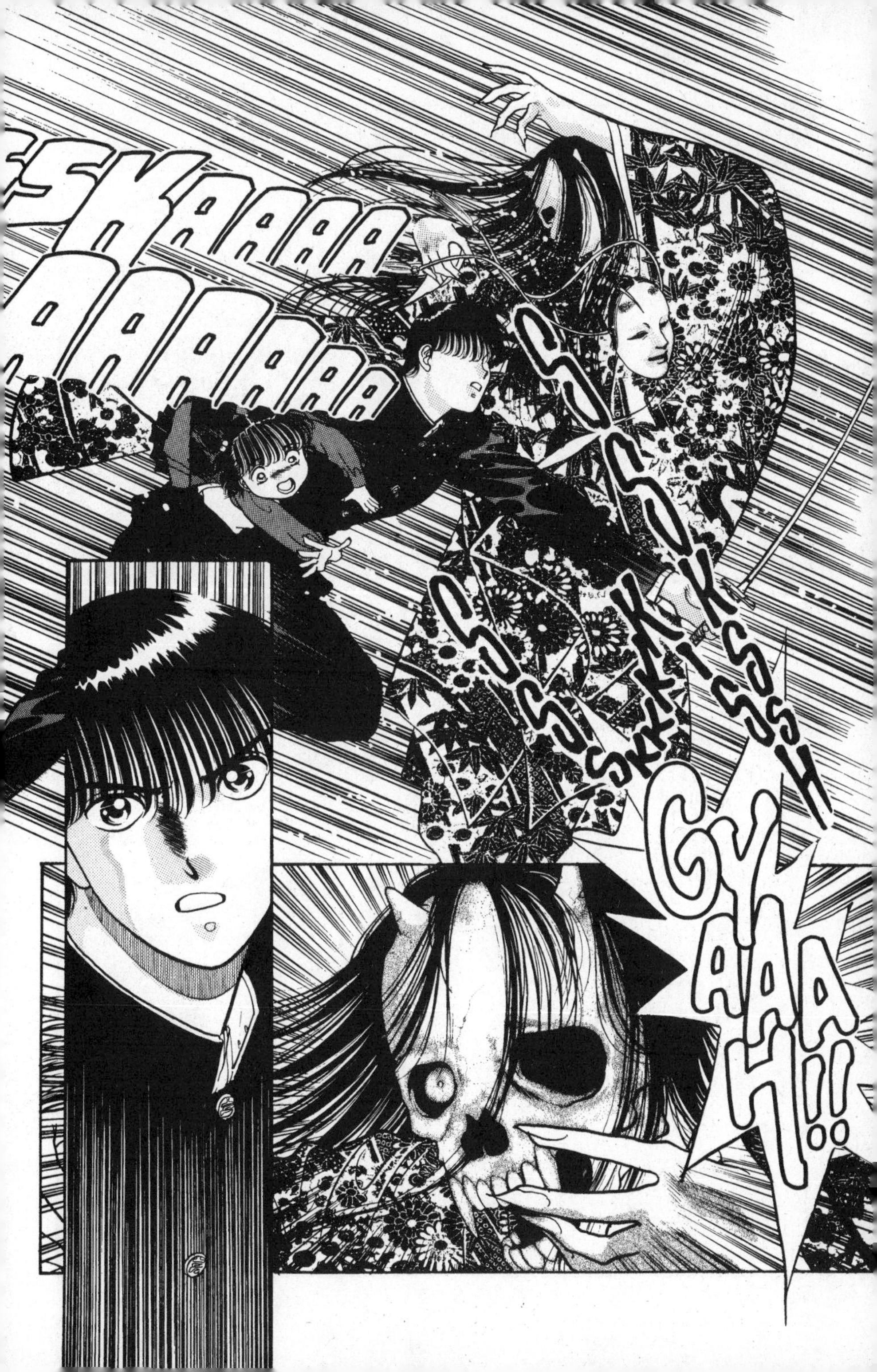
SHAAAA
AAAAAA
GYAAAH!!

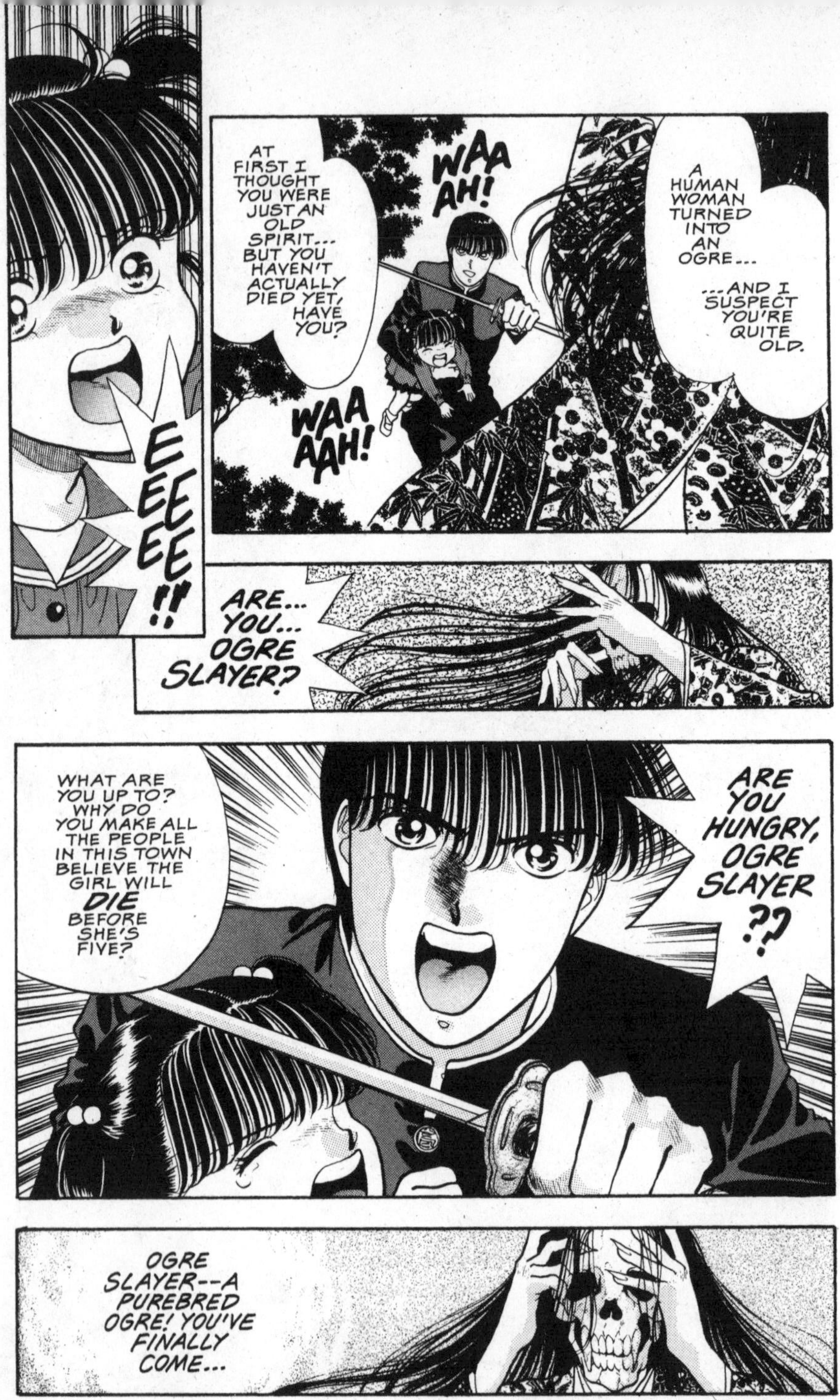
EEEEE!!
AT FIRST I THOUGHT YOU WERE JUST AN OLD SPIRIT... BUT YOU HAVEN'T ACTUALLY DIED YET, HAVE YOU?
WAA AH!
WAA AAH!
A HUMAN WOMAN TURNED INTO AN OGRE...
...AND I SUSPECT YOU'RE QUITE OLD.
ARE... YOU... OGRE SLAYER?
WHAT ARE YOU UP TO? WHY DO YOU MAKE ALL THE PEOPLE IN THIS TOWN BELIEVE THE GIRL WILL *DIE* BEFORE SHE'S FIVE?
ARE YOU HUNGRY, OGRE SLAYER??
OGRE SLAYER--A PUREBRED OGRE! YOU'VE FINALLY COME...

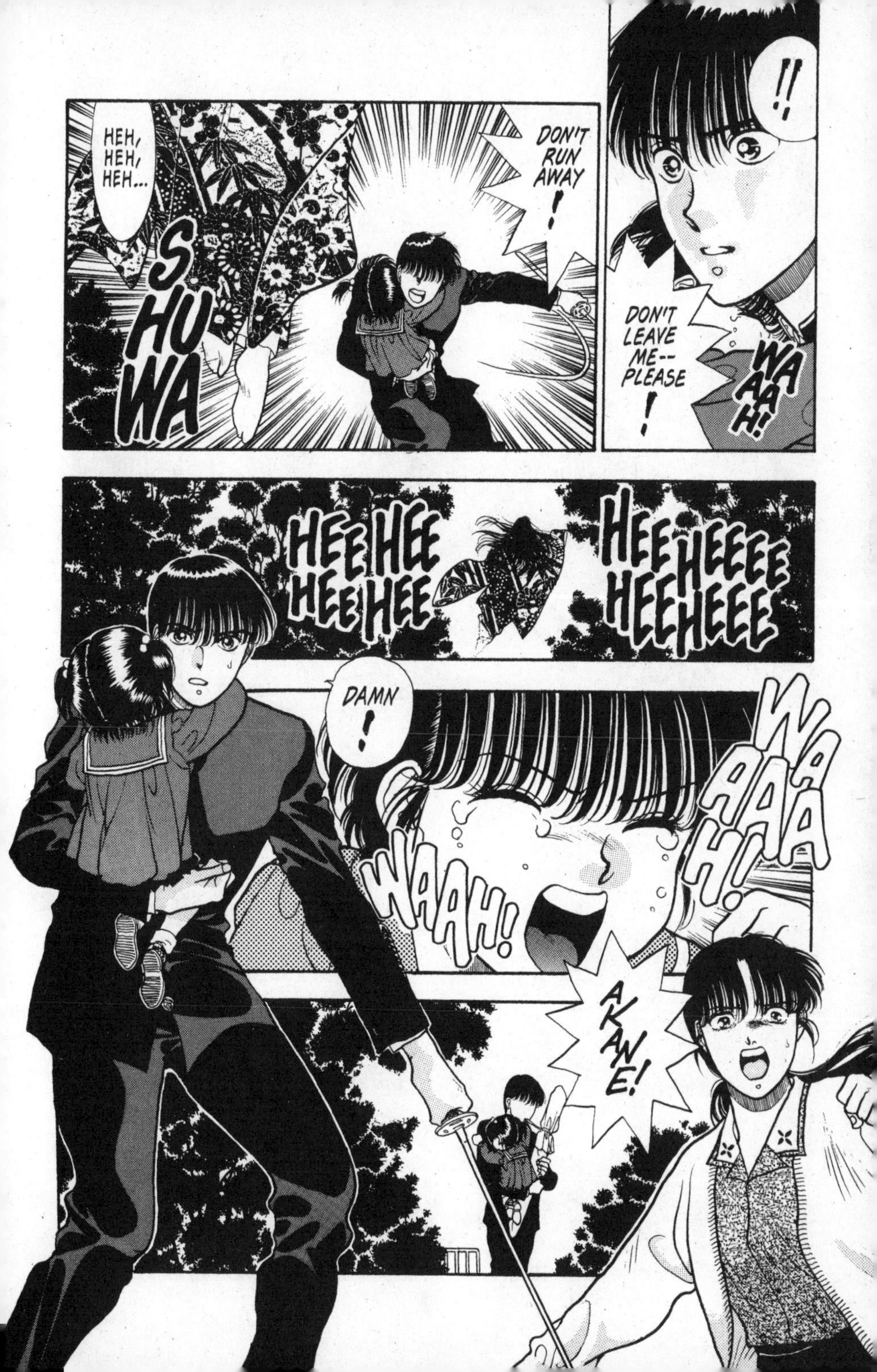
HEH, HEH, HEH...
SHUWA
DON'T RUN AWAY!
!!
DON'T LEAVE ME--PLEASE!
WAAAH!
HEE HEE HEE HEE
HEE HEEEEE HEE HEEE
DAMN!
WAAH!
WAAAAH!
AKANE!

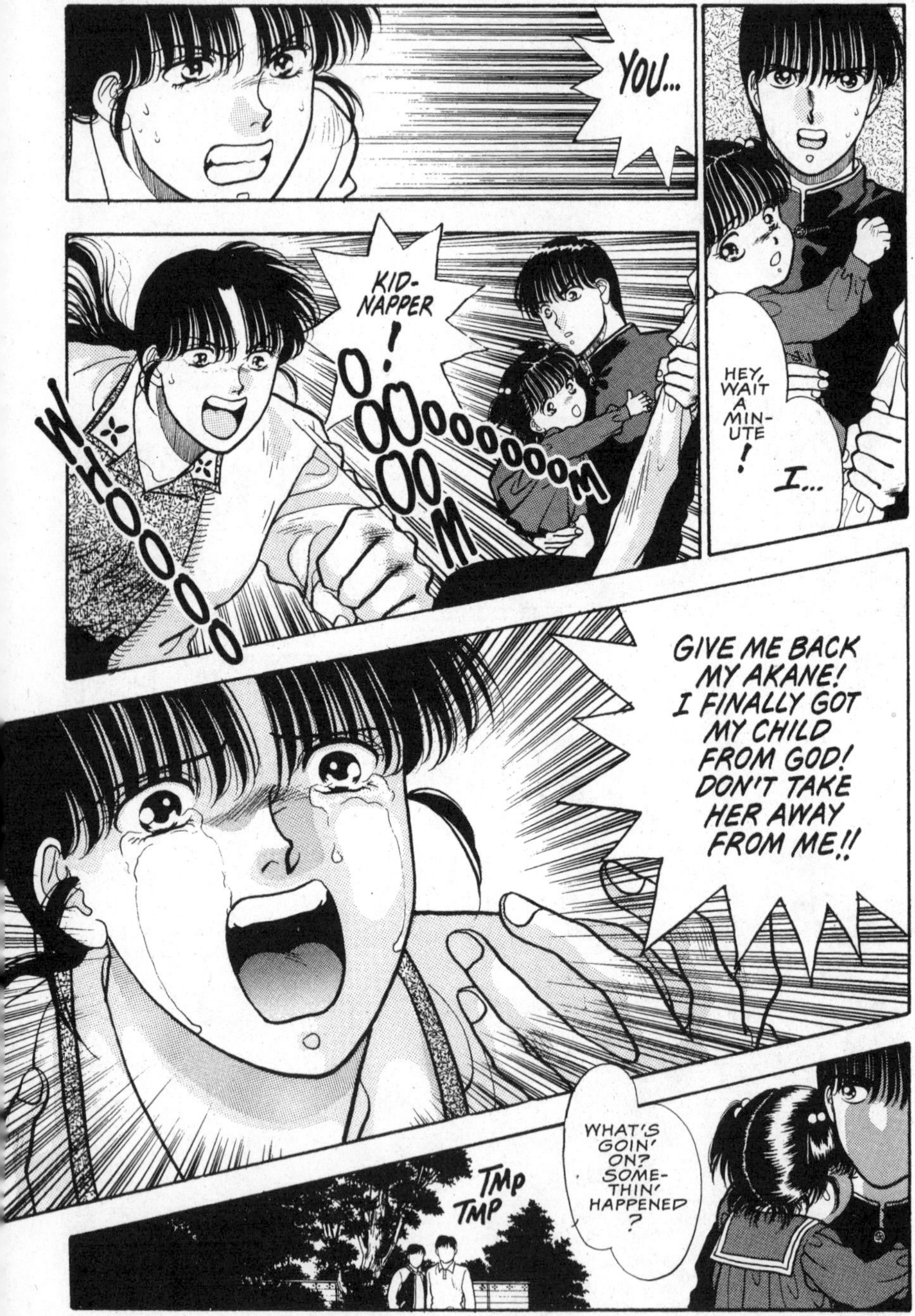
YOU...
KID-NAPPER!
WHOOOOOO
OOOOOOOOOOM
HEY, WAIT A MINUTE!
I...
GIVE ME BACK MY AKANE! I FINALLY GOT MY CHILD FROM GOD! DON'T TAKE HER AWAY FROM ME!!
TMP TMP
WHAT'S GOIN' ON? SOMETHIN' HAPPENED?

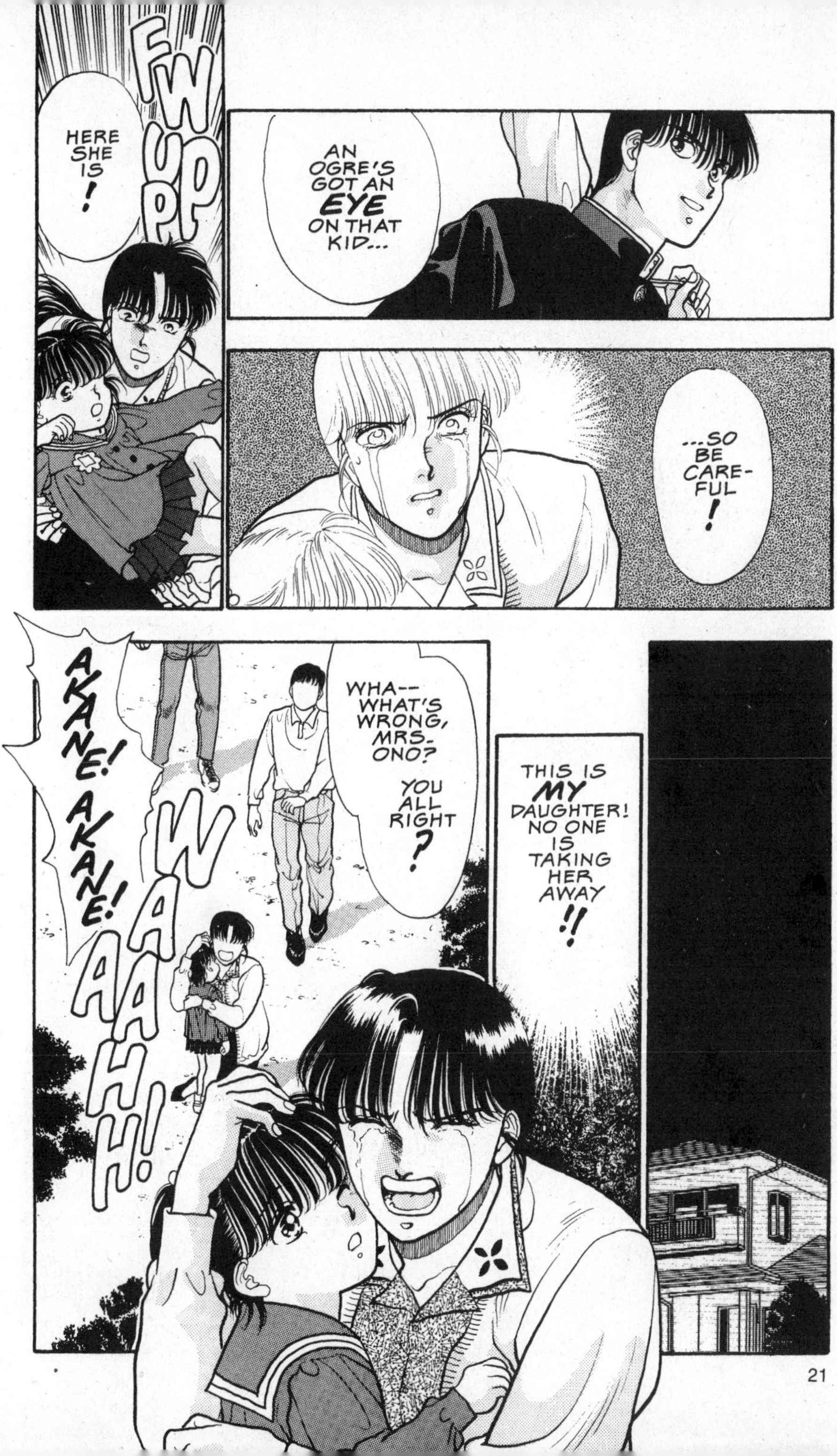
FWUPP
HERE SHE IS!
AN OGRE'S GOT AN EYE ON THAT KID...
...SO BE CAREFUL!
AKANE! AKANE! AKANE!
WAAAAHH!
WHA-- WHAT'S WRONG, MRS. ONO?
YOU ALL RIGHT?
THIS IS MY DAUGHTER! NO ONE IS TAKING HER AWAY!!

I HEARD YOU PANICKED AGAIN TODAY.

ALWAYS OVER-REACTING. IT'S SO EMBARRASSING.

WHAT DO YOU MEAN, "OVER-REACTING"? SHE'S OUR **CHILD!**

THIS IS ALL YOUR **MOTHER'S** FAULT...

DON'T, SETSUKO! IT'S A **DARK** PLACE...!

THE GIFTS OF THE SHRINE--THEY **WITHER** AND **DIE!** DON'T GO!

YOUR MOTHER BELIEVED THAT DUMB RUMOR...

...AND HER WHISPERING SPREAD IT TO **EVERYONE!**

DON'T SPEAK ILL OF THE DEAD! SHE TRIED TO STOP YOU!

IF I HADN'T GONE, WE WOULDN'T HAVE AKANE!

A COINCIDENCE!

BAM

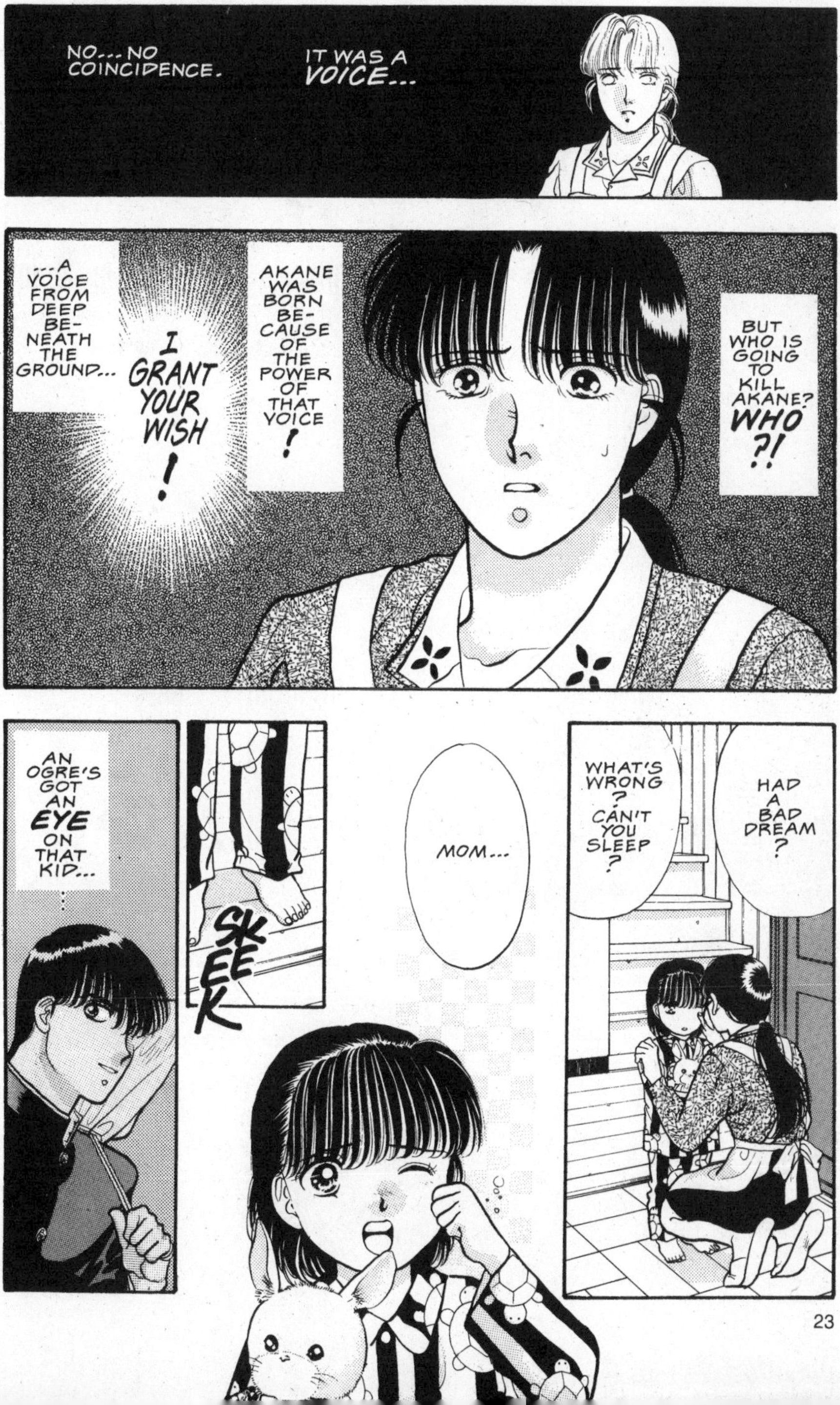

NO... NO COINCIDENCE.
IT WAS A VOICE...
...A VOICE FROM DEEP BENEATH THE GROUND...
I GRANT YOUR WISH!
AKANE WAS BORN BECAUSE OF THE POWER OF THAT VOICE!
BUT WHO IS GOING TO KILL AKANE? WHO?!
AN OGRE'S GOT AN EYE ON THAT KID...
SKEEK
MOM...
WHAT'S WRONG? CAN'T YOU SLEEP?
HAD A BAD DREAM?

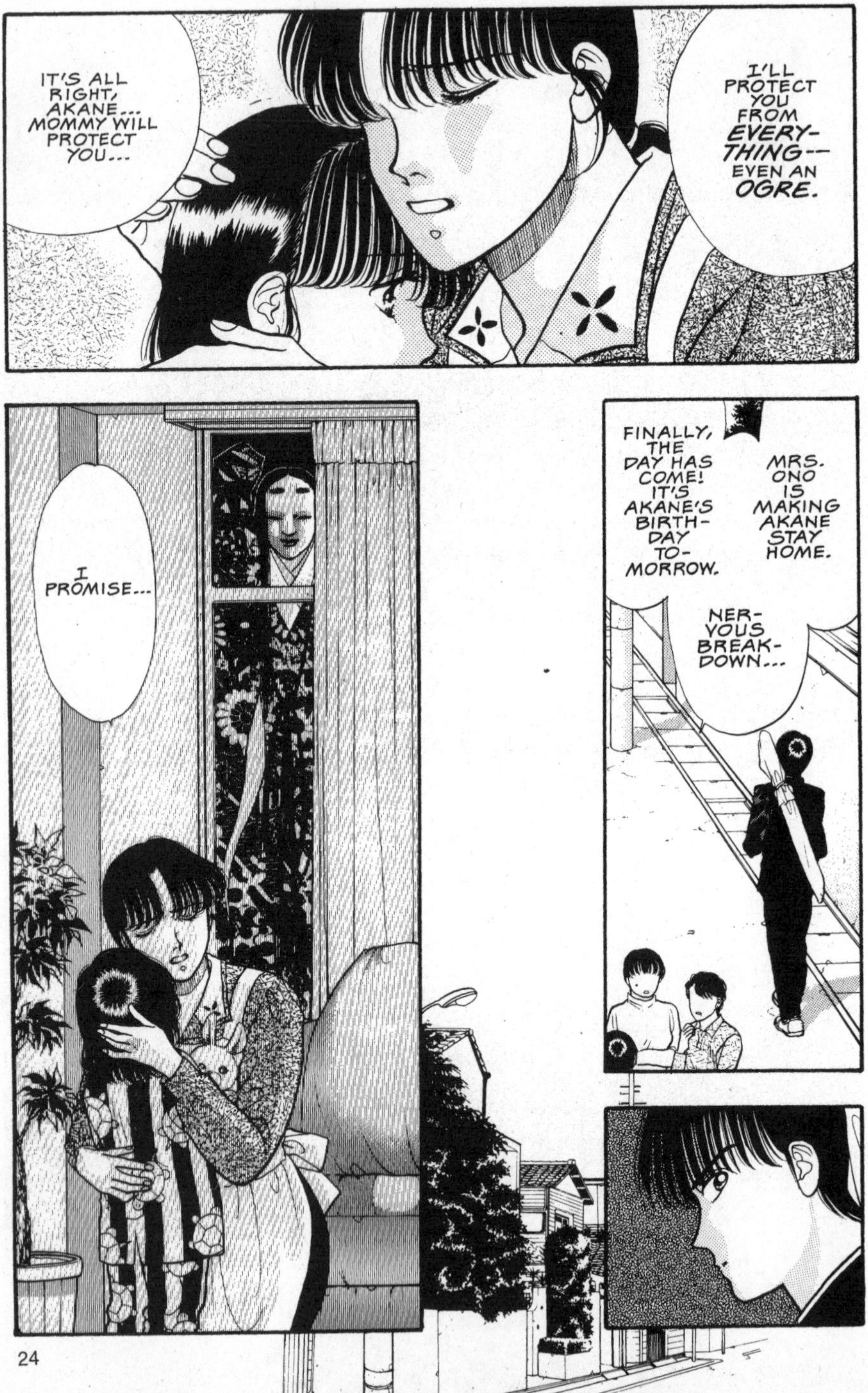

IT'S ALL RIGHT, AKANE... MOMMY WILL PROTECT YOU...
I'LL PROTECT YOU FROM EVERYTHING-- EVEN AN OGRE.
I PROMISE...
FINALLY, THE DAY HAS COME! IT'S AKANE'S BIRTHDAY TOMORROW.
MRS. ONO IS MAKING AKANE STAY HOME.
NERVOUS BREAKDOWN...

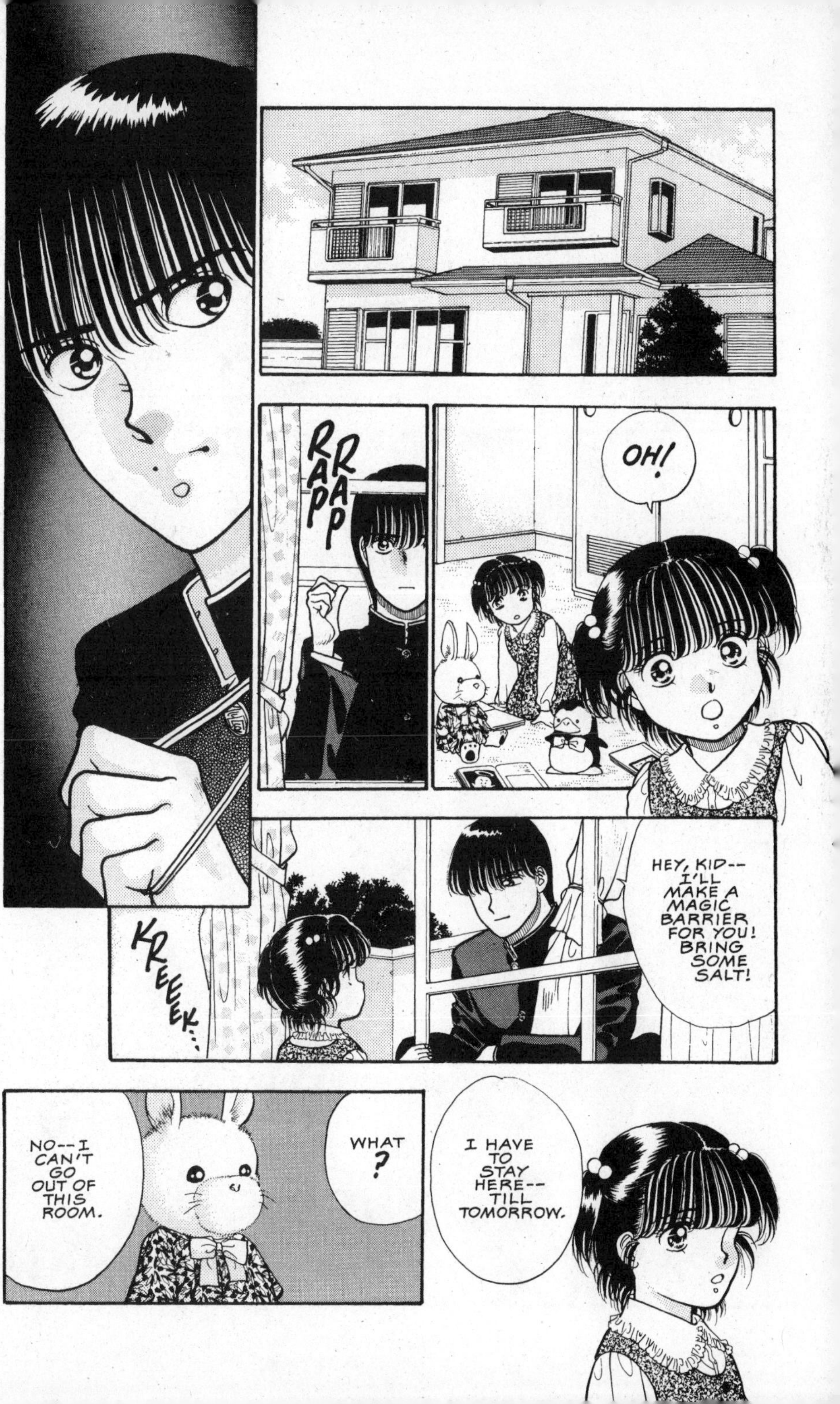
RAP RAP
OH!
KREEEEK...
HEY, KID-- I'LL MAKE A MAGIC BARRIER FOR YOU! BRING SOME SALT!
NO-- I CAN'T GO OUT OF THIS ROOM.
WHAT?
I HAVE TO STAY HERE-- TILL TOMORROW.

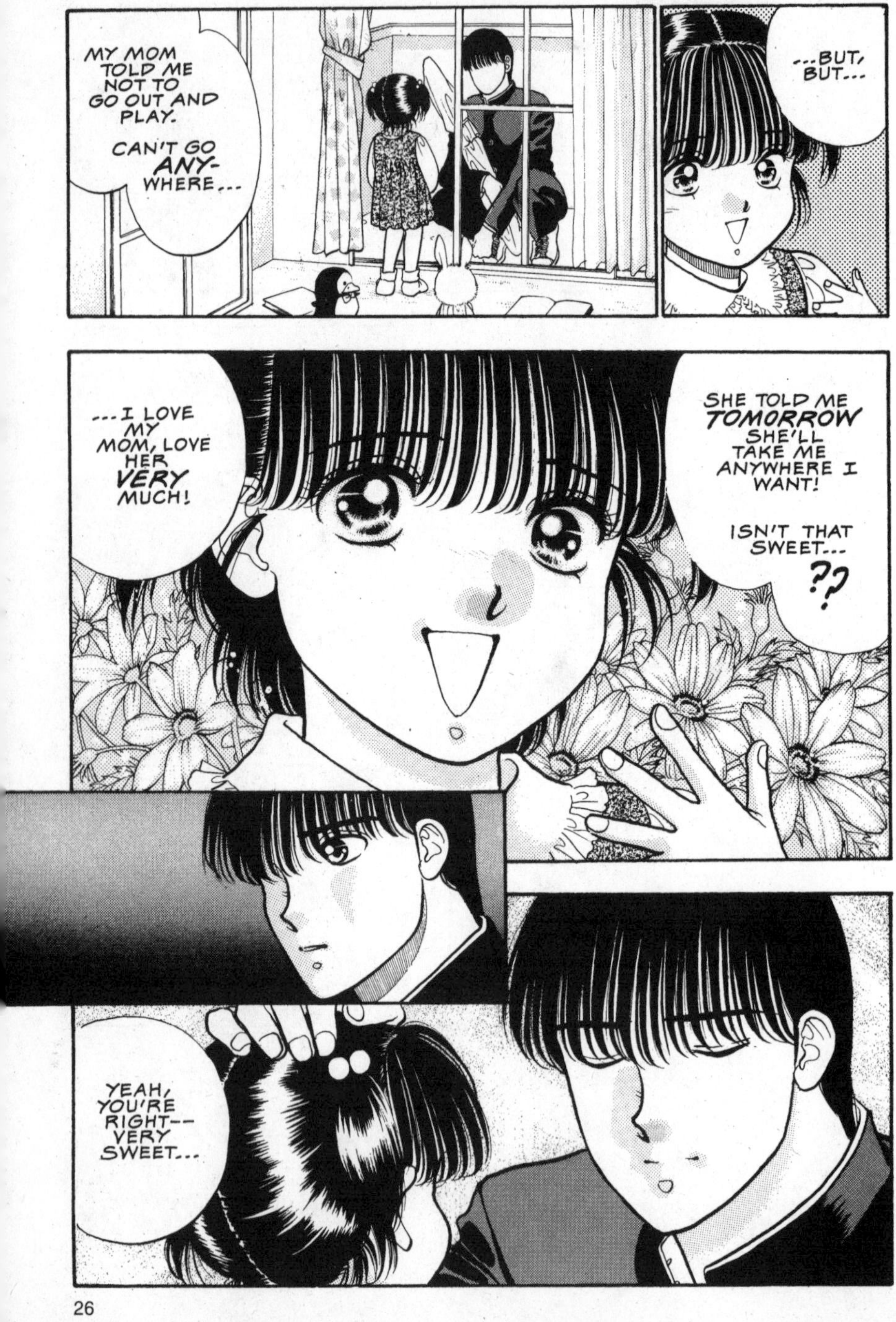
MY MOM TOLD ME NOT TO GO OUT AND PLAY.
CAN'T GO ANY-WHERE...
...BUT, BUT...
...I LOVE MY MOM, LOVE HER VERY MUCH!
SHE TOLD ME TOMORROW SHE'LL TAKE ME ANYWHERE I WANT!
ISN'T THAT SWEET... ??
YEAH, YOU'RE RIGHT-- VERY SWEET...

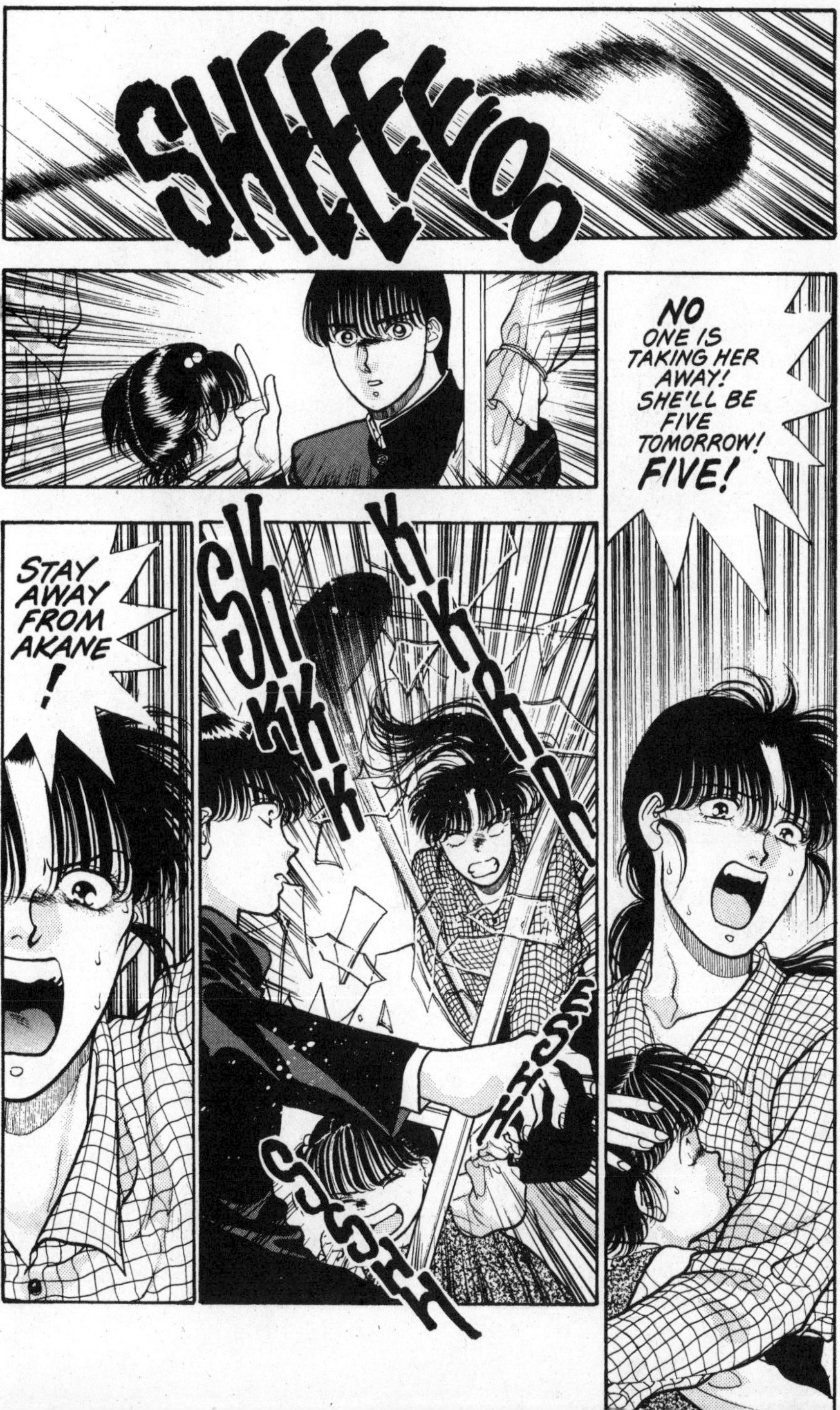
SHEEEWOO
STAY AWAY FROM AKANE!
SHKKK
KKKRRR
SSHH
SSSSH
NO ONE IS TAKING HER AWAY! SHE'LL BE FIVE TOMORROW! FIVE!

AND THEN, WHEN SHE'S SEVEN, SHE'LL GO TO ELEMENTARY SCHOOL! SHE'LL WEAR A PRETTY DRESS WHEN SHE TURNS TWENTY! SHE WON'T DIE! YOU HEAR ME?!

I DIDN'T GO TO THE SHRINE AND PRAY FOR A DAUGHTER JUST TO LET HER *DIE*!

SHRINE...?

YOU CAN'T PROTECT HER!

DON'T TALK NON-SENSE!

I SEE! SO YOU *PRAYED* FOR A CHILD, AND SHE WAS *BORN*...

YOU'RE ALREADY CAUGHT BY THE OGRE! YOUR PROMISES ARE WORTH-LESS!

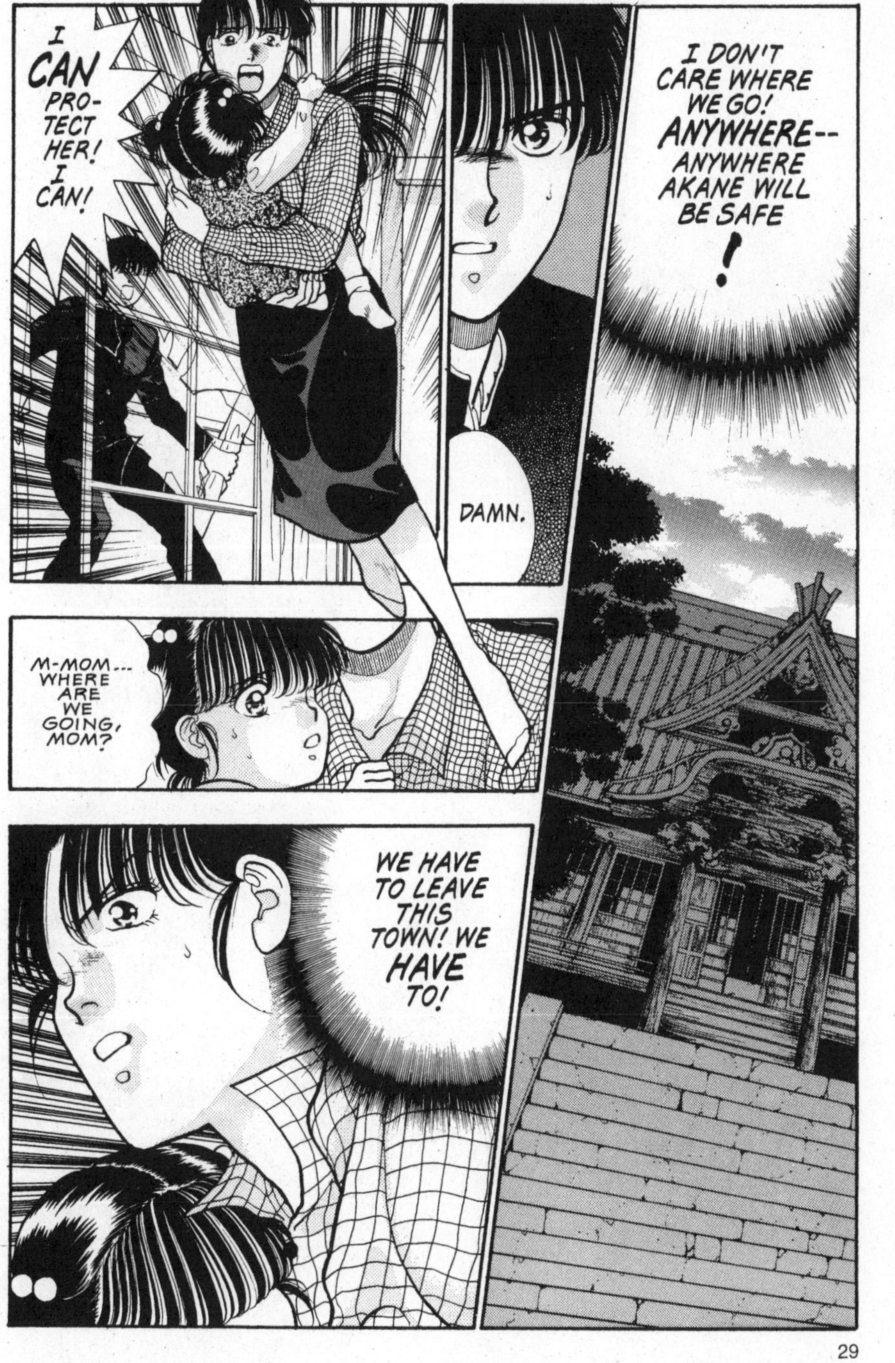
I CAN PROTECT HER! I CAN!
DAMN.
M-MOM... WHERE ARE WE GOING, MOM?
WE HAVE TO LEAVE THIS TOWN! WE HAVE TO!
I DON'T CARE WHERE WE GO! ANYWHERE-- ANYWHERE AKANE WILL BE SAFE!

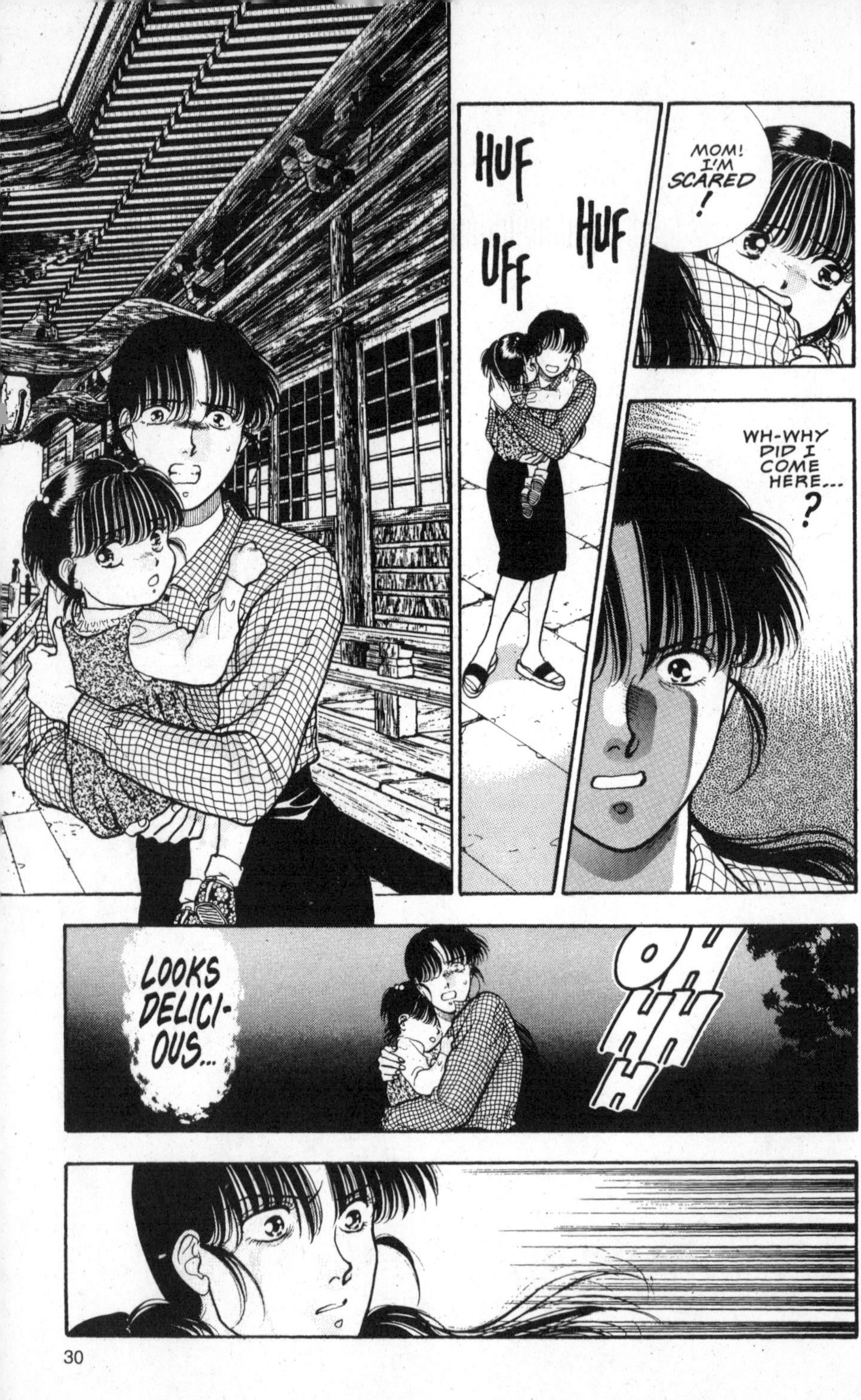
HUF
UFF
HUF
MOM! I'M SCARED!
WH-WHY DID I COME HERE...?
LOOKS DELICIOUS...
OHHHH

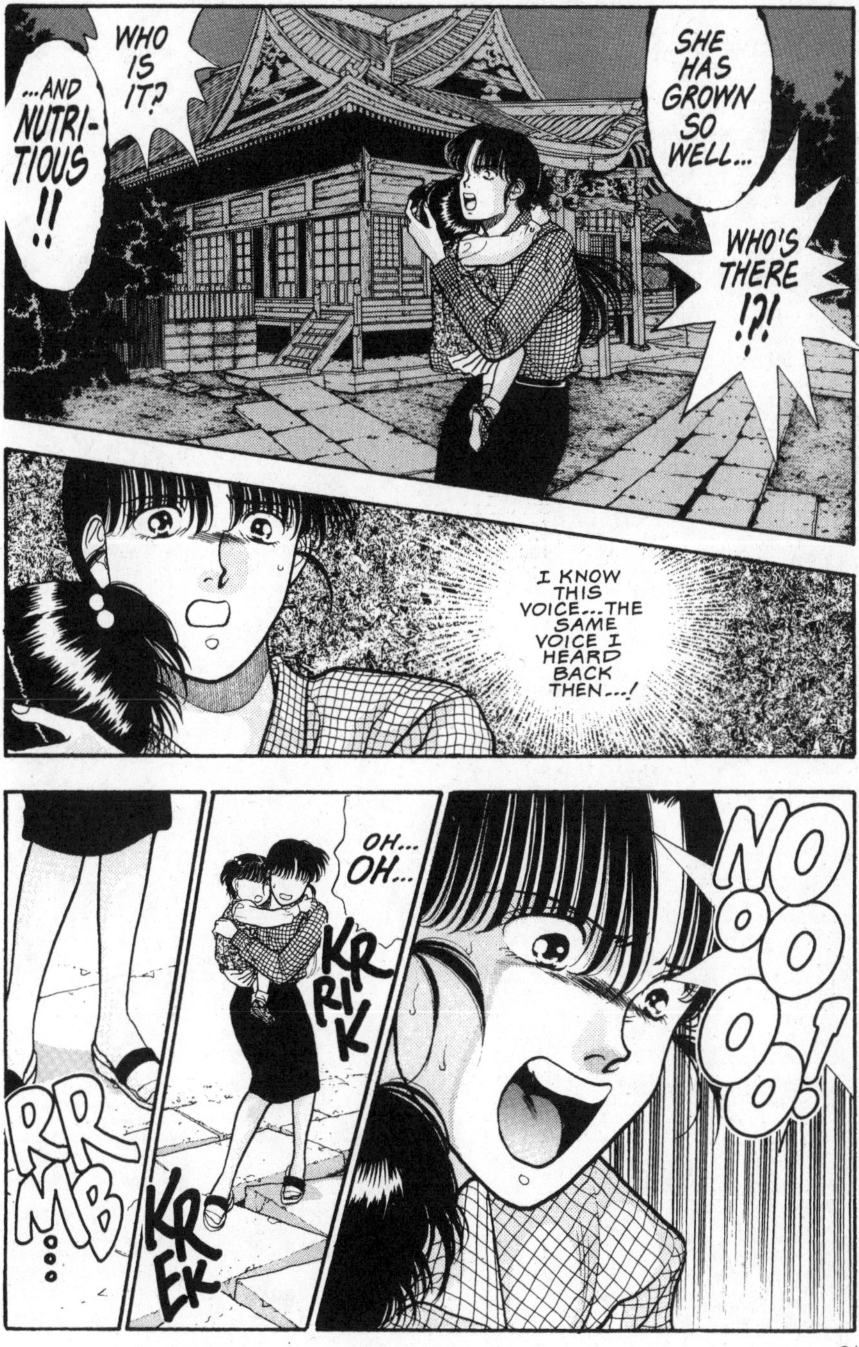
...AND NUTRITIOUS!!
WHO IS IT?
SHE HAS GROWN SO WELL...
WHO'S THERE!?!
I KNOW THIS VOICE...THE SAME VOICE I HEARD BACK THEN...!
RRMB...
OH... OH...
KRRIK
KREK
NOOOOO!

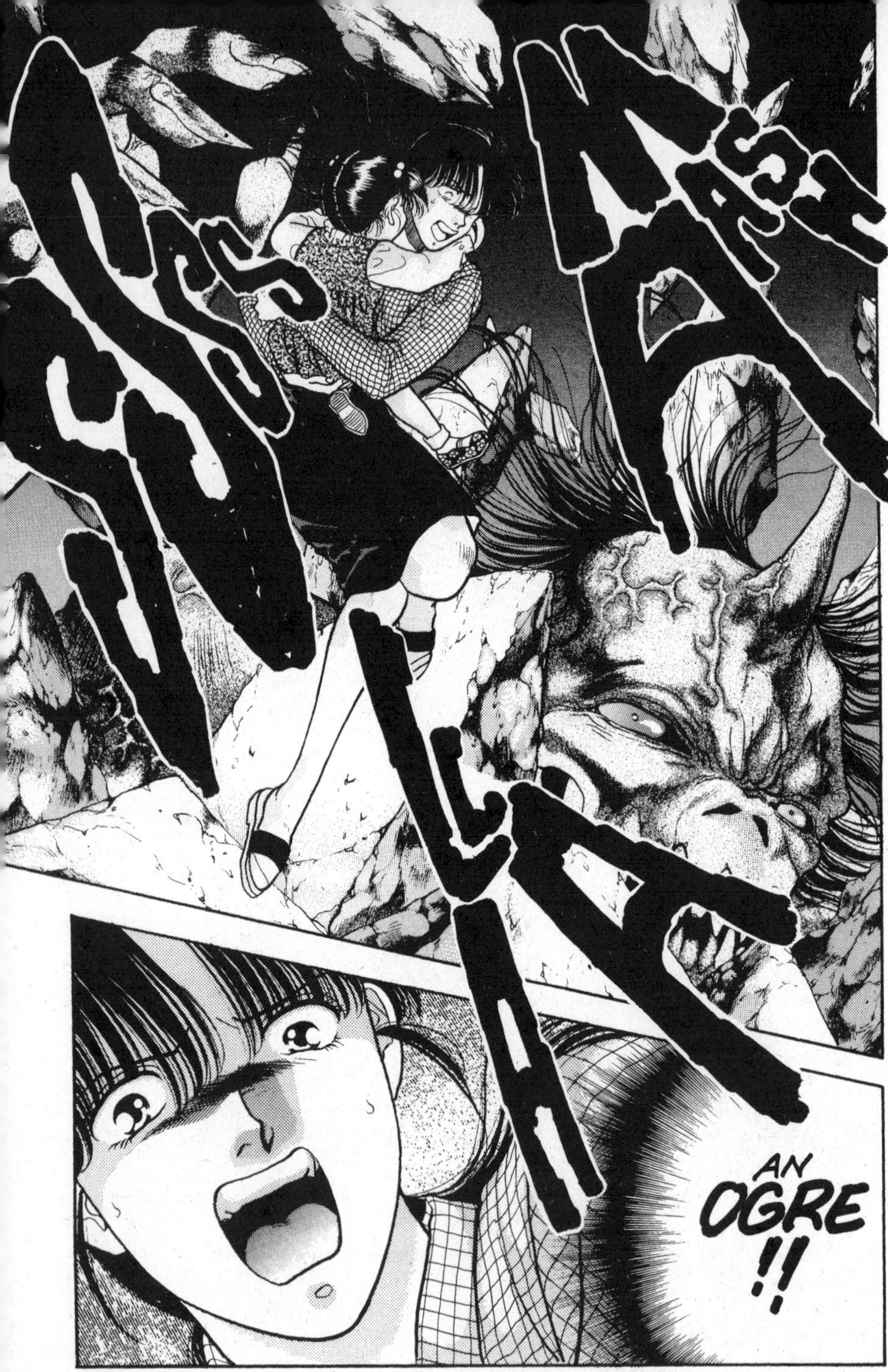
AN OGRE !!

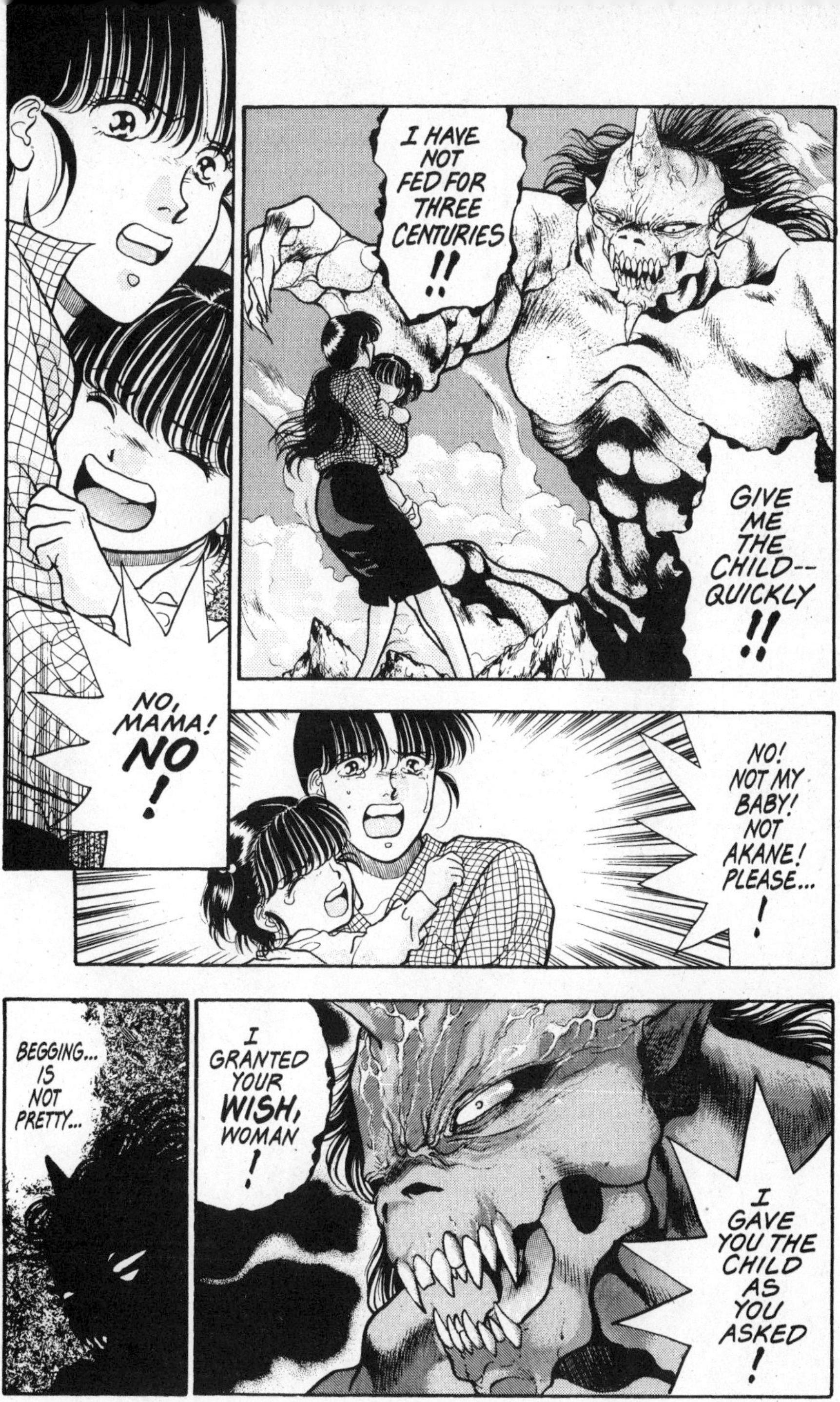
NO, MAMA! NO!
I HAVE NOT FED FOR THREE CENTURIES!!
GIVE ME THE CHILD-- QUICKLY!!
NO! NOT MY BABY! NOT AKANE! PLEASE...!
BEGGING... IS NOT PRETTY...
I GRANTED YOUR WISH, WOMAN!
I GAVE YOU THE CHILD AS YOU ASKED!

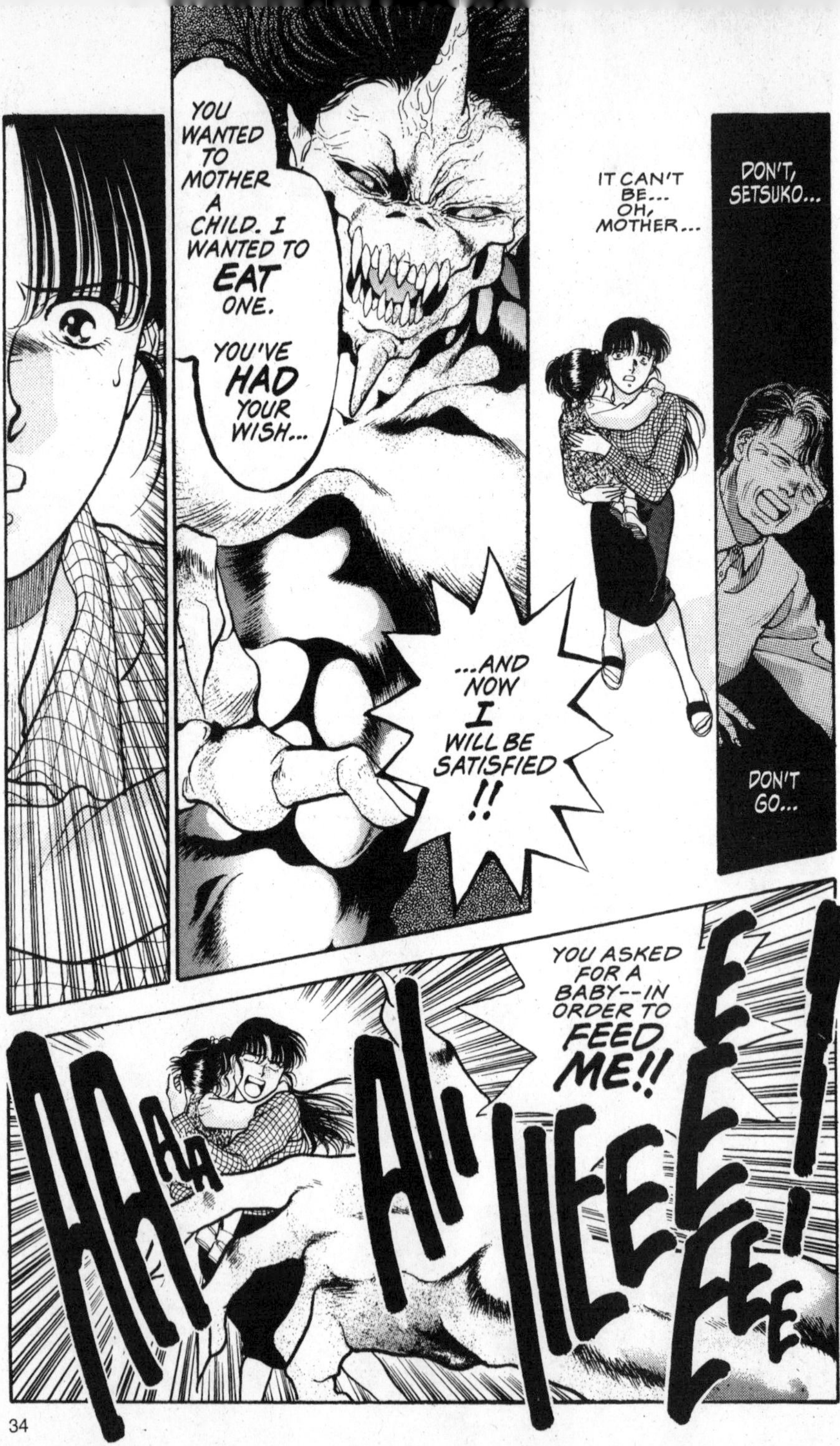
YOU WANTED TO MOTHER A CHILD. I WANTED TO EAT ONE.
YOU'VE HAD YOUR WISH...
...AND NOW I WILL BE SATISFIED!!
IT CAN'T BE... OH, MOTHER...
DON'T, SETSUKO...
DON'T GO...
HAAAA
AI... IIEEEEEEE!!
YOU ASKED FOR A BABY--IN ORDER TO FEED ME!!

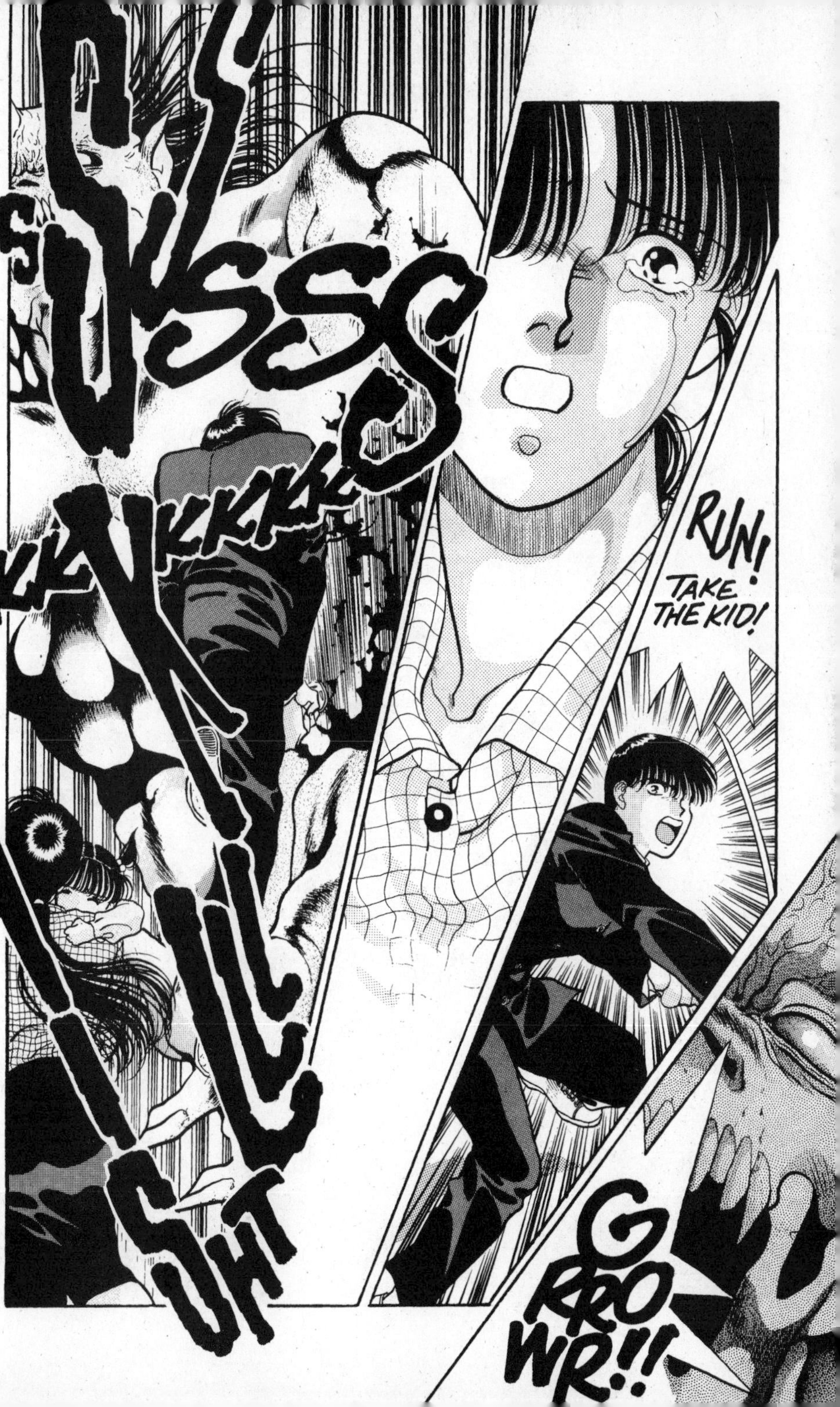
RUN!
TAKE THE KID!
G KRO WR!!

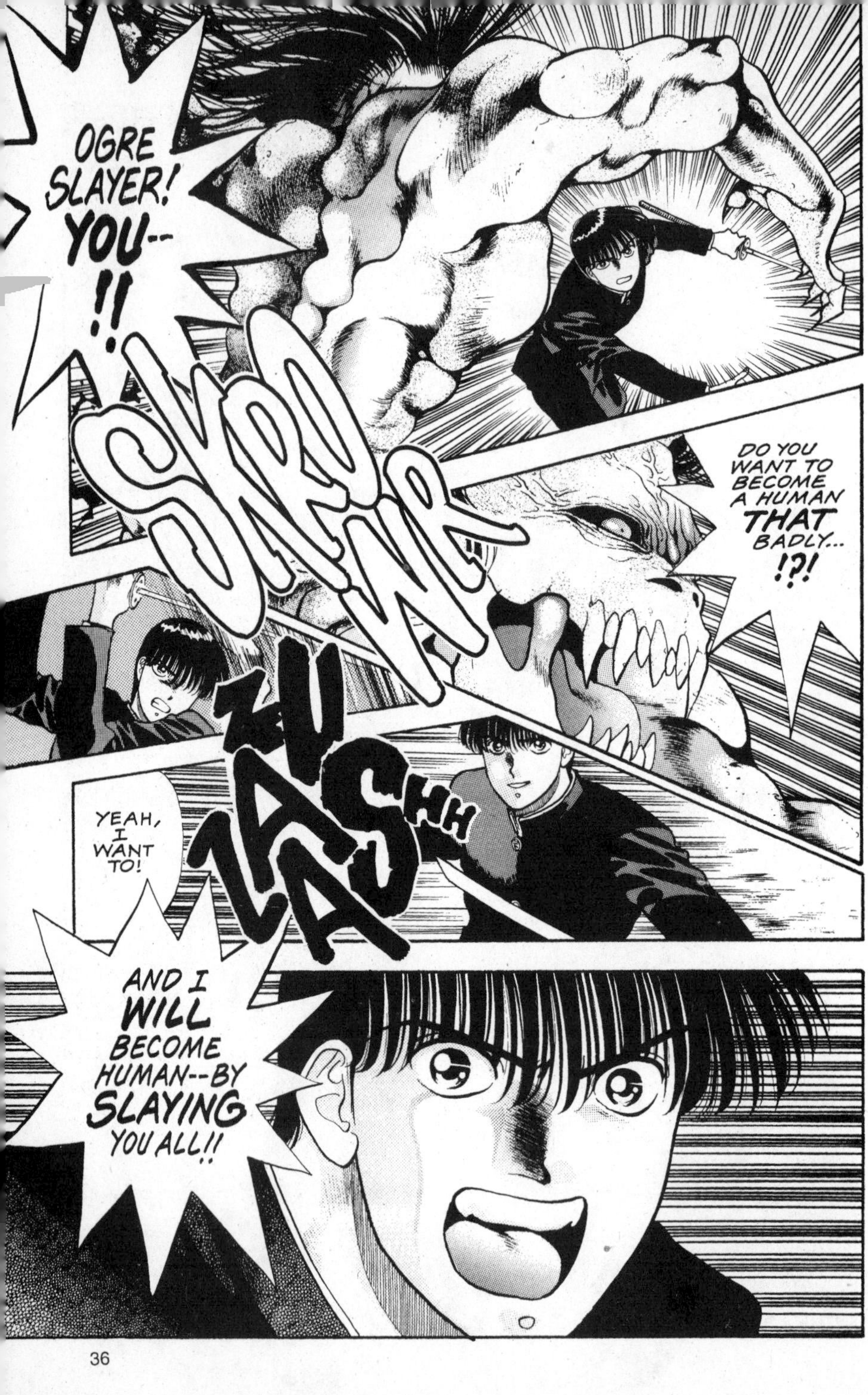
OGRE SLAYER! YOU-- !!
SKRUNCH
DO YOU WANT TO BECOME A HUMAN THAT BADLY... !?!
ZAU
ZASHH
YEAH, I WANT TO!
AND I WILL BECOME HUMAN--BY SLAYING YOU ALL!!

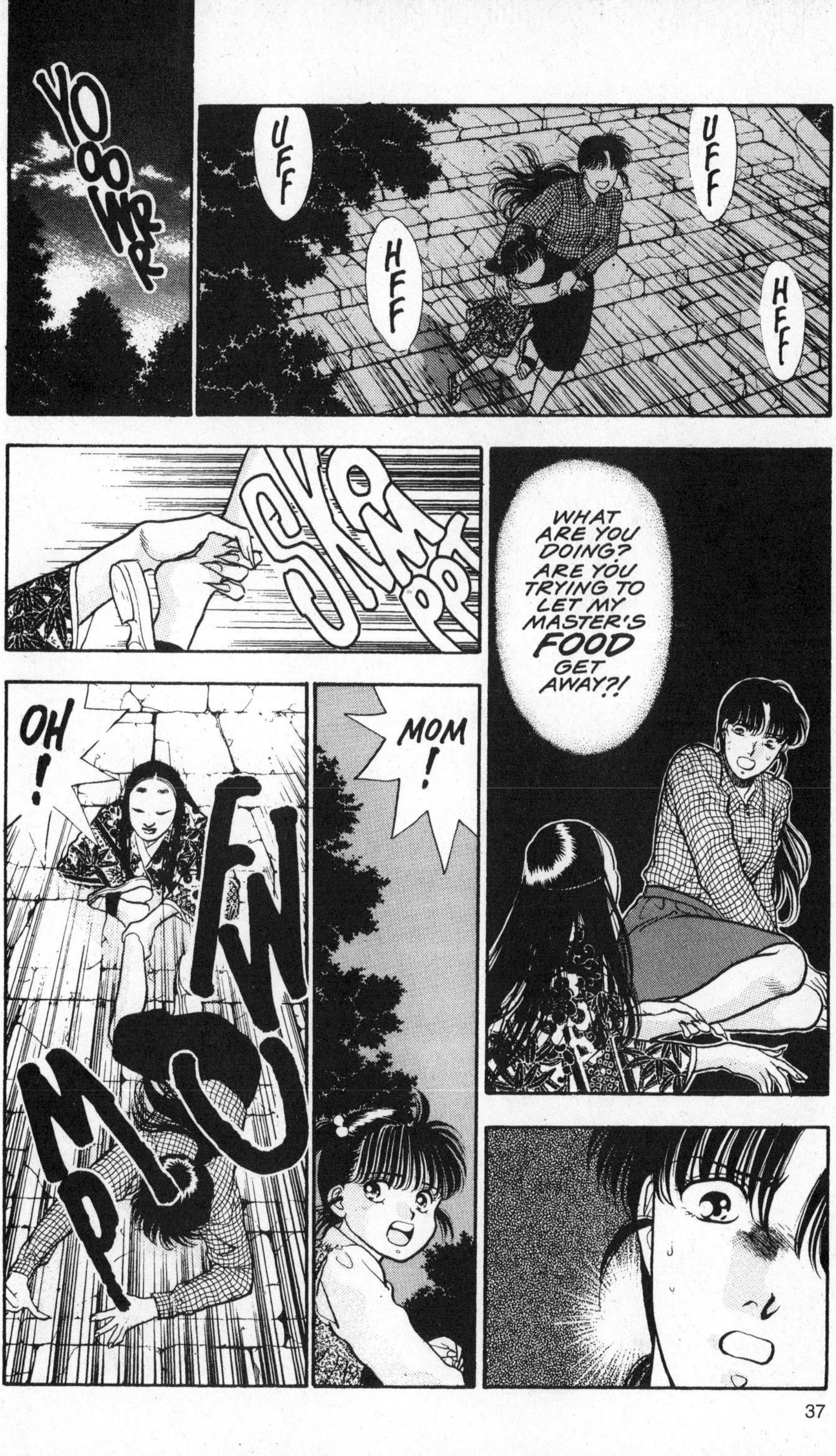
YOOOWRR
UFF
UFF
HFF
HFF
WHAT ARE YOU DOING? ARE YOU TRYING TO LET MY MASTER'S **FOOD** GET AWAY?!
OH!
MOM!

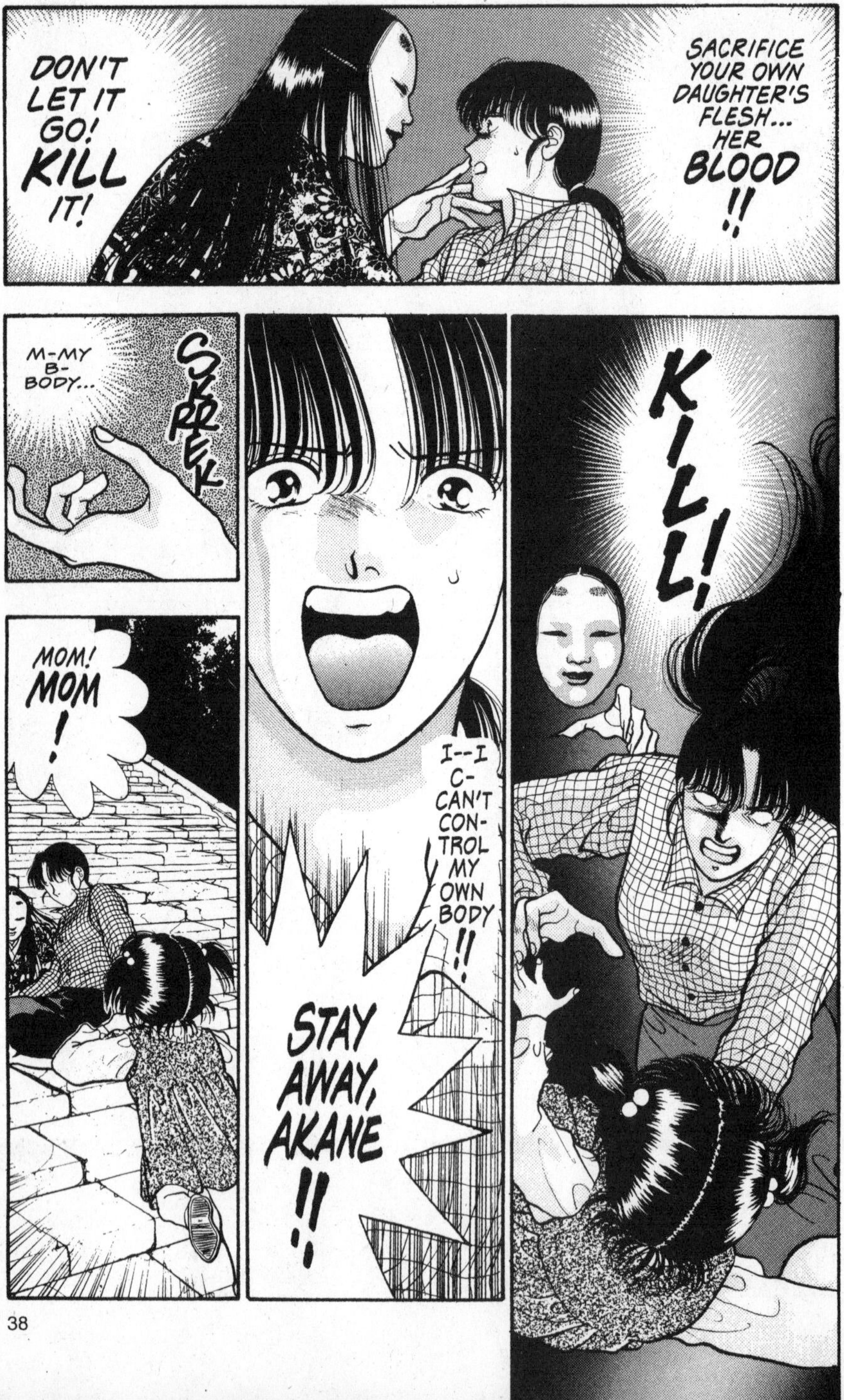

DON'T LET IT GO! KILL IT!
SACRIFICE YOUR OWN DAUGHTER'S FLESH... HER BLOOD!!
M-MY B-BODY...
SKRREK
MOM! MOM!
I--I C-CAN'T CONTROL MY OWN BODY!!
STAY AWAY, AKANE!!
KILL!

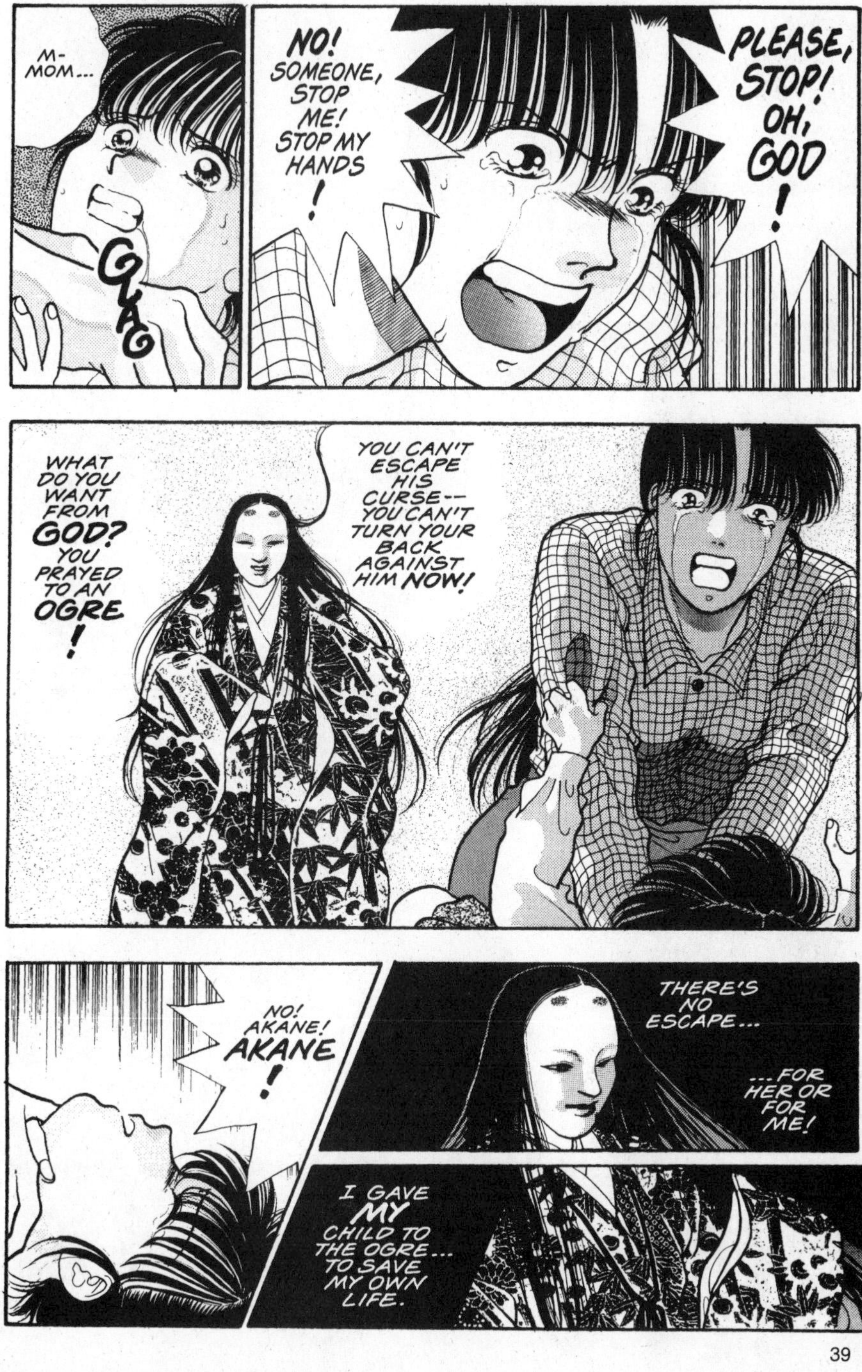
M-MOM...
GLAG
NO! SOMEONE, STOP ME! STOP MY HANDS!
PLEASE, STOP! OH, GOD!
WHAT DO YOU WANT FROM GOD? YOU PRAYED TO AN OGRE!
YOU CAN'T ESCAPE HIS CURSE-- YOU CAN'T TURN YOUR BACK AGAINST HIM NOW!
NO! AKANE! AKANE!
THERE'S NO ESCAPE...
...FOR HER OR FOR ME!
I GAVE MY CHILD TO THE OGRE... TO SAVE MY OWN LIFE.

SUCH A MOTHER HAS A SIMPLE FATE. SHE EITHER...

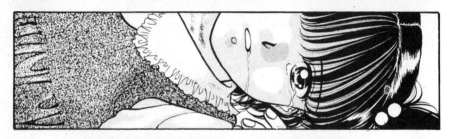

OH...

OH OH OH...

DIES...

OH!

OR ELSE...

BECOMES AN OGRE HERSELF!!

FROM NOW ON... *YOU* ARE THE ONE WHO SERVES THE OGRE!

AND NOW I CAN ESCAPE THE OGRE'S CURSE!

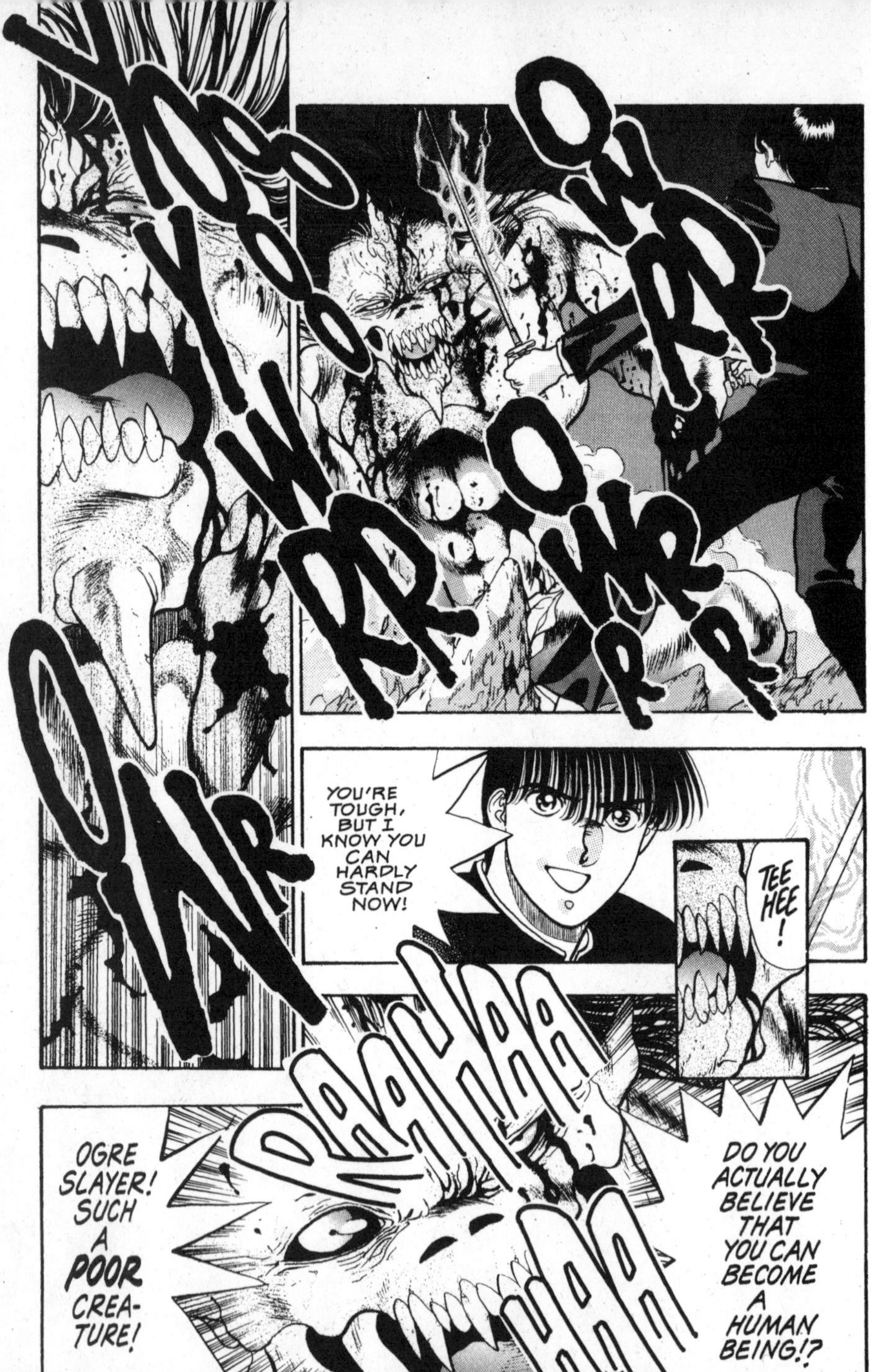
YOU'RE TOUGH, BUT I KNOW YOU CAN HARDLY STAND NOW!
TEE HEE!
OGRE SLAYER! SUCH A POOR CREATURE!
DO YOU ACTUALLY BELIEVE THAT YOU CAN BECOME A HUMAN BEING!?

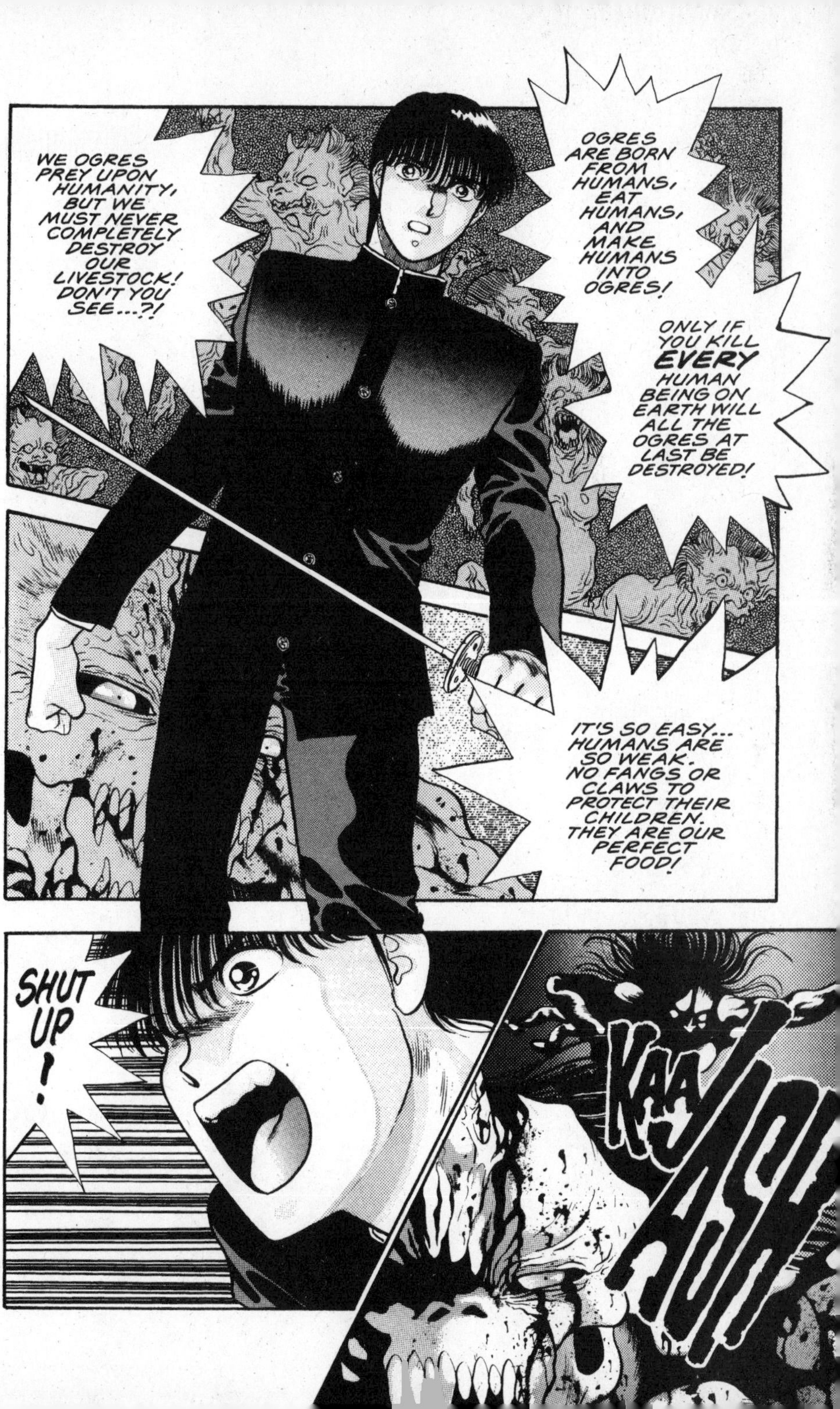
WE OGRES PREY UPON HUMANITY, BUT WE MUST NEVER COMPLETELY DESTROY OUR LIVESTOCK! DON'T YOU SEE...?!
OGRES ARE BORN FROM HUMANS, EAT HUMANS, AND MAKE HUMANS INTO OGRES!
ONLY IF YOU KILL EVERY HUMAN BEING ON EARTH WILL ALL THE OGRES AT LAST BE DESTROYED!
IT'S SO EASY... HUMANS ARE SO WEAK. NO FANGS OR CLAWS TO PROTECT THEIR CHILDREN. THEY ARE OUR PERFECT FOOD!
SHUT UP!
KAA ASH

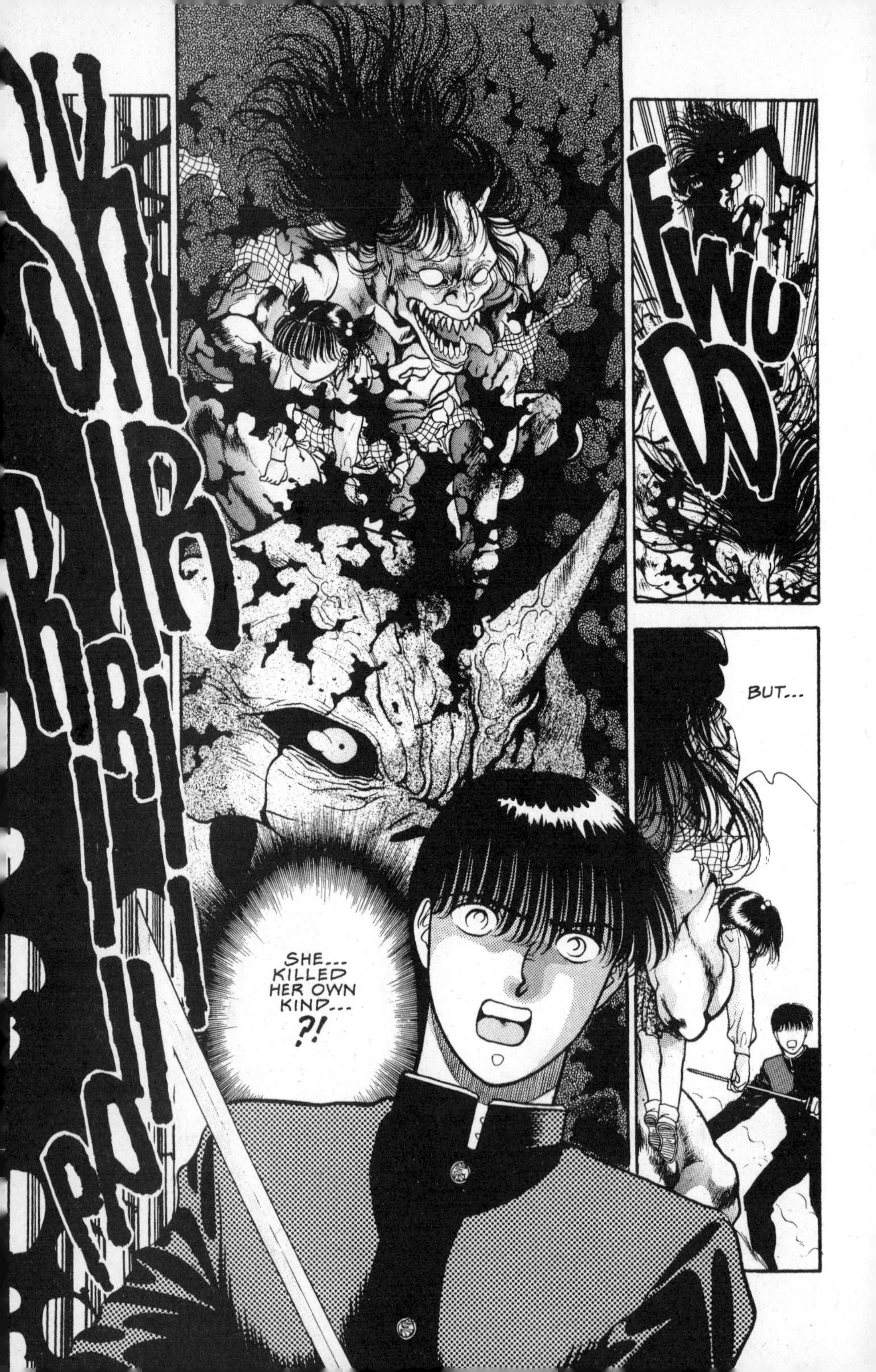
SHE... KILLED HER OWN KIND...?!
FWUDD
BUT...

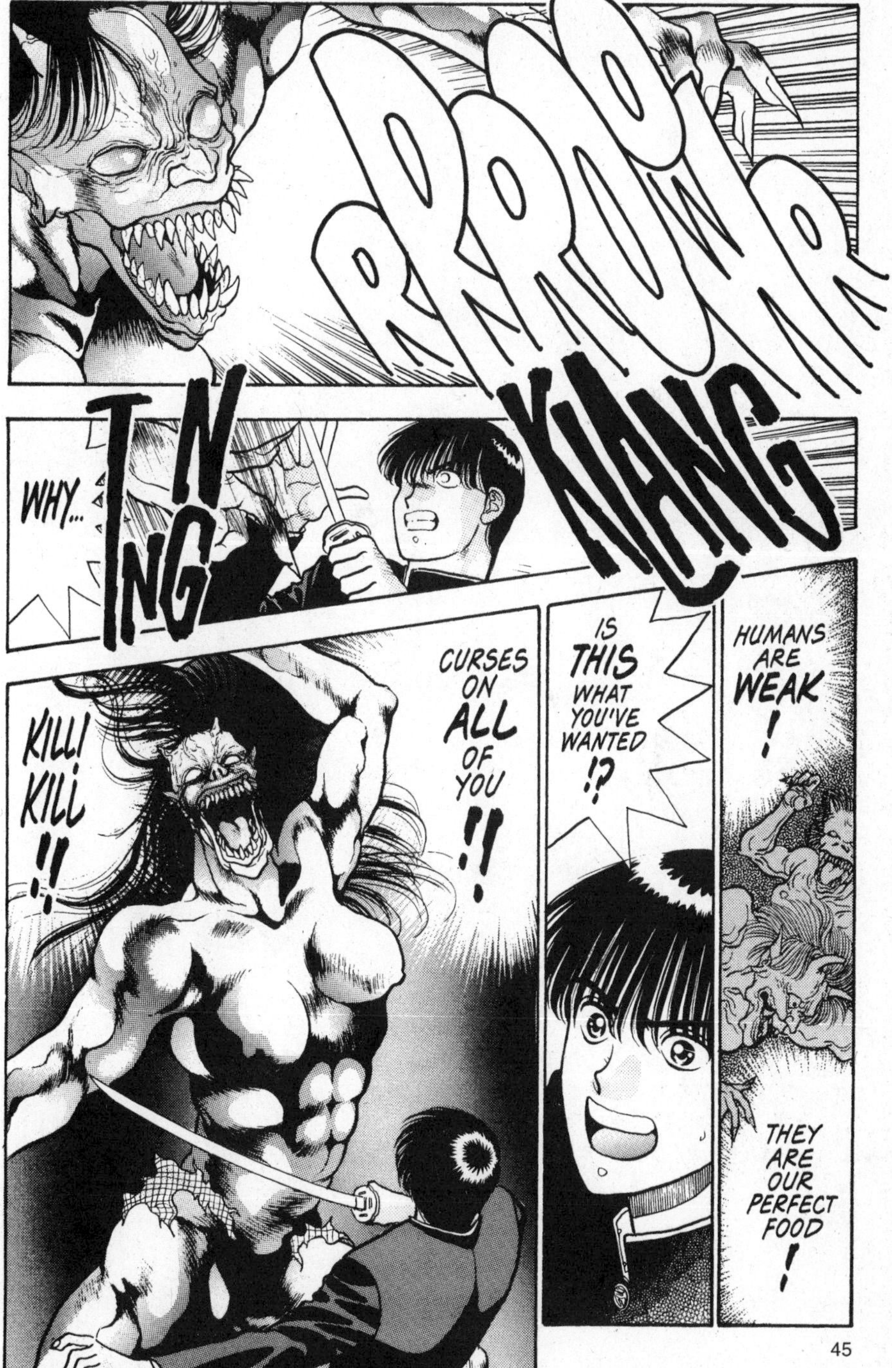
WHY...
KLANG
KILL! KILL!!
CURSES ON ALL OF YOU!!
IS THIS WHAT YOU'VE WANTED!?
HUMANS ARE WEAK!
THEY ARE OUR PERFECT FOOD!

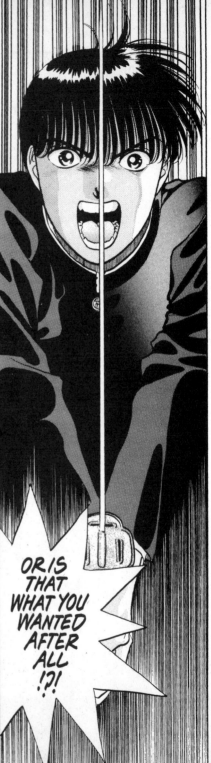

IF YOU WANT TO DESTROY THE OGRES, KILL HUMANS!

STOP! YOU NEVER ASKED TO BE AN OGRE!

OR IS THAT WHAT YOU WANTED AFTER ALL !?!

46

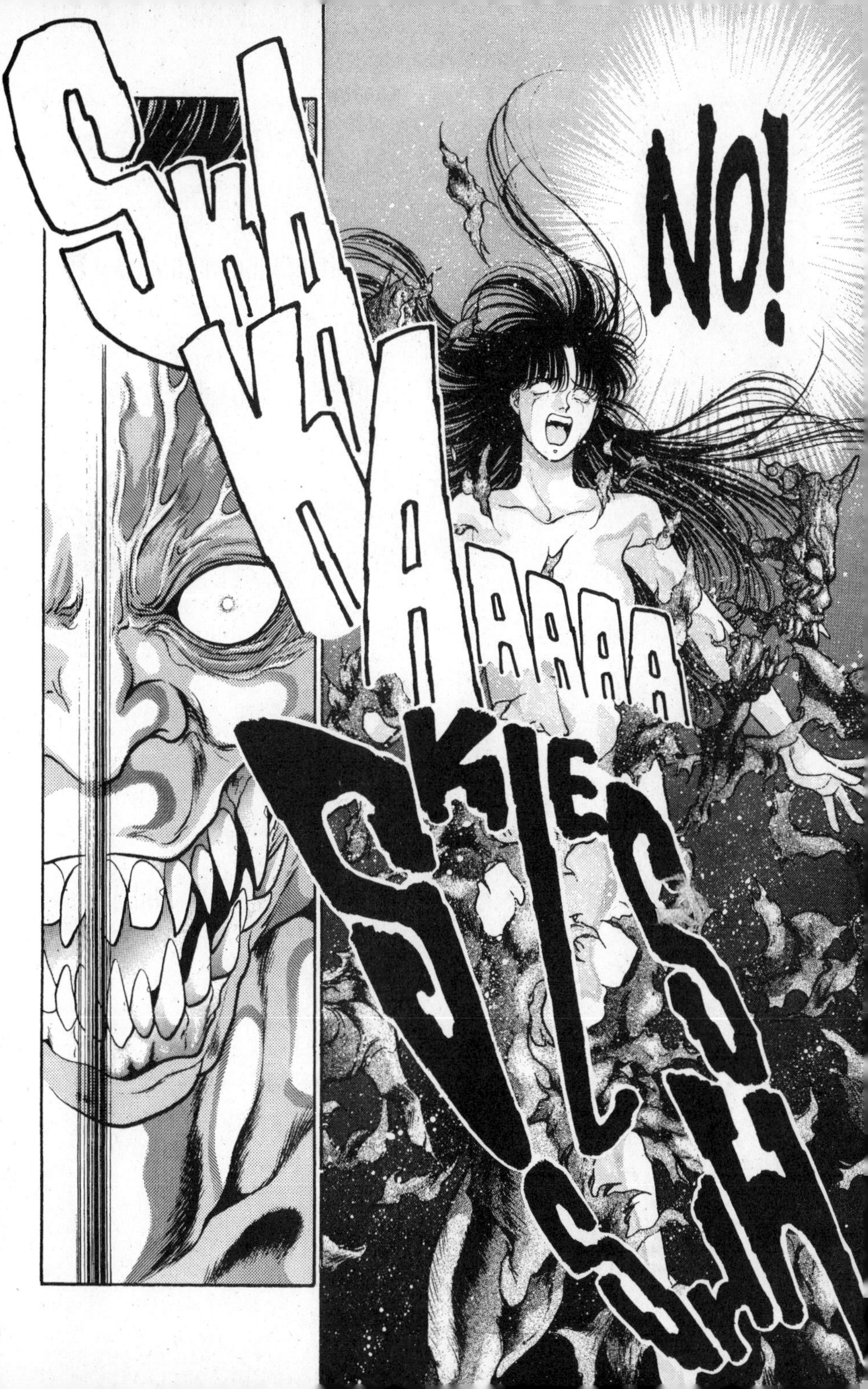
NO!

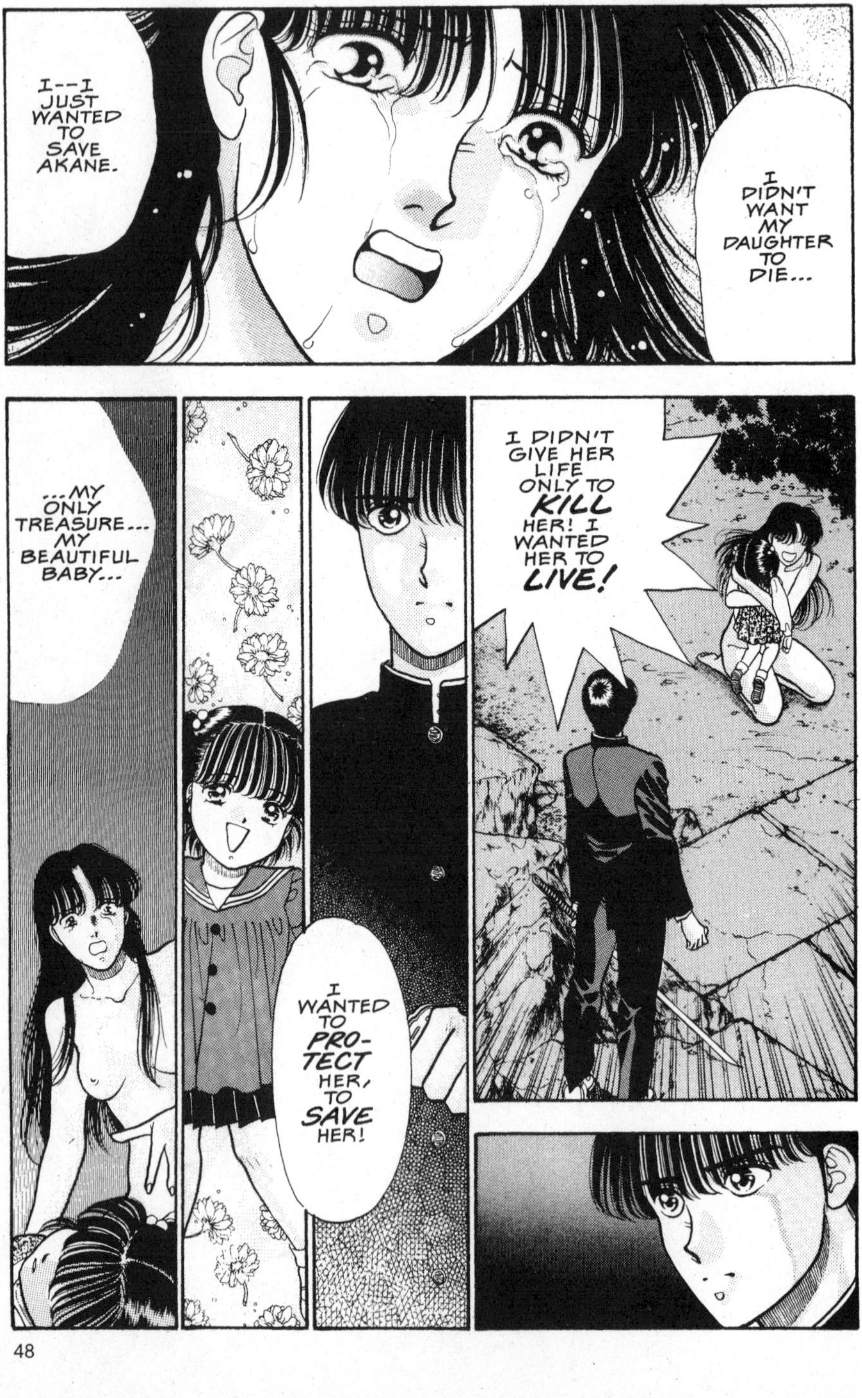
I--I JUST WANTED TO SAVE AKANE.
I DIDN'T WANT MY DAUGHTER TO DIE...
...MY ONLY TREASURE... MY BEAUTIFUL BABY...
I WANTED TO PROTECT HER, TO SAVE HER!
I DIDN'T GIVE HER LIFE ONLY TO KILL HER! I WANTED HER TO LIVE!

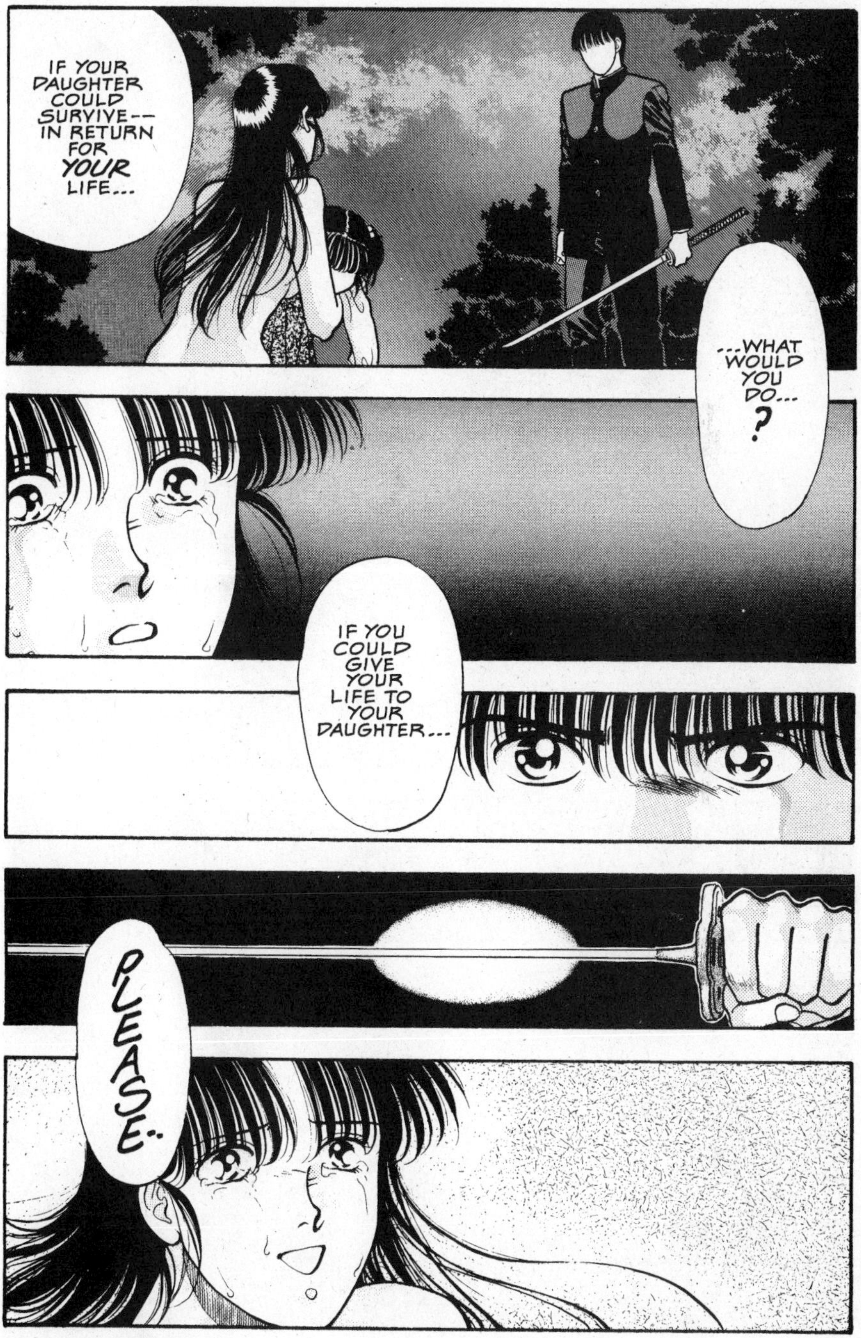
IF YOUR DAUGHTER COULD SURVIVE-- IN RETURN FOR YOUR LIFE...
...WHAT WOULD YOU DO...?
IF YOU COULD GIVE YOUR LIFE TO YOUR DAUGHTER...
PLEASE..

I WON'T STOP *KILLING* OGRES... NOT UNTIL I BECOME A HUMAN BEING...

I'M NOT CRYING...

I--I *CAN'T* CRY EACH TIME...

I HAVE DONE THIS BEFORE AND WILL DO THIS AGAIN...

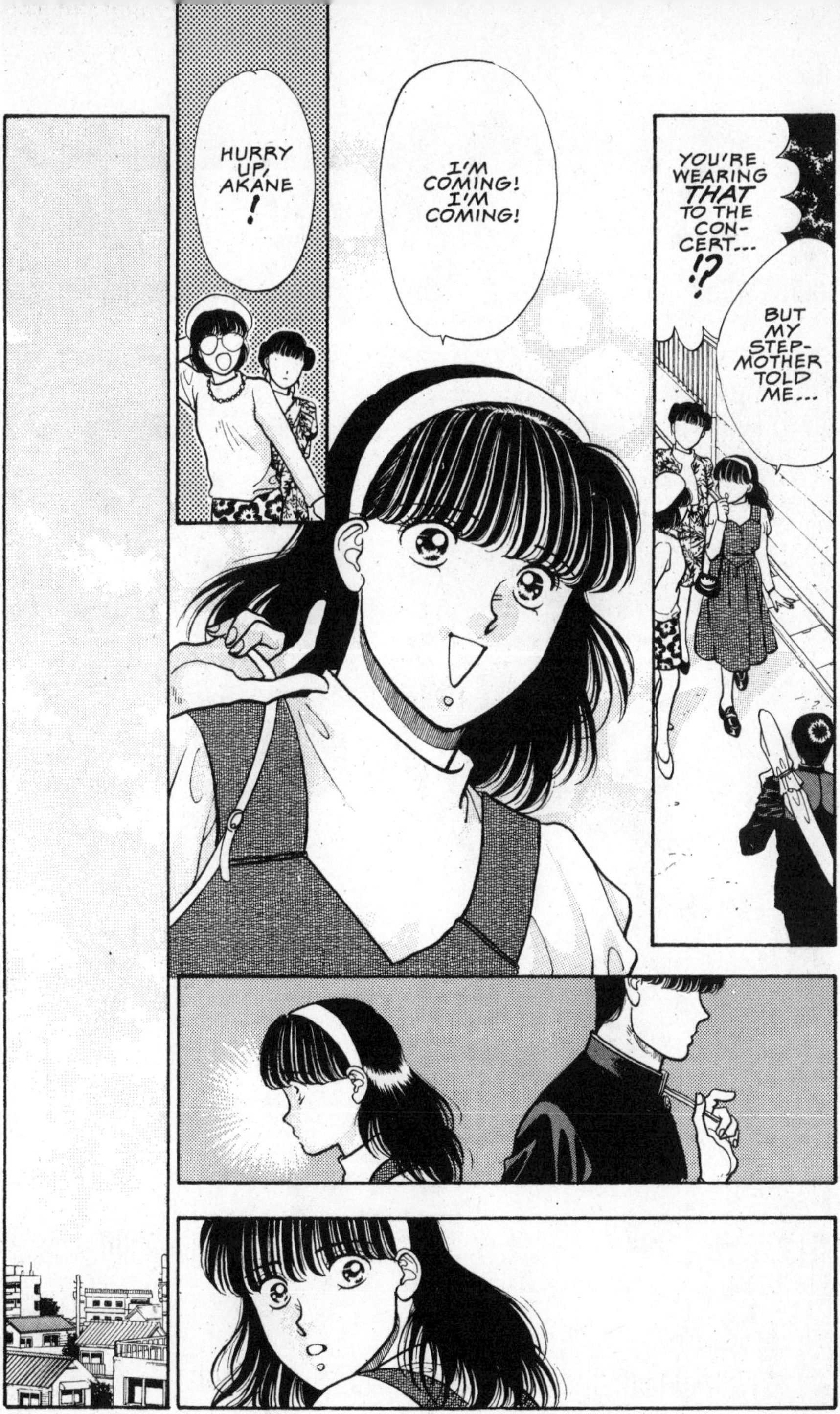
HURRY UP, AKANE!
I'M COMING! I'M COMING!
YOU'RE WEARING THAT TO THE CONCERT...!?
BUT MY STEP-MOTHER TOLD ME...

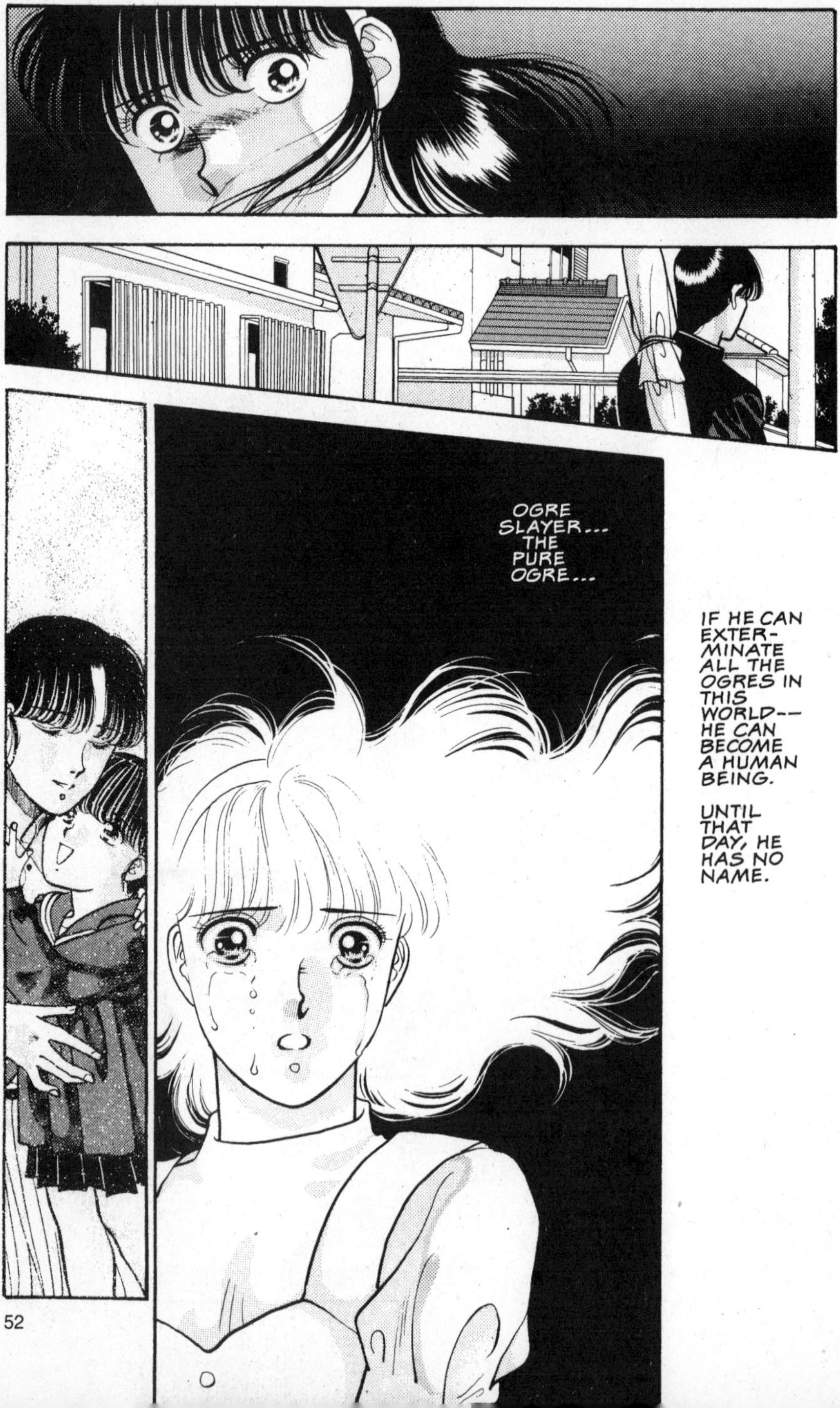
OGRE SLAYER... THE PURE OGRE...
IF HE CAN EXTERMINATE ALL THE OGRES IN THIS WORLD-- HE CAN BECOME A HUMAN BEING.
UNTIL THAT DAY, HE HAS NO NAME.

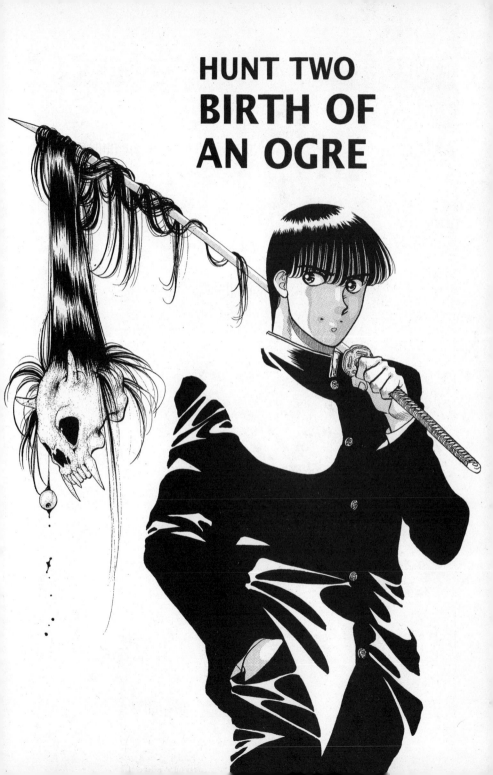

HUNT TWO
BIRTH OF
AN OGRE

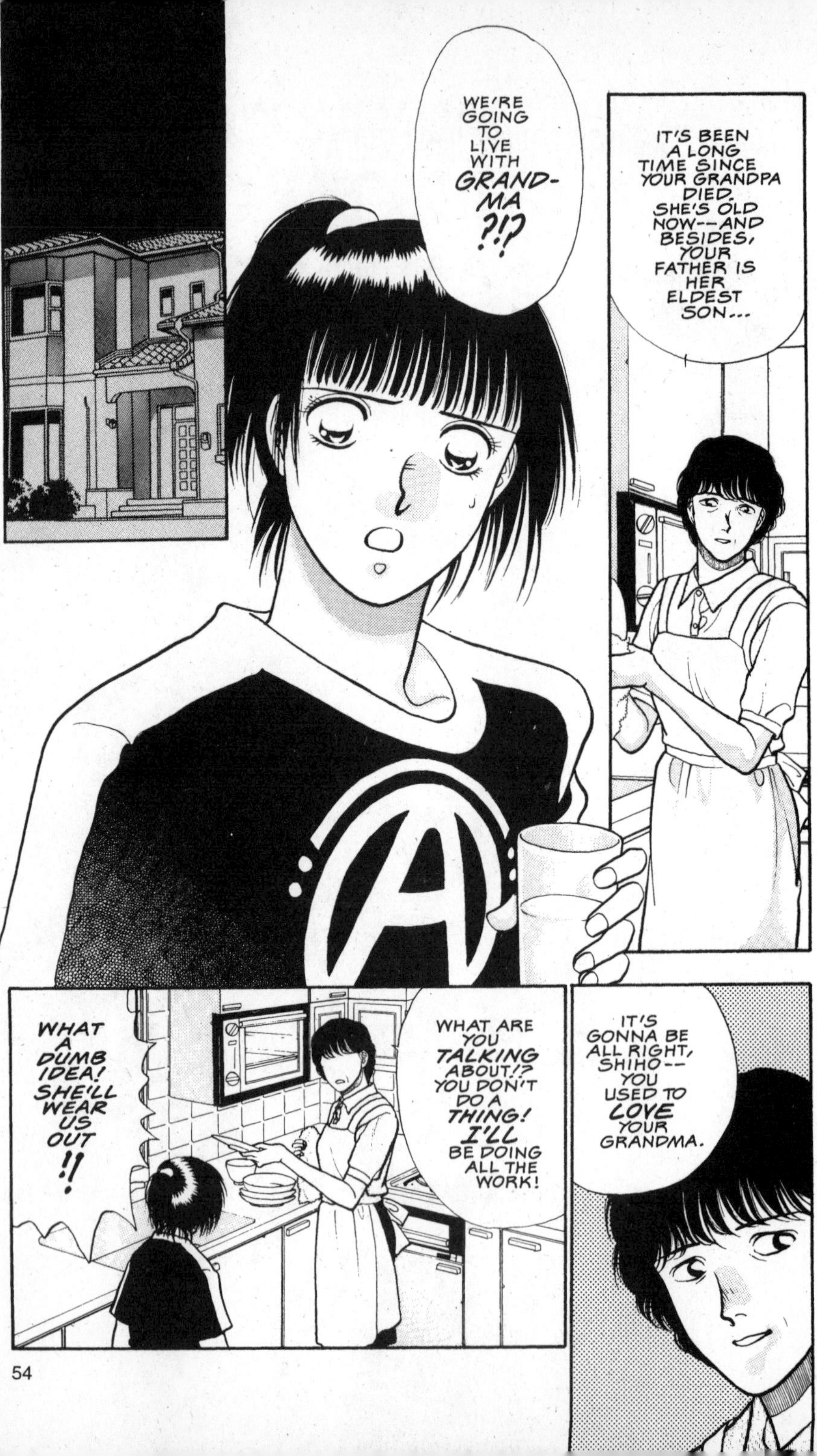
WE'RE GOING TO LIVE WITH GRANDMA?!?
IT'S BEEN A LONG TIME SINCE YOUR GRANDPA DIED. SHE'S OLD NOW--AND BESIDES, YOUR FATHER IS HER ELDEST SON...
WHAT A DUMB IDEA! SHE'LL WEAR US OUT!!
WHAT ARE YOU TALKING ABOUT!? YOU DON'T DO A THING! I'LL BE DOING ALL THE WORK!
IT'S GONNA BE ALL RIGHT, SHIHO--YOU USED TO LOVE YOUR GRANDMA.

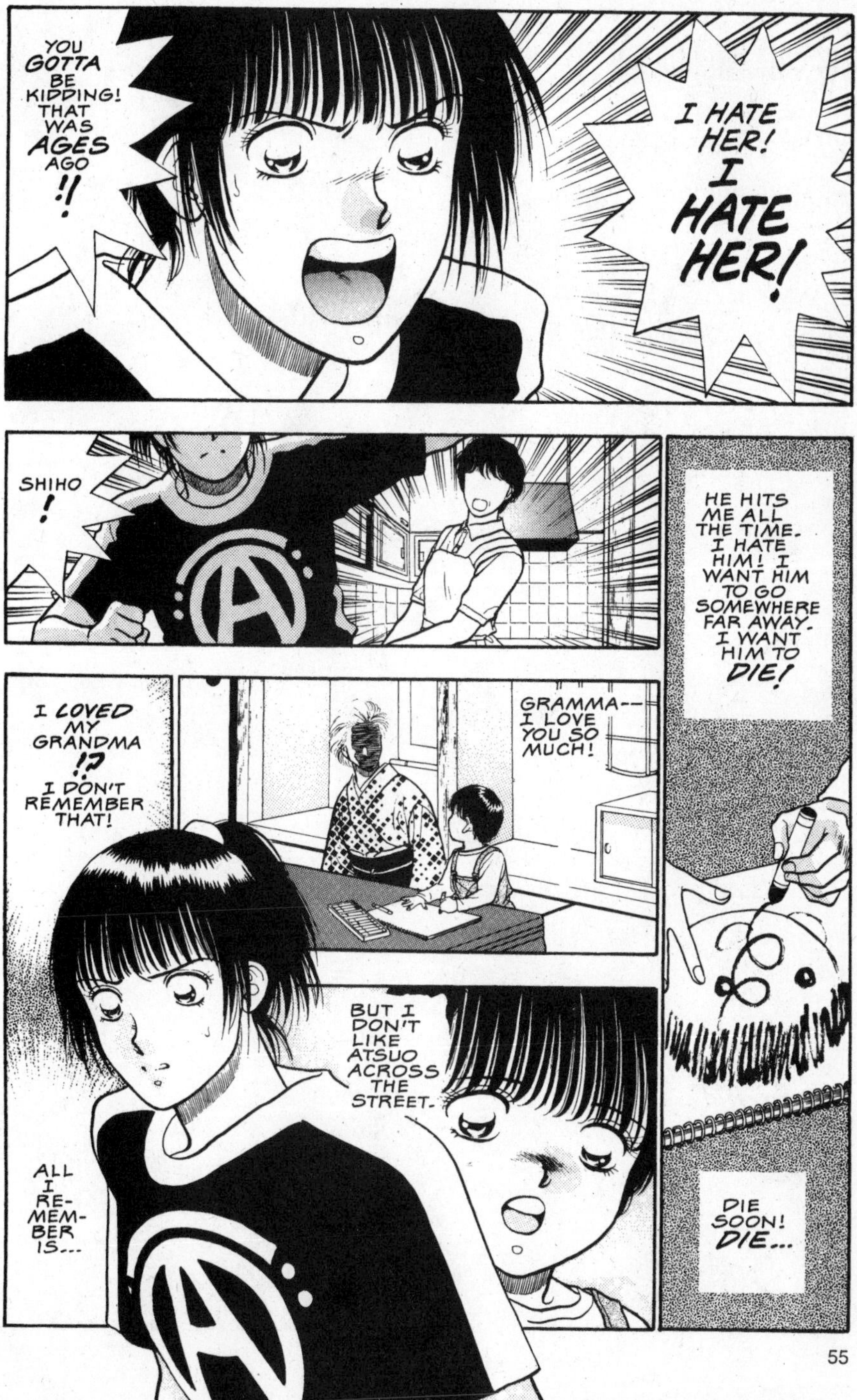
YOU GOTTA BE KIDDING! THAT WAS AGES AGO!!
I HATE HER! I HATE HER!
SHIHO!
I LOVED MY GRANDMA!? I DON'T REMEMBER THAT!
GRAMMA-- I LOVE YOU SO MUCH!
ALL I RE-MEM-BER IS...
BUT I DON'T LIKE ATSUO ACROSS THE STREET.
HE HITS ME ALL THE TIME. I HATE HIM! I WANT HIM TO GO SOMEWHERE FAR AWAY. I WANT HIM TO DIE!
DIE SOON! DIE...

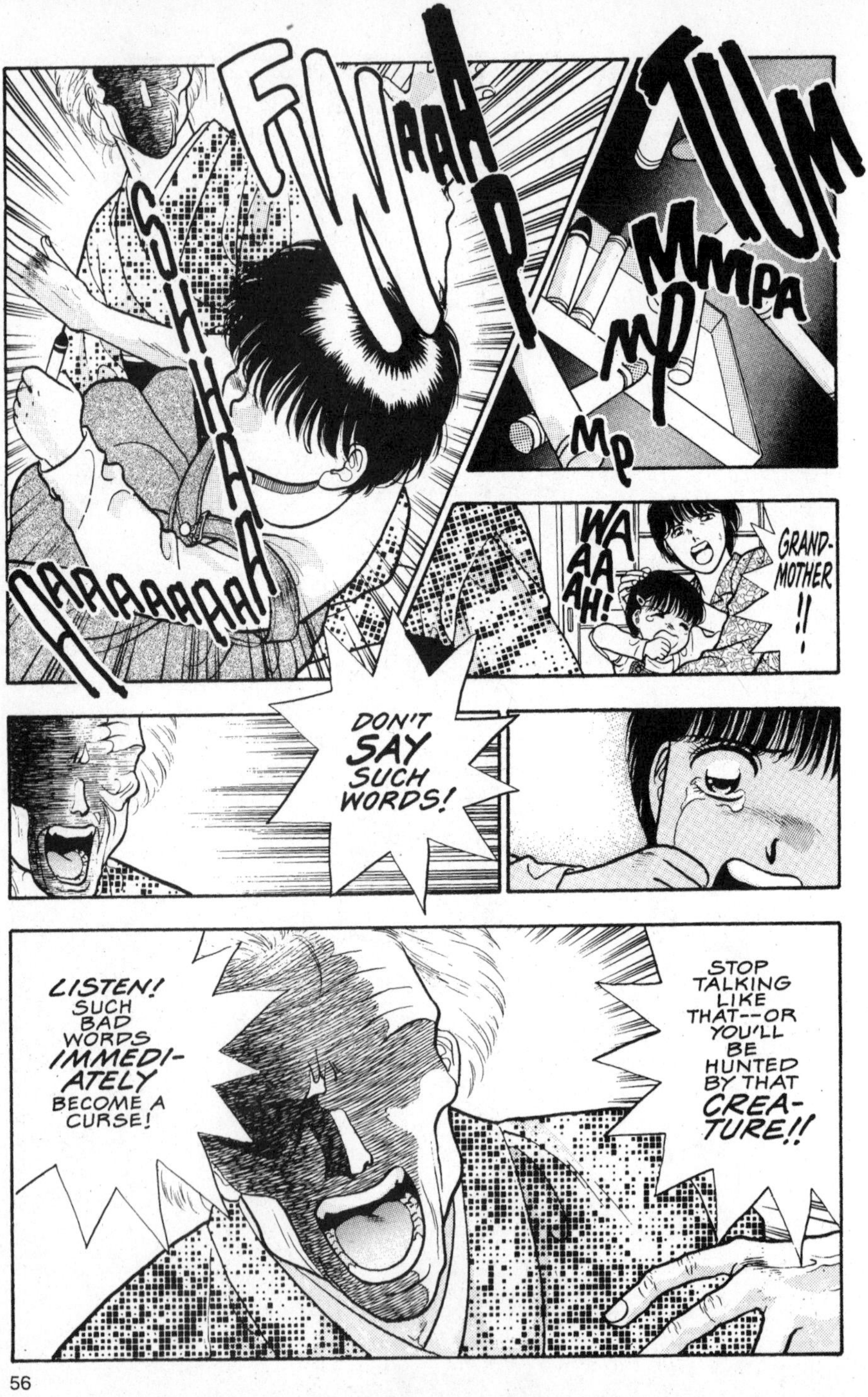
FWAAAP
SHHAAA
AAAAAAAH
TUUM
MMPA
MP
MP
WAAAAH!
GRAND-MOTHER!!
DON'T SAY SUCH WORDS!
STOP TALKING LIKE THAT--OR YOU'LL BE HUNTED BY THAT CREATURE!!
LISTEN! SUCH BAD WORDS IMMEDIATELY BECOME A CURSE!

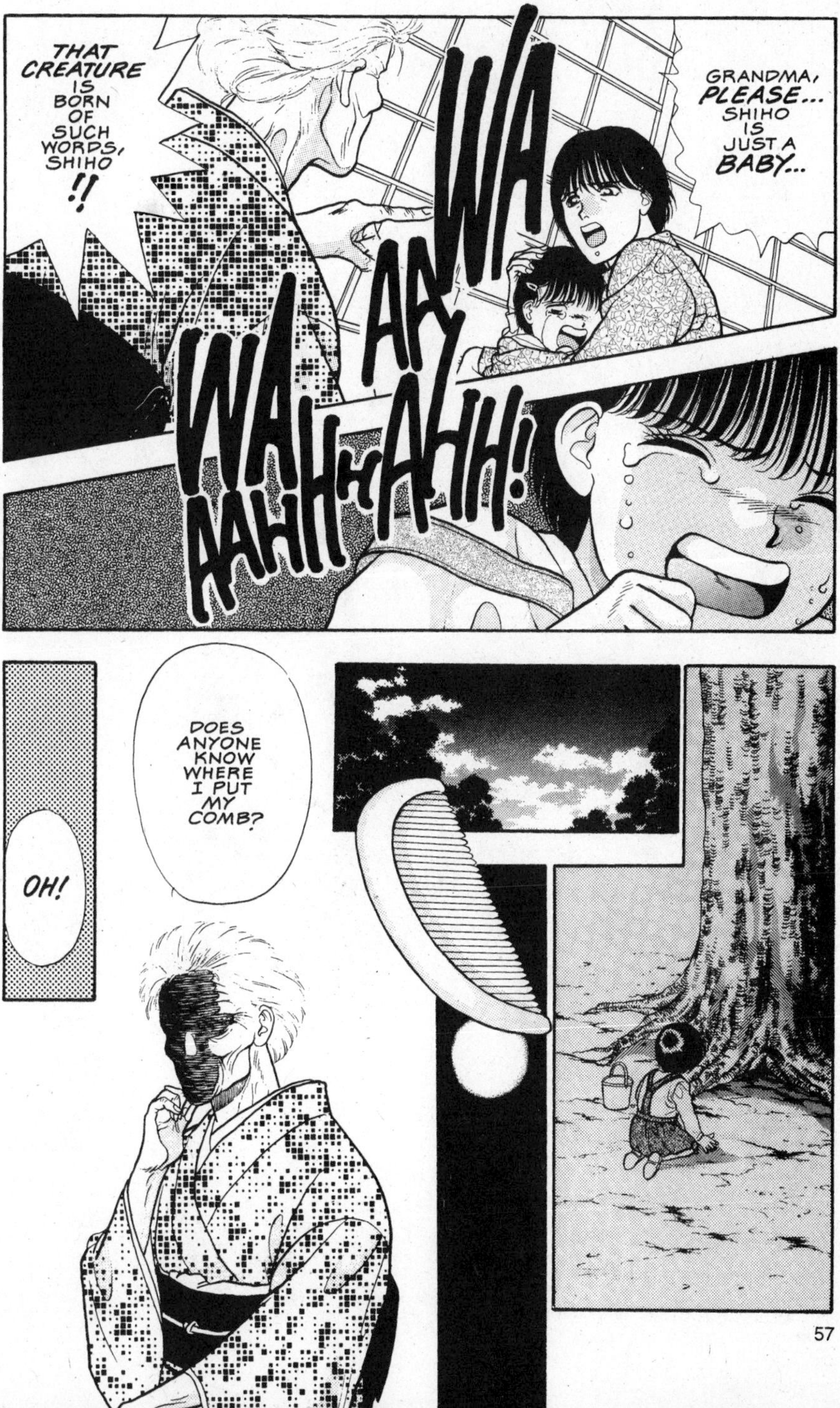
THAT CREATURE IS BORN OF SUCH WORDS, SHIHO !!
GRANDMA, PLEASE... SHIHO IS JUST A BABY...
WA WA AA AAHH AHH!
OH!
DOES ANYONE KNOW WHERE I PUT MY COMB?

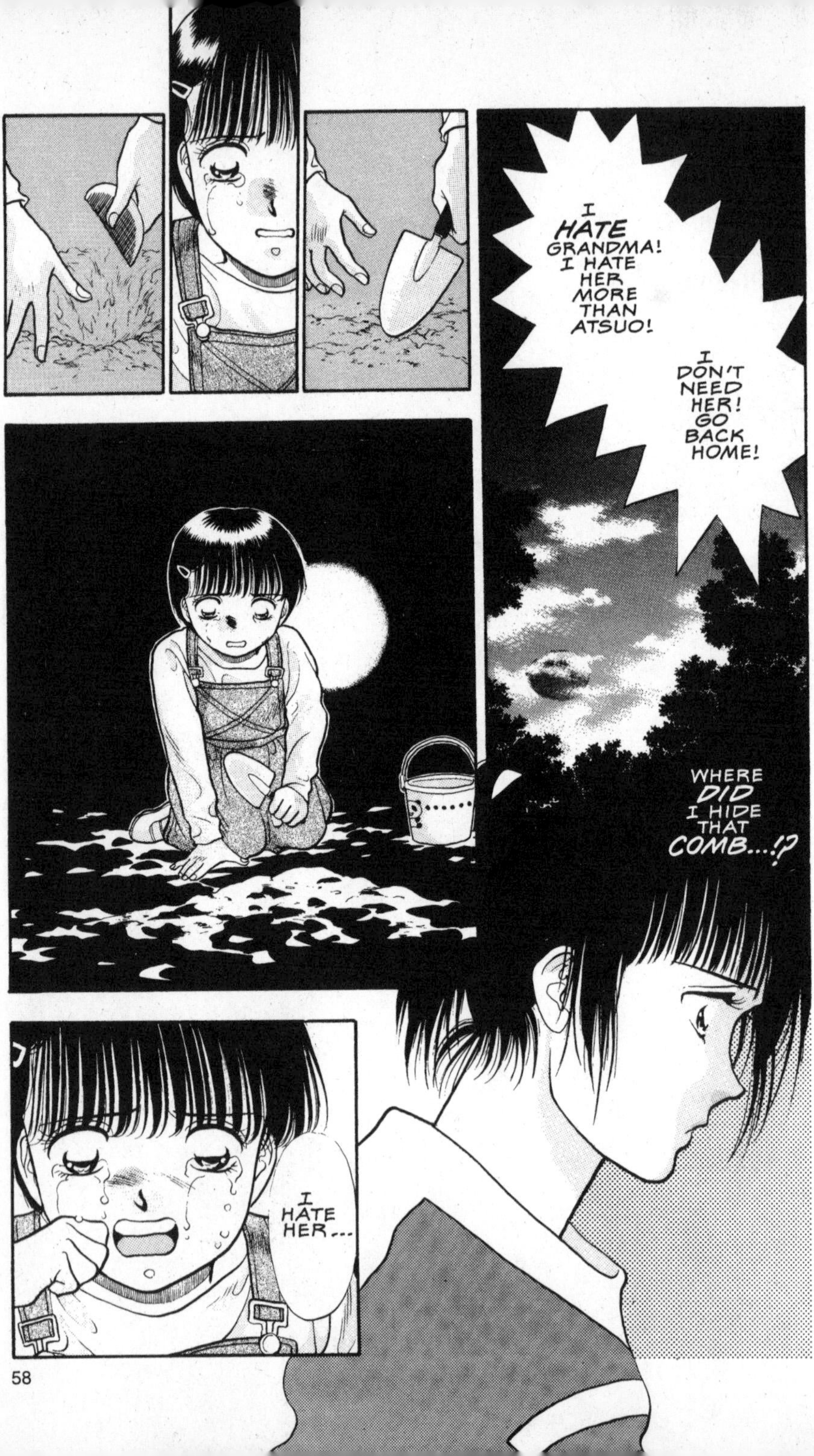
I HATE GRANDMA! I HATE HER MORE THAN ATSUO!
I DON'T NEED HER! GO BACK HOME!
WHERE DID I HIDE THAT COMB...!?
I HATE HER...

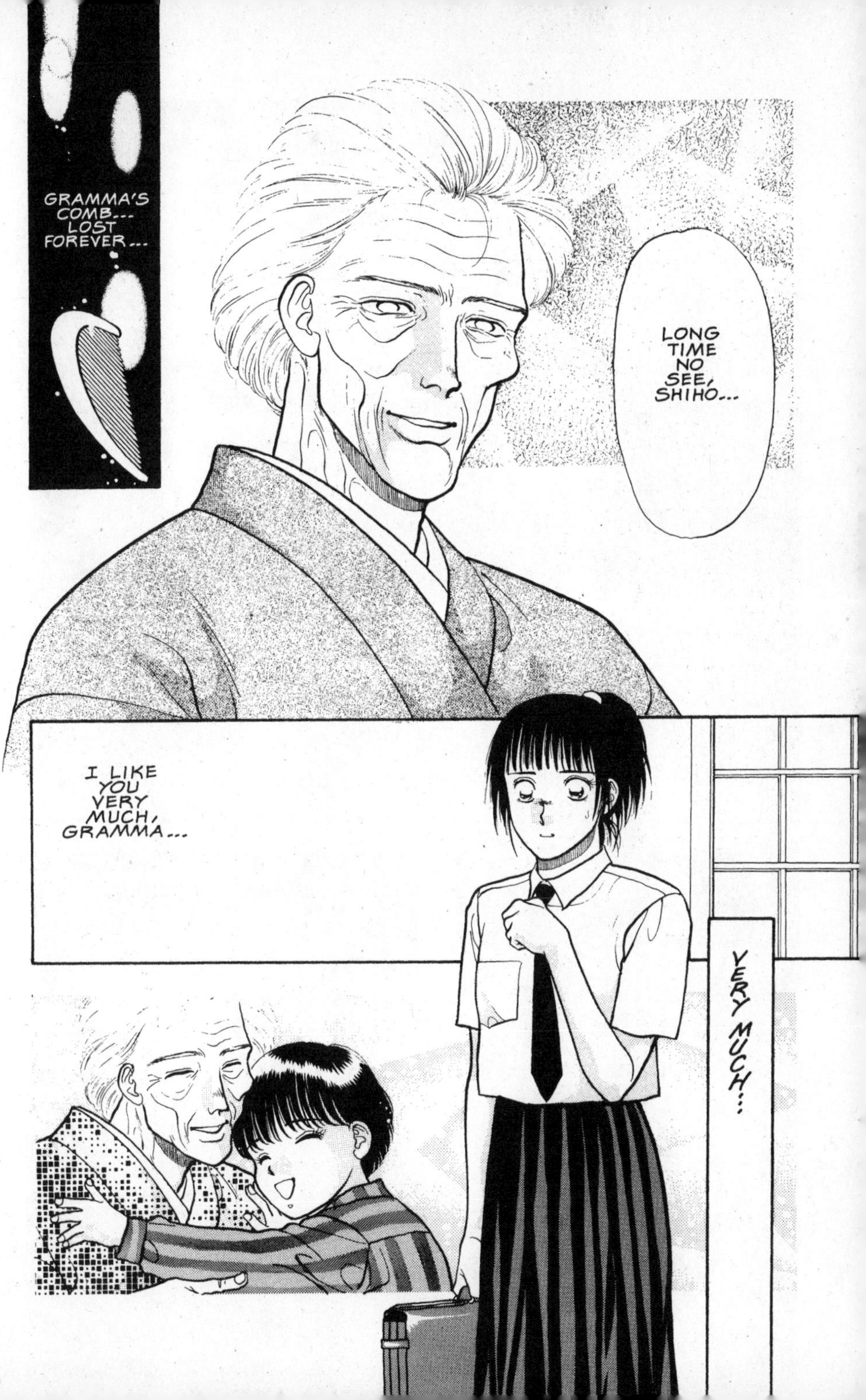
GRAMMA'S COMB... LOST FOREVER...
LONG TIME NO SEE, SHIHO...
I LIKE YOU VERY MUCH, GRAMMA...
VERY MUCH...

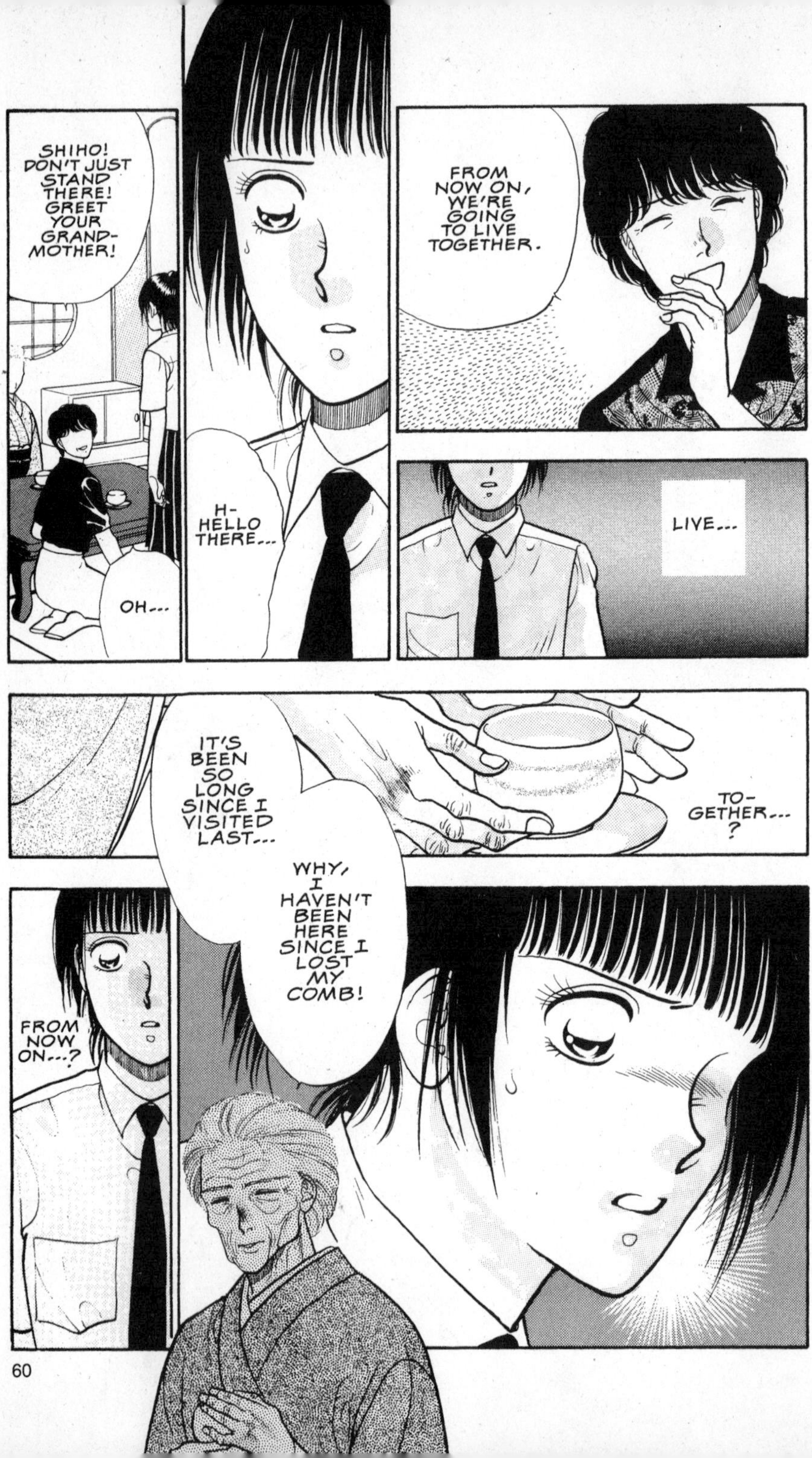
SHIHO! DON'T JUST STAND THERE! GREET YOUR GRAND-MOTHER!
OH...
H-HELLO THERE...
FROM NOW ON, WE'RE GOING TO LIVE TOGETHER.
LIVE...
IT'S BEEN SO LONG SINCE I VISITED LAST...
TO-GETHER...?
FROM NOW ON...?
WHY, I HAVEN'T BEEN HERE SINCE I LOST MY COMB!

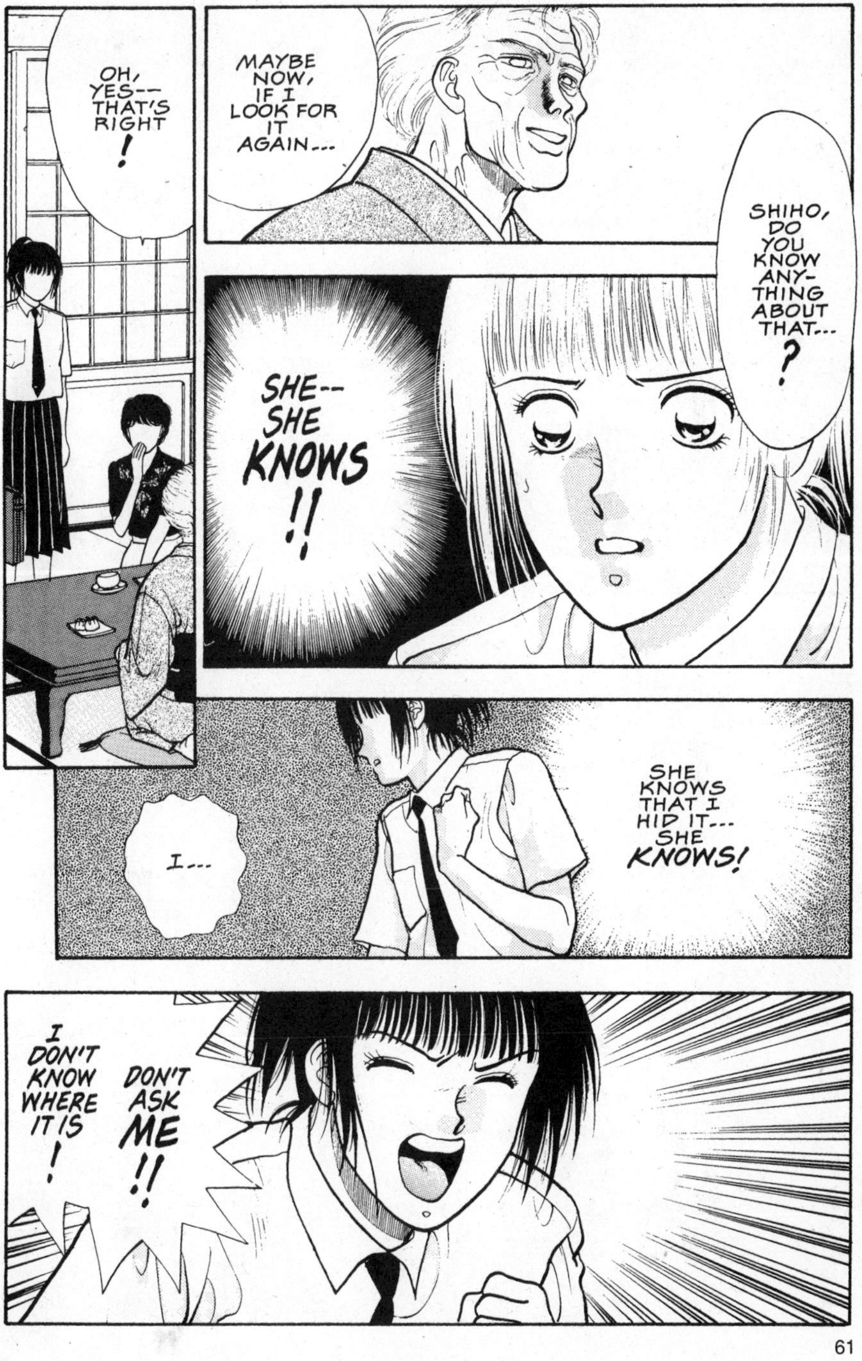

OH, YES-- THAT'S RIGHT!
MAYBE NOW, IF I LOOK FOR IT AGAIN...
SHIHO, DO YOU KNOW ANYTHING ABOUT THAT...?
SHE-- SHE KNOWS!!
I...
SHE KNOWS THAT I HID IT... SHE KNOWS!
I DON'T KNOW WHERE IT IS!
DON'T ASK ME!!

SHIHO! DINNER'S READY!

MOM, I'M EATING IN MY ROOM FROM NOW ON!

...SHE WON'T BE CAUGHT BY *THAT CREATURE.*

AS LONG AS SHE REMEMBERS WHAT I TOLD HER...

I... I'M SORRY ABOUT THIS...

THAT'S ALL RIGHT.

?

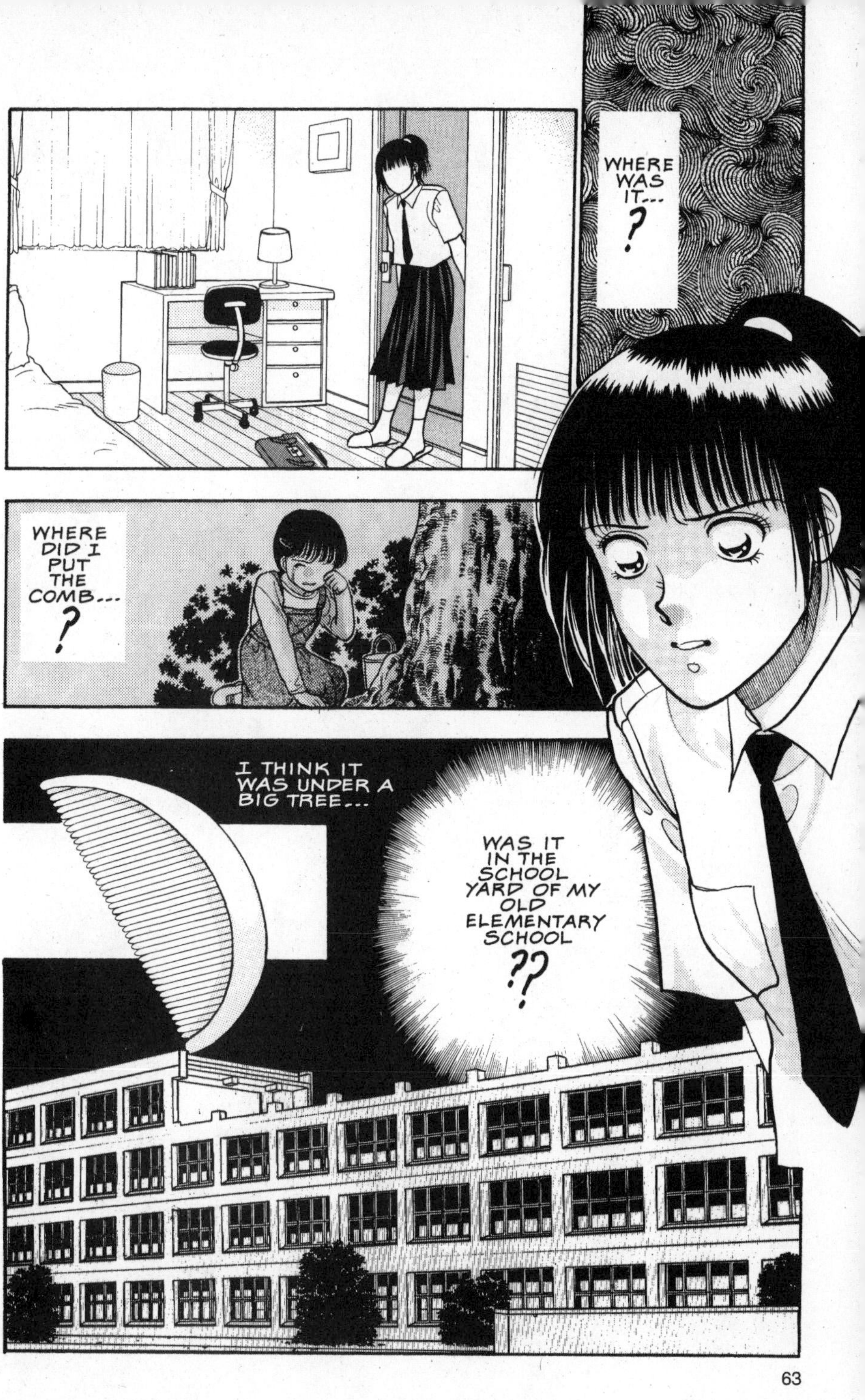
WHERE WAS IT...?
WHERE DID I PUT THE COMB...?
I THINK IT WAS UNDER A BIG TREE...
WAS IT IN THE SCHOOL YARD OF MY OLD ELEMENTARY SCHOOL??

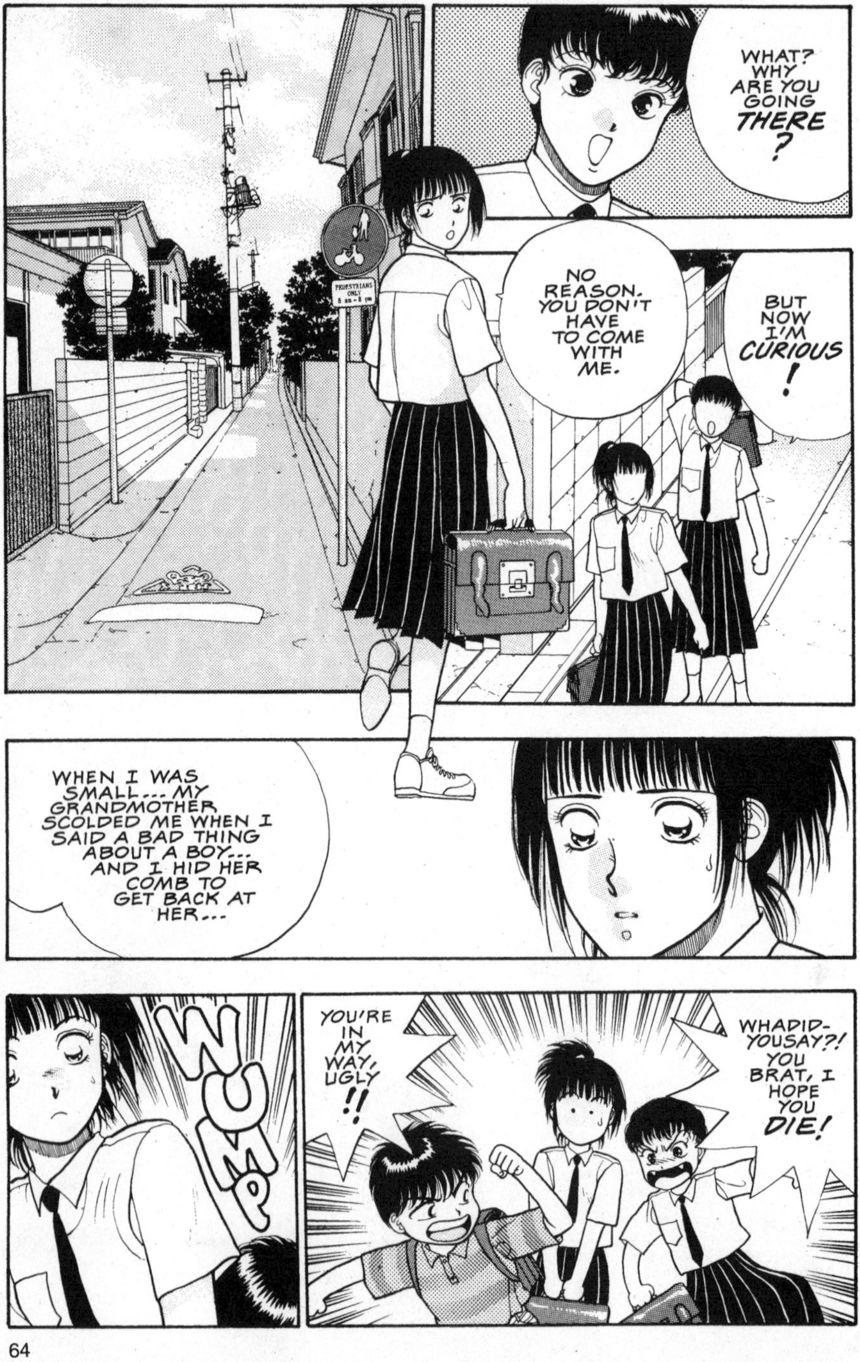
PEDESTRIANS ONLY
WHAT? WHY ARE YOU GOING THERE?
NO REASON. YOU DON'T HAVE TO COME WITH ME.
BUT NOW I'M CURIOUS!
WHEN I WAS SMALL... MY GRANDMOTHER SCOLDED ME WHEN I SAID A BAD THING ABOUT A BOY... AND I HID HER COMB TO GET BACK AT HER...
WUMP
YOU'RE IN MY WAY, UGLY!!
WHADID-YOUSAY?! YOU BRAT, I HOPE YOU DIE!

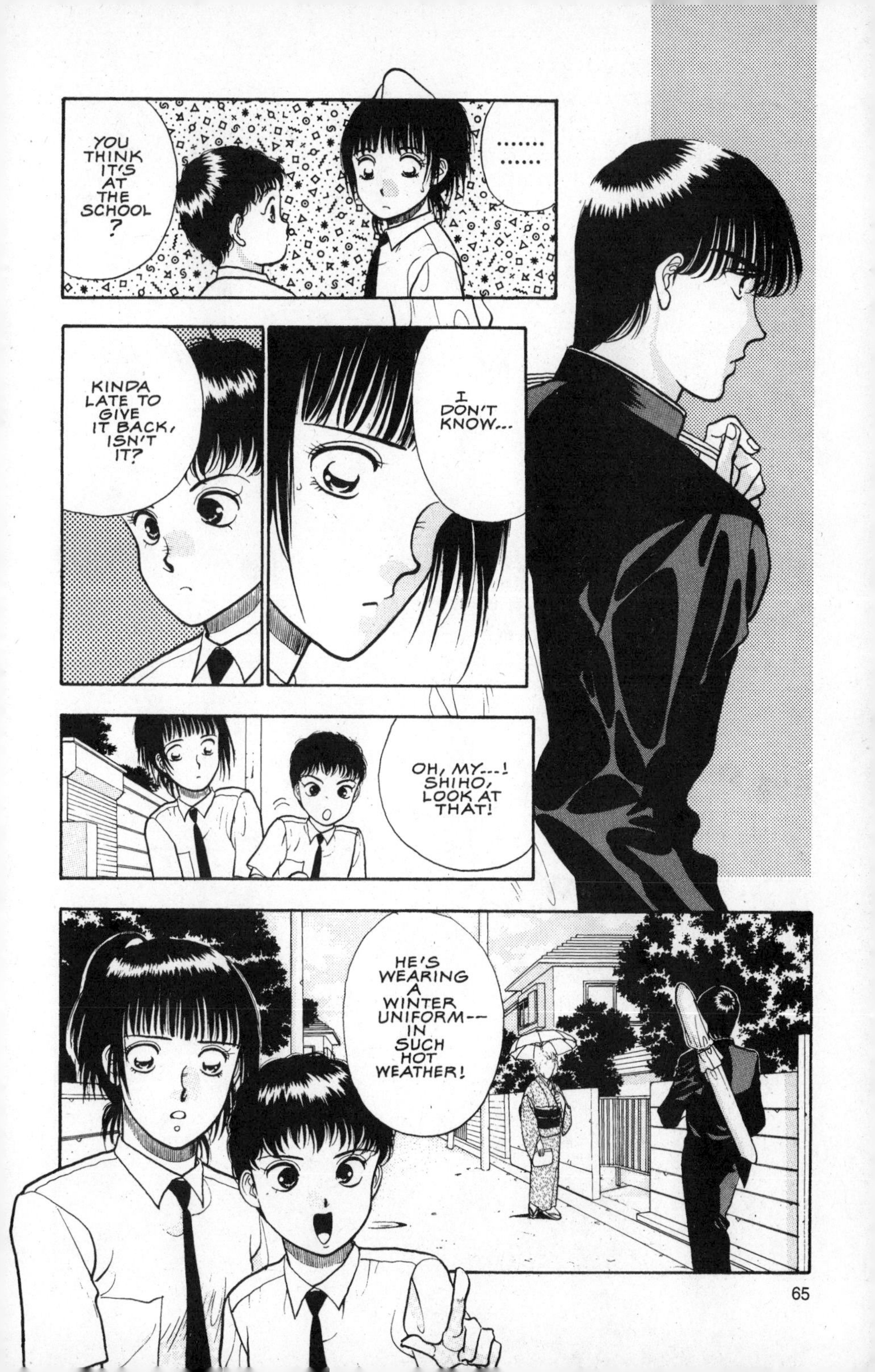
YOU THINK IT'S AT THE SCHOOL?
......
......
KINDA LATE TO GIVE IT BACK, ISN'T IT?
I DON'T KNOW...
OH, MY...! SHIHO, LOOK AT THAT!
HE'S WEARING A WINTER UNIFORM-- IN SUCH HOT WEATHER!

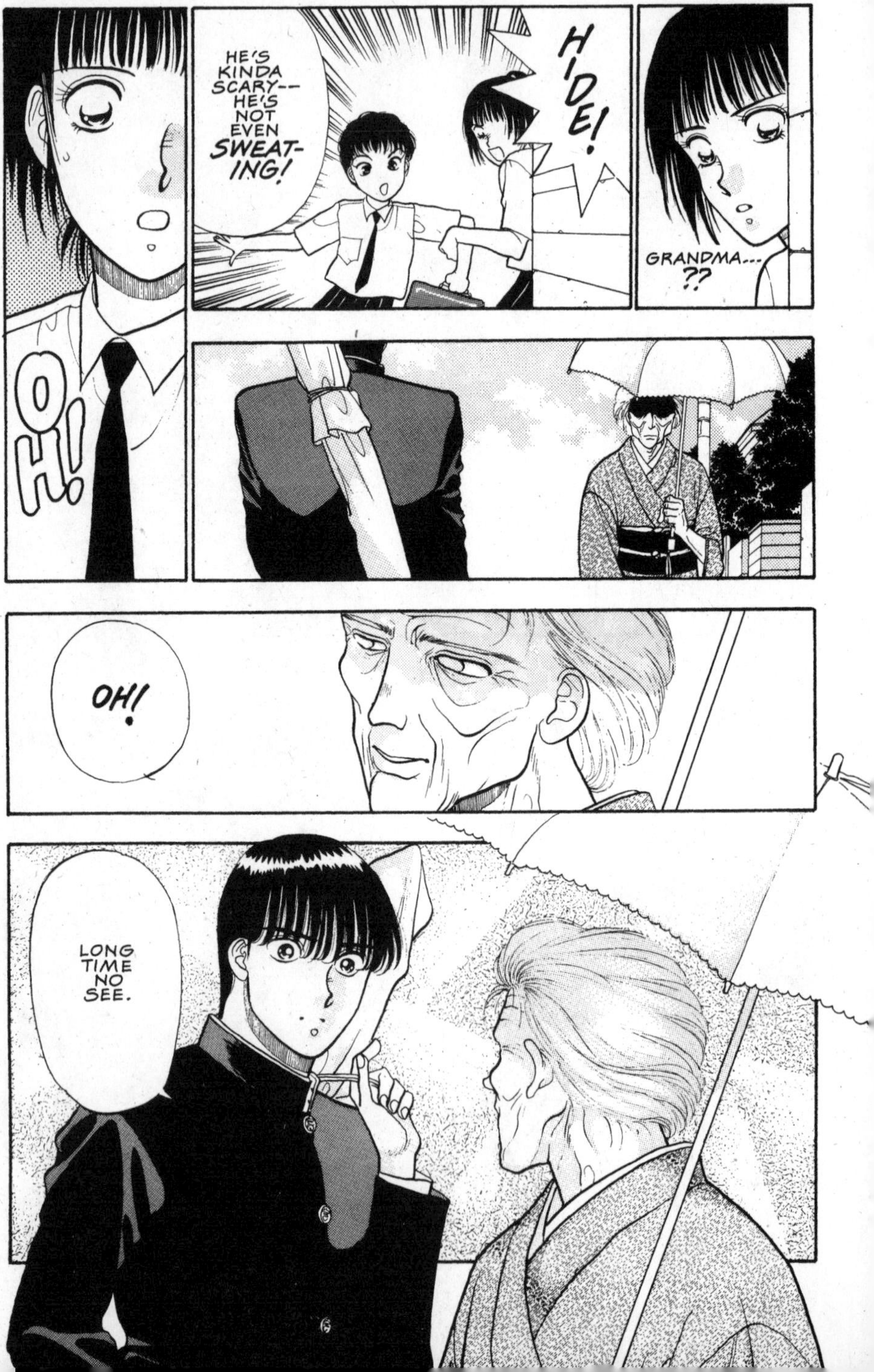
OH!
HE'S KINDA SCARY-- HE'S NOT EVEN SWEATING!
HIDE!
GRANDMA...??
OH!
LONG TIME NO SEE.

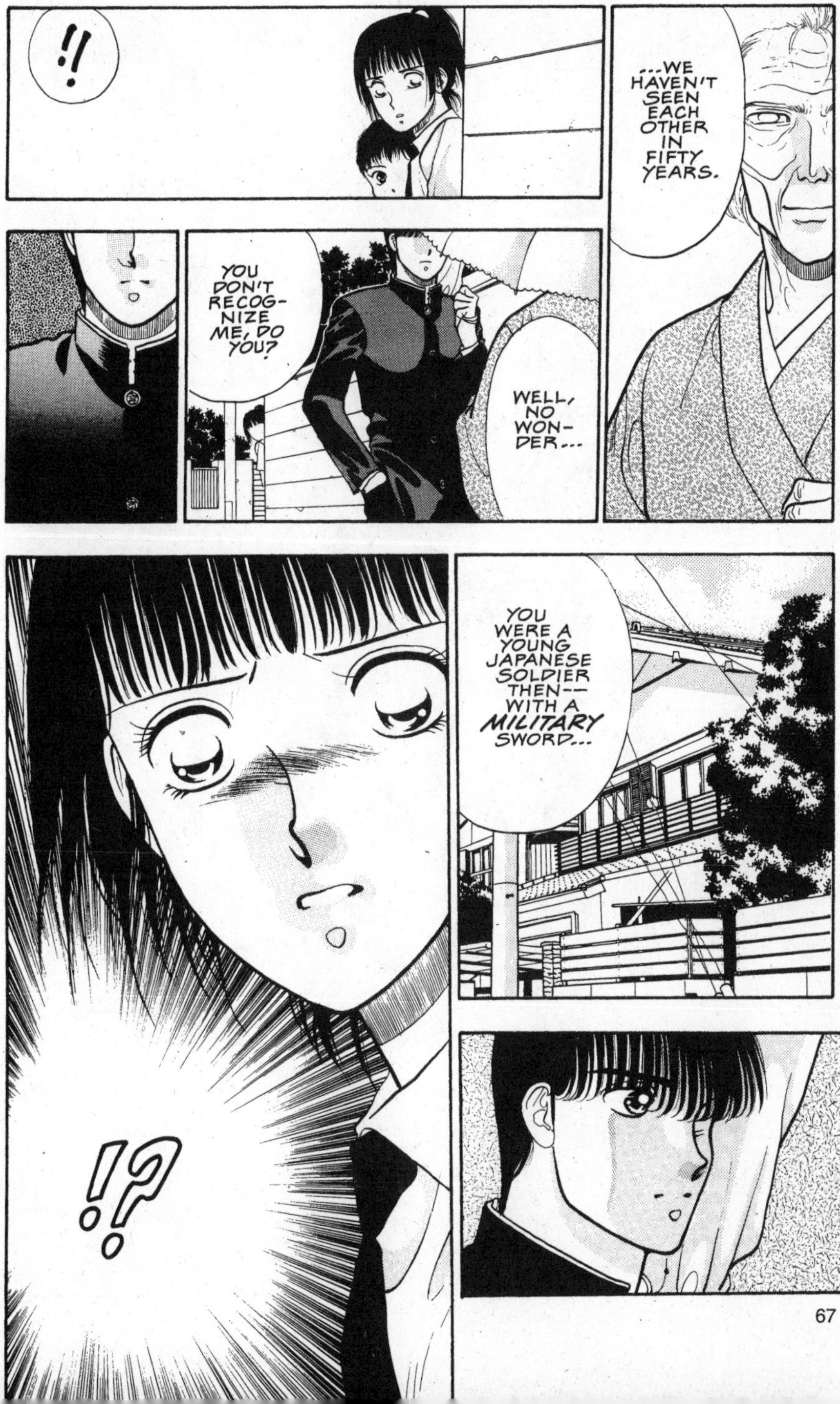
!!
...WE HAVEN'T SEEN EACH OTHER IN FIFTY YEARS.
YOU DON'T RECOG-NIZE ME, DO YOU?
WELL, NO WON-DER...
!?
YOU WERE A YOUNG JAPANESE SOLDIER THEN-- WITH A *MILITARY* SWORD...

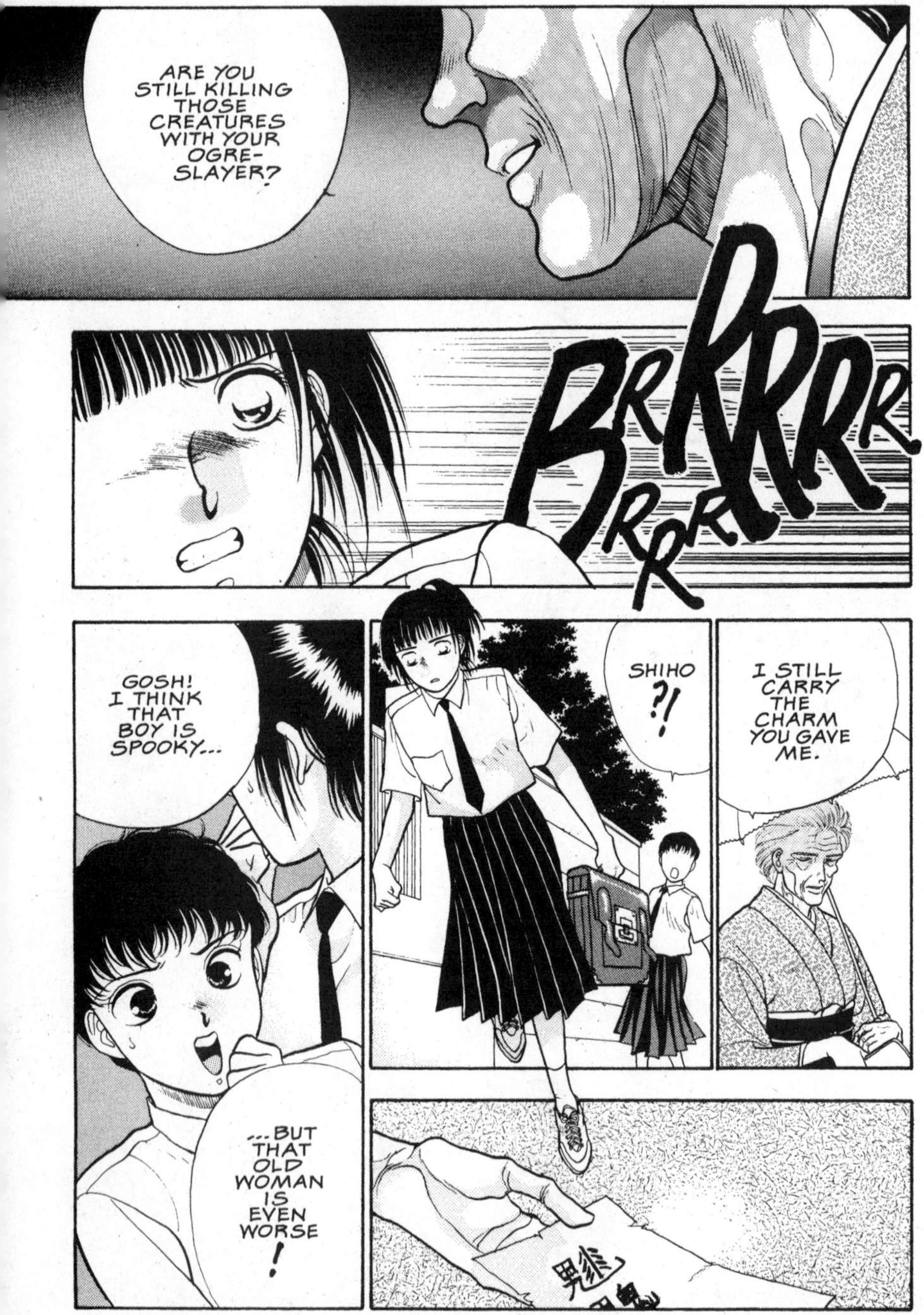
ARE YOU STILL KILLING THOSE CREATURES WITH YOUR OGRE-SLAYER?
BRRRRRR
RRRR
GOSH! I THINK THAT BOY IS SPOOKY...
...BUT THAT OLD WOMAN IS EVEN WORSE!
SHIHO ?!
I STILL CARRY THE CHARM YOU GAVE ME.

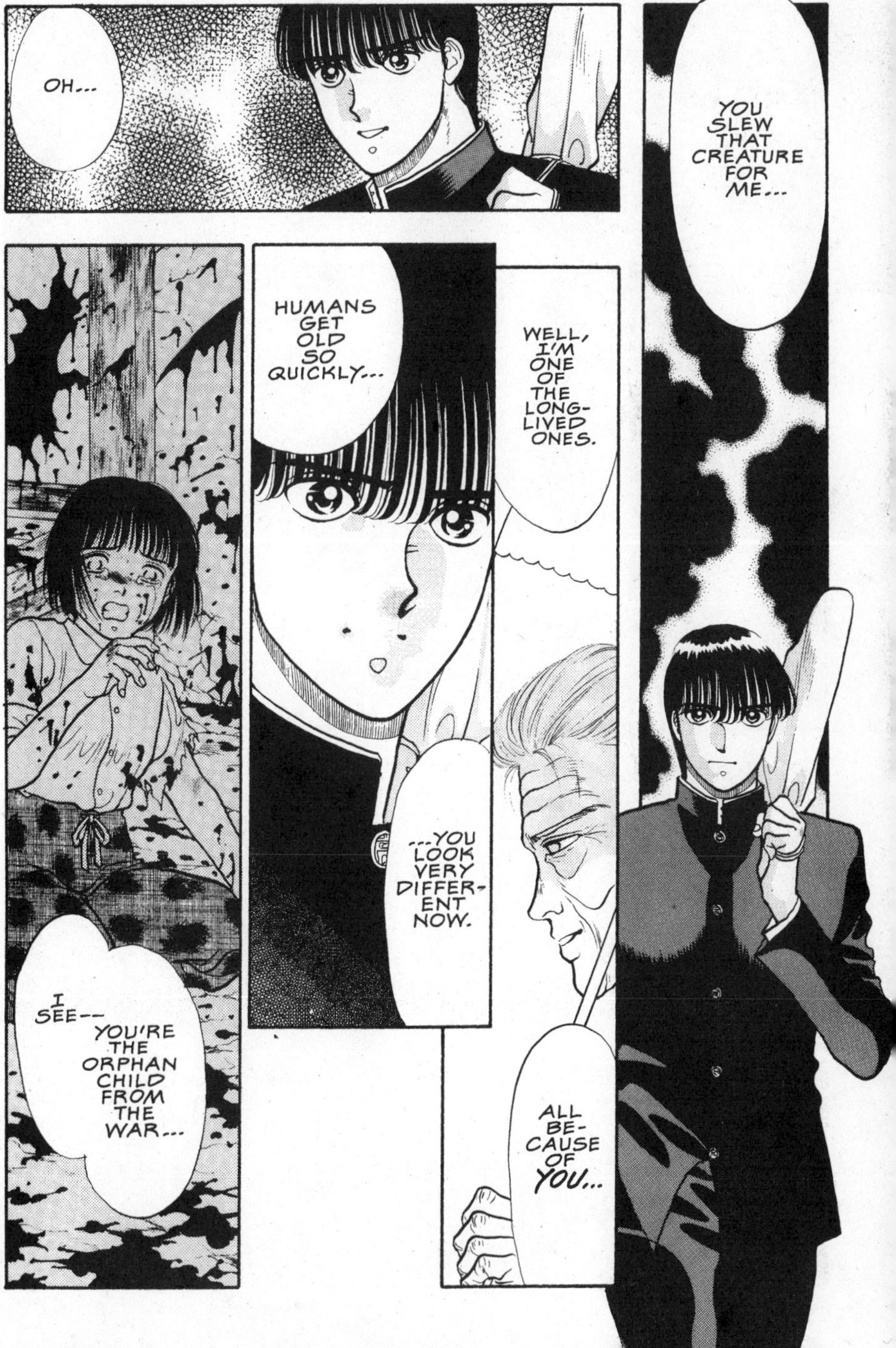
OH...
I SEE-- YOU'RE THE ORPHAN CHILD FROM THE WAR...
HUMANS GET OLD SO QUICKLY...
...YOU LOOK VERY DIFFERENT NOW.
WELL, I'M ONE OF THE LONG-LIVED ONES.
ALL BECAUSE OF YOU...
YOU SLEW THAT CREATURE FOR ME...

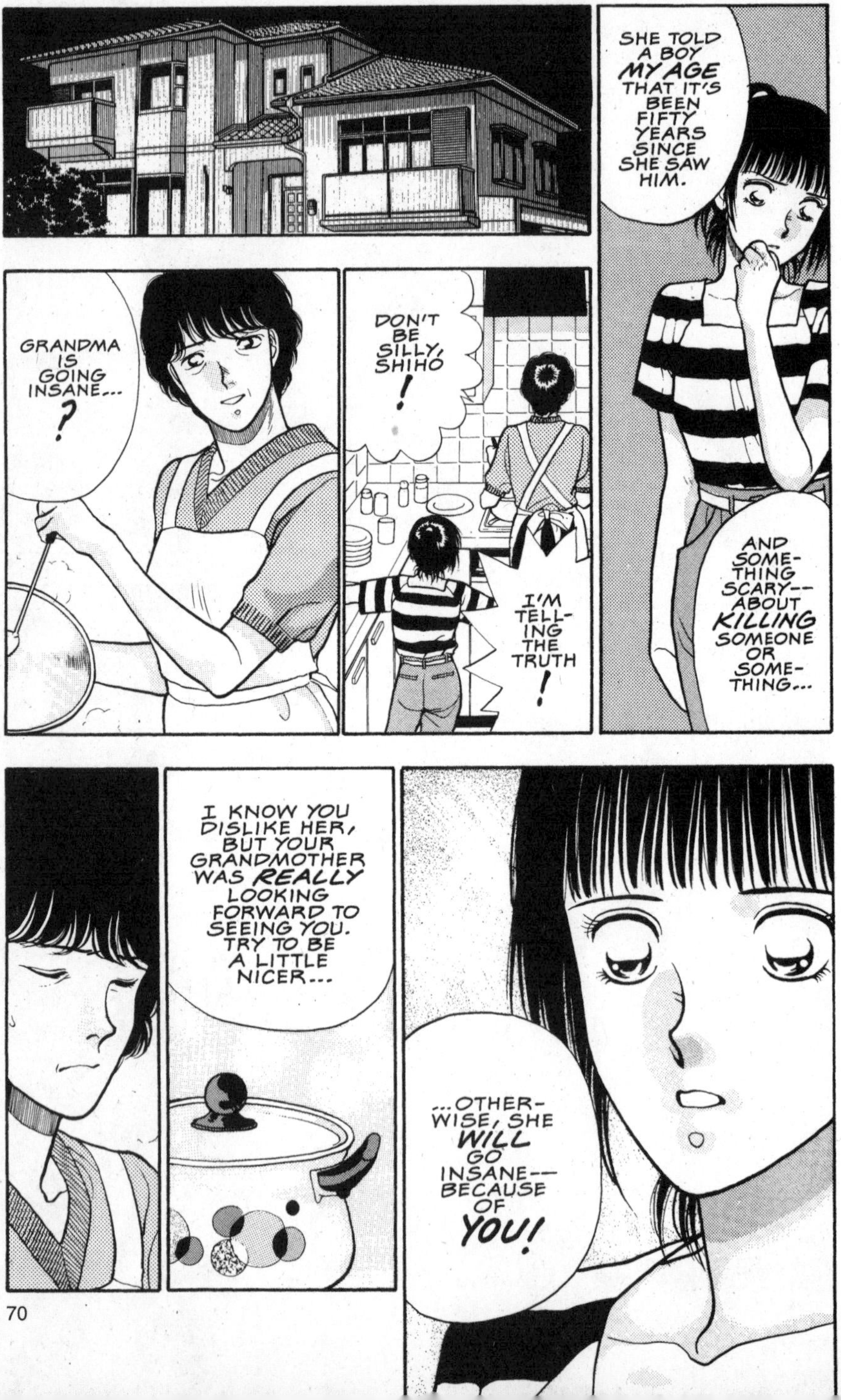
GRANDMA IS GOING INSANE...?
DON'T BE SILLY, SHIHO!
I'M TELL-ING THE TRUTH!
SHE TOLD A BOY MY AGE THAT IT'S BEEN FIFTY YEARS SINCE SHE SAW HIM.
AND SOME-THING SCARY-- ABOUT KILLING SOMEONE OR SOME-THING...
I KNOW YOU DISLIKE HER, BUT YOUR GRANDMOTHER WAS REALLY LOOKING FORWARD TO SEEING YOU. TRY TO BE A LITTLE NICER...
...OTHER-WISE, SHE WILL GO INSANE-- BECAUSE OF YOU!

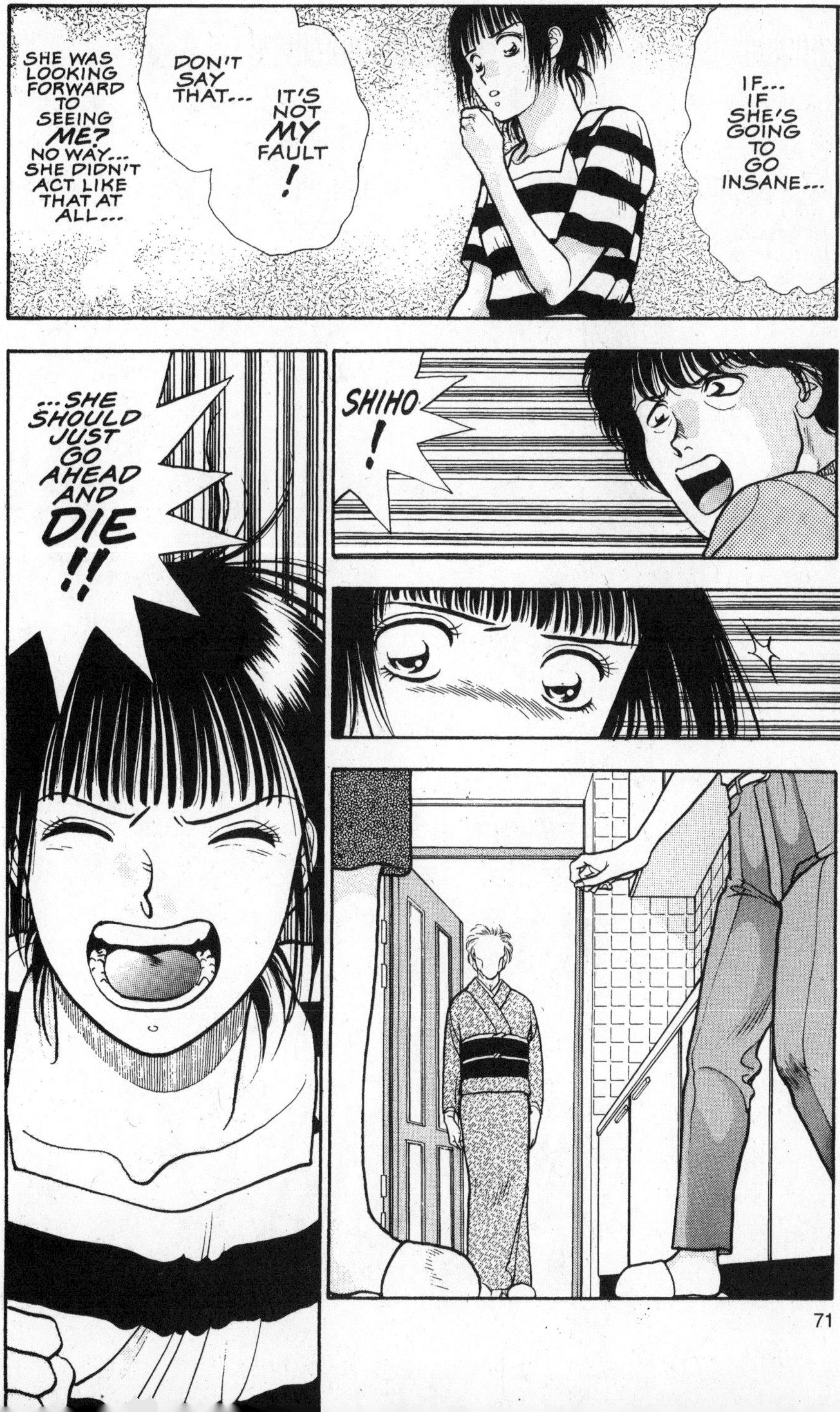
SHE WAS LOOKING FORWARD TO SEEING ME? NO WAY... SHE DIDN'T ACT LIKE THAT AT ALL...
DON'T SAY THAT...
IT'S NOT MY FAULT!
IF... IF SHE'S GOING TO GO INSANE...
...SHE SHOULD JUST GO AHEAD AND DIE!!
SHIHO!

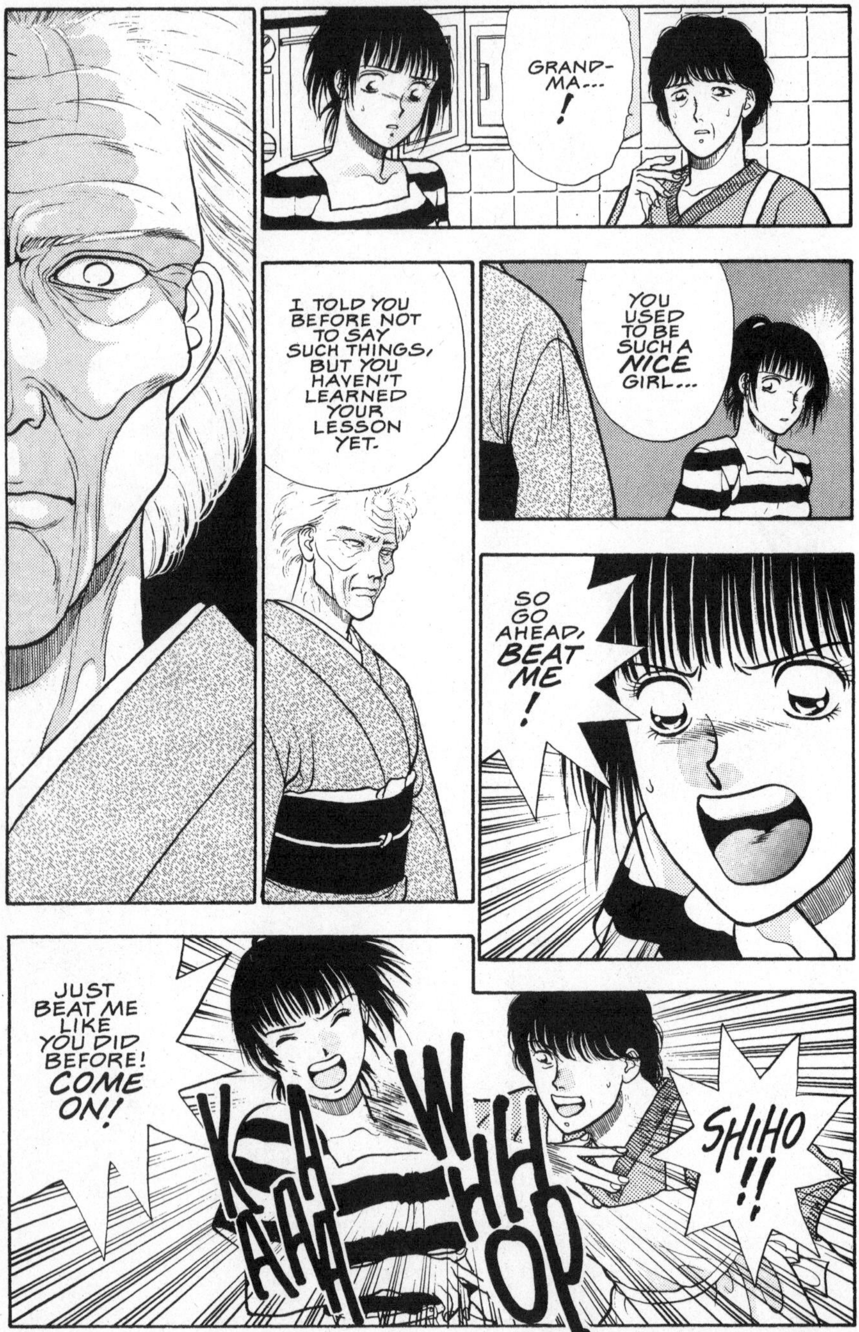
GRAND-MA...!
I TOLD YOU BEFORE NOT TO SAY SUCH THINGS, BUT YOU HAVEN'T LEARNED YOUR LESSON YET.
YOU USED TO BE SUCH A NICE GIRL...
SO GO AHEAD, BEAT ME!
JUST BEAT ME LIKE YOU DID BEFORE! COME ON!
KAAAAA
WHHOP
SHIHO!!

WEE GOE WEE GOE WEE GOE

...EVER SINCE GRAND-MA CAME!

IT'S ALL HER FAULT!

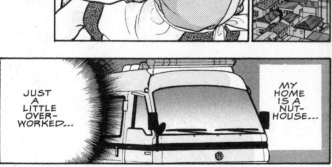

JUST A LITTLE OVER-WORKED...

MY HOME IS A NUT-HOUSE...

...THERE'S NO PLACE I CAN RELAX...

...BUT WE'LL STILL WANT TO KEEP HER A WHILE FOR OBSERVA-TION.

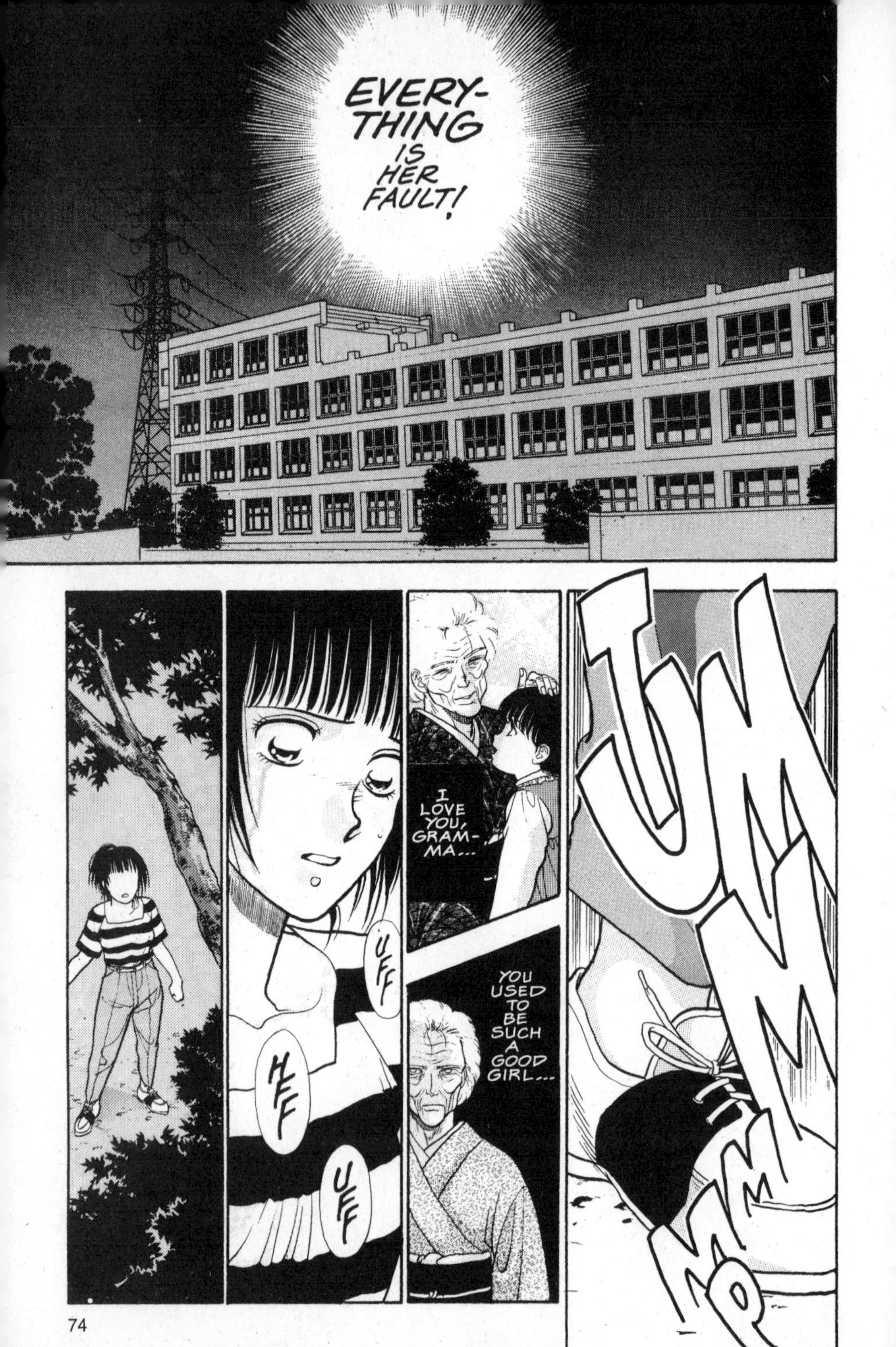
EVERY-THING IS HER FAULT!
UFF
HFF
UFF
I LOVE YOU, GRAM-MA...
YOU USED TO BE SUCH A GOOD GIRL...
THUMMMMP

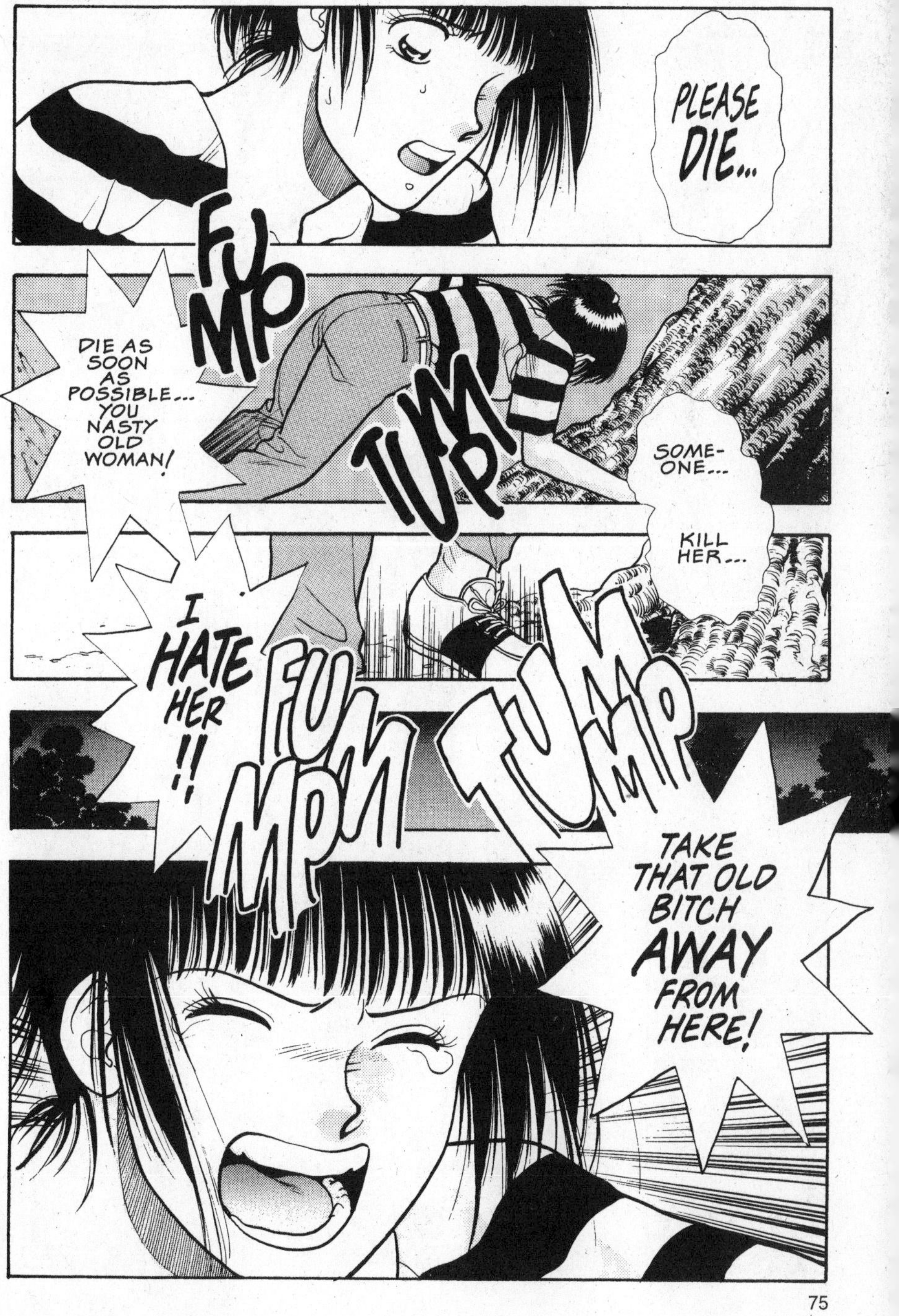
PLEASE DIE...
FUMP
DIE AS SOON AS POSSIBLE... YOU NASTY OLD WOMAN!
TUMP
SOME-ONE...
KILL HER...
I HATE HER!!
FUMP
TUMP
TAKE THAT OLD BITCH AWAY FROM HERE!

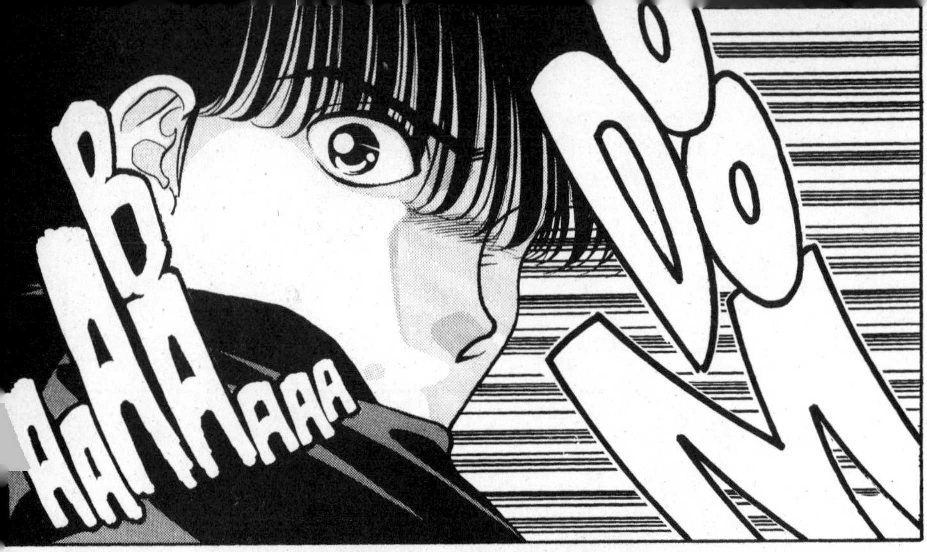
BAHAHAAA
DOOM

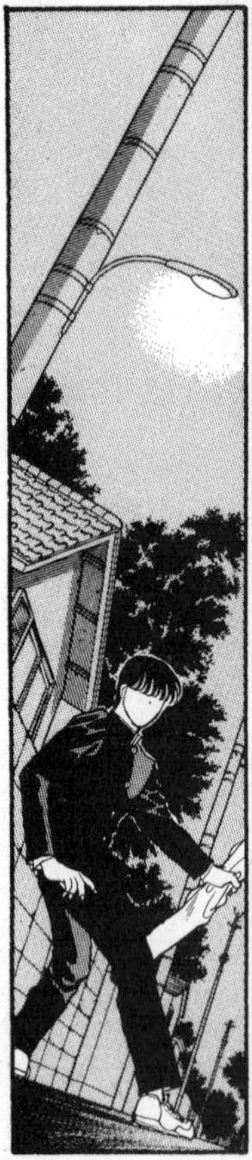

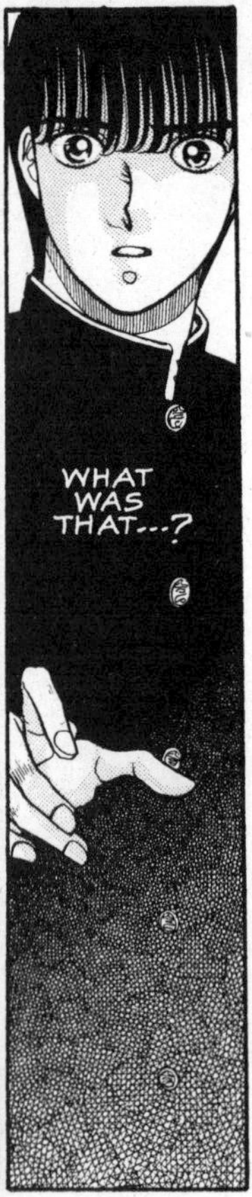
WHAT WAS THAT...?

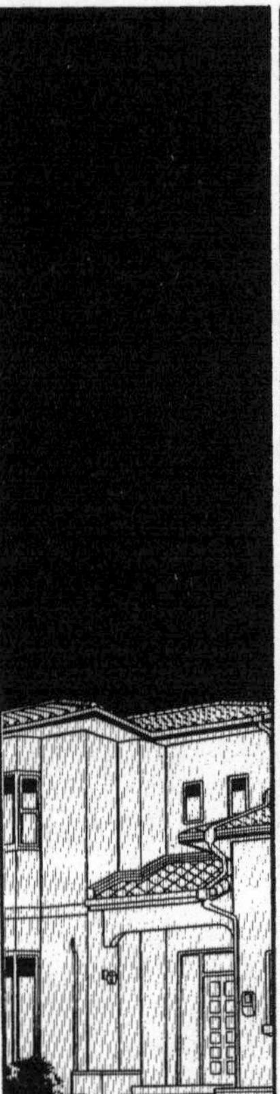

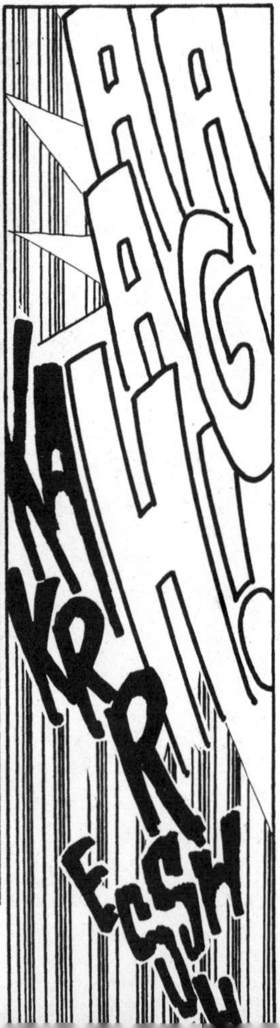
AAAAAGH
KAKRRRESSH

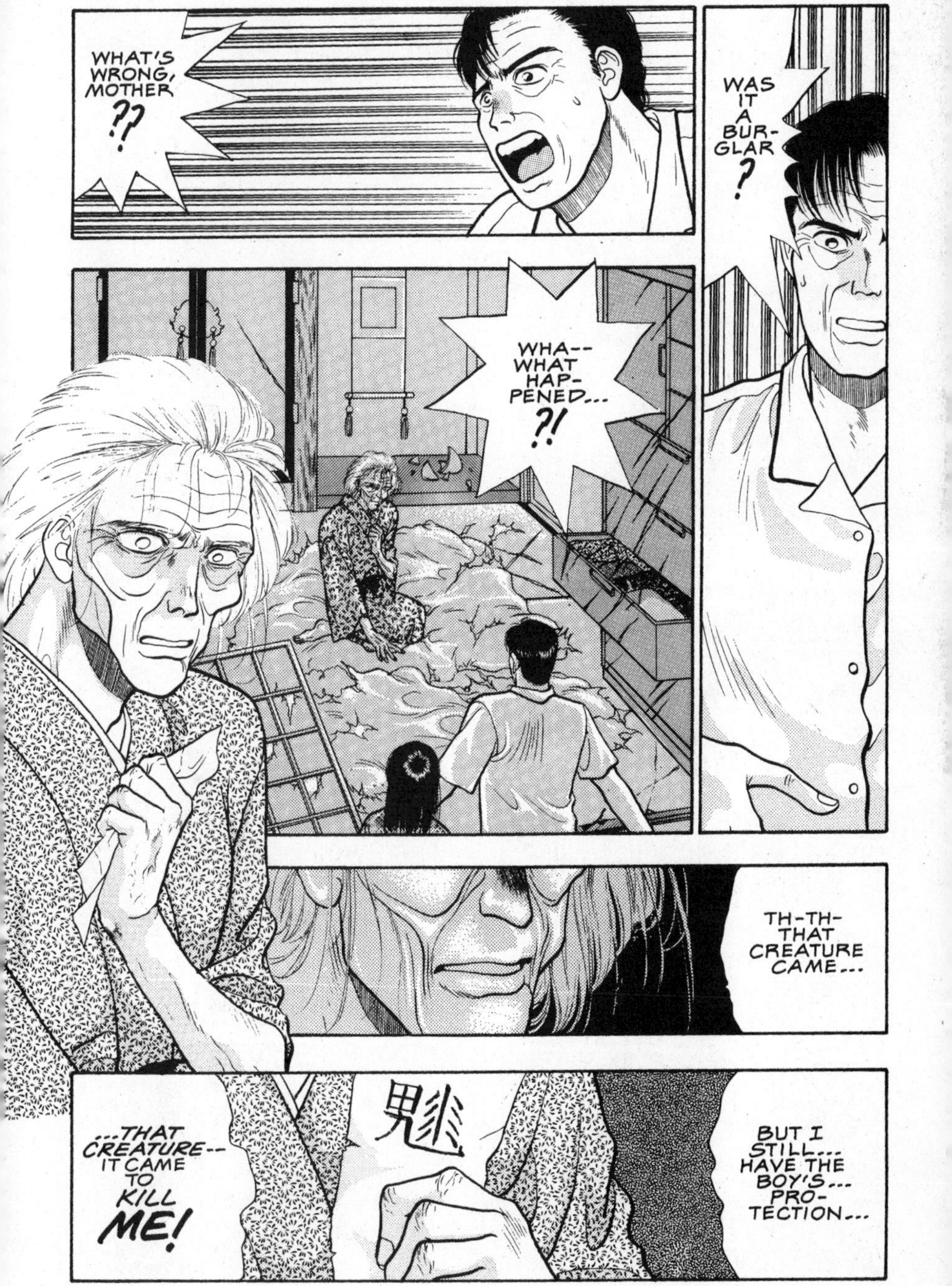
WHAT'S WRONG, MOTHER??
WHA-- WHAT HAPPENED...?!
WAS IT A BURGLAR?
TH-TH-THAT CREATURE CAME...
...THAT CREATURE-- IT CAME TO KILL ME!
BUT I STILL... HAVE THE BOY'S... PROTECTION...

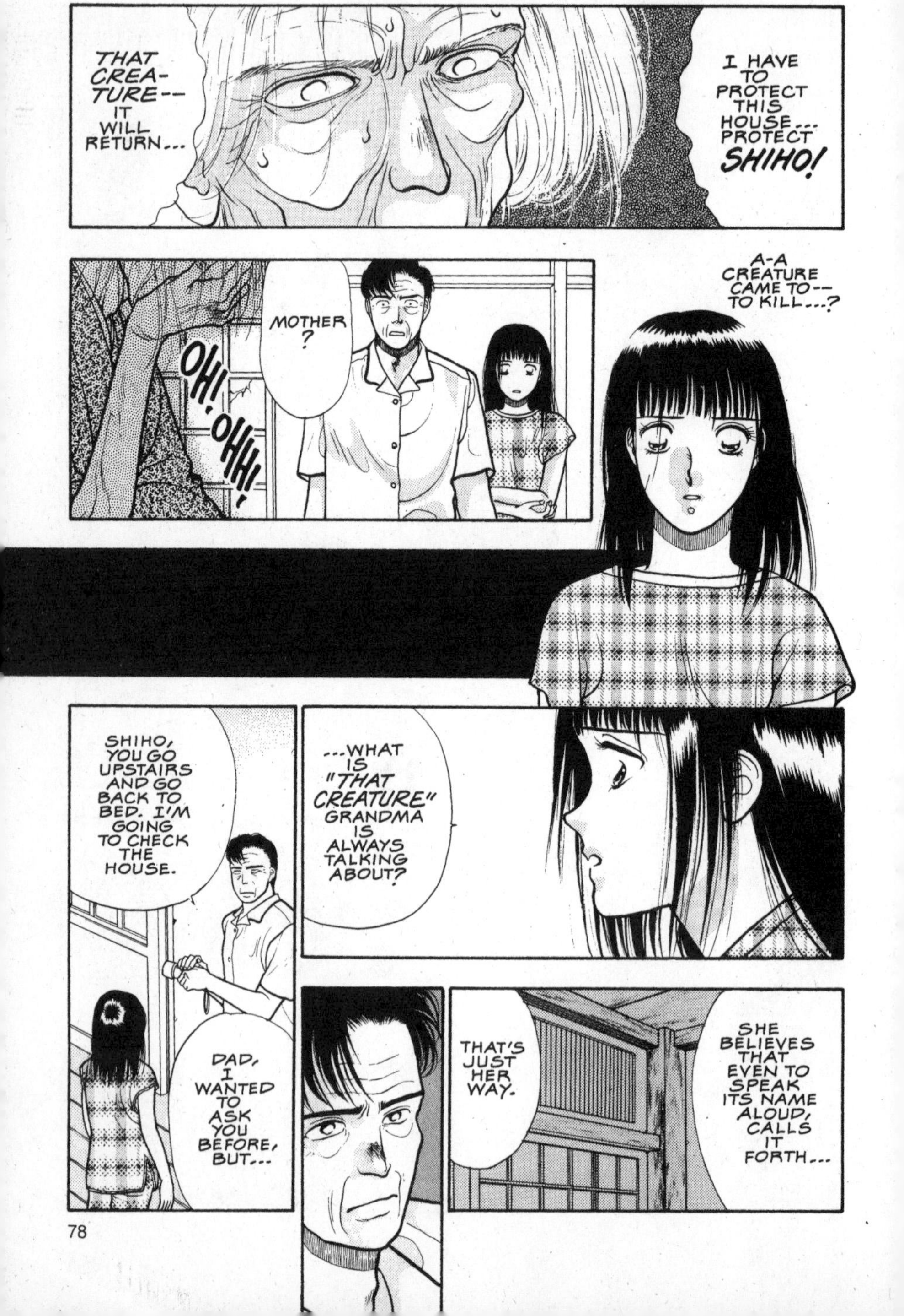
THAT CREATURE-- IT WILL RETURN...
I HAVE TO PROTECT THIS HOUSE... PROTECT SHIHO!
MOTHER?
OH! OHH!
A-A CREATURE CAME TO-- TO KILL...?
SHIHO, YOU GO UPSTAIRS AND GO BACK TO BED. I'M GOING TO CHECK THE HOUSE.
...WHAT IS "THAT CREATURE" GRANDMA IS ALWAYS TALKING ABOUT?
DAD, I WANTED TO ASK YOU BEFORE, BUT...
THAT'S JUST HER WAY.
SHE BELIEVES THAT EVEN TO SPEAK ITS NAME ALOUD, CALLS IT FORTH...

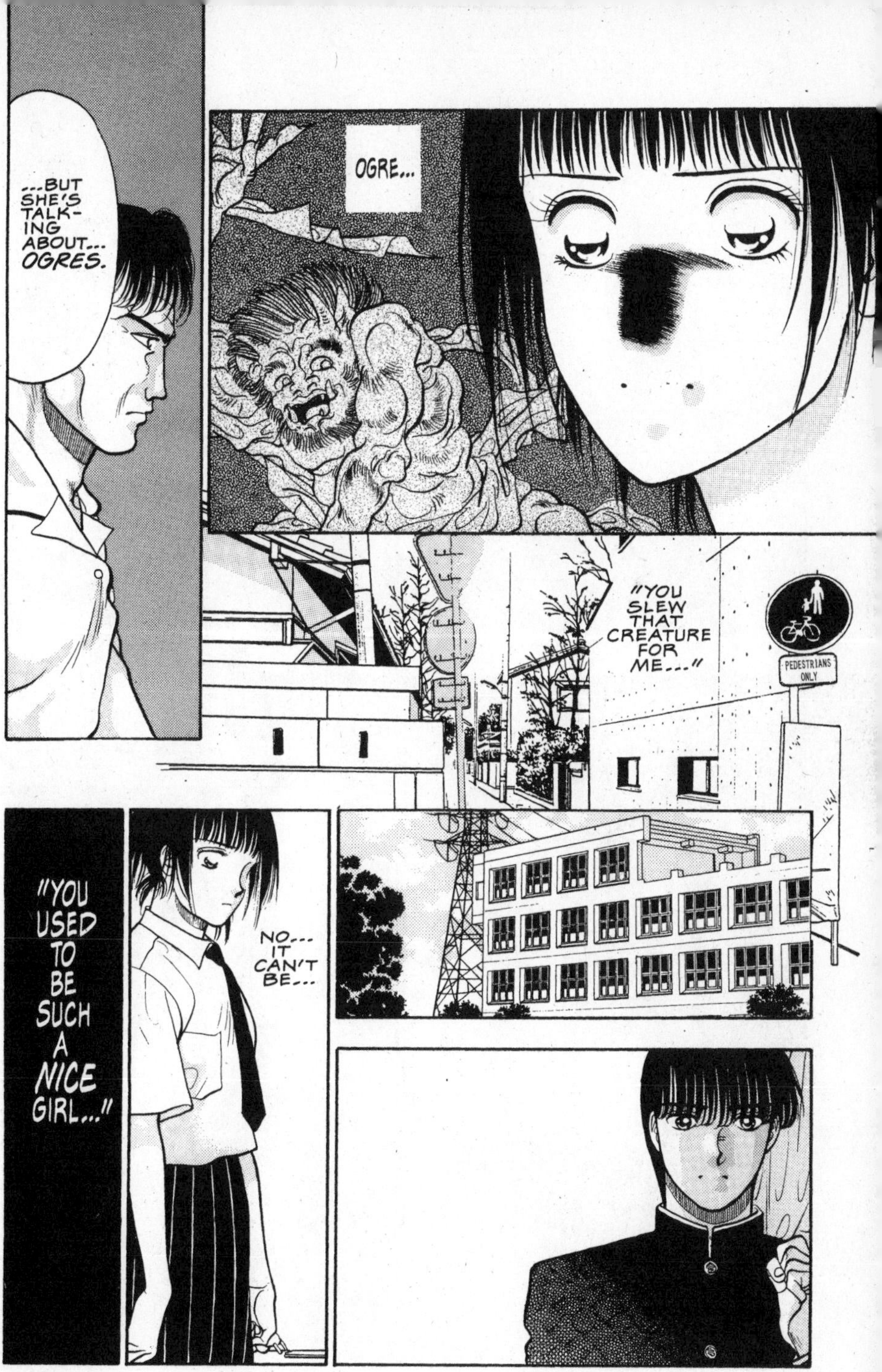

...BUT SHE'S TALKING ABOUT... OGRES.
OGRE...
"YOU SLEW THAT CREATURE FOR ME..."
PEDESTRIANS ONLY
"YOU USED TO BE SUCH A NICE GIRL..."
NO... IT CAN'T BE...

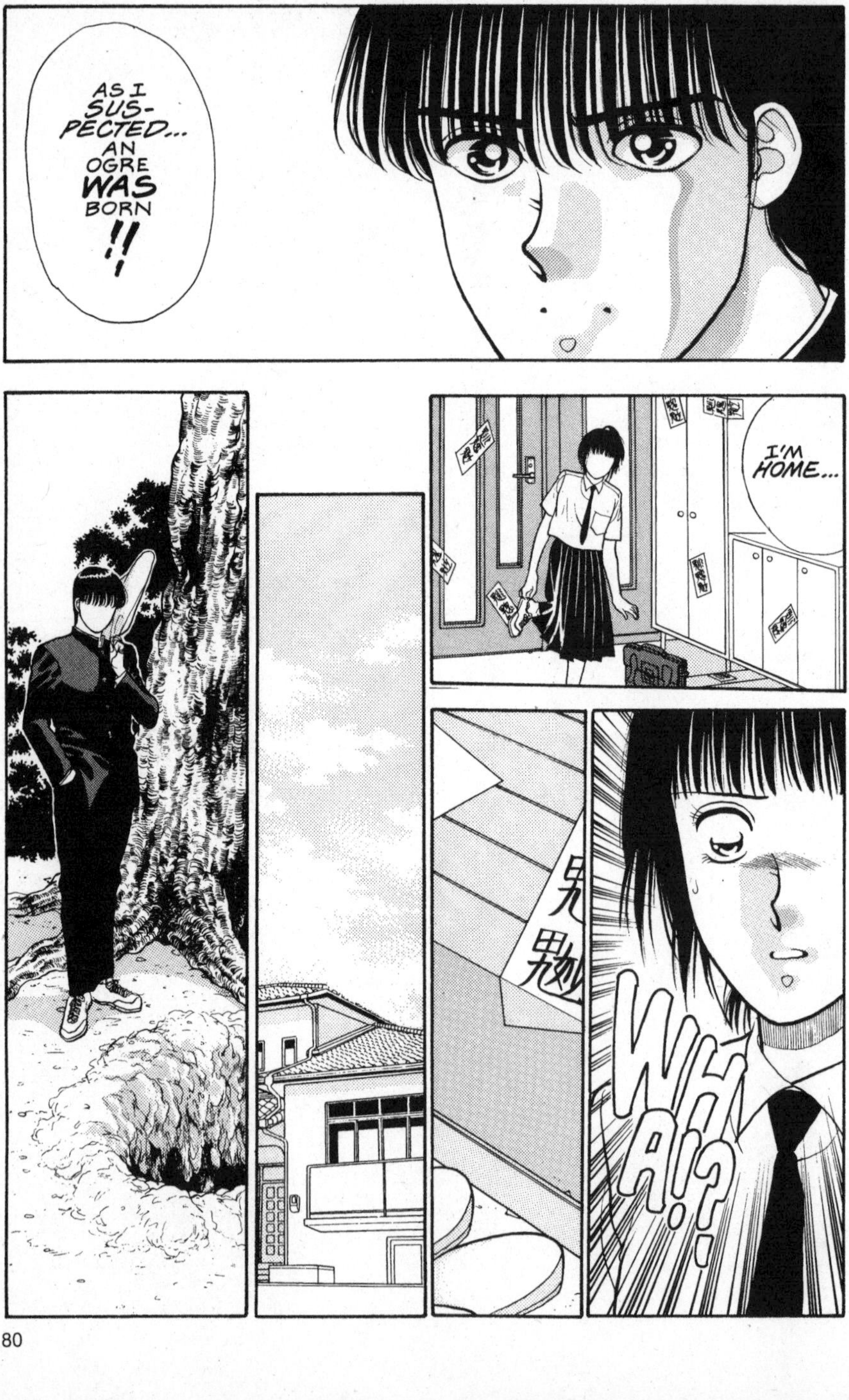
AS I SUS-PECTED... AN OGRE WAS BORN !!
I'M HOME...
WHA!?

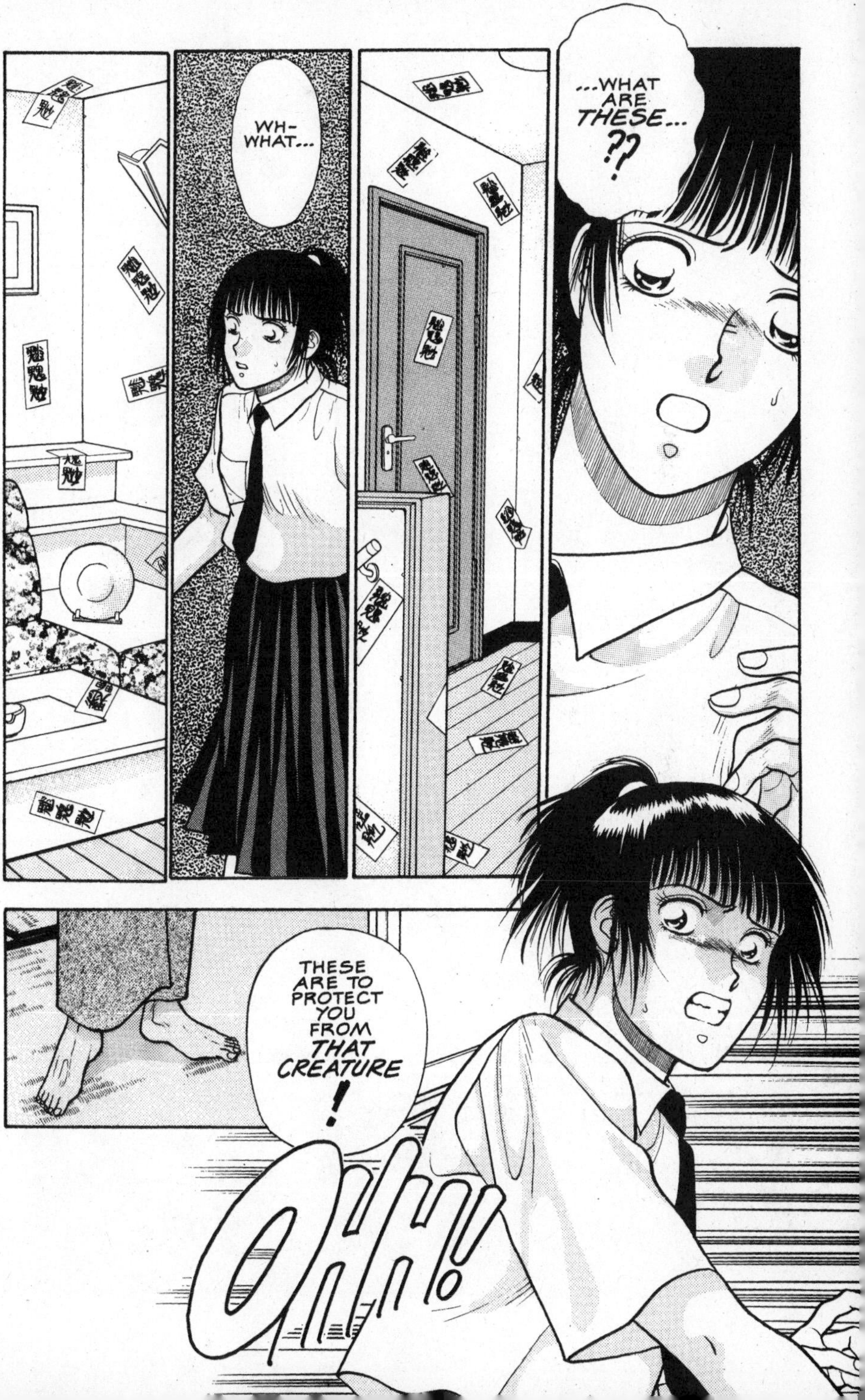
WH- WHAT...
...WHAT ARE THESE... ??
THESE ARE TO PROTECT YOU FROM THAT CREATURE!
OH!

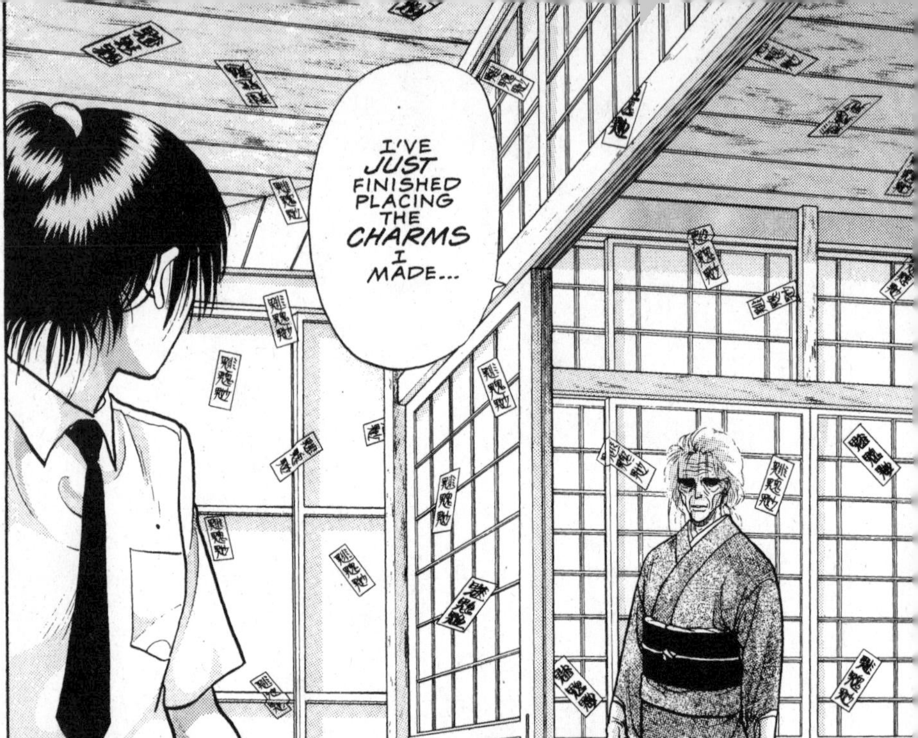
I'VE JUST FINISHED PLACING THE CHARMS I MADE...

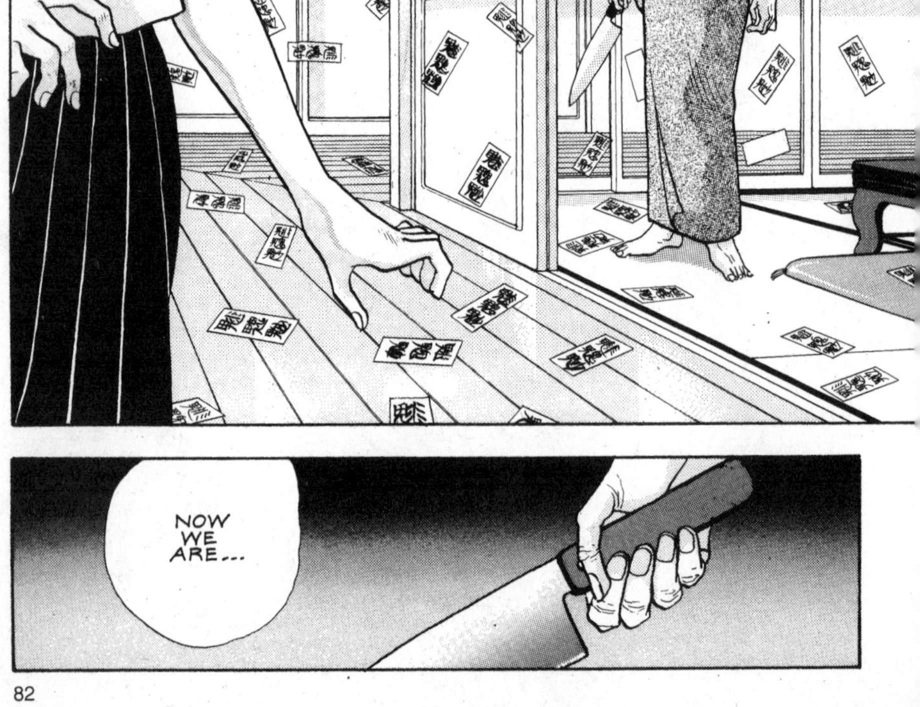
NOW WE ARE...

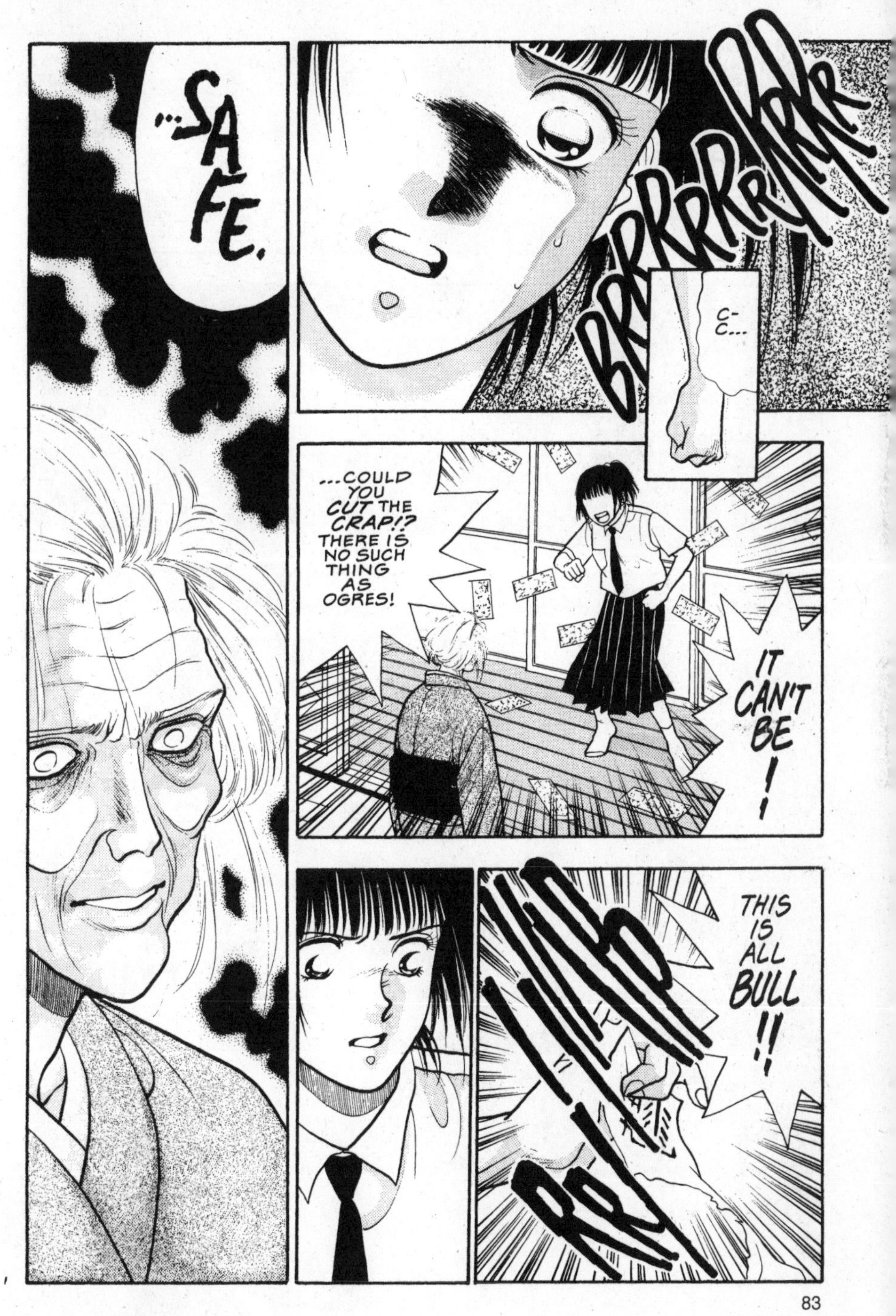
...SAFE.
C- C...
...COULD YOU CUT THE CRAP!? THERE IS NO SUCH THING AS OGRES!
IT CAN'T BE!!
THIS IS ALL BULL!!

STOP!

WHAT ARE YOU DOING?!

I CAN'T *TAKE* THIS ANY-MORE!

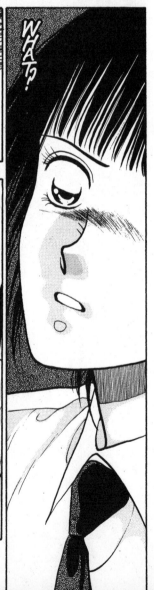

WHAT?!

PLEASE, GRANDMA! STOP *SCARING* ME!

I *KNOW* THAT CREATURE EXISTS!

I'VE SEEN IT, SHIHO! I-I'VE CREATED... AN *OGRE* BEFORE.

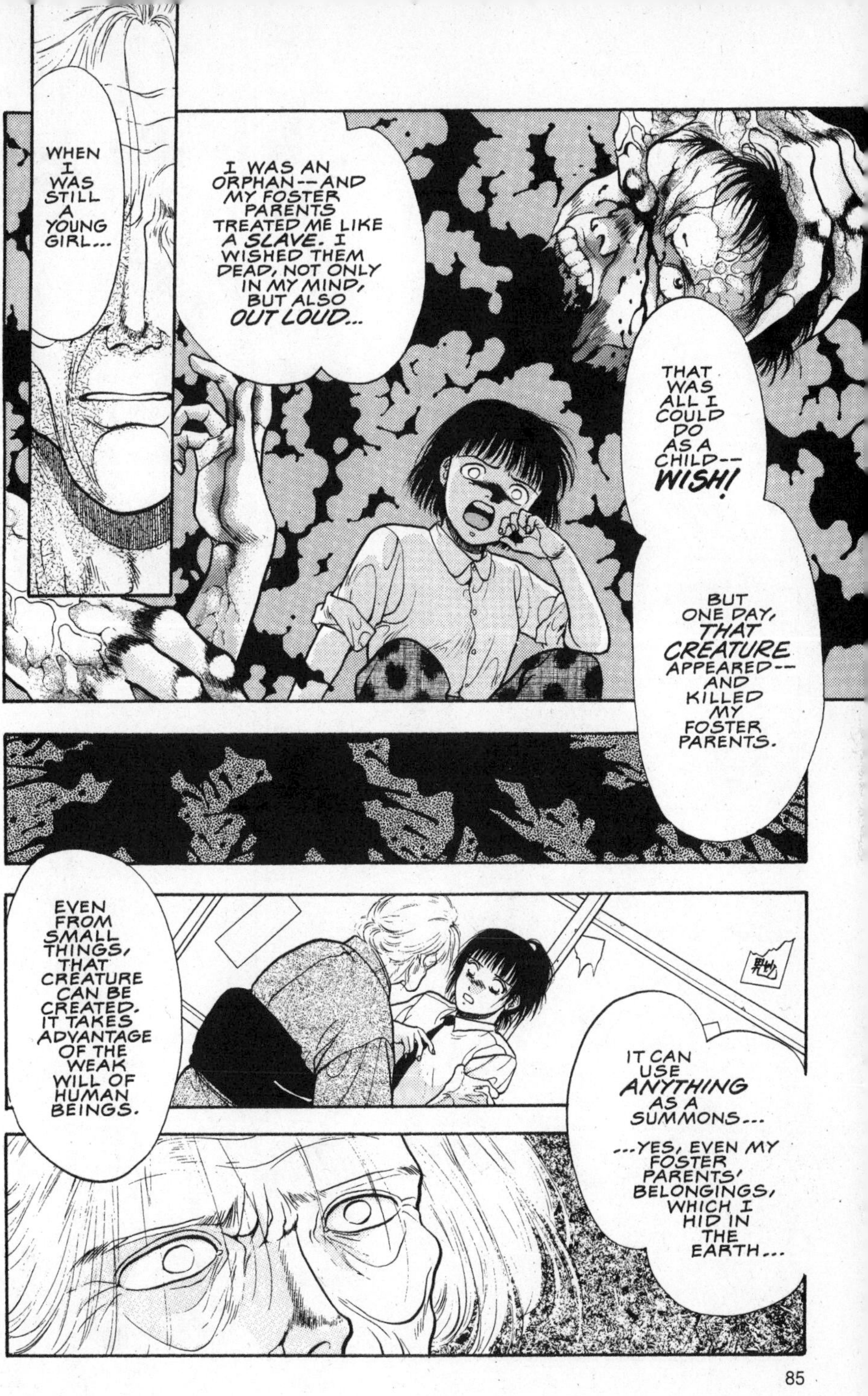
WHEN I WAS STILL A YOUNG GIRL...
I WAS AN ORPHAN--AND MY FOSTER PARENTS TREATED ME LIKE A SLAVE. I WISHED THEM DEAD, NOT ONLY IN MY MIND, BUT ALSO OUT LOUD...
THAT WAS ALL I COULD DO AS A CHILD--WISH!
BUT ONE DAY, THAT CREATURE APPEARED--AND KILLED MY FOSTER PARENTS.
EVEN FROM SMALL THINGS, THAT CREATURE CAN BE CREATED. IT TAKES ADVANTAGE OF THE WEAK WILL OF HUMAN BEINGS.
IT CAN USE ANYTHING AS A SUMMONS...
...YES, EVEN MY FOSTER PARENTS' BELONGINGS, WHICH I HID IN THE EARTH...

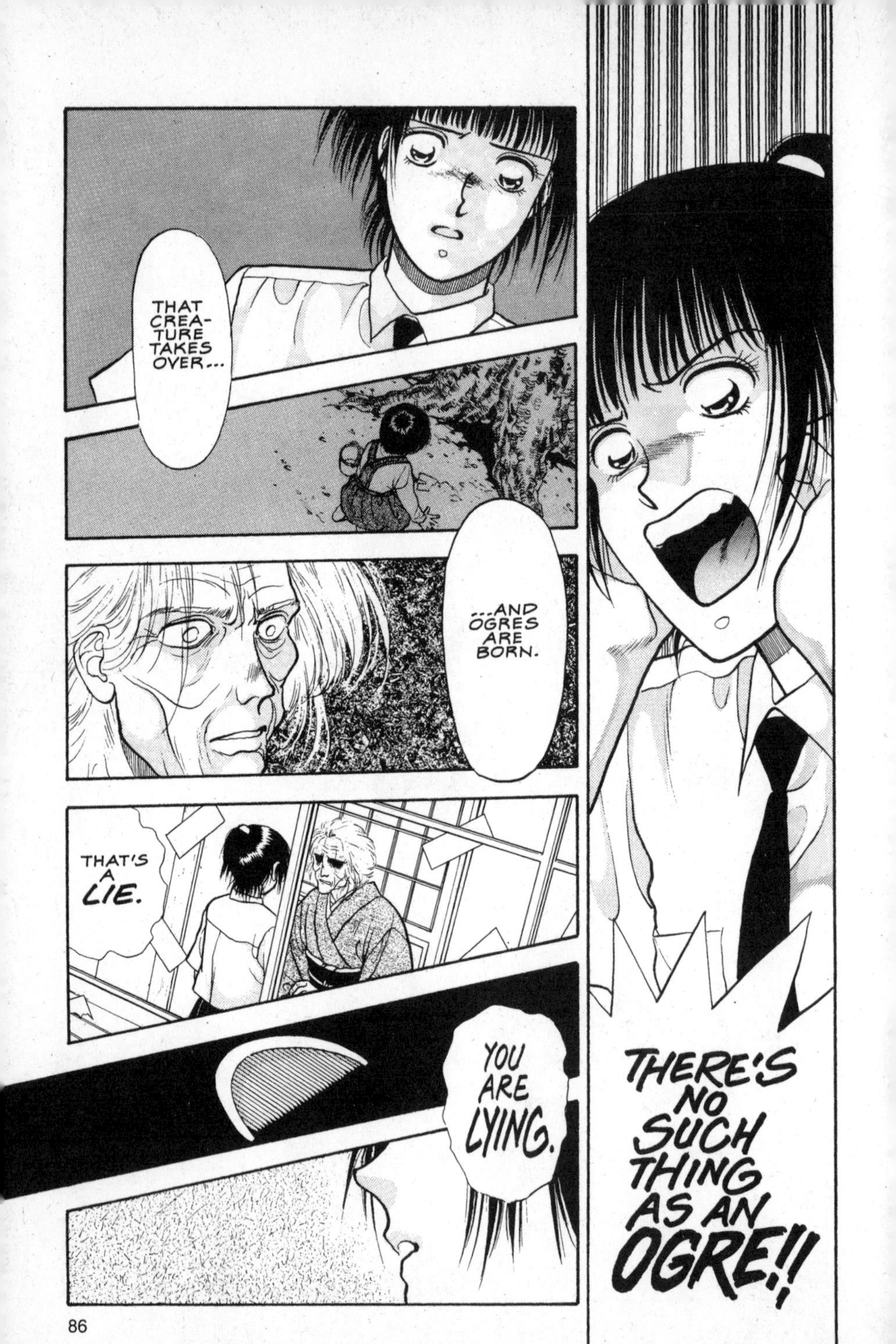
THAT CREATURE TAKES OVER...
...AND OGRES ARE BORN.
THAT'S A LIE.
YOU ARE LYING.
THERE'S NO SUCH THING AS AN OGRE!!

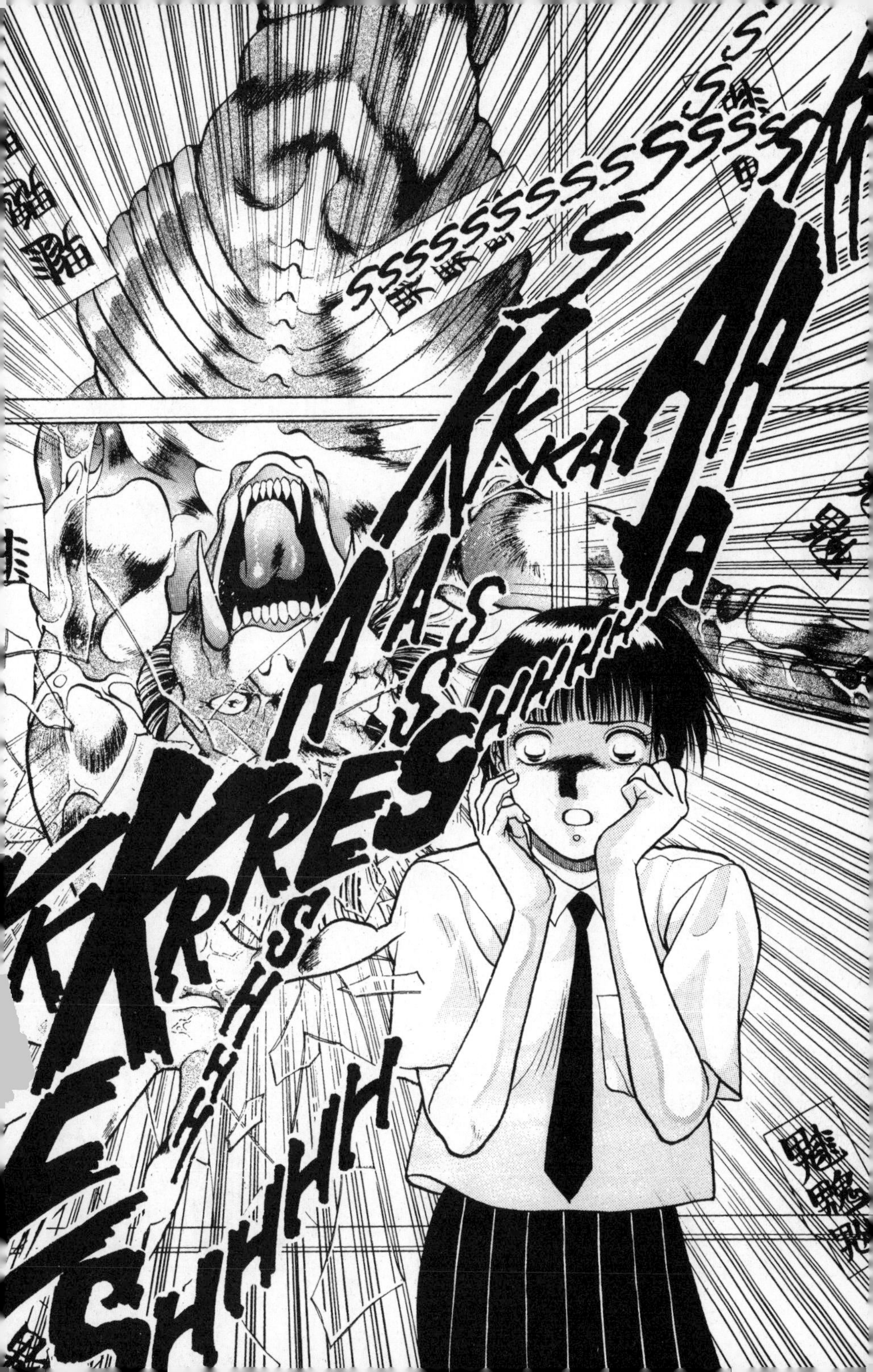

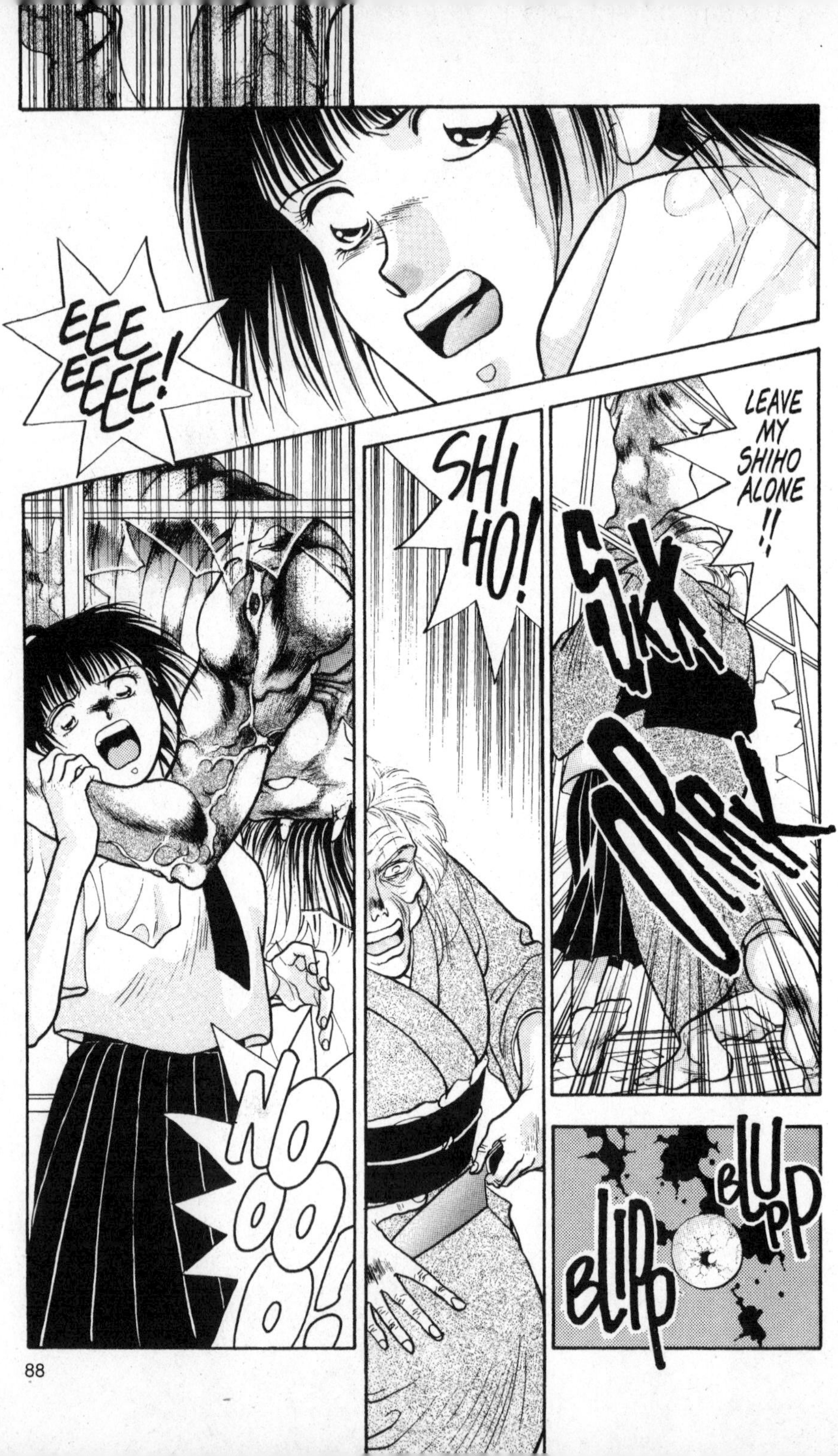
EEEEEEE!
NOOOOO!
SHIHO!
LEAVE MY SHIHO ALONE!!
SKK
DRRK
BLIPP
BLUPP

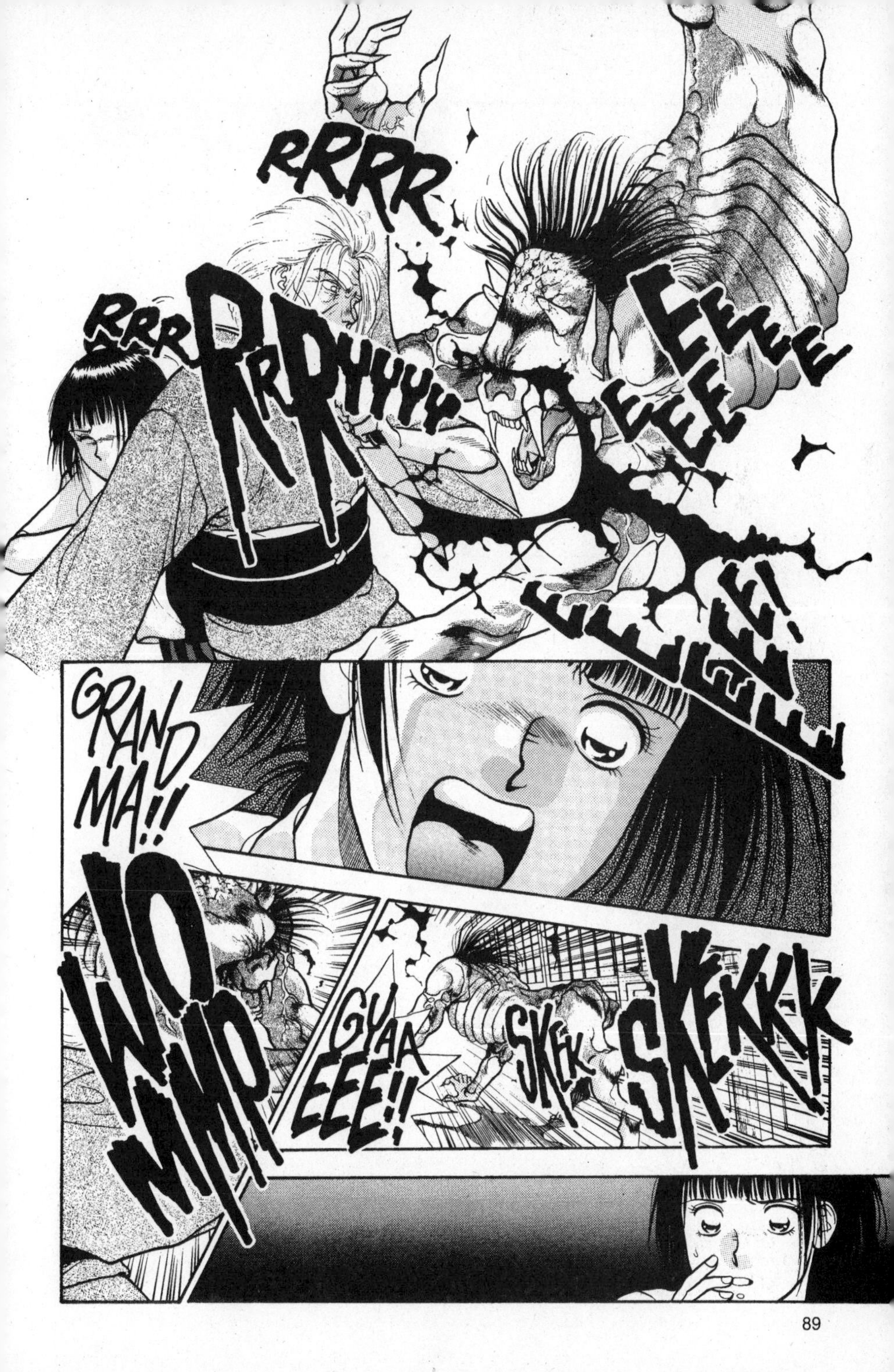
RRRR
RRRRRRRYYYYYEEEEEEEEEEEEEEE!
GRANDMA!!
WOMMP
GYAAEEE!!
SKEK SKEKKK

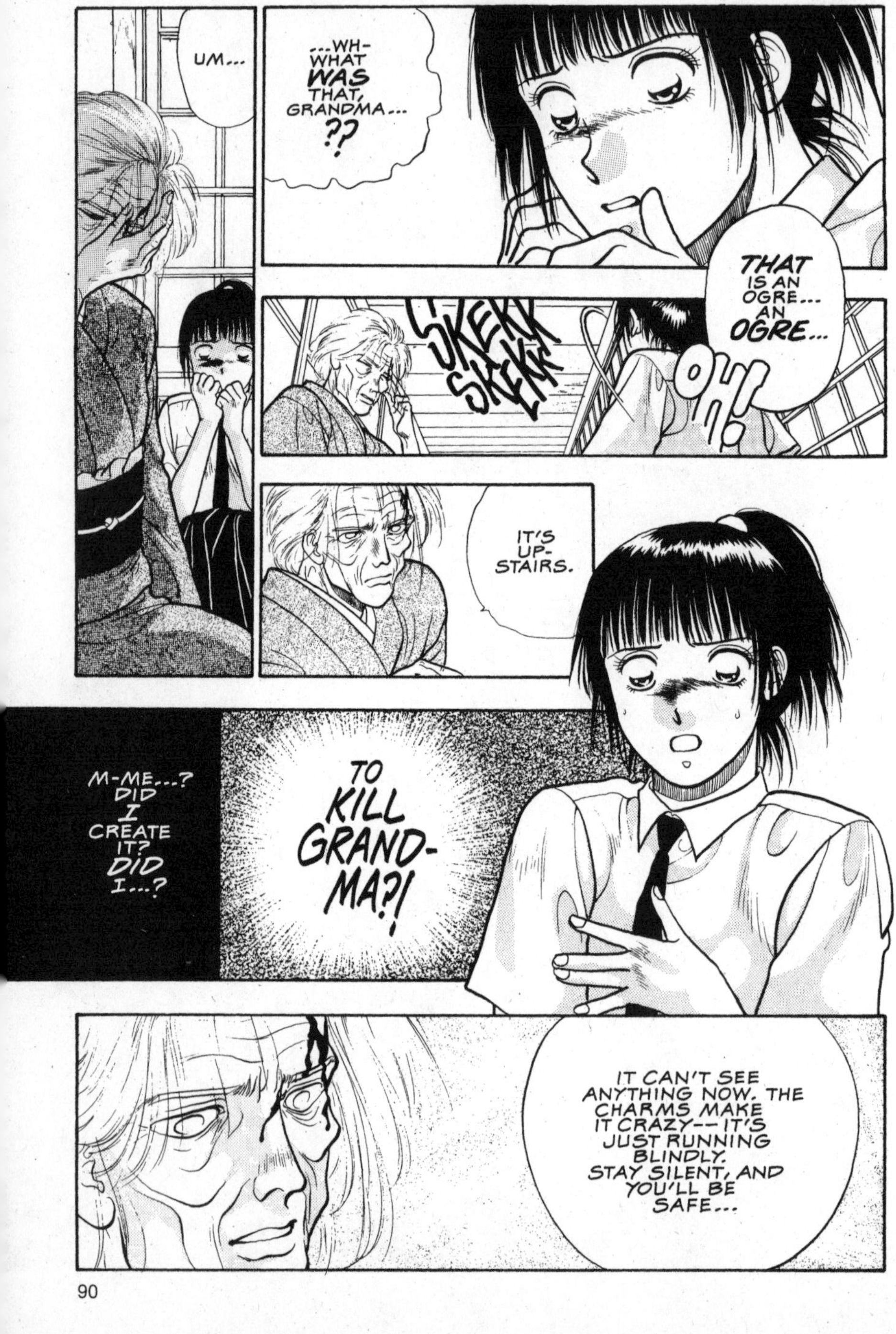
UM...
...WH-WHAT WAS THAT, GRANDMA...??
THAT IS AN OGRE... AN OGRE...
SKEKK SKEKK
OH!
IT'S UP-STAIRS.
M-ME...? DID I CREATE IT? DID I...?
TO KILL GRAND-MA?!
IT CAN'T SEE ANYTHING NOW. THE CHARMS MAKE IT CRAZY-- IT'S JUST RUNNING BLINDLY. STAY SILENT, AND YOU'LL BE SAFE...

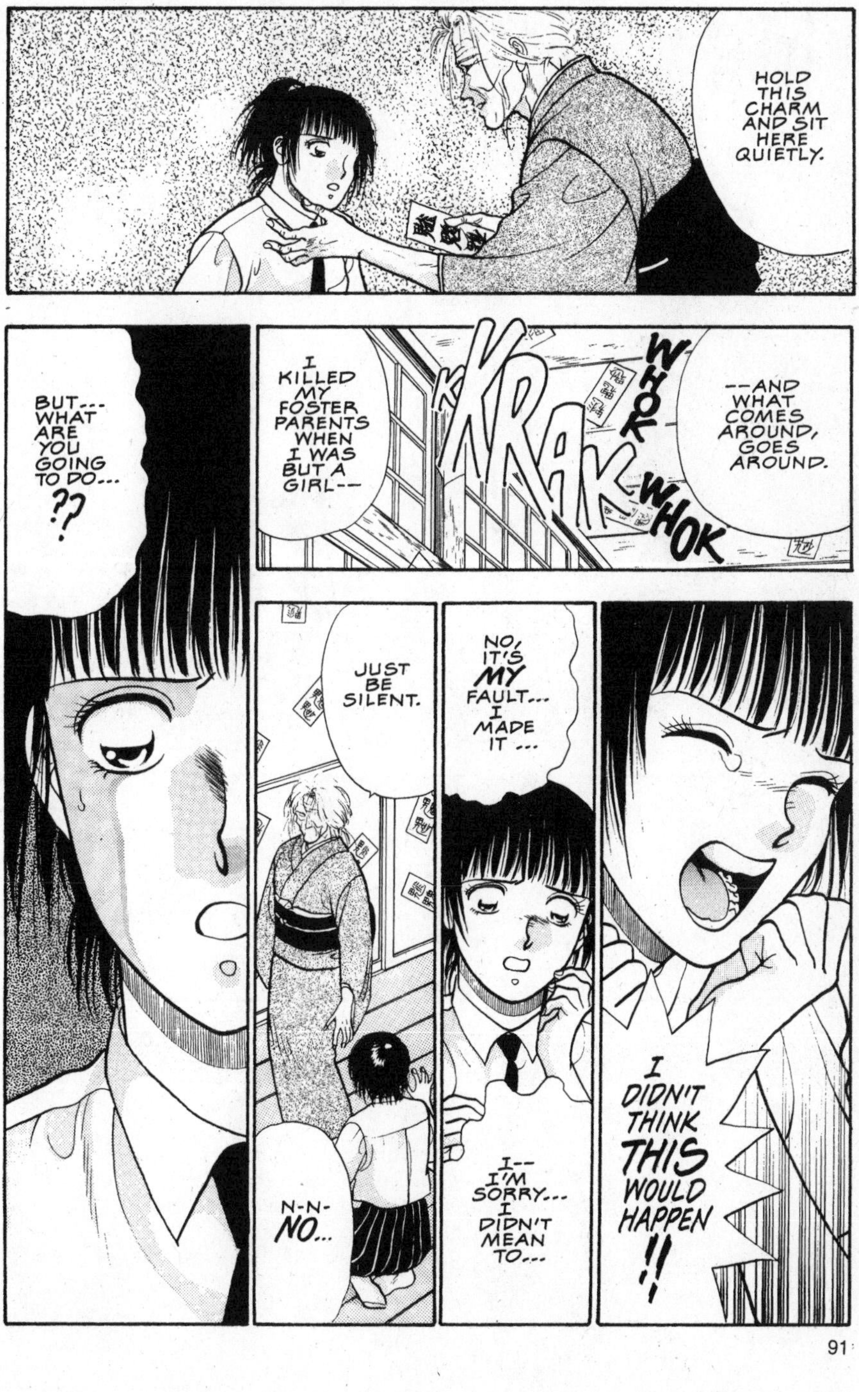
HOLD THIS CHARM AND SIT HERE QUIETLY.
BUT--- WHAT ARE YOU GOING TO DO...??
I KILLED MY FOSTER PARENTS WHEN I WAS BUT A GIRL--
KKRAK
WHOK
WHOK
WHOK
--AND WHAT COMES AROUND, GOES AROUND.
JUST BE SILENT.
N-N-NO...
NO, IT'S MY FAULT... I MADE IT ...
I-- I'M SORRY... I DIDN'T MEAN TO...
I DIDN'T THINK THIS WOULD HAPPEN!!

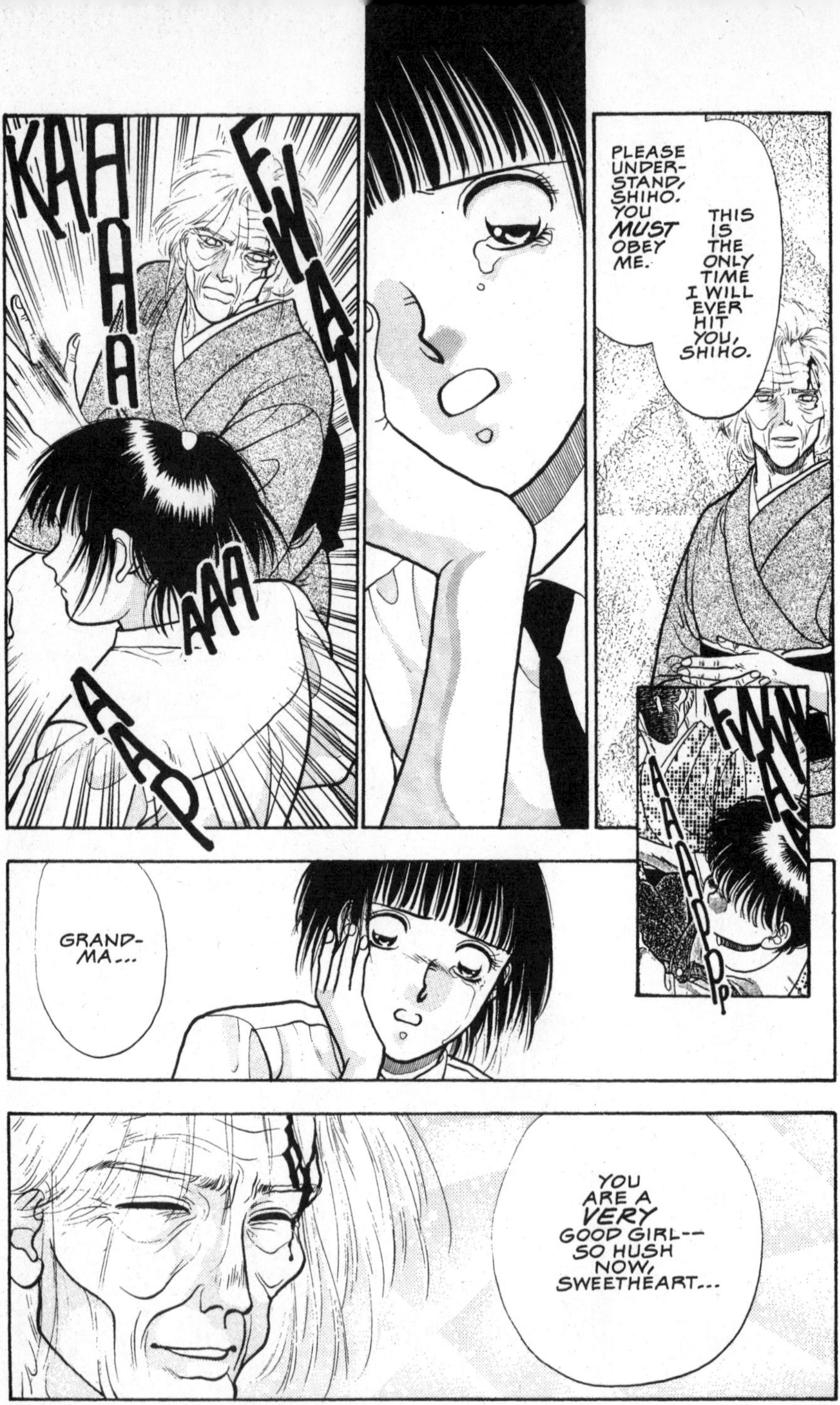
KAAAAAA
FWAA
AAA
AAAP
PLEASE UNDER-STAND, SHIHO. YOU MUST OBEY ME.
THIS IS THE ONLY TIME I WILL EVER HIT YOU, SHIHO.
FWAA
AAAAAAPp
GRAND-MA...
YOU ARE A VERY GOOD GIRL-- SO HUSH NOW, SWEETHEART...

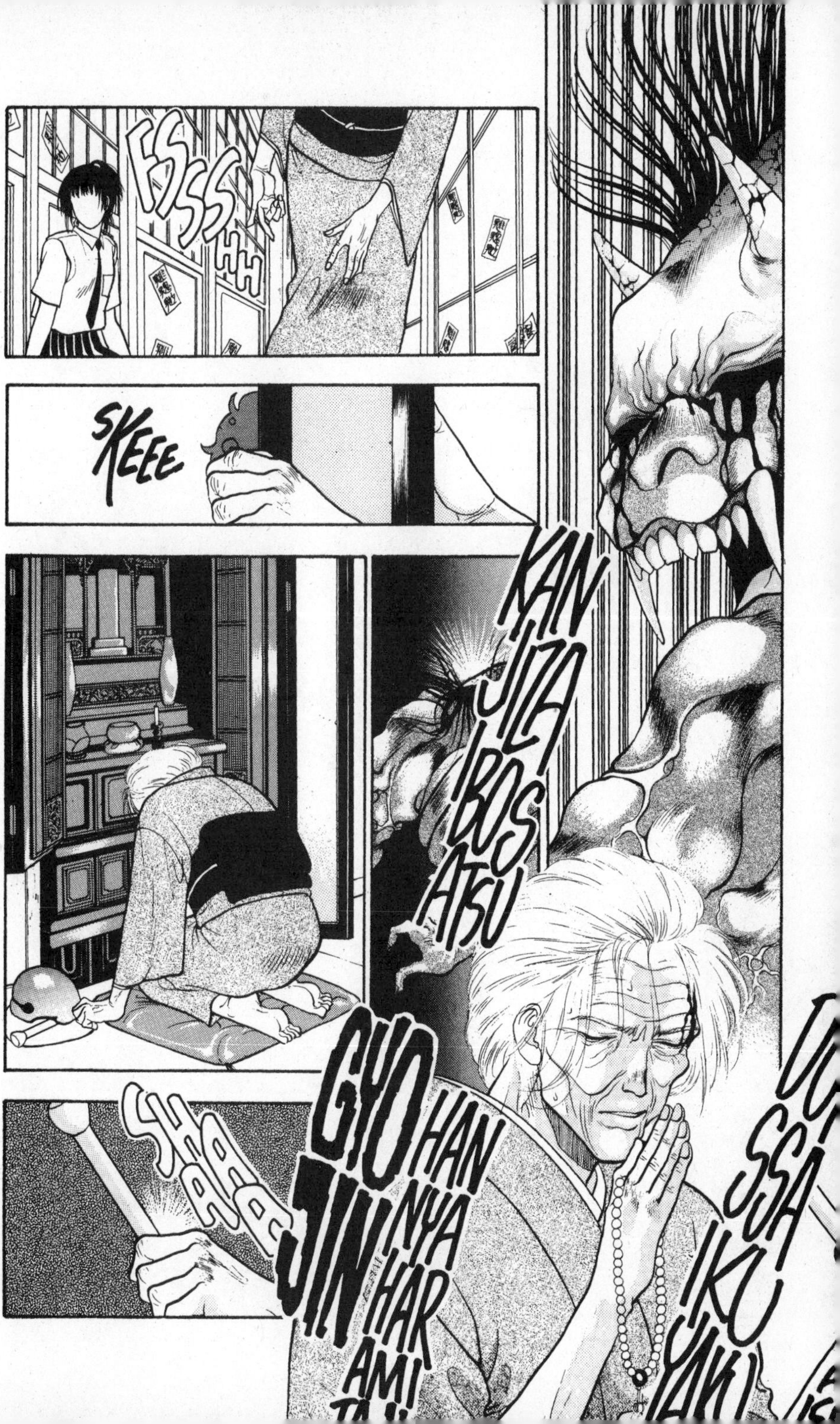
FSSSHHH
SKEEE
KAN JIZA IBOSATSU
GYO JIN
HAN NYA HAR AMI
SSA IKU

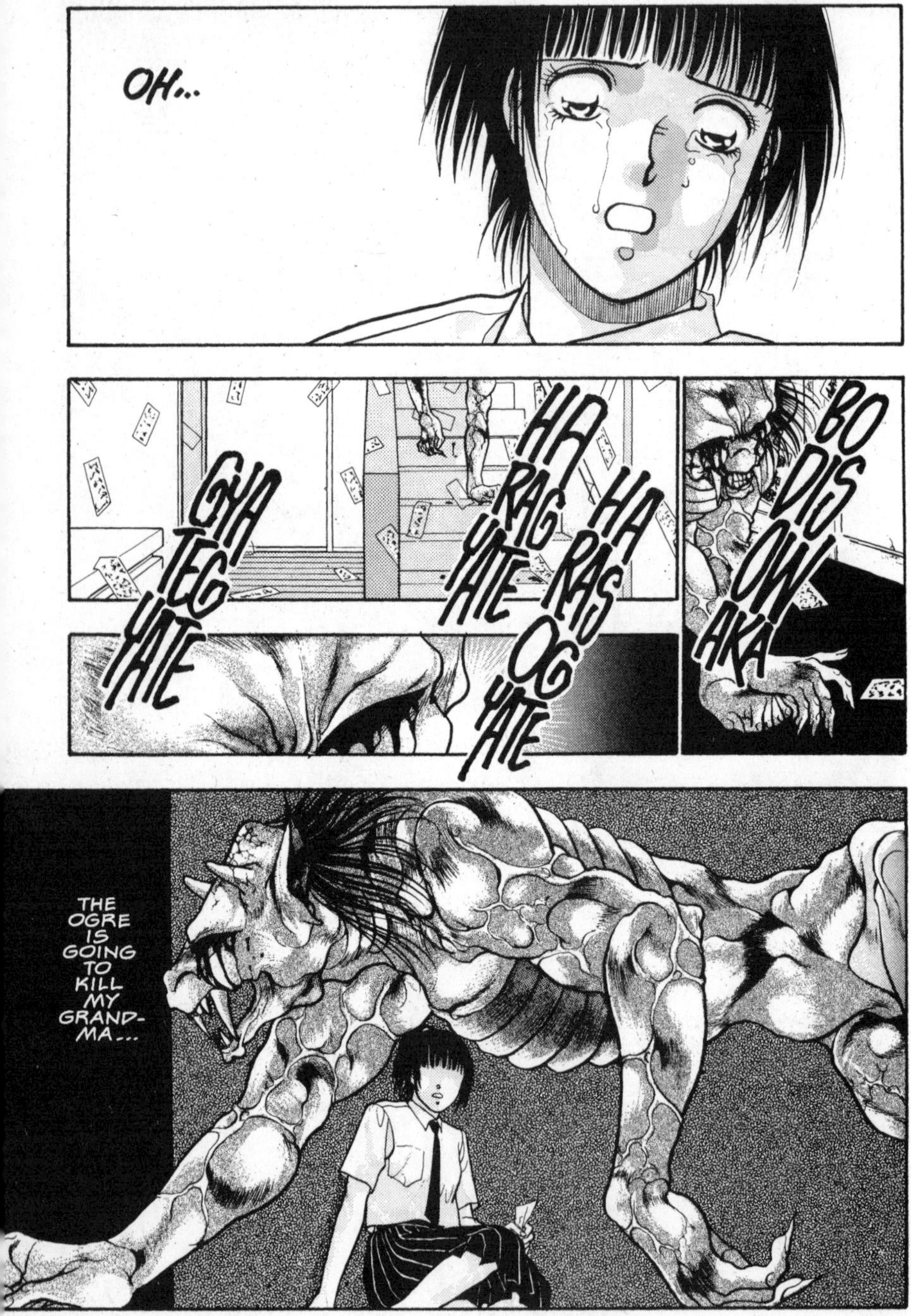
OH...
GHA TEG YATE
HA RAG YATE
HA RAS OG YATE
BO DIS OW AKA
THE OGRE IS GOING TO KILL MY GRAND-MA...

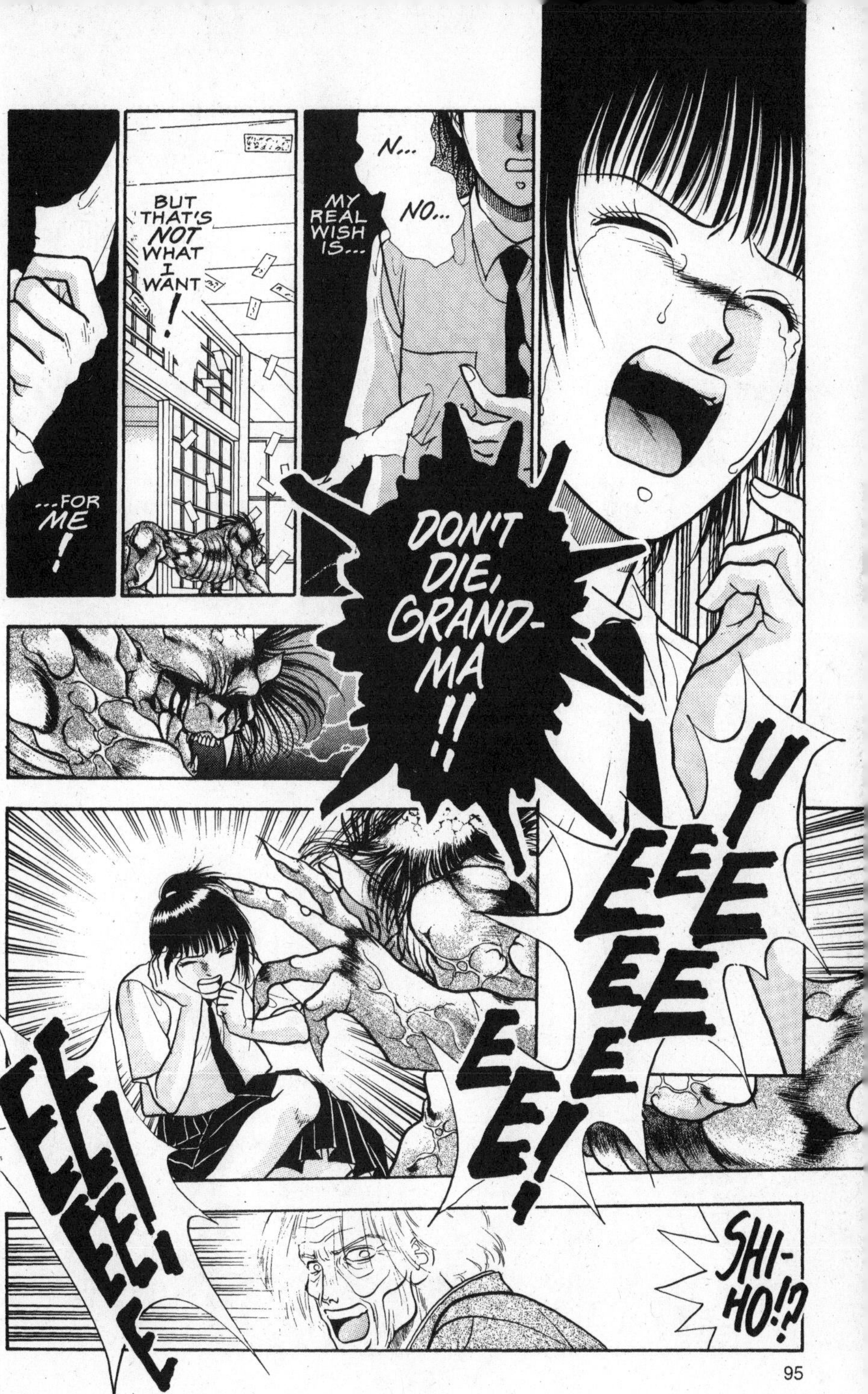
...FOR ME!
BUT THAT'S NOT WHAT I WANT!
MY REAL WISH IS...
N...
NO...
DON'T DIE, GRANDMA!!
YEEEEEEEEE!
EEEEEE!
SHIHO!?

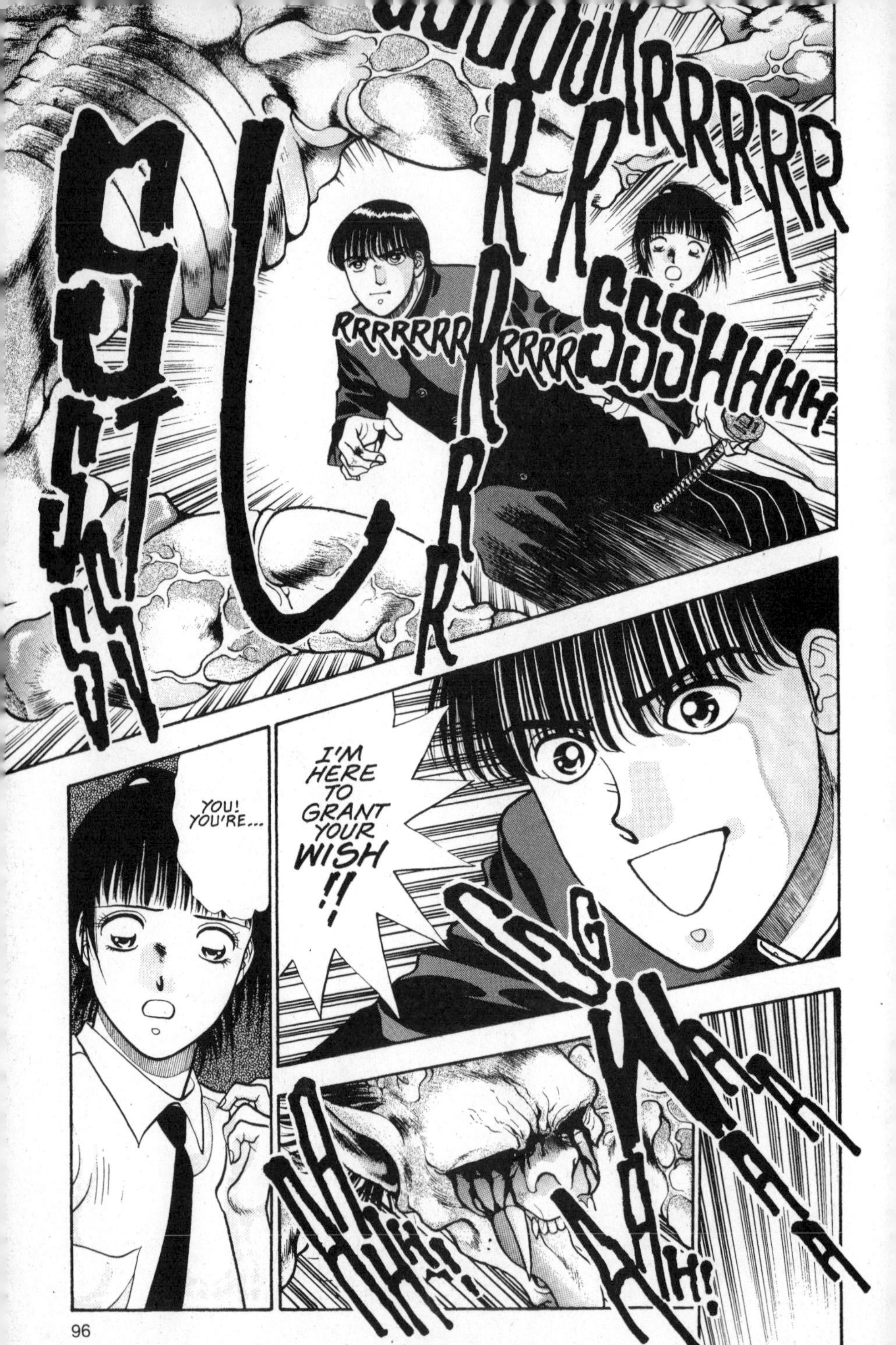
RRRRRRR
RRRRRRRR
RRRRR
SSSHHHHH
I'M HERE TO GRANT YOUR WISH!!
YOU! YOU'RE...

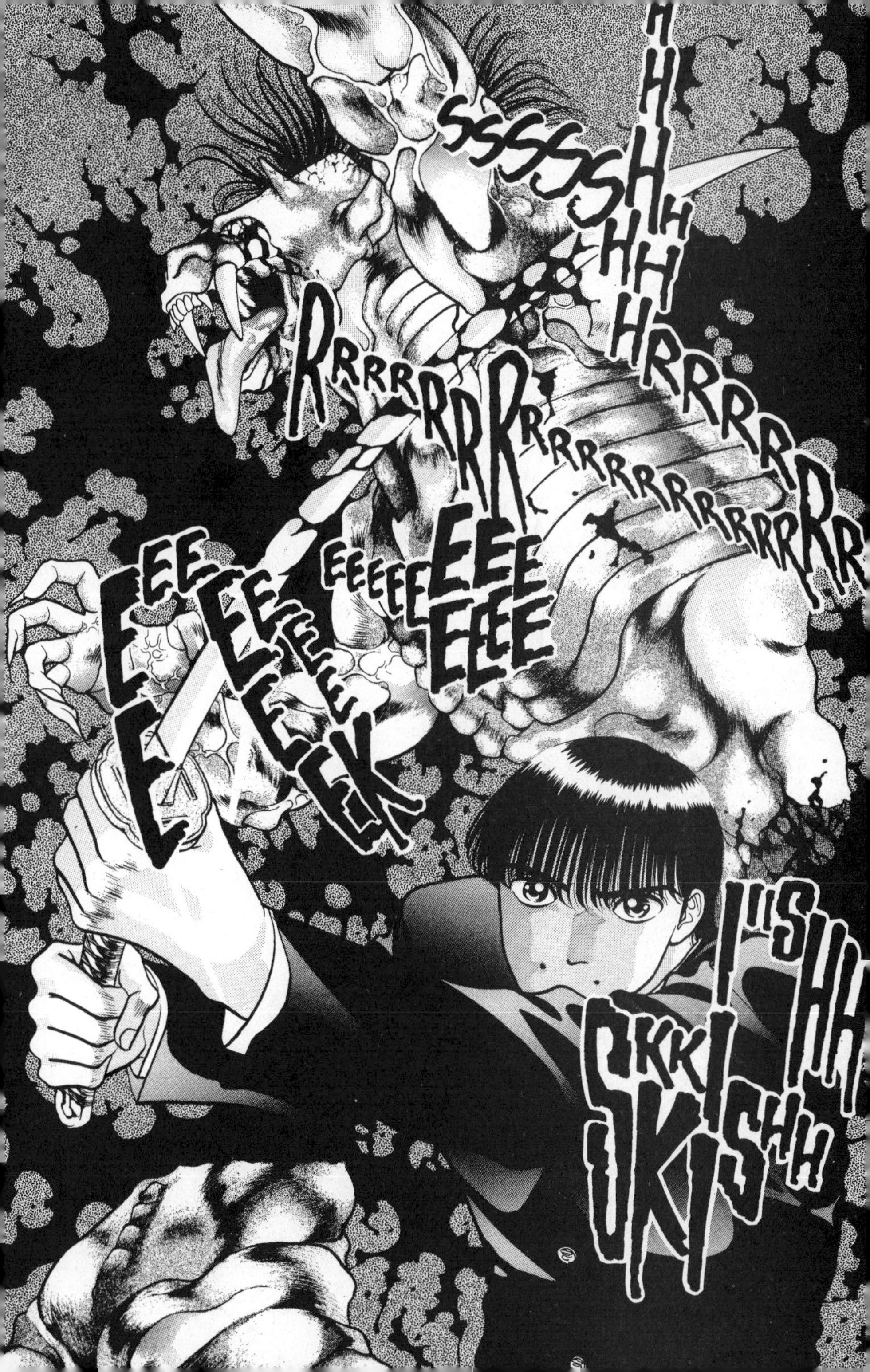
SSSSSSHHHHHHHHRRRRRRRRRR
RRRRRRRRRRRRRRRRRRRRRRR
EEEEEEEEEEEEEEEEEEEEEK
SKKISHH
SKISHH

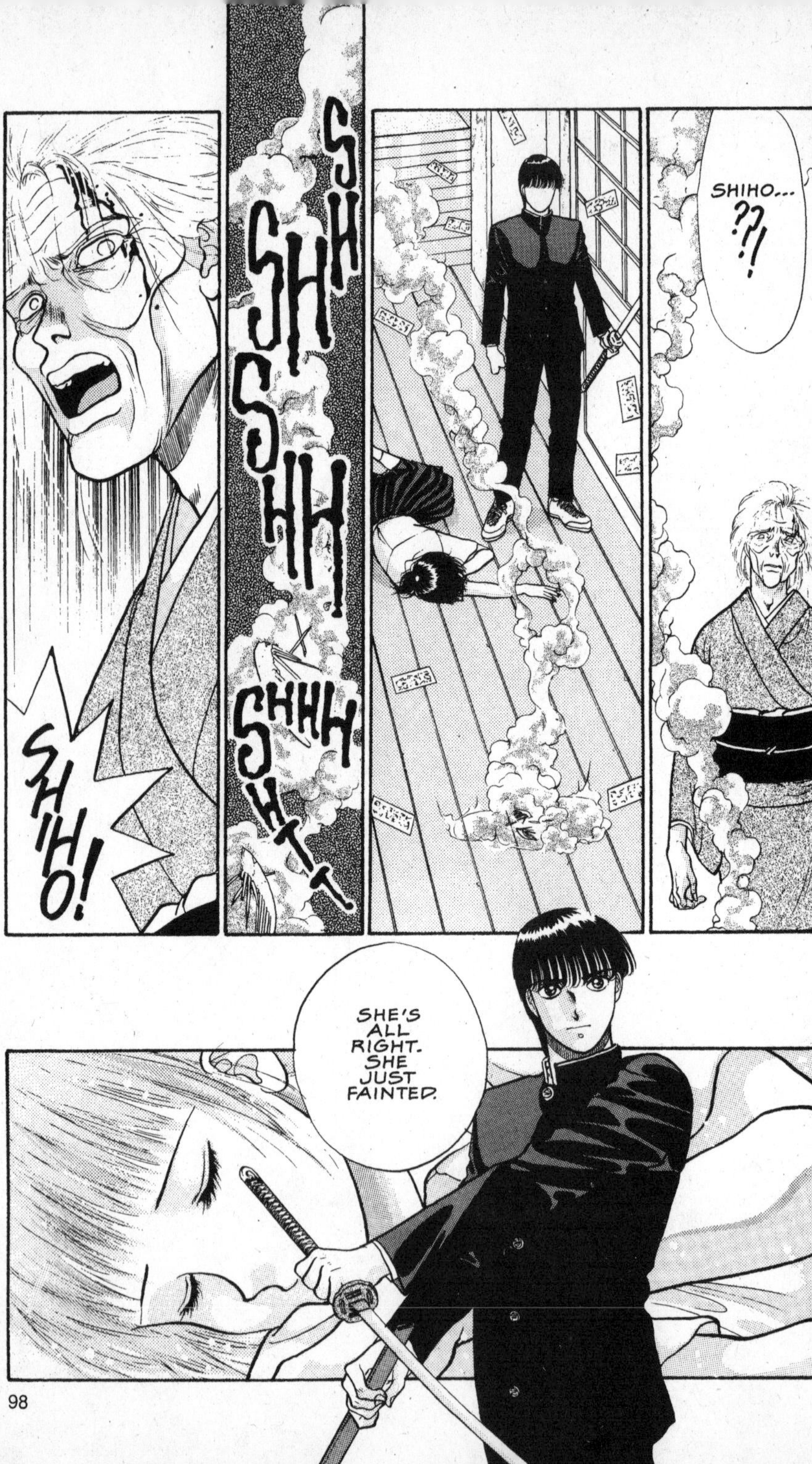
SHIHO!
SHHH SHHH SHHHH SHHHHHHT
SHIHO...
??!
SHE'S ALL RIGHT. SHE JUST FAINTED.

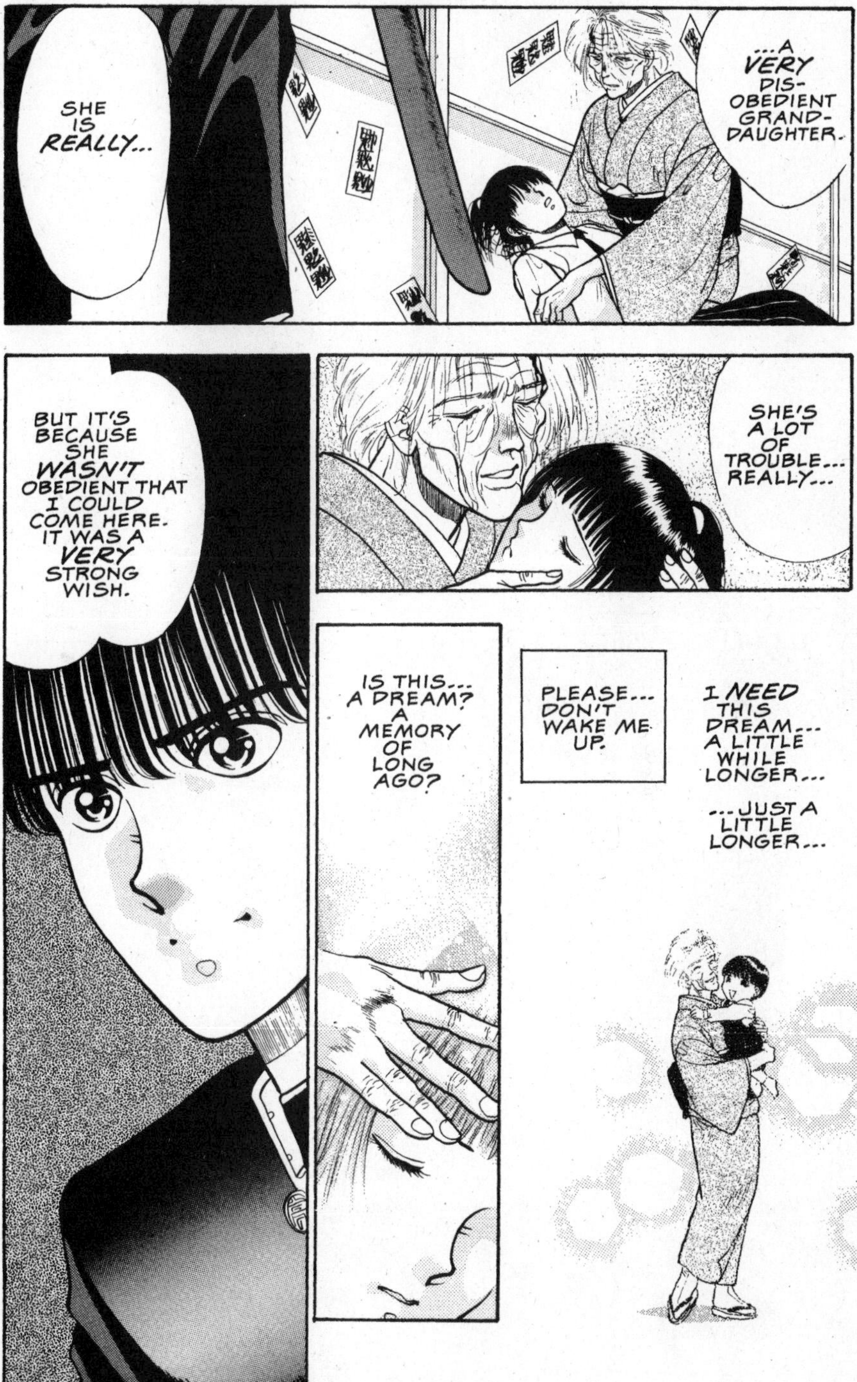
SHE IS *REALLY*...
...A *VERY* DISOBEDIENT GRANDDAUGHTER.
BUT IT'S BECAUSE SHE *WASN'T* OBEDIENT THAT I COULD COME HERE. IT WAS A *VERY* STRONG WISH.
SHE'S A LOT OF TROUBLE... REALLY...
IS THIS... A DREAM? A MEMORY OF LONG AGO?
PLEASE... DON'T WAKE ME UP.
I *NEED* THIS DREAM... A LITTLE WHILE LONGER...
...JUST A LITTLE LONGER...

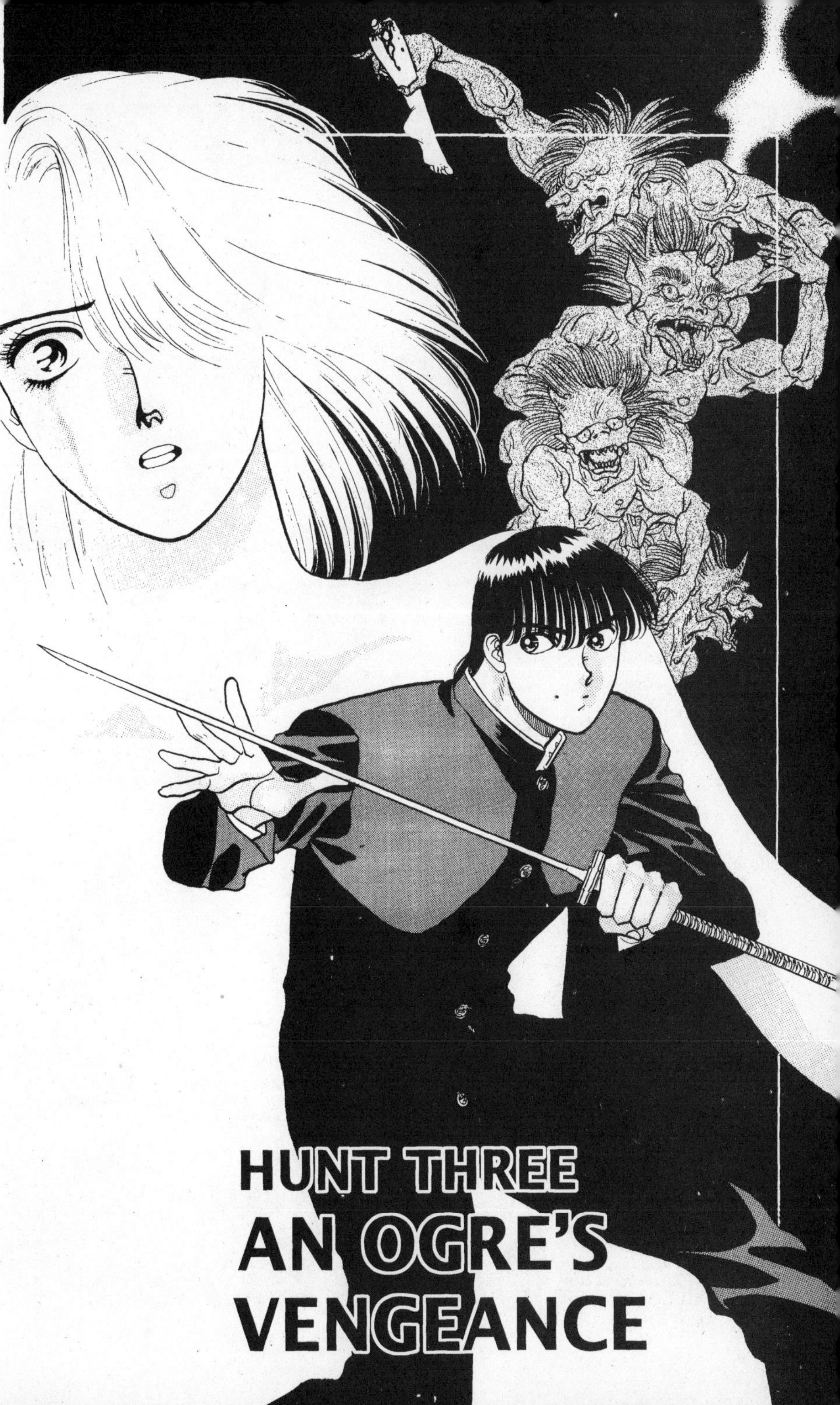

HUNT THREE
AN OGRE'S VENGEANCE

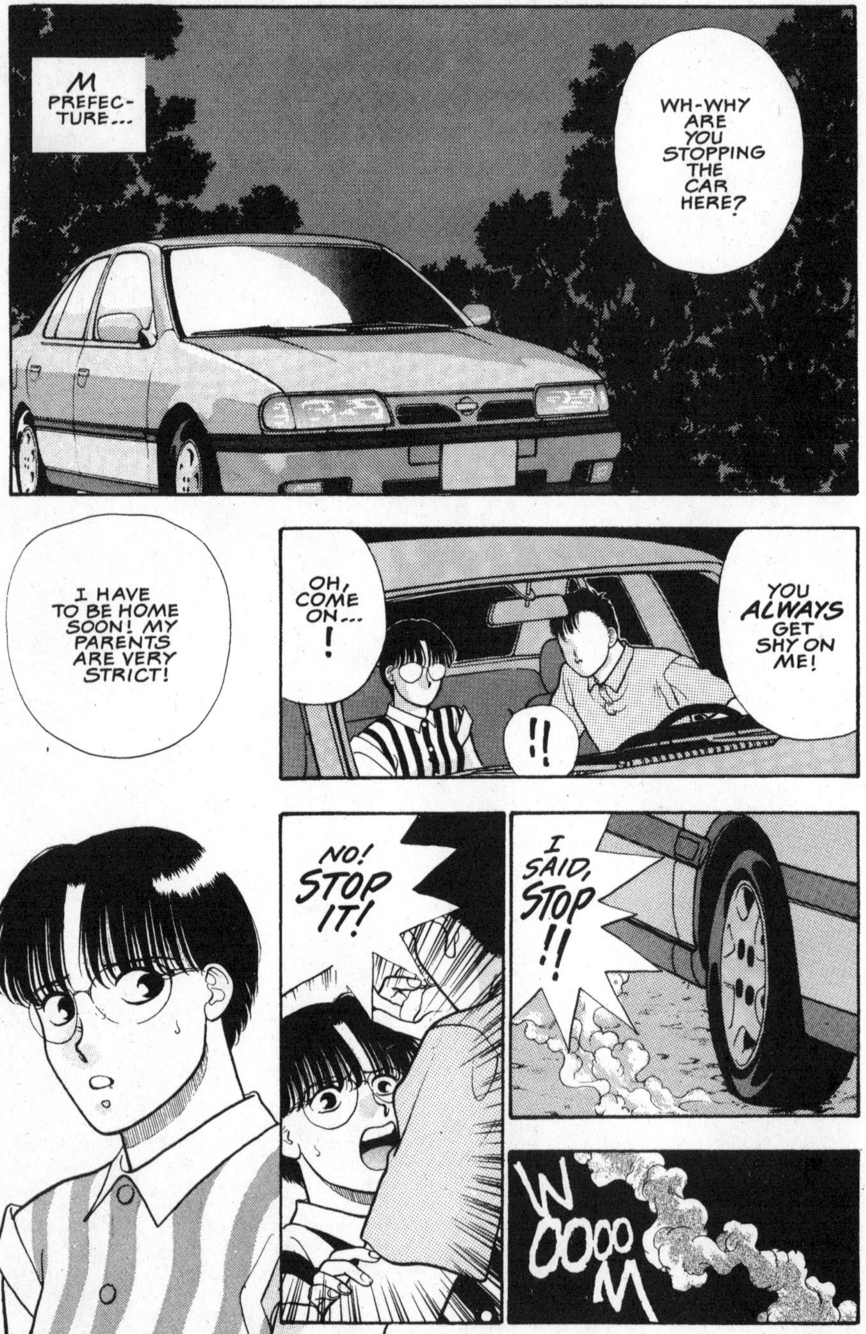
M PREFECTURE...
WH-WHY ARE YOU STOPPING THE CAR HERE?
I HAVE TO BE HOME SOON! MY PARENTS ARE VERY STRICT!
OH, COME ON... !
YOU ALWAYS GET SHY ON ME!
!!
NO! STOP IT!
I SAID, STOP!!
WOOOOM

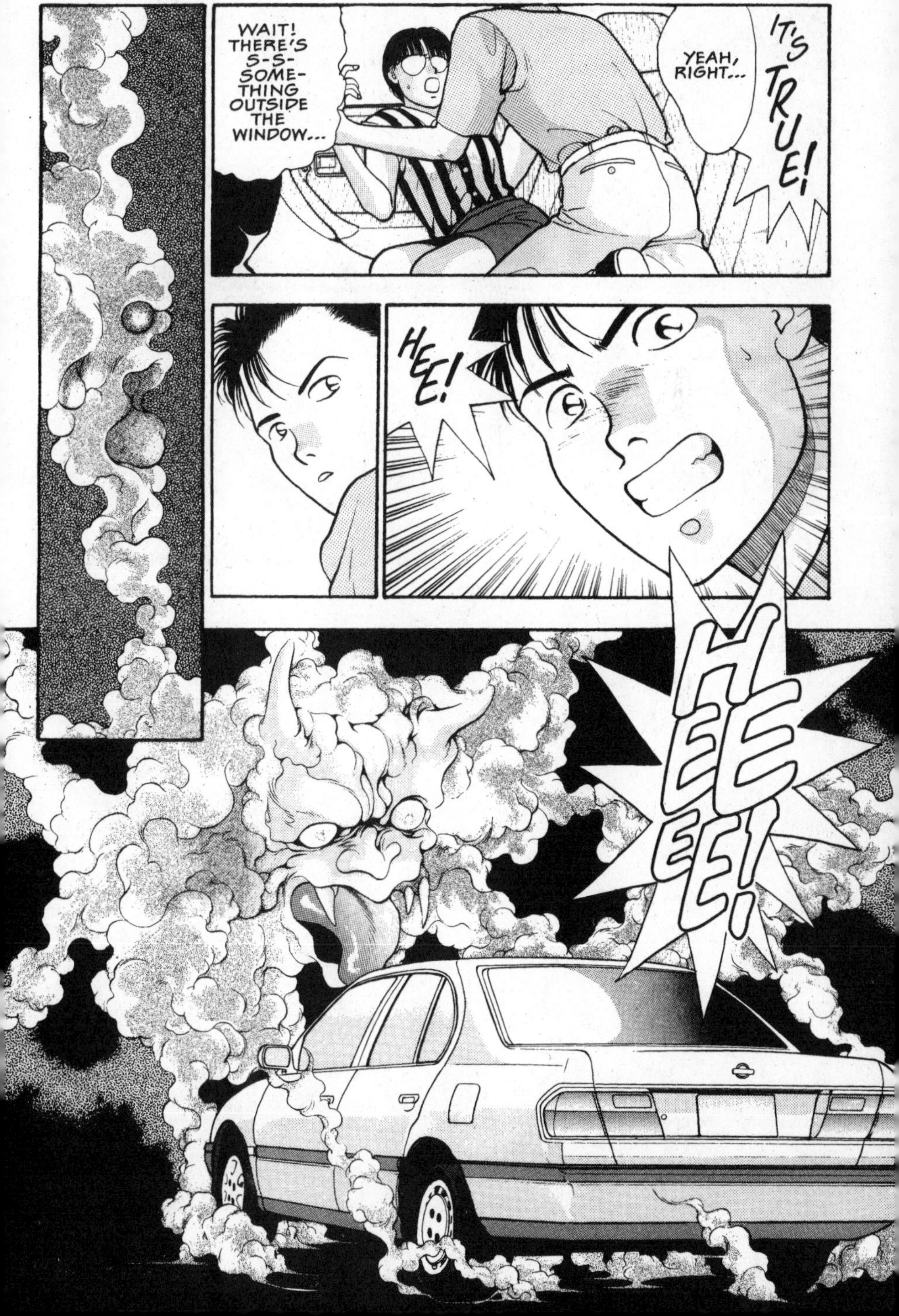
WAIT! THERE'S S-S-SOMETHING OUTSIDE THE WINDOW...
YEAH, RIGHT...
IT'S TRUE!
HEE!
HEEEEEE!

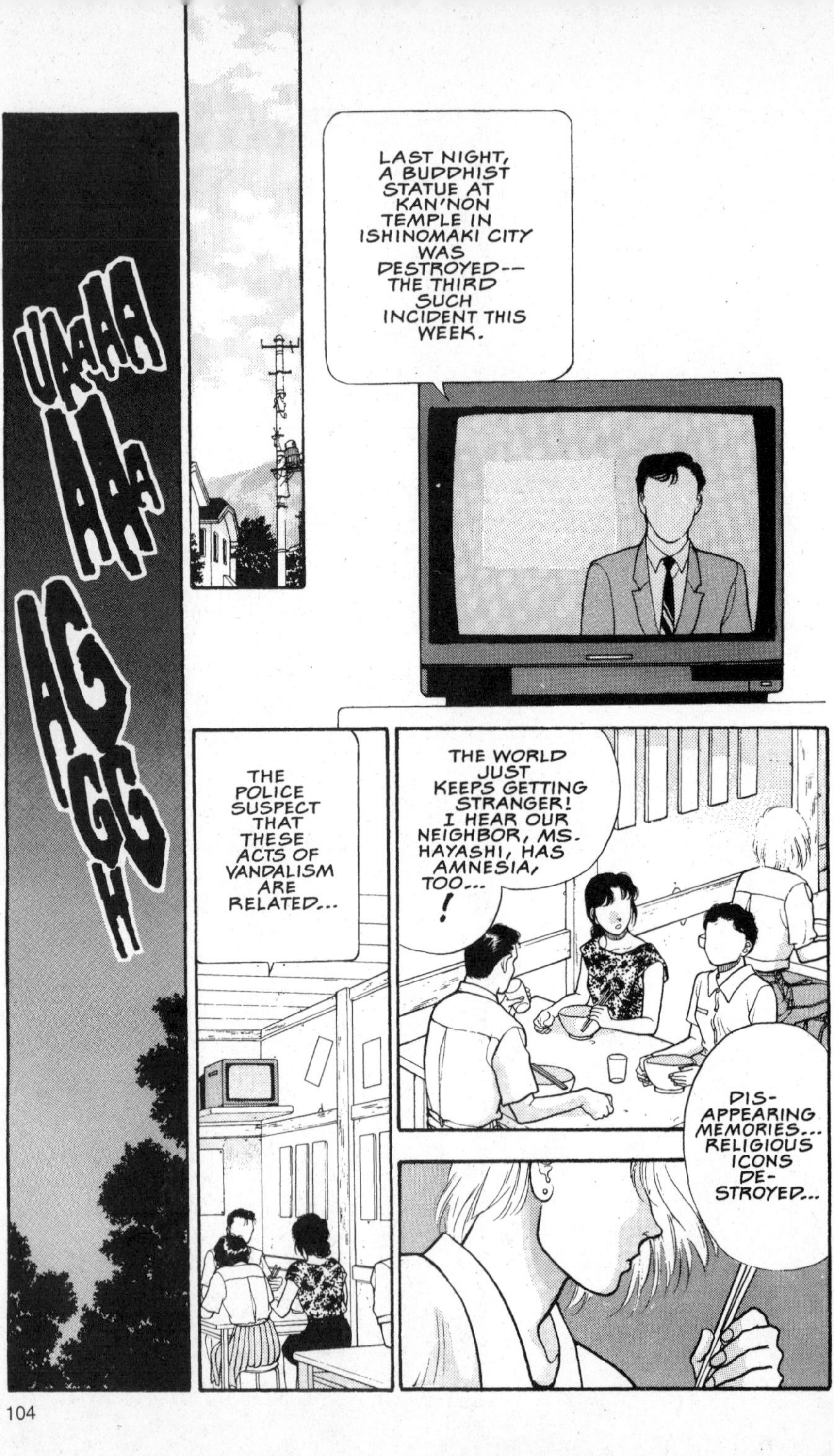
UAAAAAAAAAGGGHH
LAST NIGHT, A BUDDHIST STATUE AT KAN'NON TEMPLE IN ISHINOMAKI CITY WAS DESTROYED-- THE THIRD SUCH INCIDENT THIS WEEK.
THE POLICE SUSPECT THAT THESE ACTS OF VANDALISM ARE RELATED...
THE WORLD JUST KEEPS GETTING STRANGER! I HEAR OUR NEIGHBOR, MS. HAYASHI, HAS AMNESIA, TOO...
!
DIS-APPEARING MEMORIES... RELIGIOUS ICONS DE-STROYED...

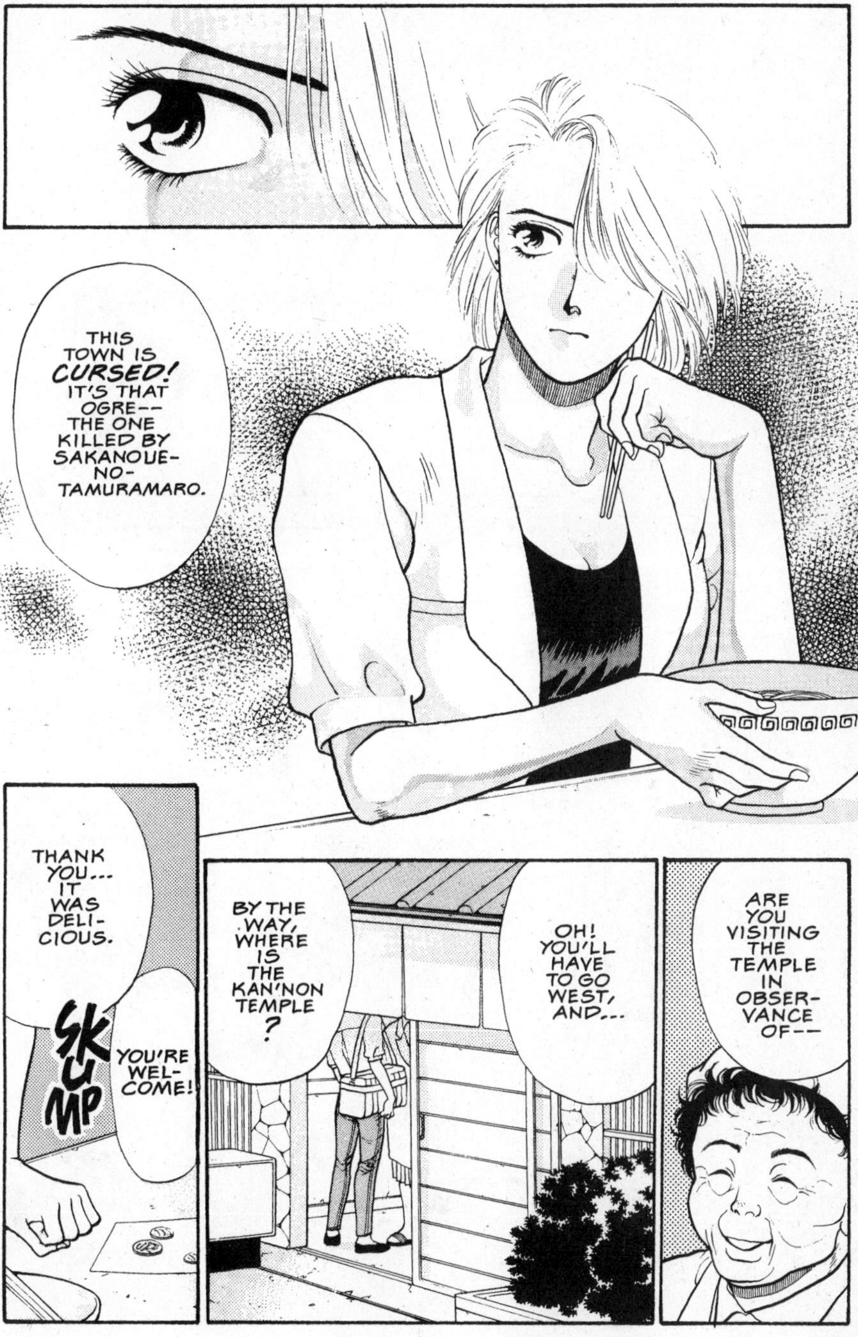

THIS TOWN IS CURSED! IT'S THAT OGRE-- THE ONE KILLED BY SAKANOUE-NO-TAMURAMARO.
THANK YOU... IT WAS DELICIOUS.
SKUMP
YOU'RE WELCOME!
BY THE WAY, WHERE IS THE KAN'NON TEMPLE?
OH! YOU'LL HAVE TO GO WEST, AND...
ARE YOU VISITING THE TEMPLE IN OBSERVANCE OF--

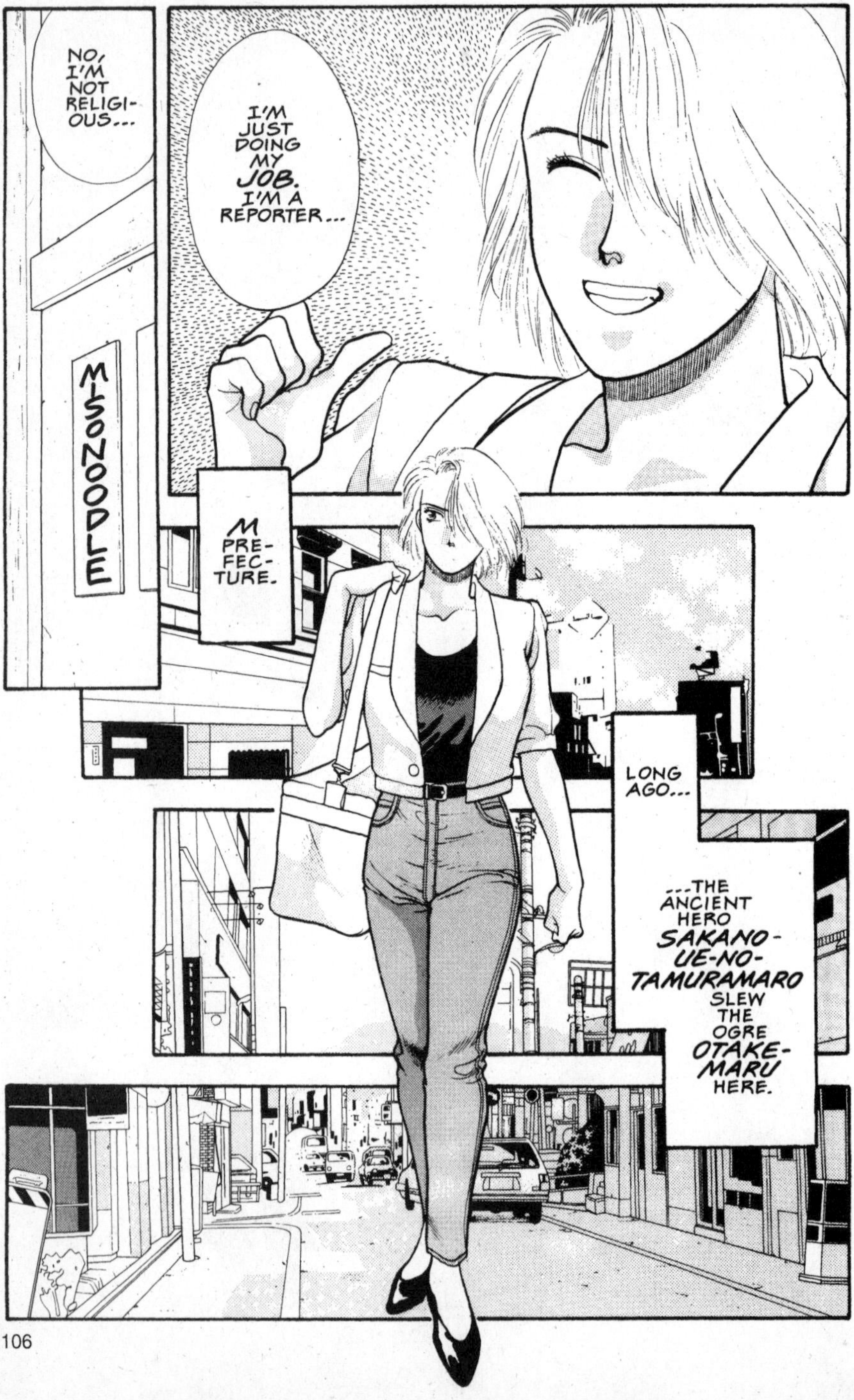
NO, I'M NOT RELIGIOUS...
MISONOODLE
I'M JUST DOING MY JOB. I'M A REPORTER...
M PREFECTURE.
LONG AGO...
...THE ANCIENT HERO SAKANO-UE-NO-TAMURAMARO SLEW THE OGRE OTAKE-MARU HERE.

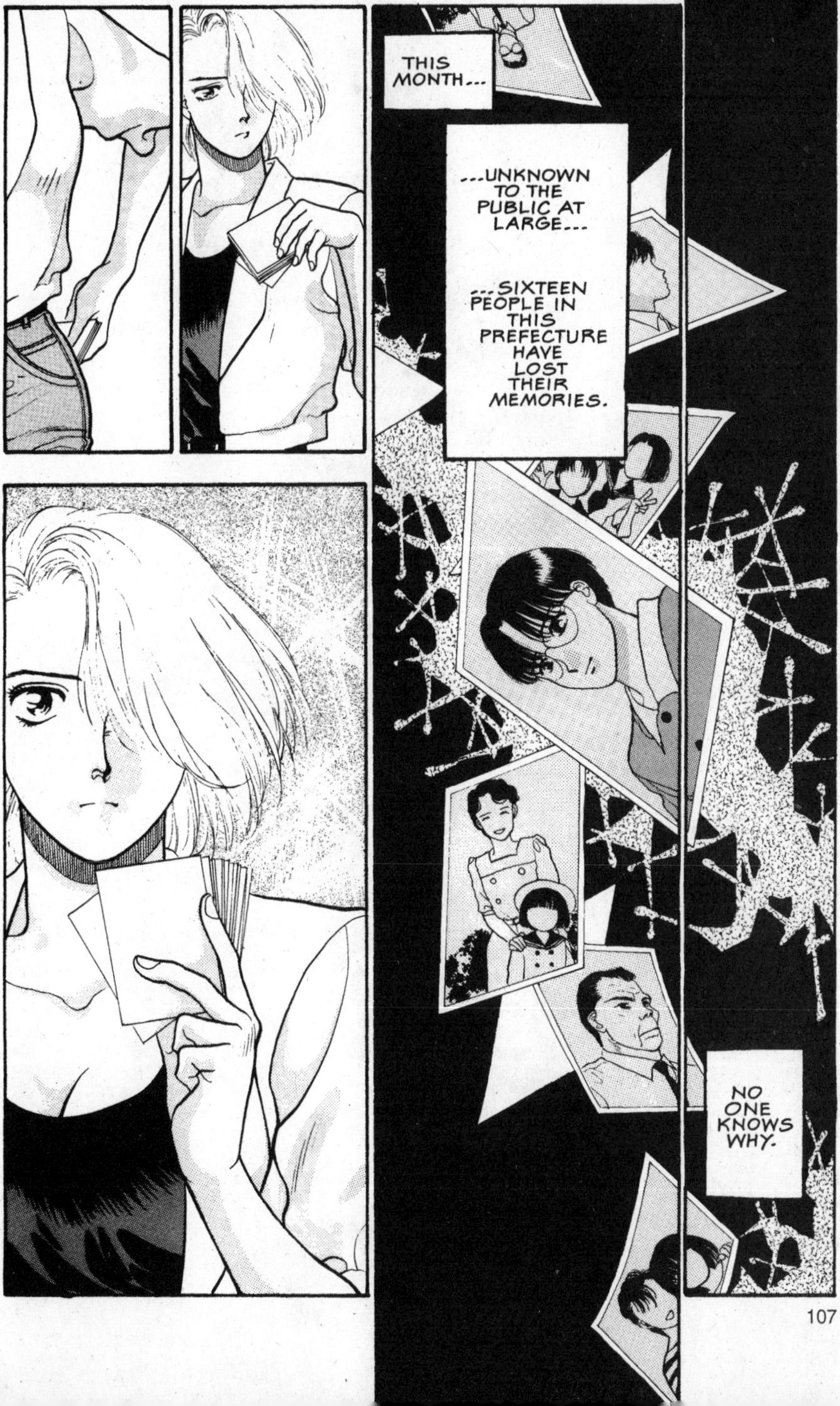
THIS MONTH...
...UNKNOWN TO THE PUBLIC AT LARGE...
...SIXTEEN PEOPLE IN THIS PREFECTURE HAVE LOST THEIR MEMORIES.
NO ONE KNOWS WHY.

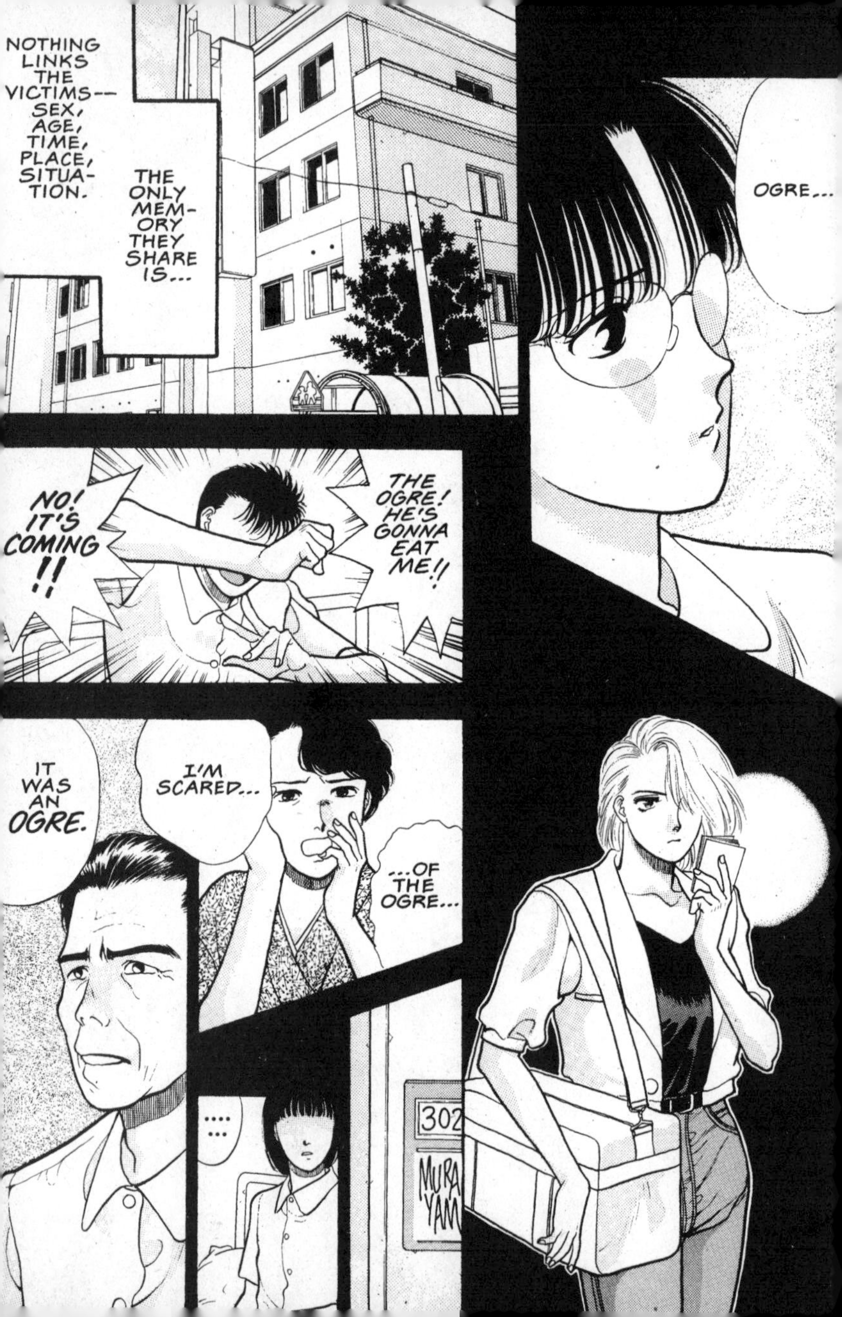
NOTHING LINKS THE VICTIMS--SEX, AGE, TIME, PLACE, SITUATION.
THE ONLY MEMORY THEY SHARE IS...
NO! IT'S COMING!!
THE OGRE! HE'S GONNA EAT ME!!
OGRE...
IT WAS AN OGRE.
I'M SCARED...
...OF THE OGRE...
....
....
302

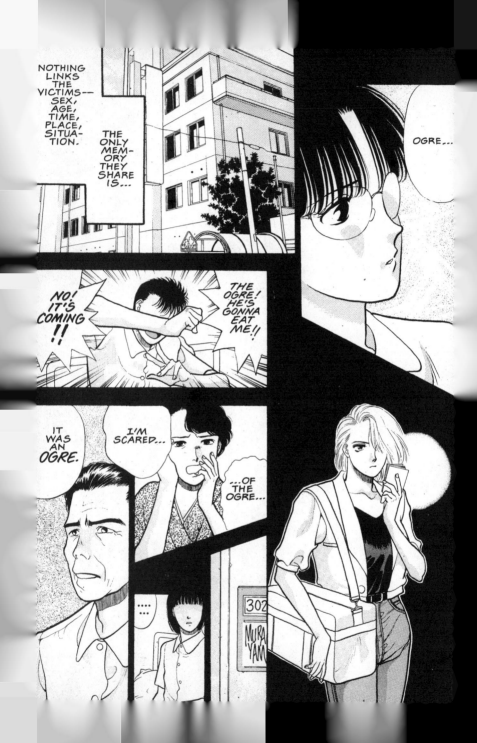

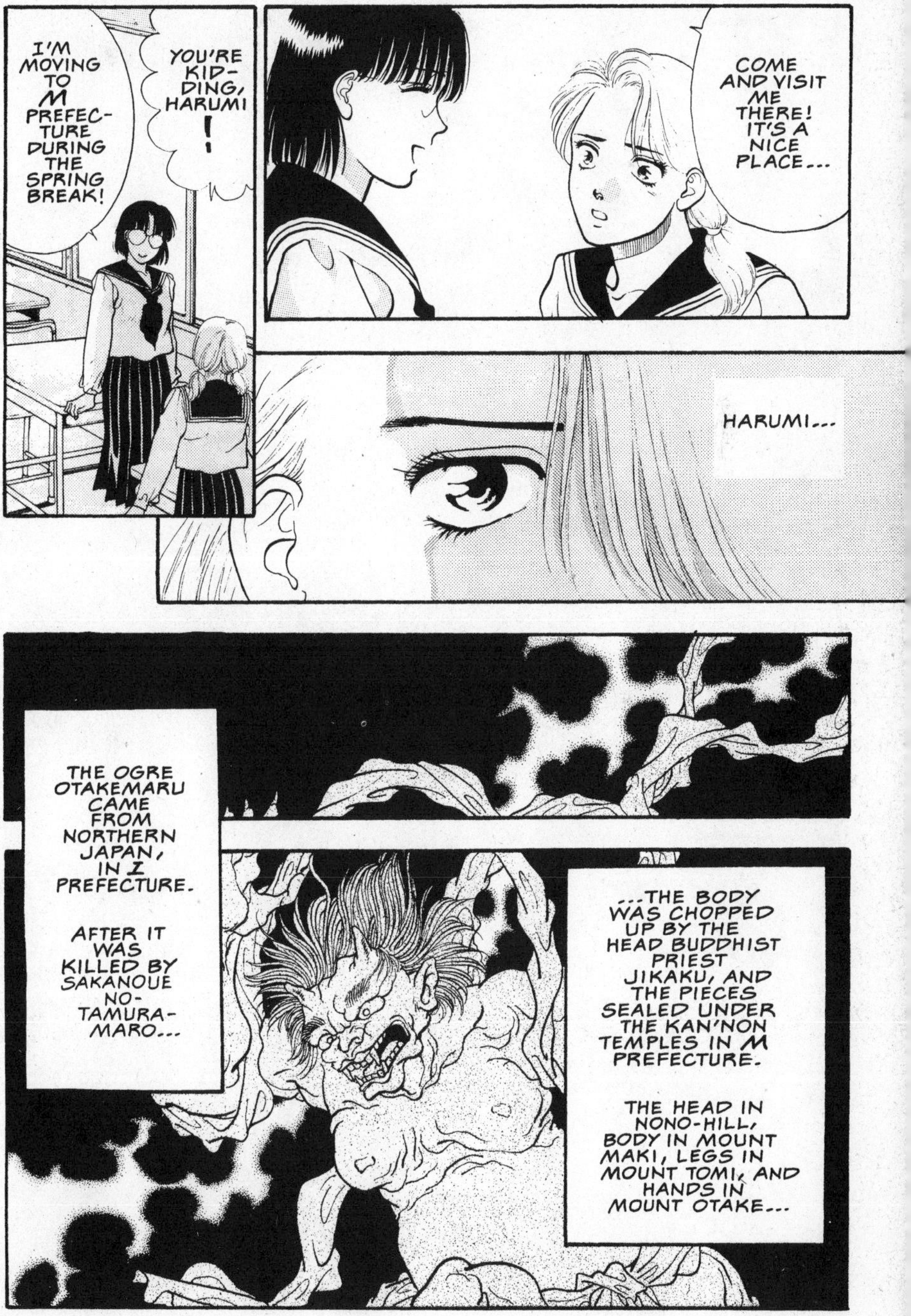
I'M MOVING TO M PREFECTURE DURING THE SPRING BREAK!
YOU'RE KIDDING, HARUMI!
COME AND VISIT ME THERE! IT'S A NICE PLACE...
HARUMI...
THE OGRE OTAKEMARU CAME FROM NORTHERN JAPAN, IN I PREFECTURE.
AFTER IT WAS KILLED BY SAKANOUE NO-TAMURA-MARO...
...THE BODY WAS CHOPPED UP BY THE HEAD BUDDHIST PRIEST JIKAKU, AND THE PIECES SEALED UNDER THE KAN'NON TEMPLES IN M PREFECTURE.
THE HEAD IN NONO-HILL, BODY IN MOUNT MAKI, LEGS IN MOUNT TOMI, AND HANDS IN MOUNT OTAKE...

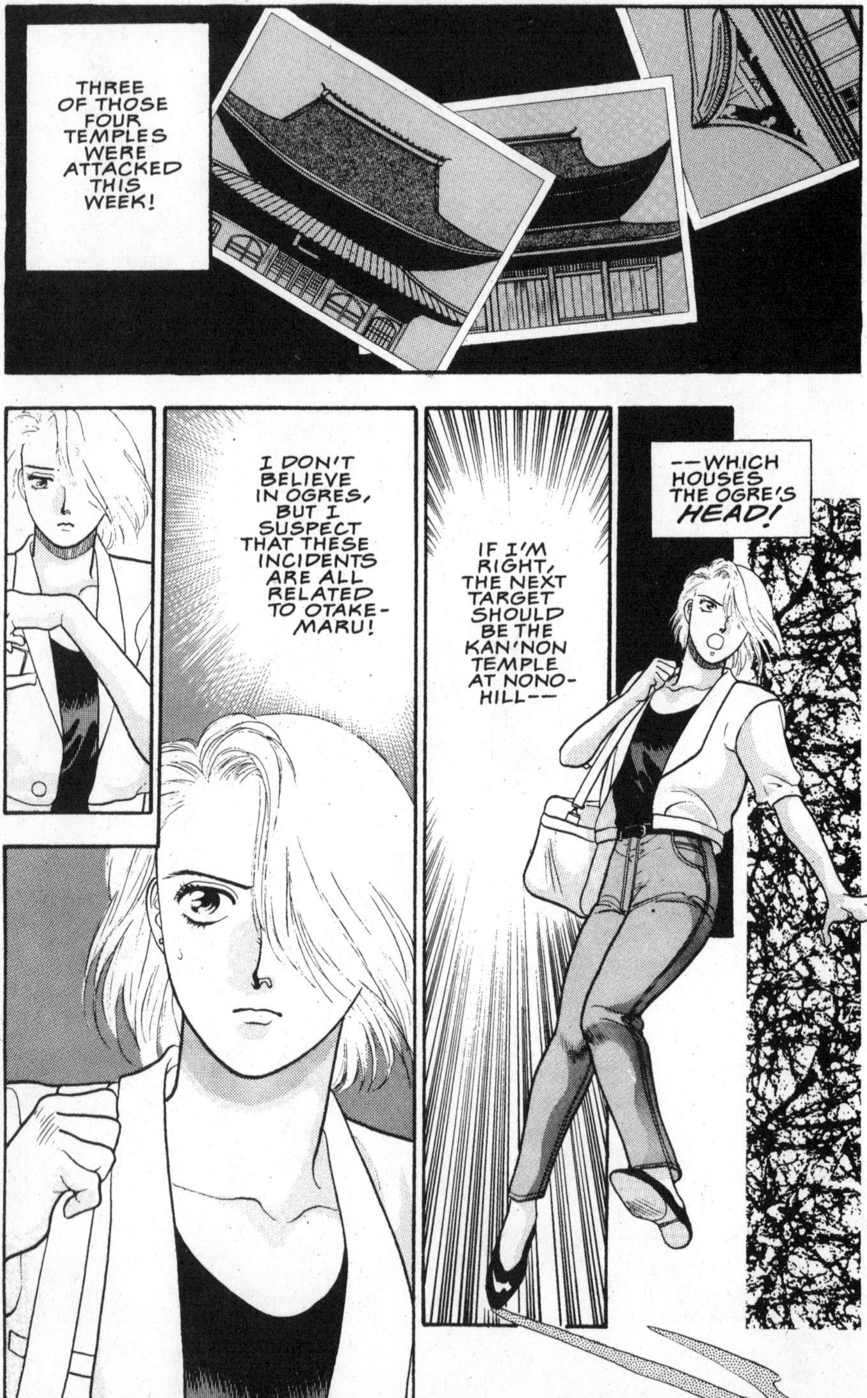
THREE OF THOSE FOUR TEMPLES WERE ATTACKED THIS WEEK!
I DON'T BELIEVE IN OGRES, BUT I SUSPECT THAT THESE INCIDENTS ARE ALL RELATED TO OTAKE-MARU!
IF I'M RIGHT, THE NEXT TARGET SHOULD BE THE KAN'NON TEMPLE AT NONO-HILL--
--WHICH HOUSES THE OGRE'S HEAD!

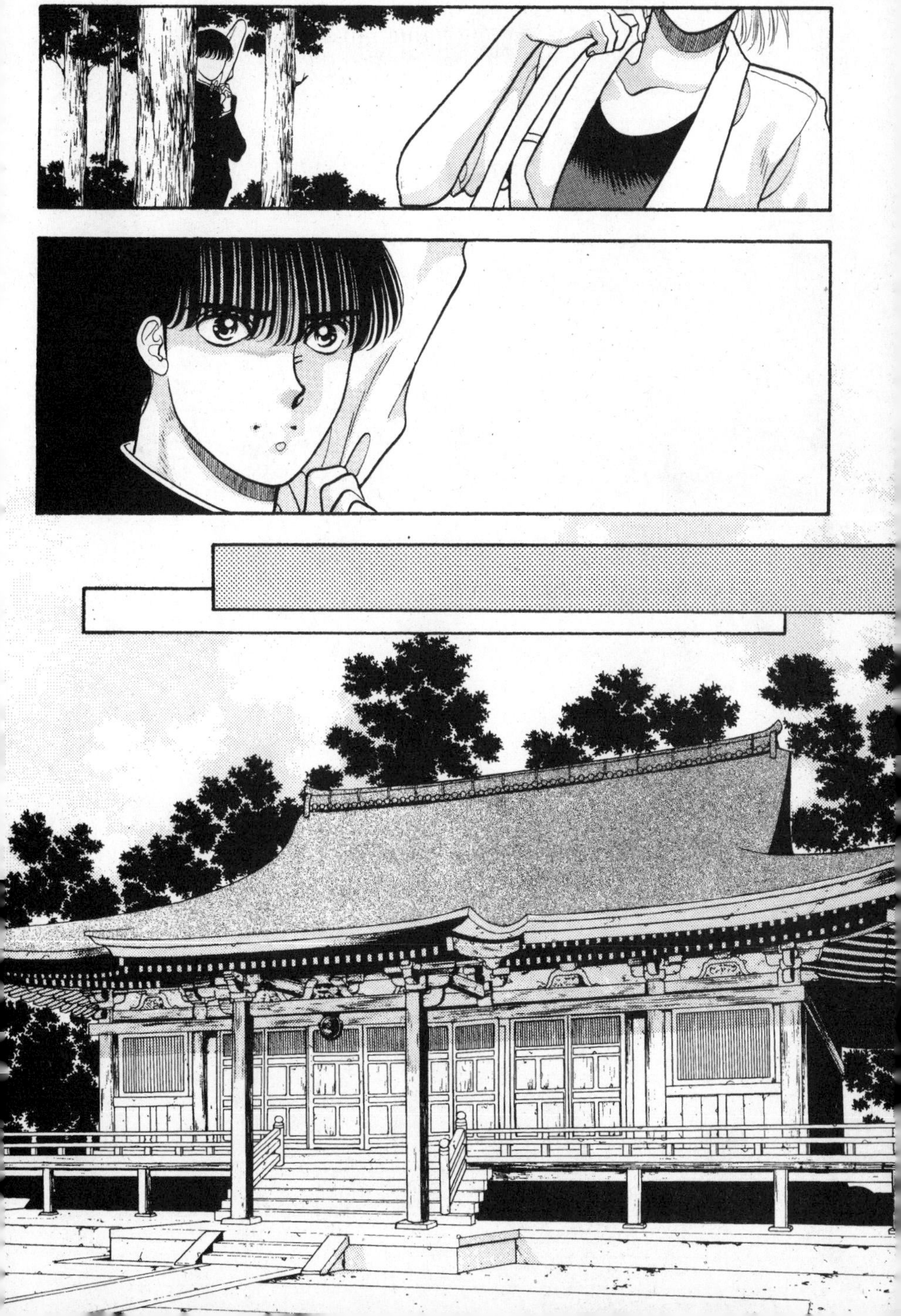

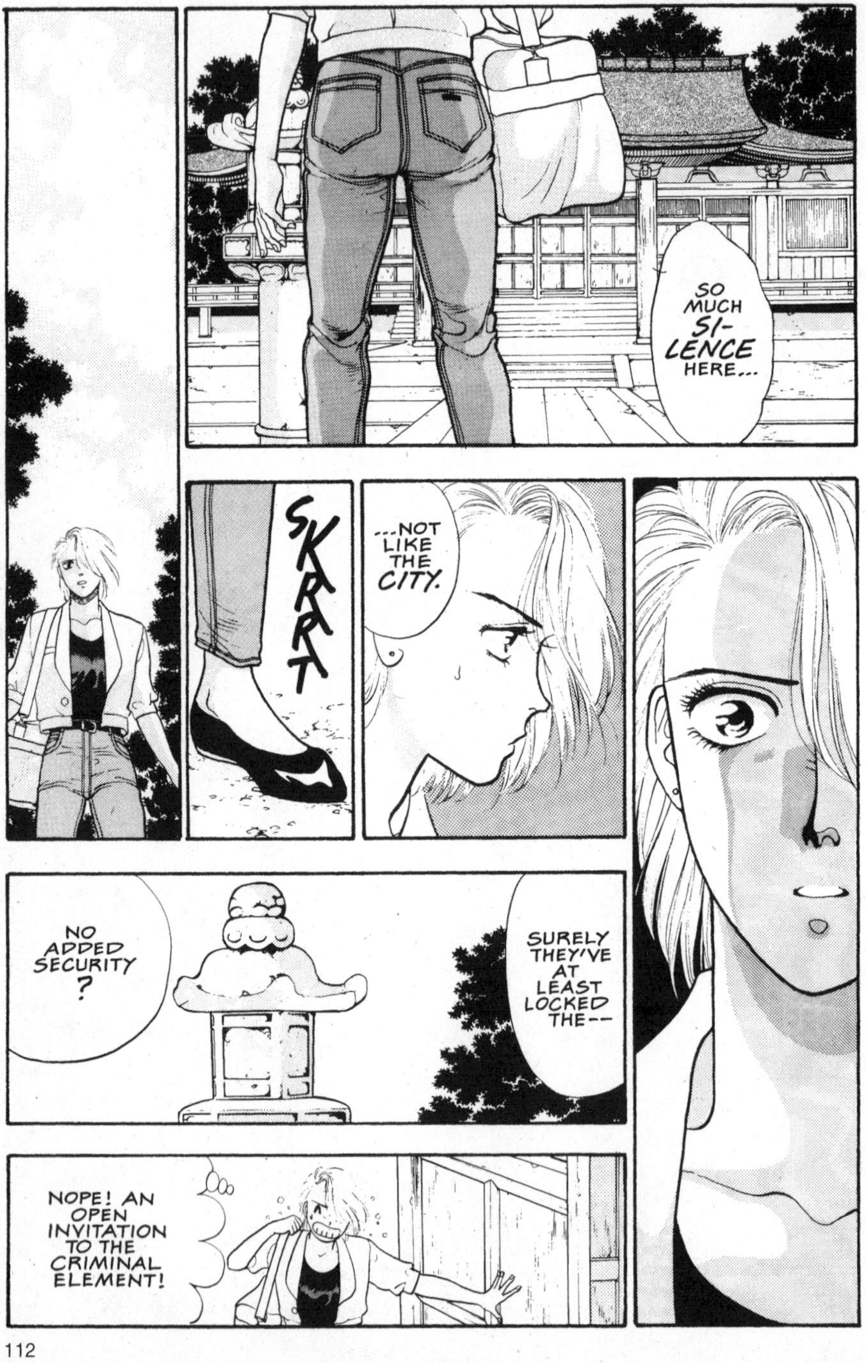
SO MUCH SI-LENCE HERE...
SKRRT
...NOT LIKE THE CITY.
NO ADDED SECURITY?
SURELY THEY'VE AT LEAST LOCKED THE--
NOPE! AN OPEN INVITATION TO THE CRIMINAL ELEMENT!

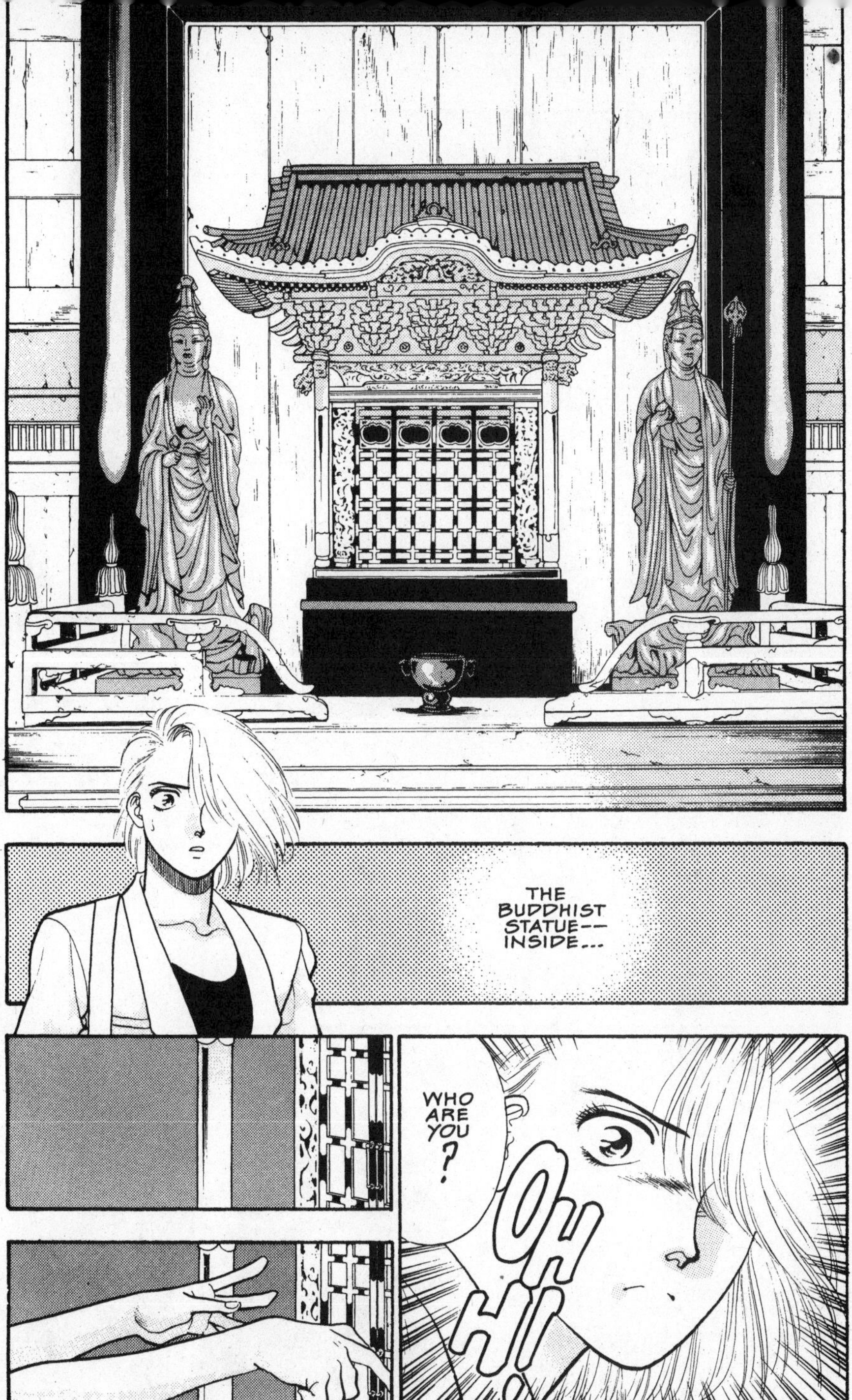
THE BUDDHIST STATUE-- INSIDE...
WHO ARE YOU?
OH HI!

NO, NO, NO!

I'M NOT THE ONE!!

IT'S NOT WHAT YOU THINK! I'M JUST A WRITER-- SAE GOTOH!

I....I WAS JUST DOING RESEARCH, 'CAUSE I THOUGHT THIS TEMPLE MIGHT BE RELATED TO THE OTHER...

OH--?! TH-THEN THERE *IS* A PURPOSE BEHIND THESE INCIDENTS... ??

I SEE... SO YOU ARE THE WRITER.

YOU'RE QUITE RIGHT. OTAKEMARU'S HEAD IS SEALED IN HERE---

---SO THIS TEMPLE WILL BE THE NEXT TARGET.

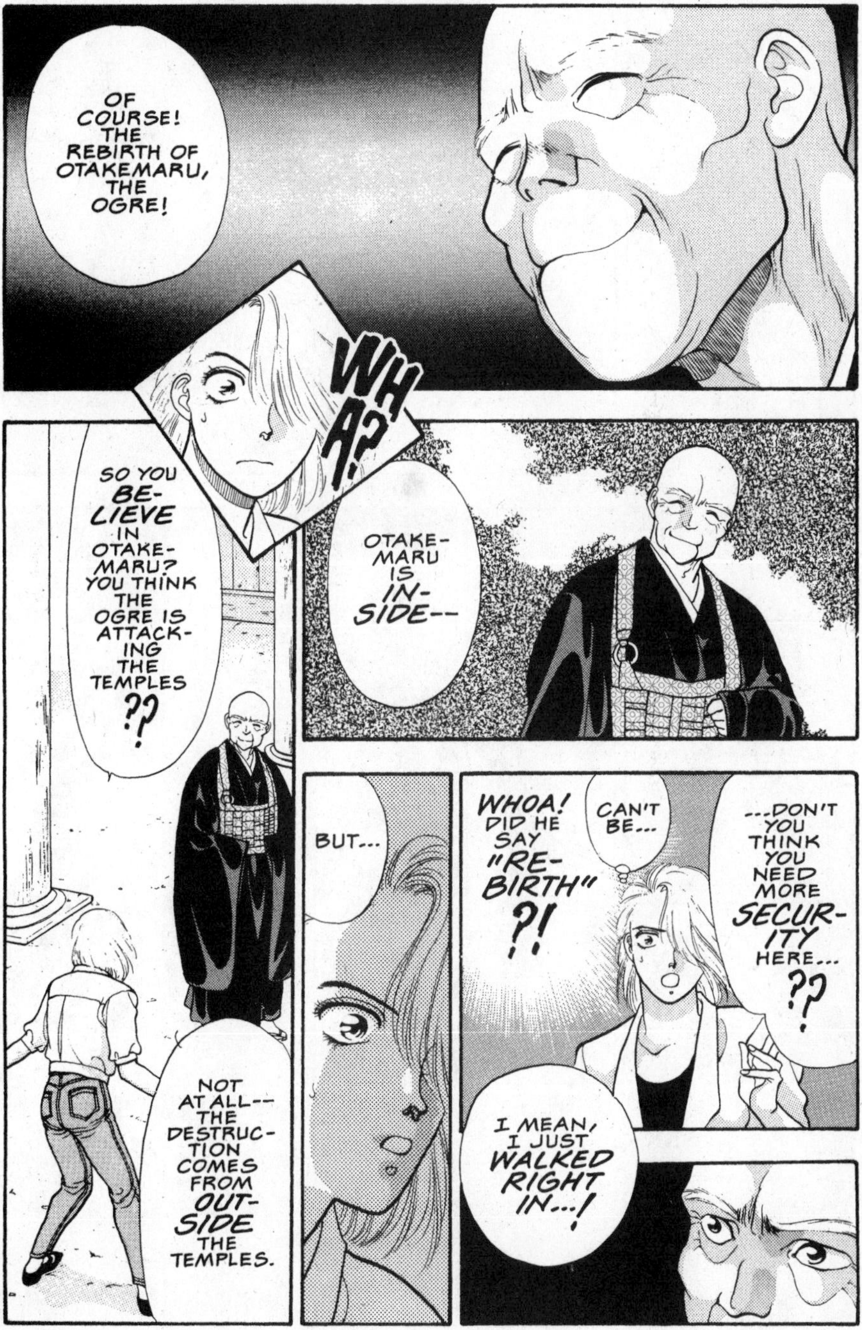
OF COURSE! THE REBIRTH OF OTAKEMARU, THE OGRE!
WHA?
SO YOU BELIEVE IN OTAKEMARU? YOU THINK THE OGRE IS ATTACKING THE TEMPLES ??
NOT AT ALL-- THE DESTRUCTION COMES FROM OUTSIDE THE TEMPLES.
OTAKEMARU IS INSIDE--
BUT...
WHOA! DID HE SAY "REBIRTH" ?!
CAN'T BE...
...DON'T YOU THINK YOU NEED MORE SECURITY HERE... ??
I MEAN, I JUST WALKED RIGHT IN...!

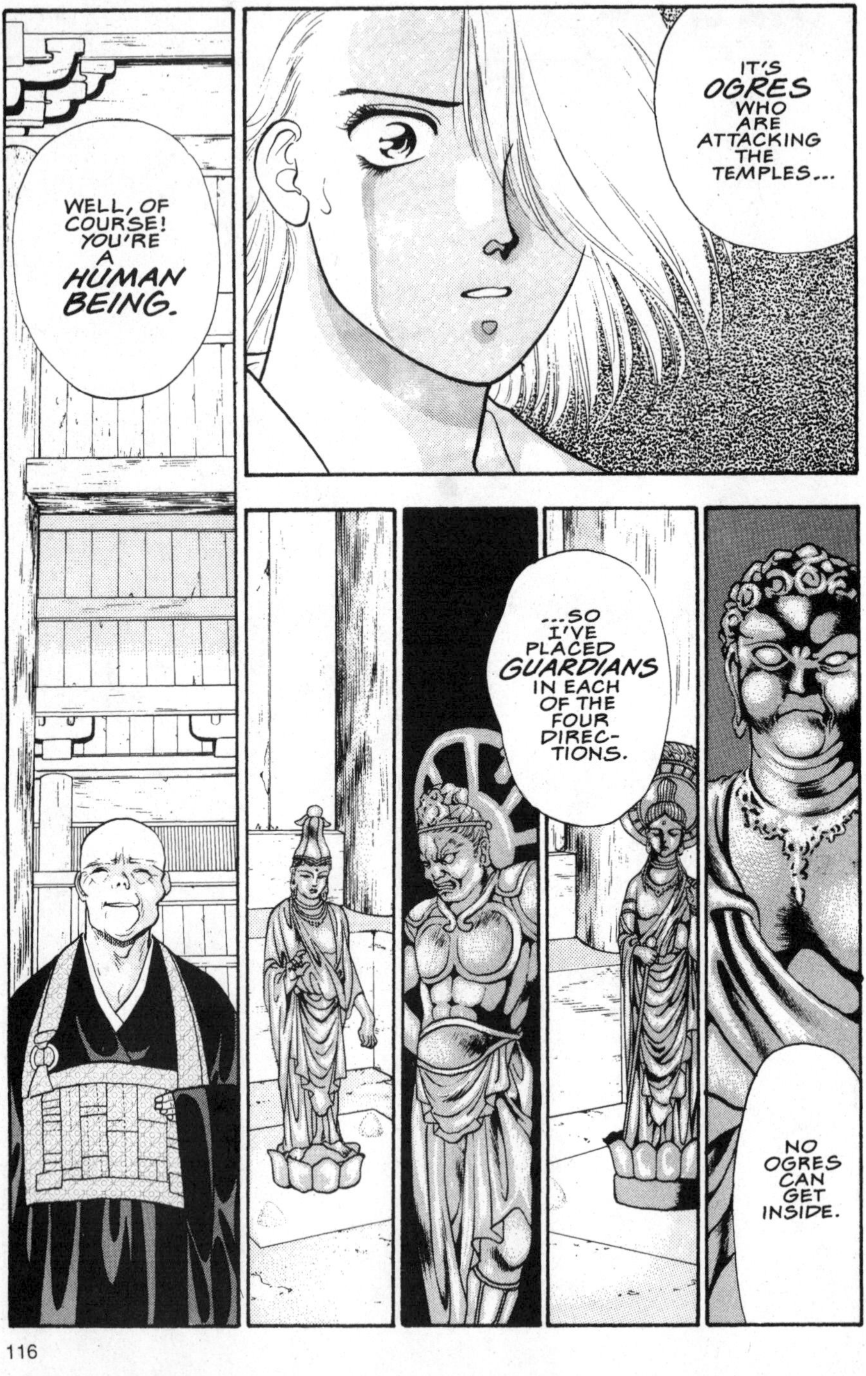
WELL, OF COURSE! YOU'RE A HUMAN BEING.
IT'S OGRES WHO ARE ATTACKING THE TEMPLES...
...SO I'VE PLACED GUARDIANS IN EACH OF THE FOUR DIREC-TIONS.
NO OGRES CAN GET INSIDE.

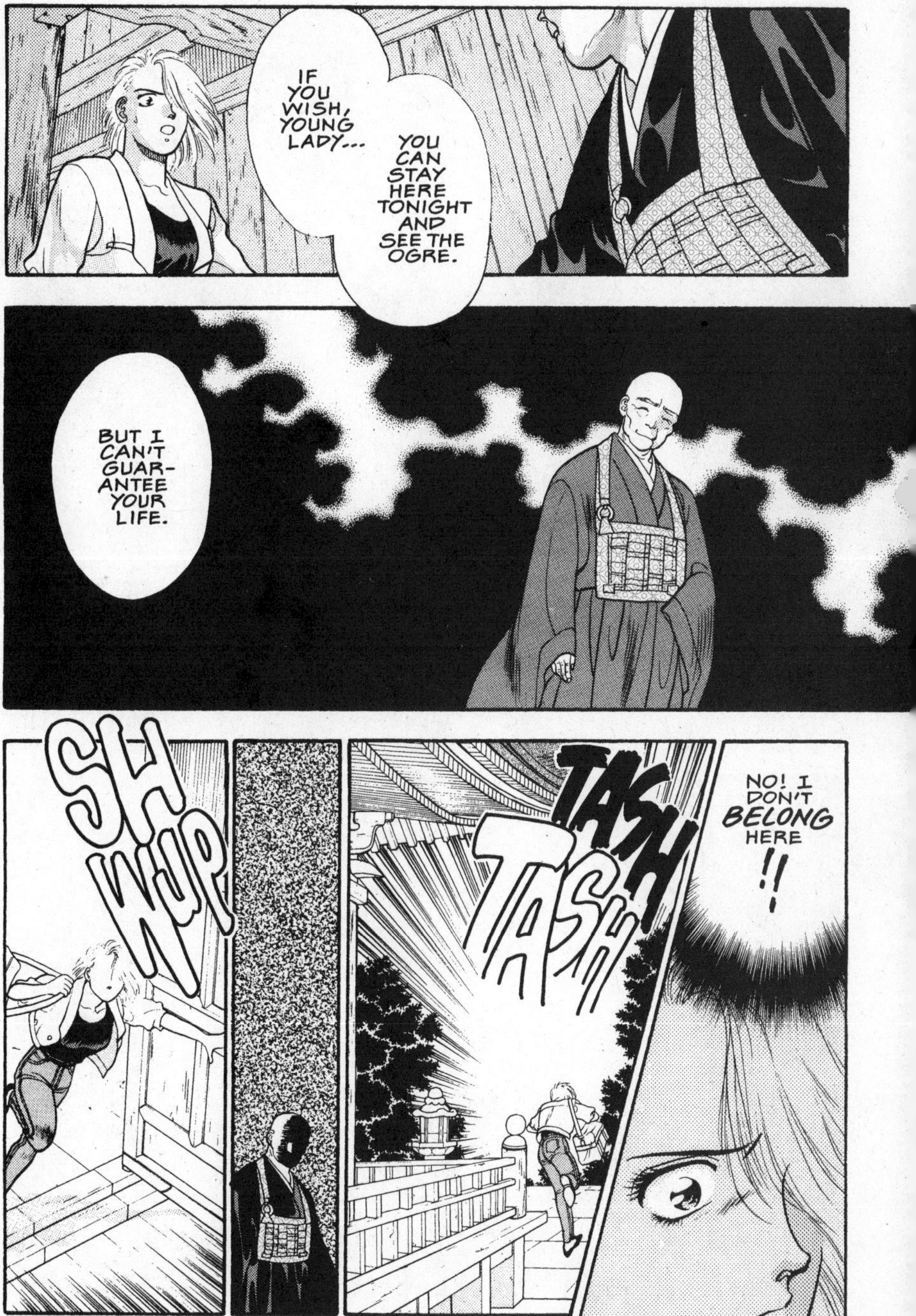
IF YOU WISH, YOUNG LADY...
YOU CAN STAY HERE TONIGHT AND SEE THE OGRE.
BUT I CAN'T GUARANTEE YOUR LIFE.
SHWUP
TASH TASH
NO! I DON'T BELONG HERE !!

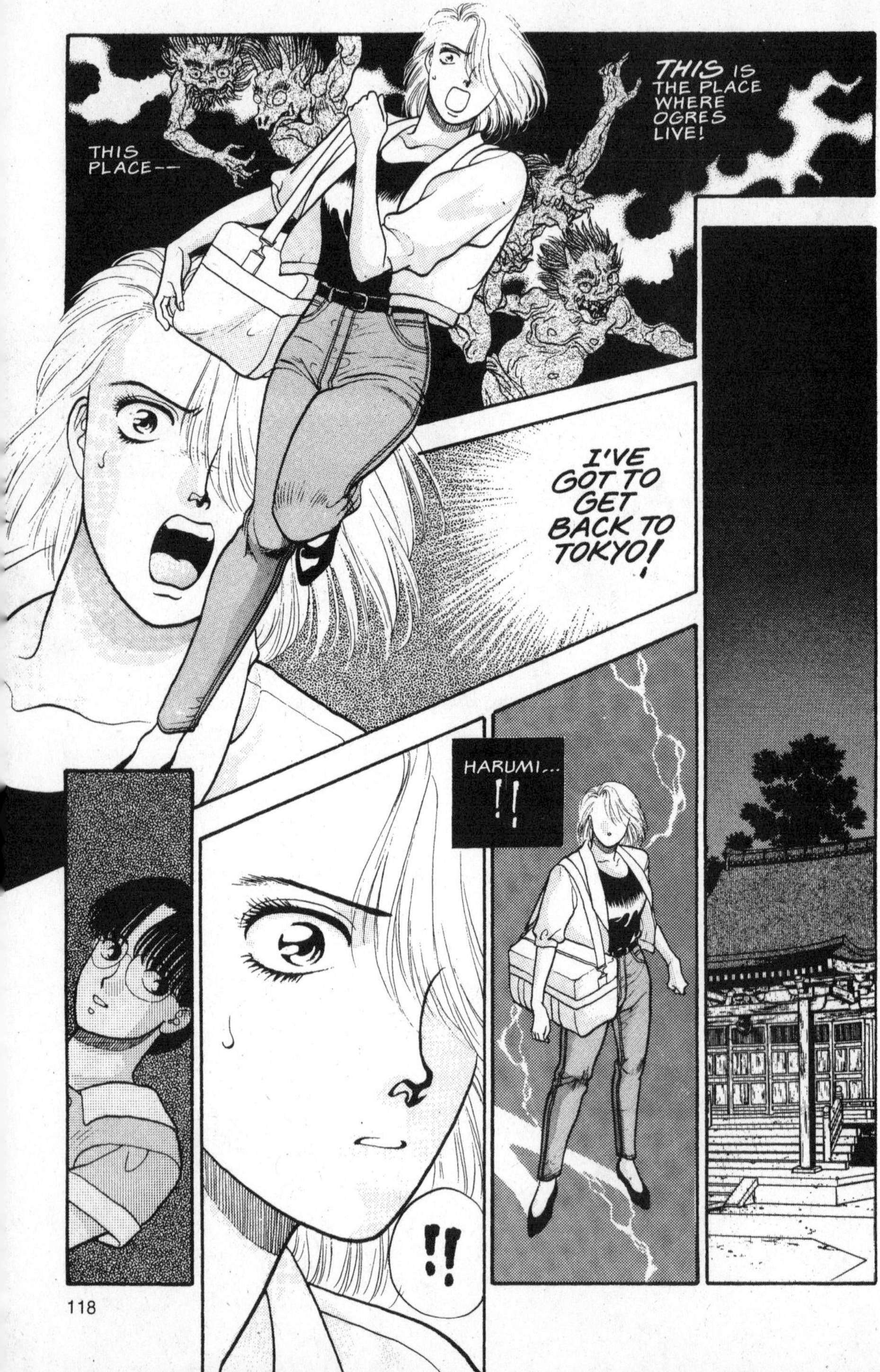
THIS PLACE--
THIS IS THE PLACE WHERE OGRES LIVE!
I'VE GOT TO GET BACK TO TOKYO!
HARUMI...
!!
!!

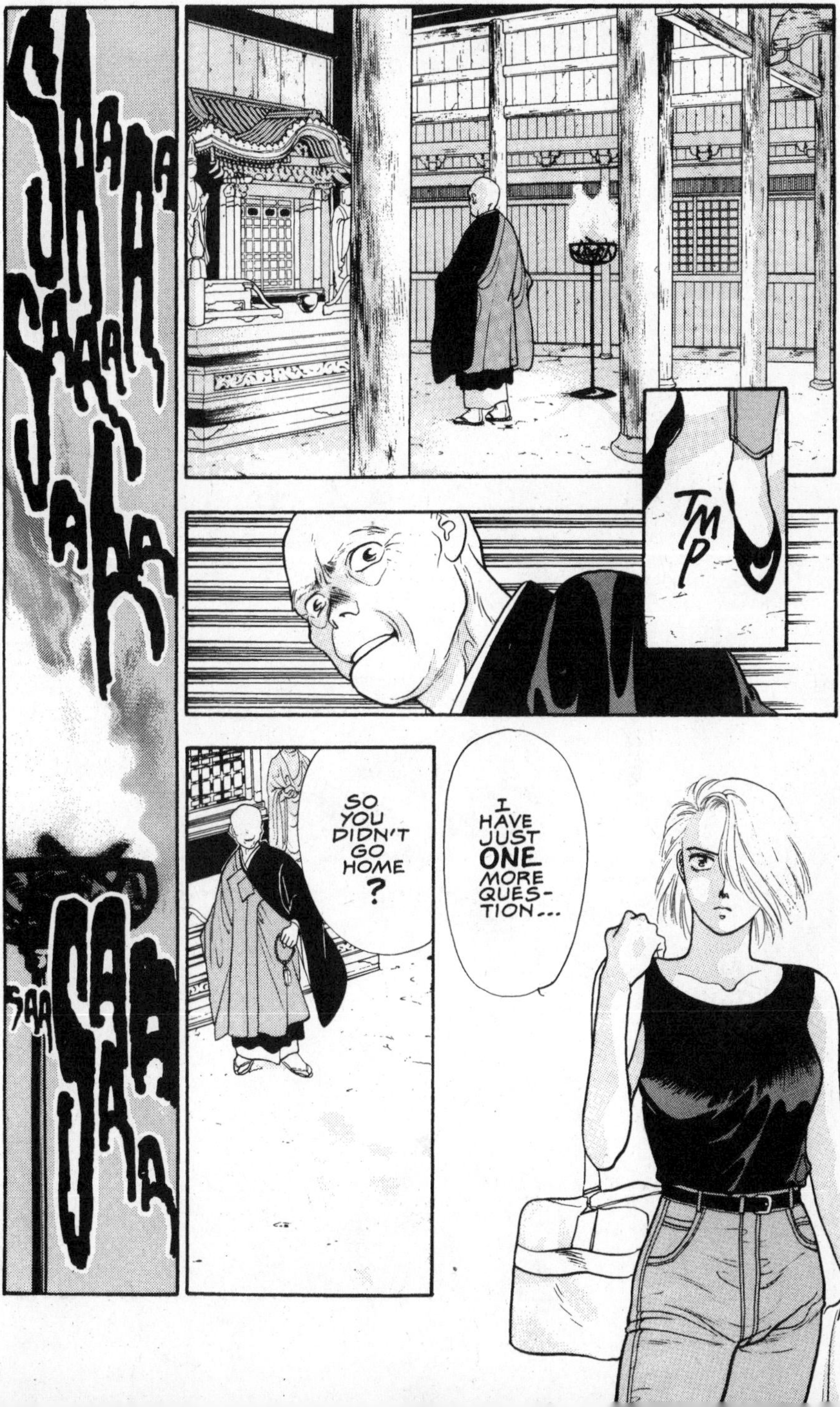
TMP
SO YOU DIDN'T GO HOME?
I HAVE JUST **ONE** MORE QUESTION...

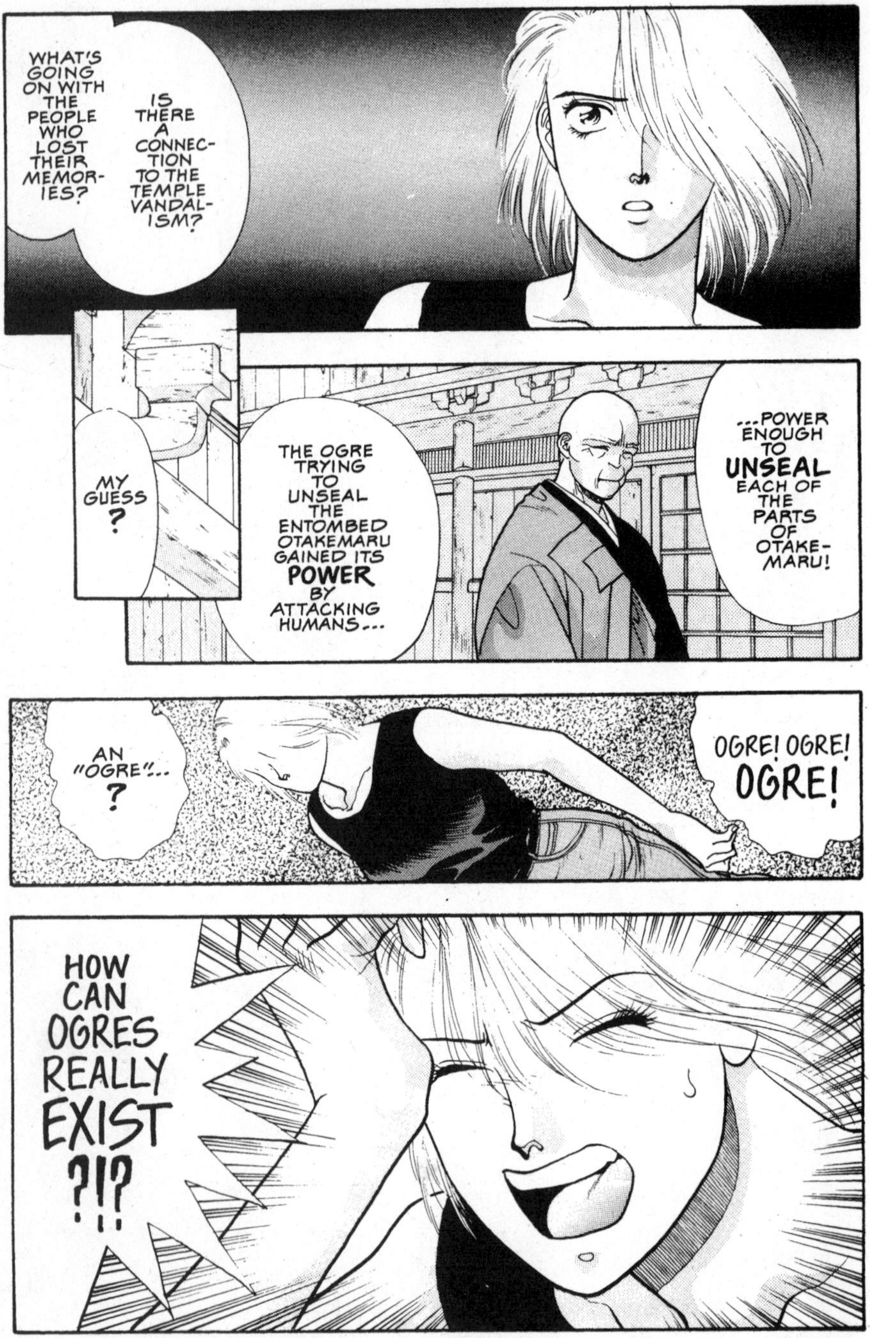
WHAT'S GOING ON WITH THE PEOPLE WHO LOST THEIR MEMORIES?
IS THERE A CONNECTION TO THE TEMPLE VANDALISM?
MY GUESS?
THE OGRE TRYING TO UNSEAL THE ENTOMBED OTAKEMARU GAINED ITS POWER BY ATTACKING HUMANS...
...POWER ENOUGH TO UNSEAL EACH OF THE PARTS OF OTAKEMARU!
AN "OGRE"...?
OGRE! OGRE! OGRE!
HOW CAN OGRES REALLY EXIST?!?

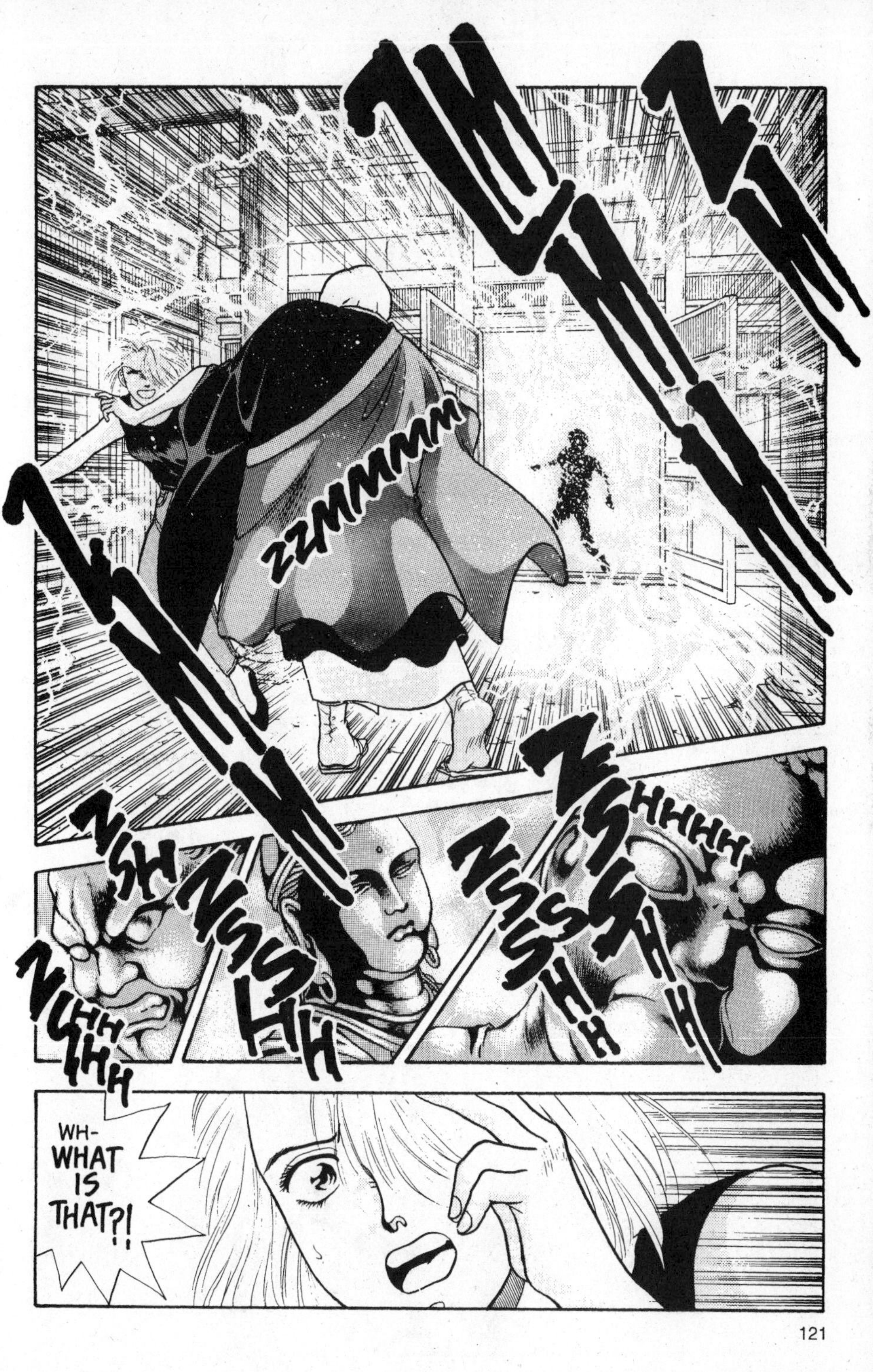
ZZMMMMM
WH- WHAT IS THAT?!

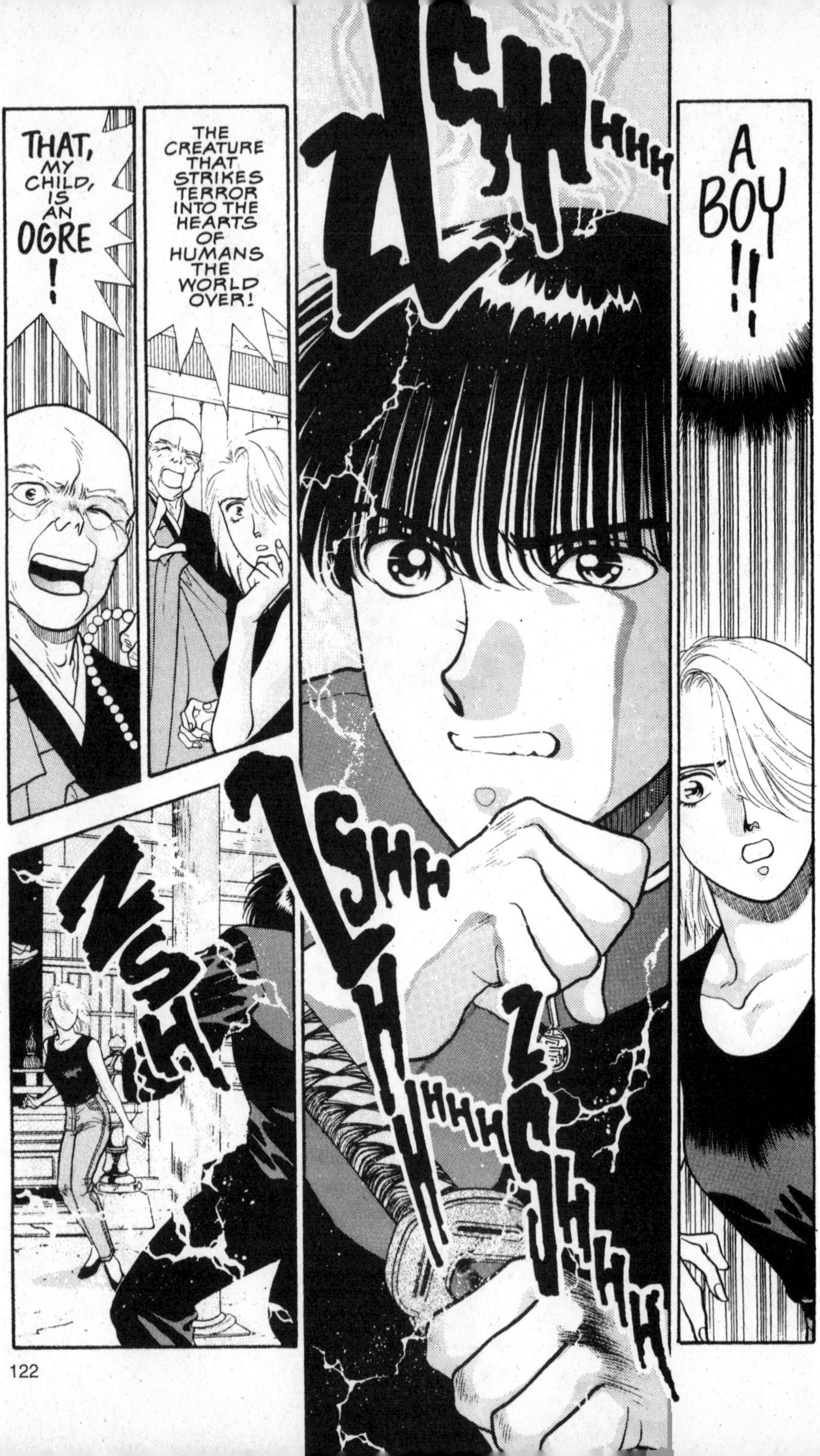
THAT, MY CHILD, IS AN OGRE!
THE CREATURE THAT STRIKES TERROR INTO THE HEARTS OF HUMANS THE WORLD OVER!
ZSHH
ZSHHHH
ZSHHHHHH
ZSHHHHH
A BOY!!

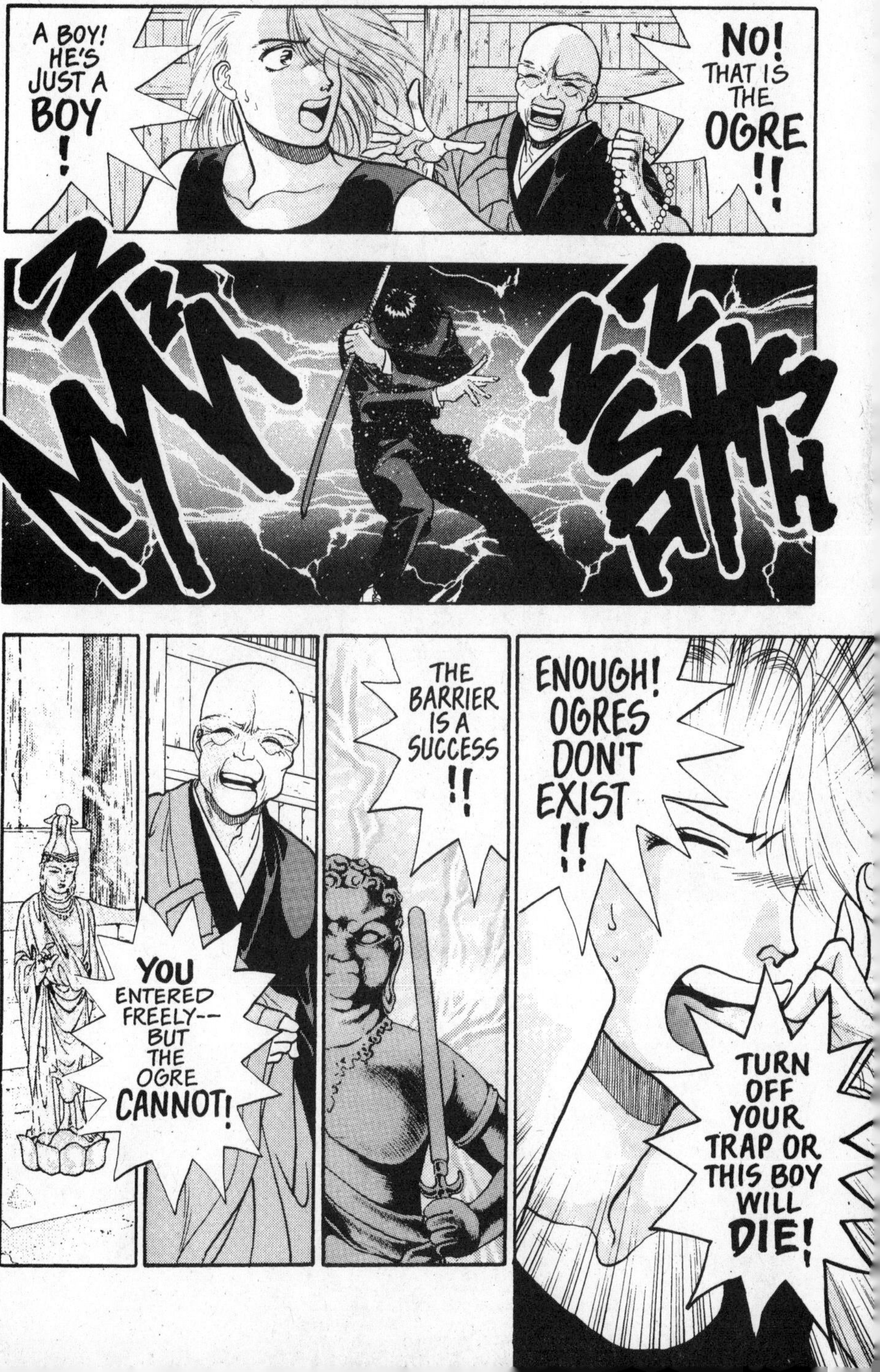
A BOY! HE'S JUST A BOY!
NO! THAT IS THE OGRE!!
YOU ENTERED FREELY-- BUT THE OGRE CANNOT!
THE BARRIER IS A SUCCESS!!
ENOUGH! OGRES DON'T EXIST!!
TURN OFF YOUR TRAP OR THIS BOY WILL DIE!

OGRES... EXIST...

...LIKE... OTAKE-MARU...

EVEN FROM ITS ENTRAPPED SLUMBER, THE OGRE **DREAMS** ITS **DREAM** AND ATTACKS HUMANS!

PEOPLE HAVE BEEN LOSING THEIR MEMORIES BECAUSE OTAKEMARU RELEASED ITS VILE NIGHTMARES TO CAPTURE THEM! ENTOMBING IS JUST ENTOMBING, AFTER ALL--NOT **ANNIHILATION!**

SHUT UP, OGRE! DON'T LISTEN TO THE OGRE'S WORDS!

TRUST ME!

ONIKIRI-MARU...

DESTROY THIS BARRIER BEFORE ANOTHER PERSON FALLS VICTIM TO ITS NIGHTMARE...

I'LL SLAY THE OGRE WITH MY SWORD--

--ONIKIRI-MARU! BUT TO DO IT, I NEED TO **UNSEAL** OTAKEMARU!!

ISN'T THAT THE SWORD OF THE ANCIENT HERO **WATANABE-NO-TSUNA,** THE SWORD WHICH CAN PIERCE AND KILL AN OGRE'S FLESH--?!

GRAH

HAHH

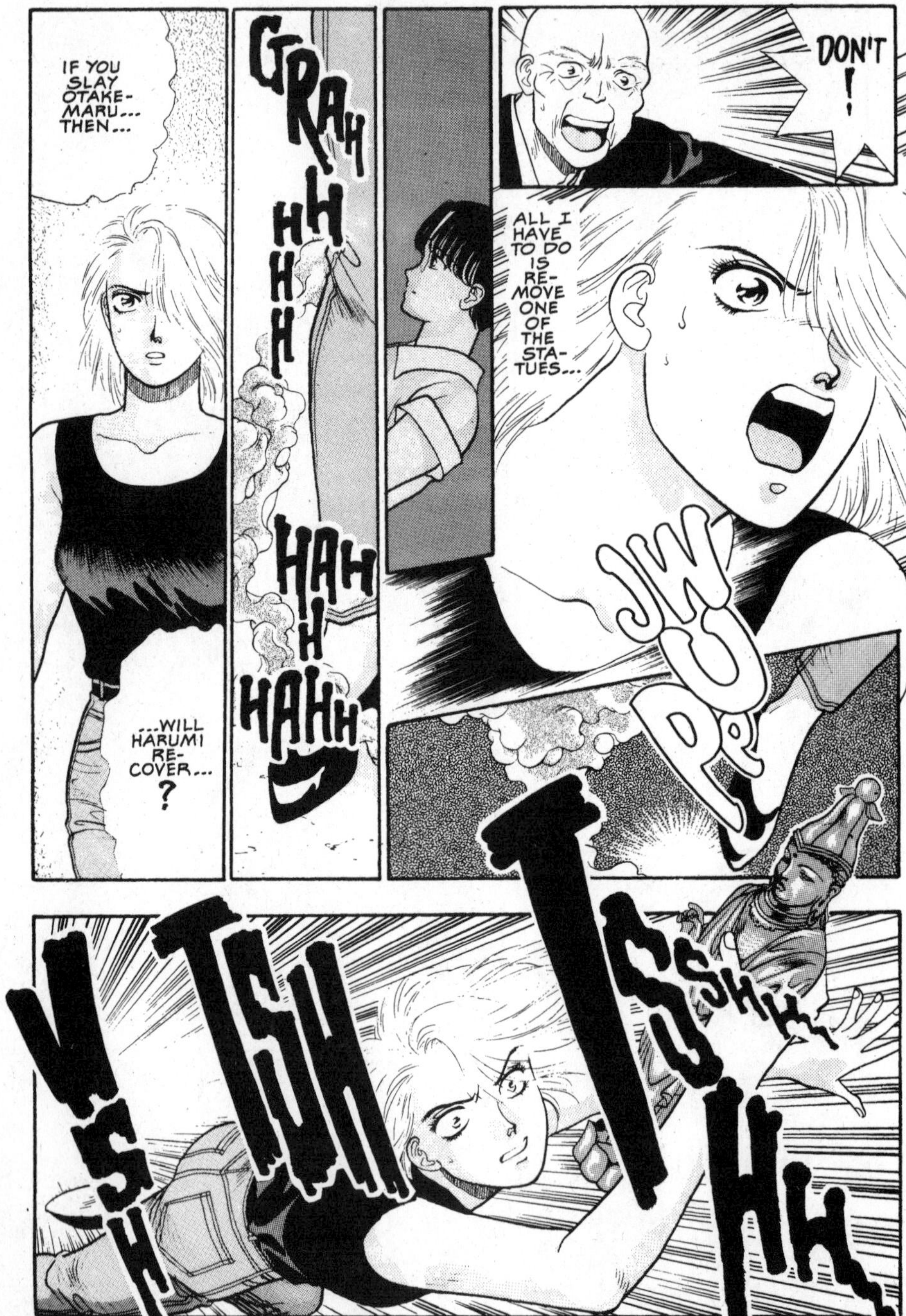
IF YOU SLAY OTAKE-MARU... THEN...
...WILL HARUMI RE-COVER...?
GRAHHHHHH
HAHHHAHH
DON'T!
ALL I HAVE TO DO IS RE-MOVE ONE OF THE STA-TUES...

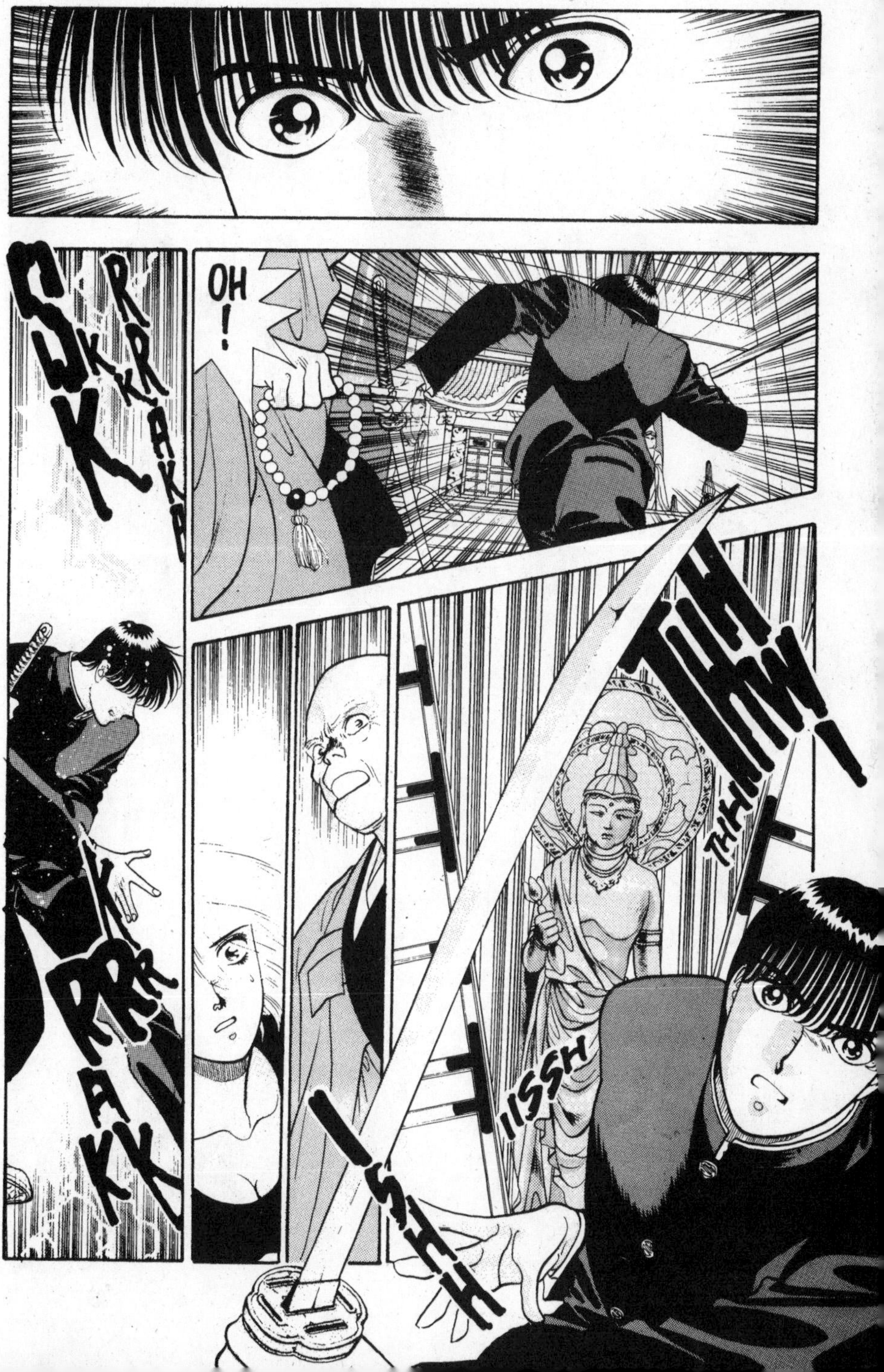
OH!
THH
IISSH

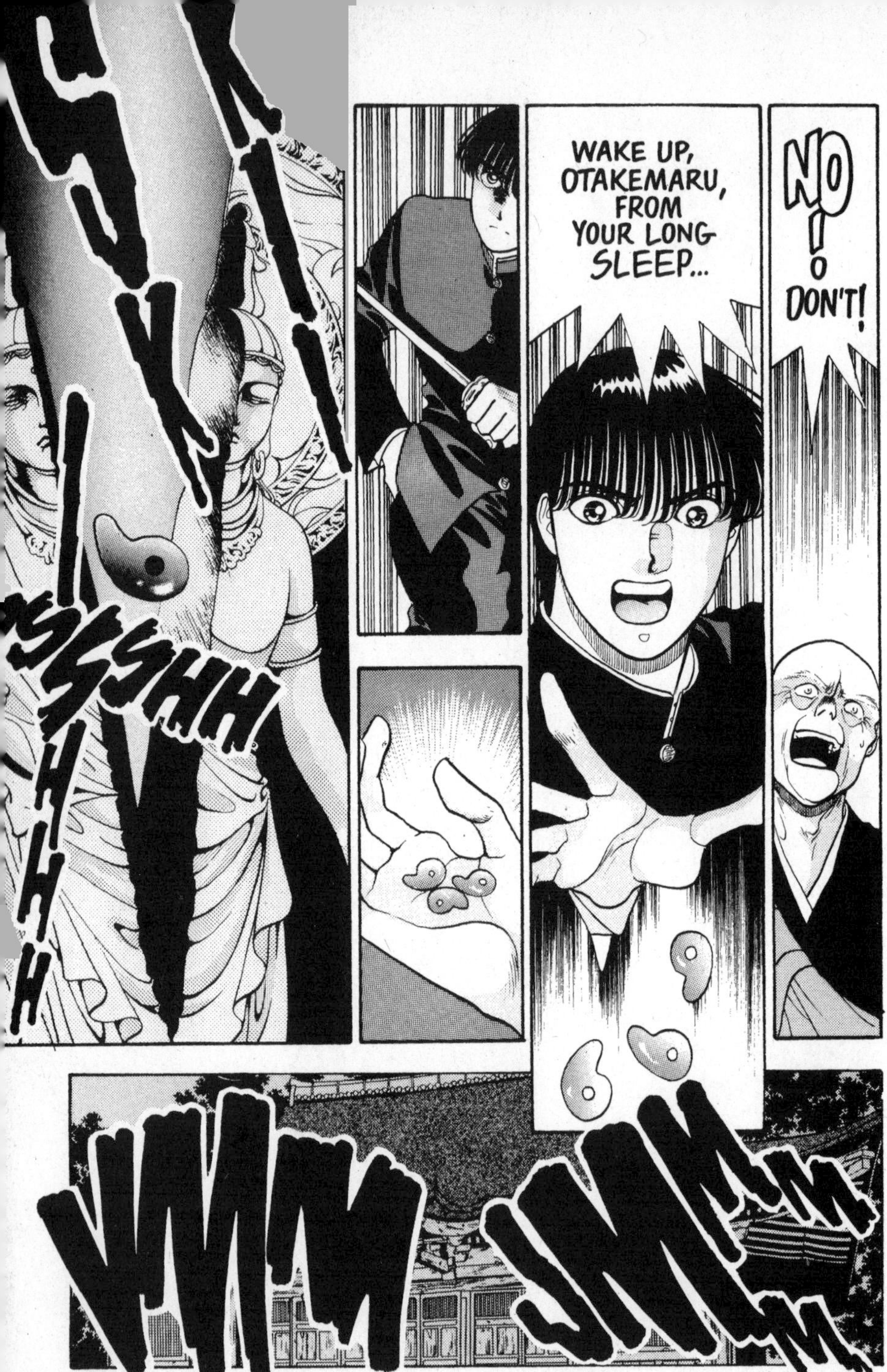
WAKE UP, OTAKEMARU, FROM YOUR LONG SLEEP...
NO! O DON'T!

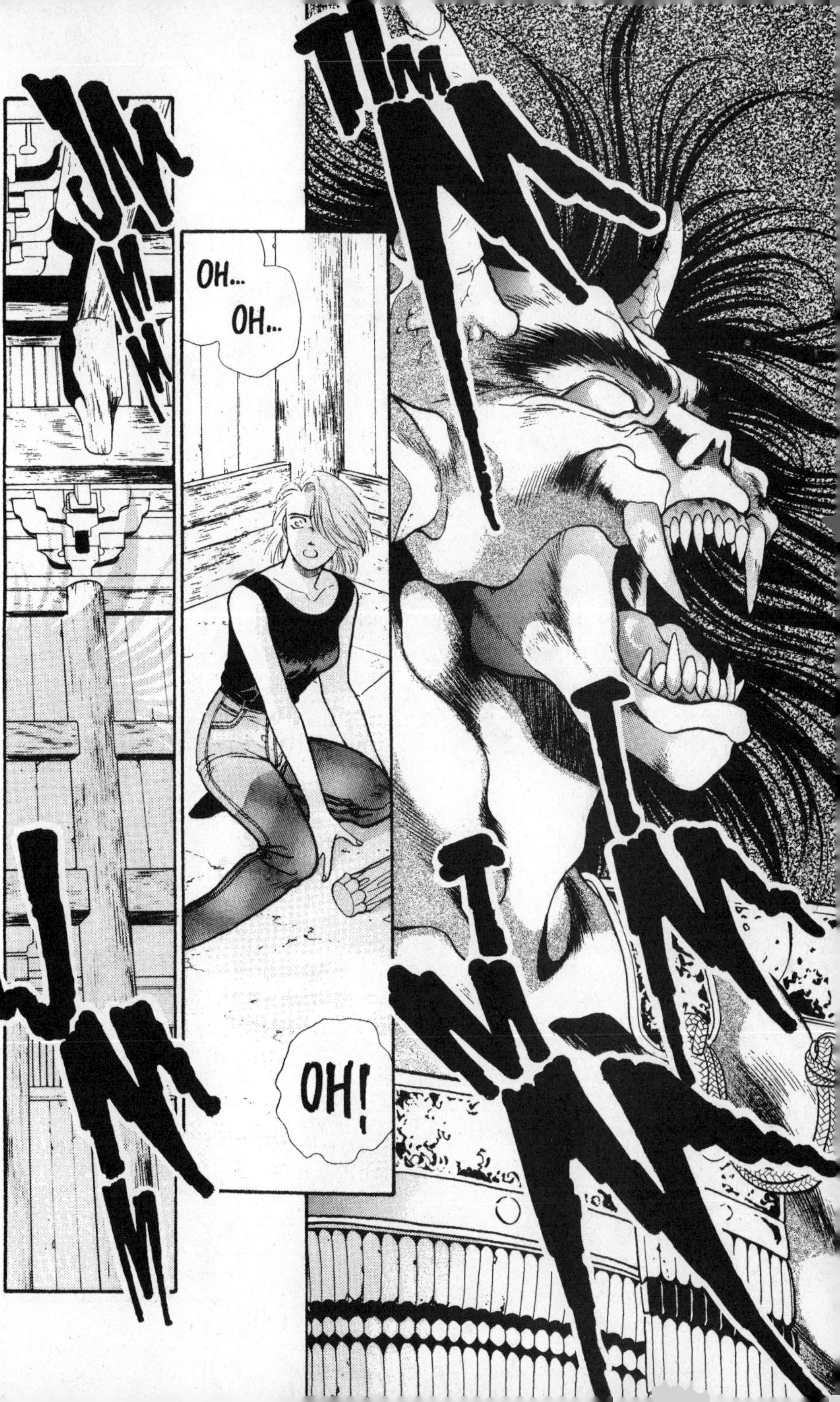
OH... OH...
OH!

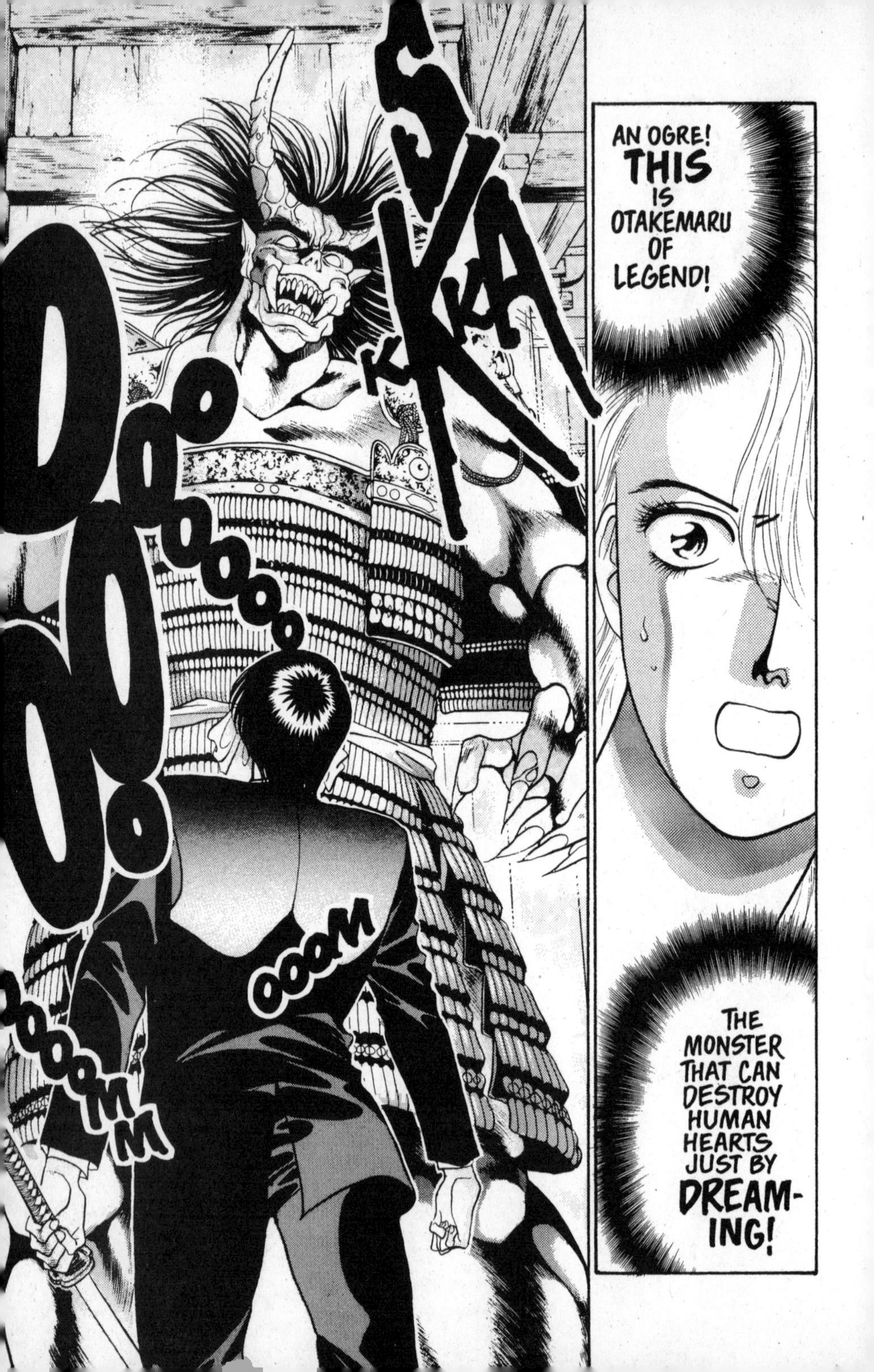
oooM
AN OGRE! **THIS** IS OTAKEMARU OF LEGEND!
THE MONSTER THAT CAN DESTROY HUMAN HEARTS JUST BY **DREAMING!**

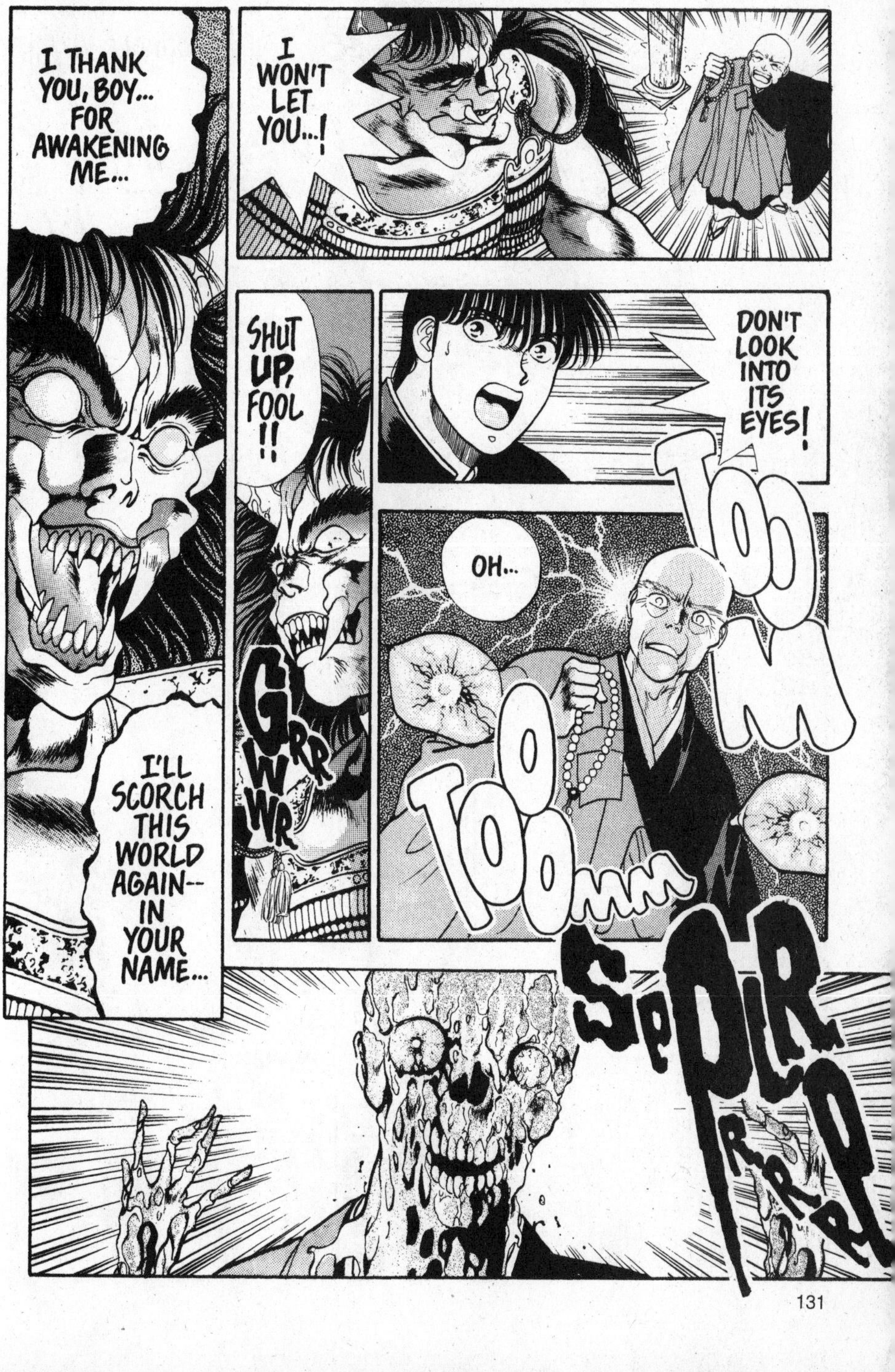
I THANK YOU, BOY... FOR AWAKENING ME...
I'LL SCORCH THIS WORLD AGAIN-- IN YOUR NAME...
I WON'T LET YOU...!
SHUT UP, FOOL!!
GRRR
WWR
DON'T LOOK INTO ITS EYES!
OH...
TOOOM
TOOOOMM
SPLRRRRP

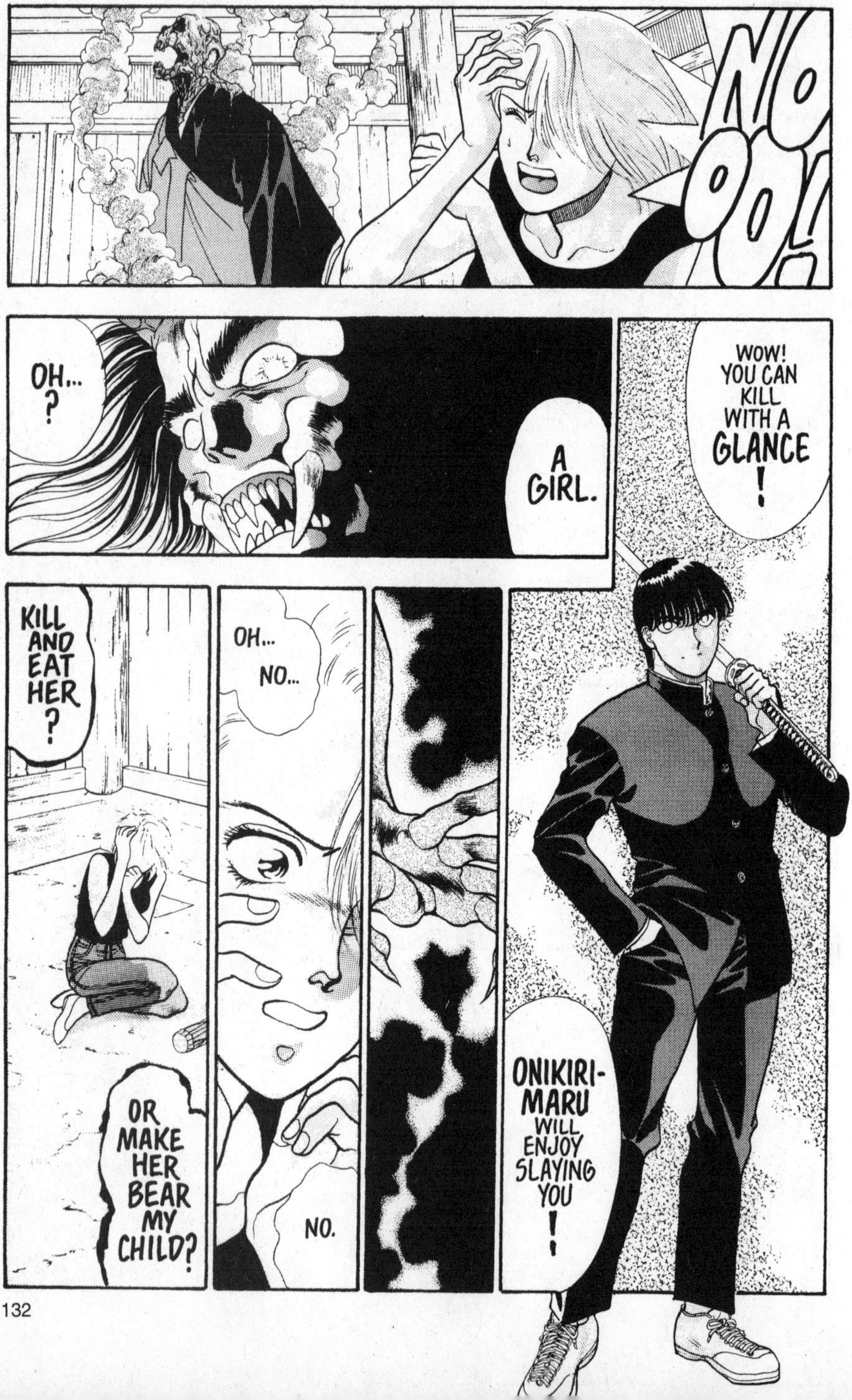
NOOOO!!
OH... ?
A GIRL.
WOW! YOU CAN KILL WITH A GLANCE!
KILL AND EAT HER?
OR MAKE HER BEAR MY CHILD?
OH... NO...
NO.
ONIKIRI-MARU WILL ENJOY SLAYING YOU!

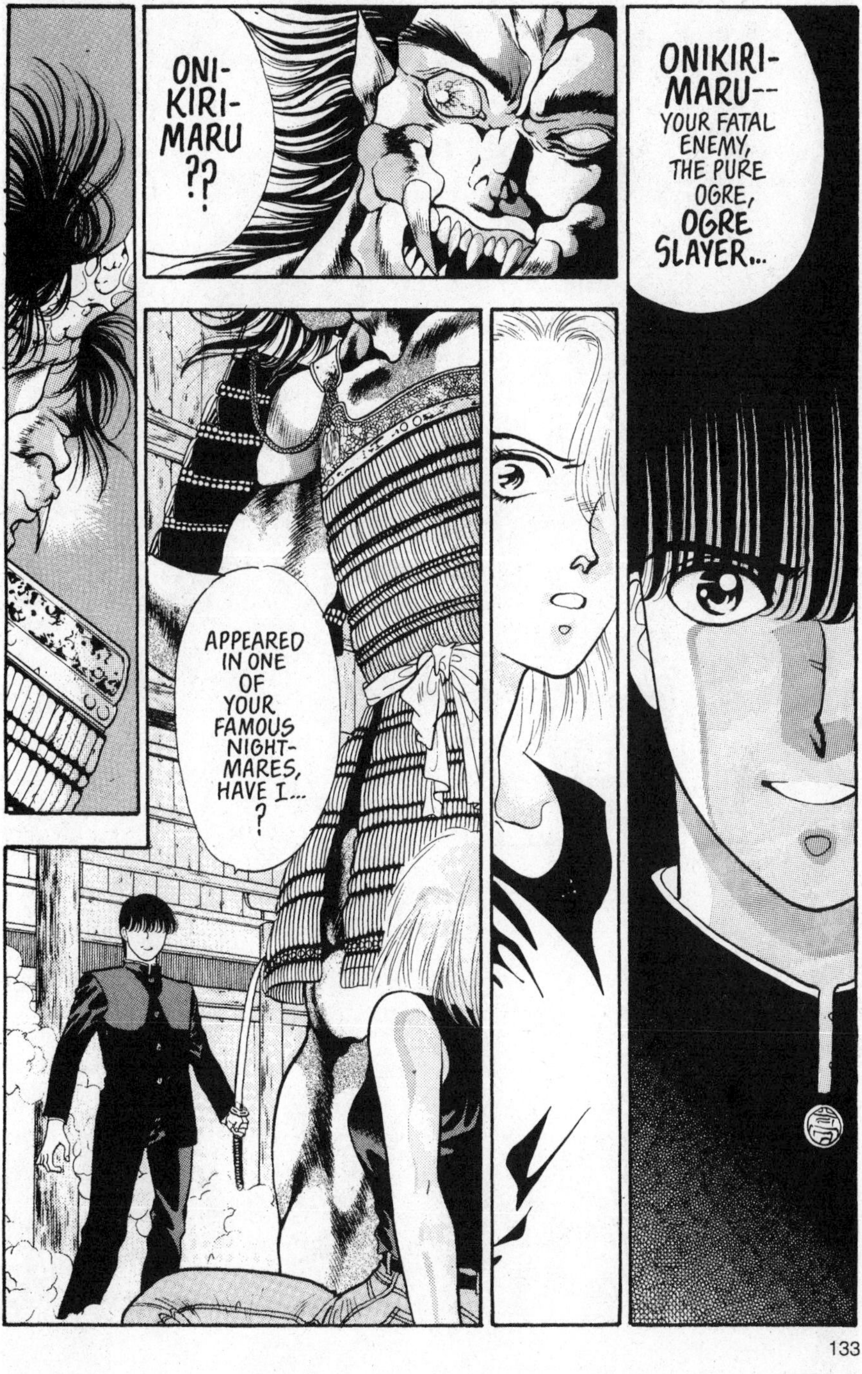
ONI-
KIRI-
MARU
??
ONIKIRI-
MARU--
YOUR FATAL
ENEMY,
THE PURE
OGRE,
OGRE
SLAYER...
APPEARED
IN ONE
OF
YOUR
FAMOUS
NIGHT-
MARES,
HAVE I...
?

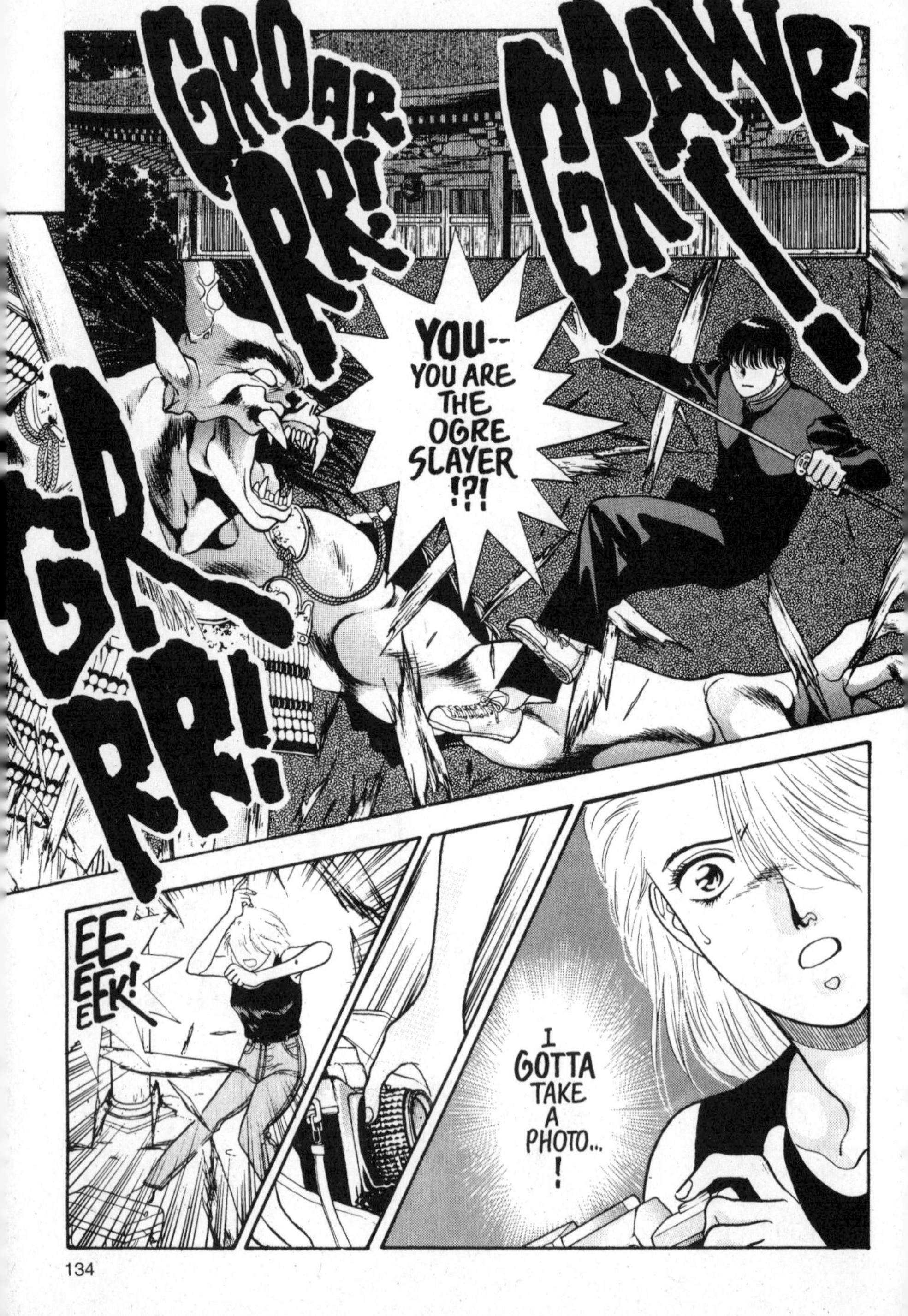
GROAR RR!
GRAWR GR!!
GR RR!!
YOU-- YOU ARE THE OGRE SLAYER !?!
EE EE EEK!
I GOTTA TAKE A PHOTO... !

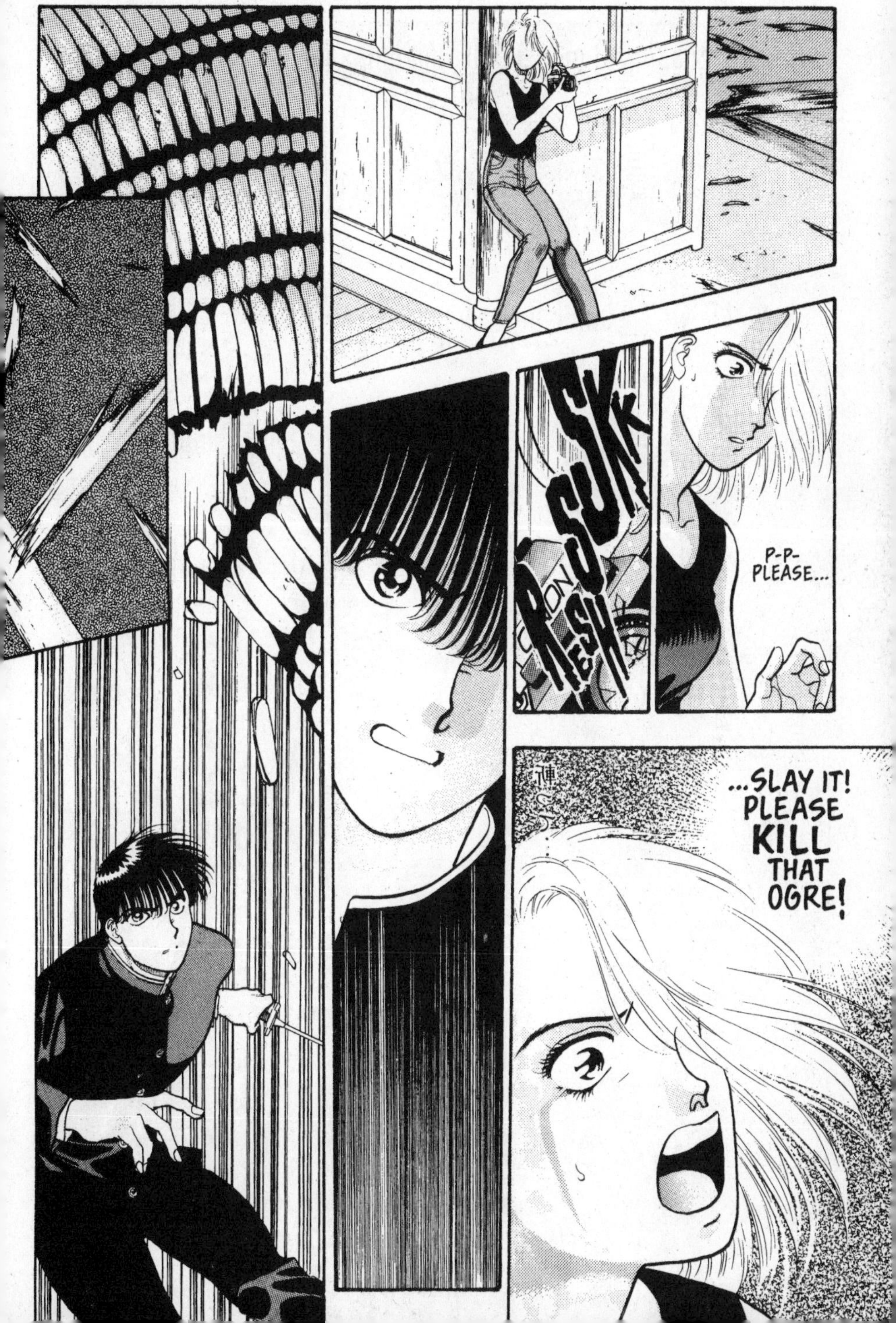
P-P-
PLEASE...
...SLAY IT! PLEASE KILL THAT OGRE!

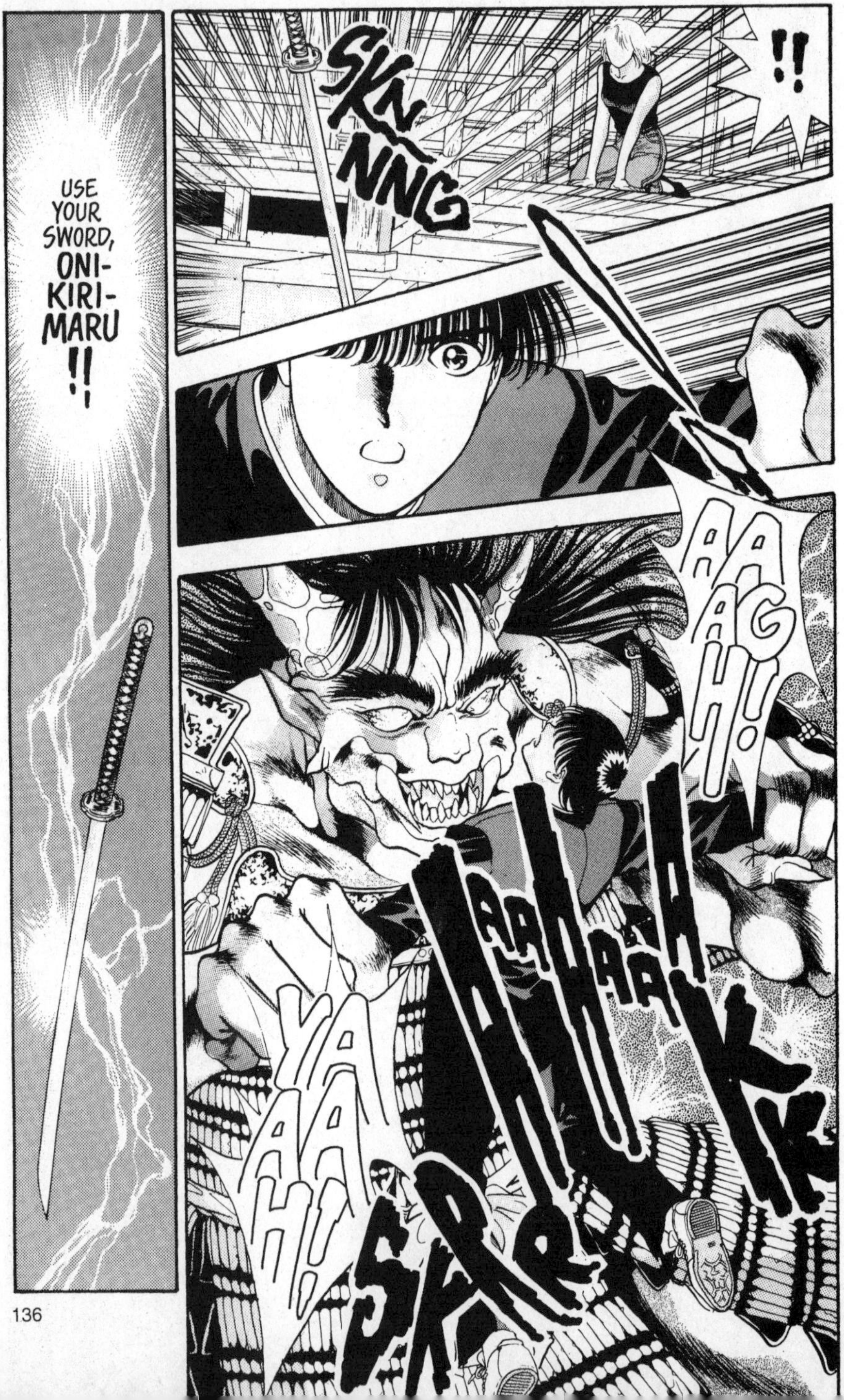
USE YOUR SWORD, ONI-KIRI-MARU!!
SKNNNG
!!
AAAGH!
YAAAH

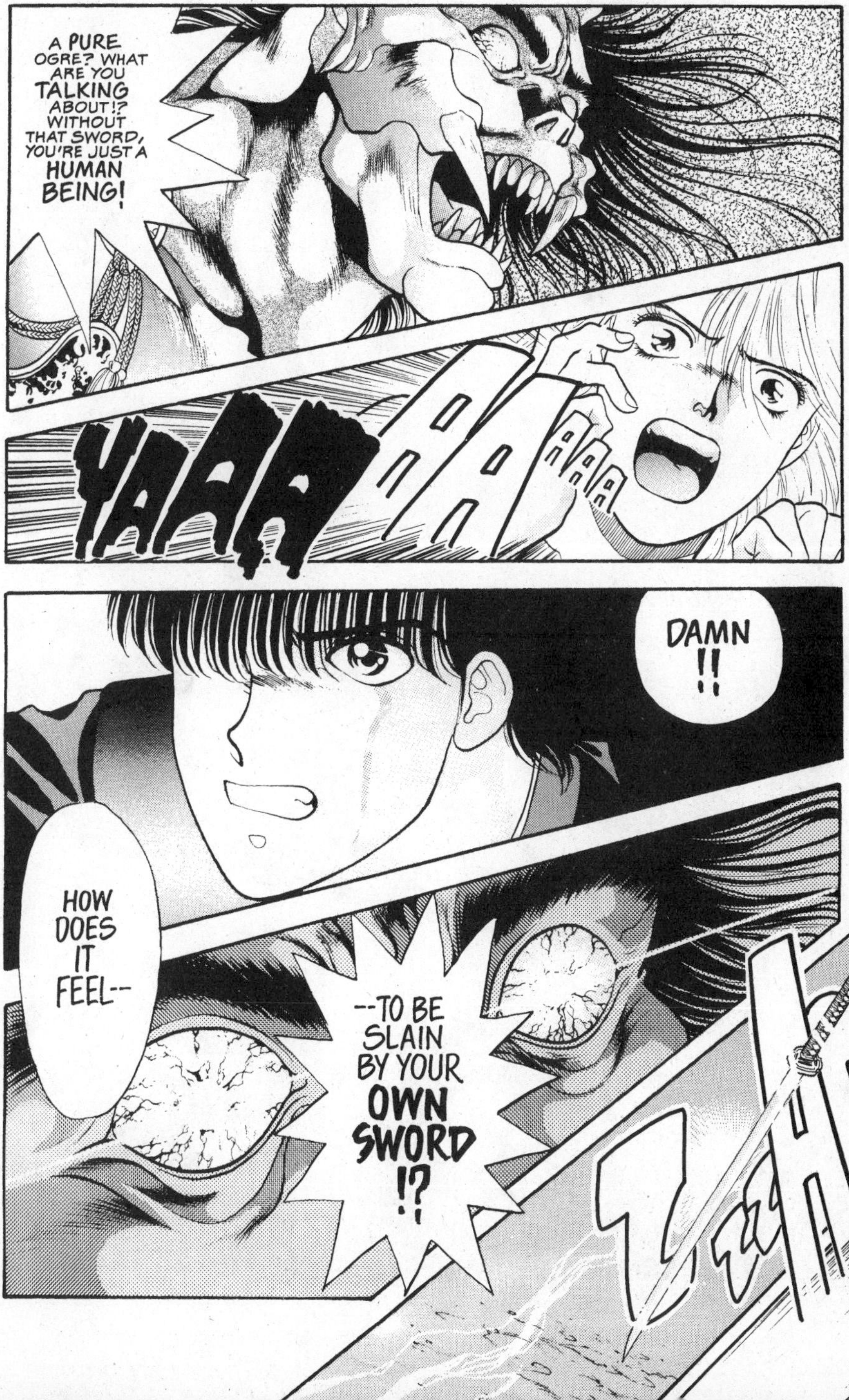
A PURE OGRE? WHAT ARE YOU TALKING ABOUT!? WITHOUT THAT SWORD, YOU'RE JUST A HUMAN BEING!
YAAAAAAAAAA
DAMN !!
HOW DOES IT FEEL--
--TO BE SLAIN BY YOUR OWN SWORD !?
ZAP

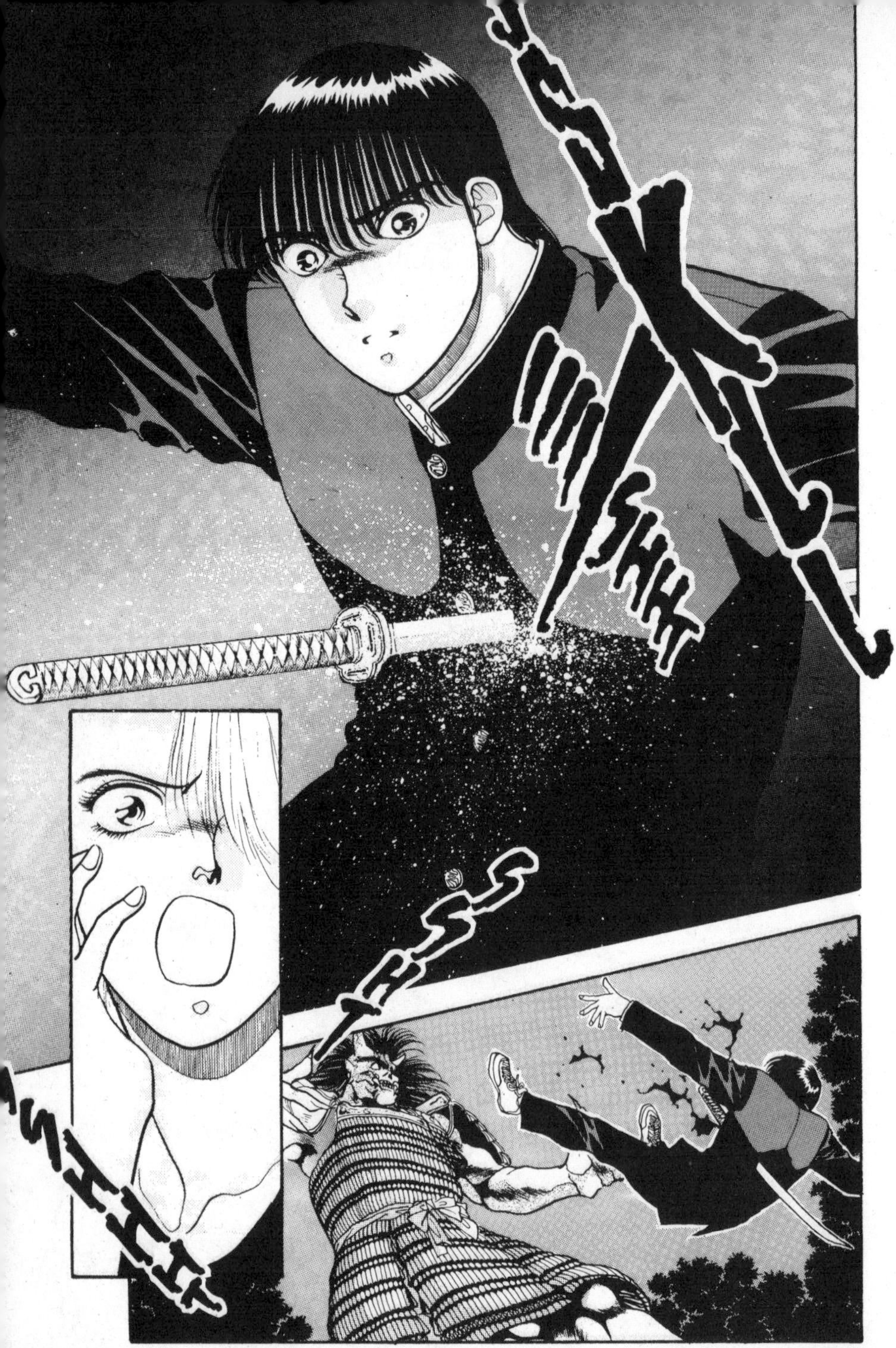
SHHH

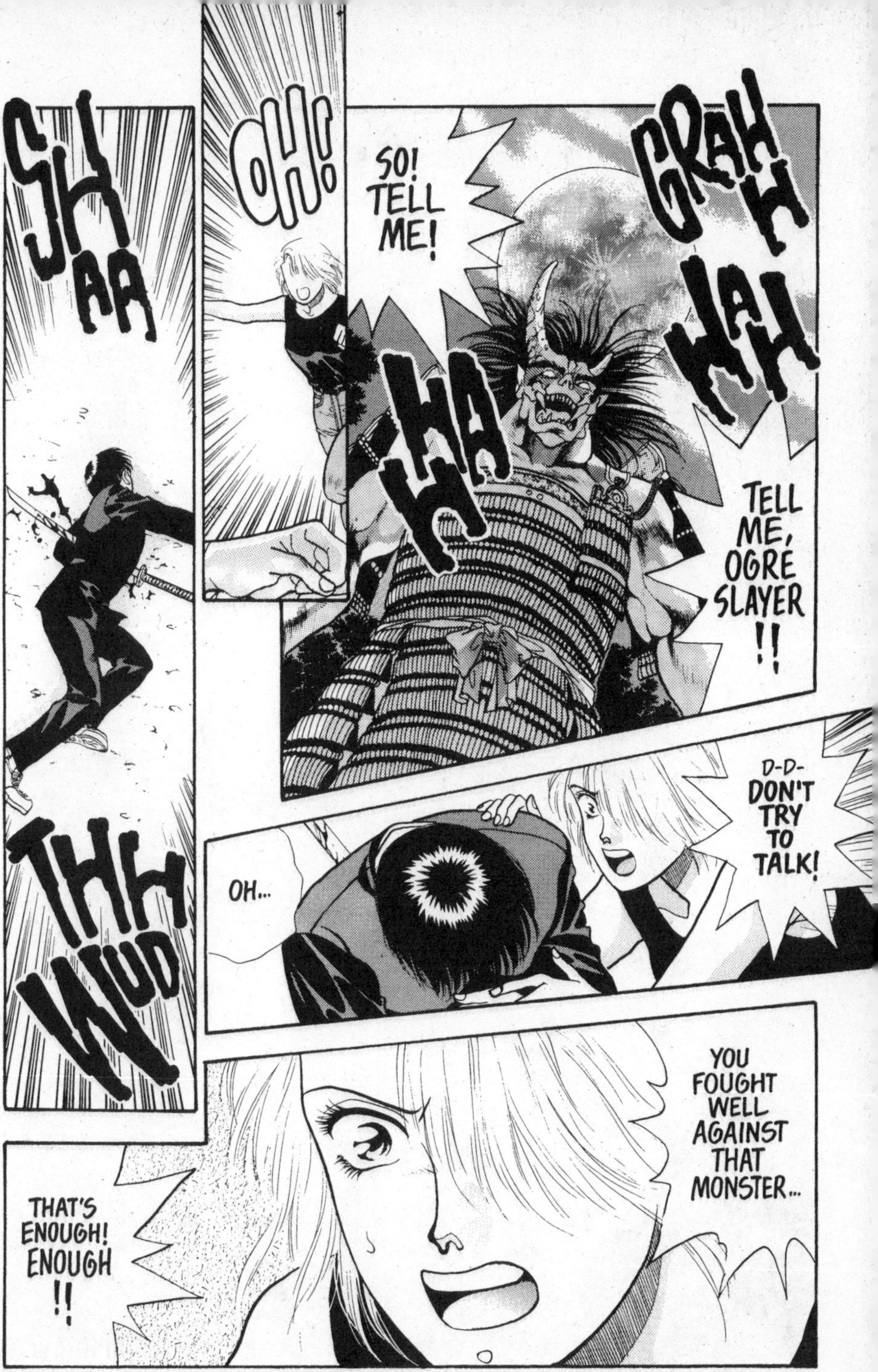
SHAA
THHUD
OH!
SO! TELL ME!
GRAHH HAH HAH
HAHAH
TELL ME, OGRE SLAYER !!
OH...
D-D-DON'T TRY TO TALK!
THAT'S ENOUGH! ENOUGH !!
YOU FOUGHT WELL AGAINST THAT MONSTER...

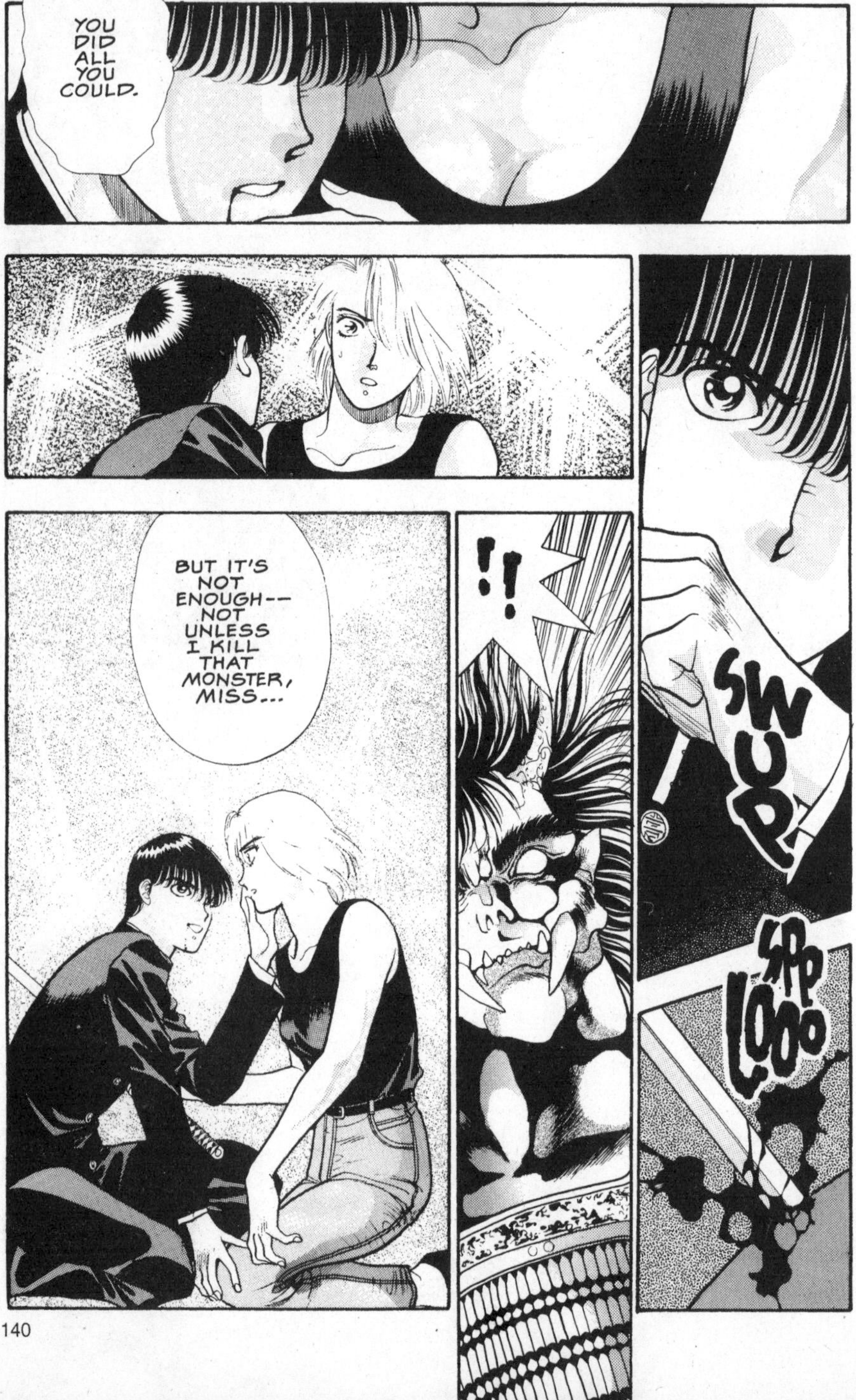

YOU DID ALL YOU COULD.
BUT IT'S NOT ENOUGH-- NOT UNLESS I KILL THAT MONSTER, MISS...
!!
SWUP
SPPLOOO

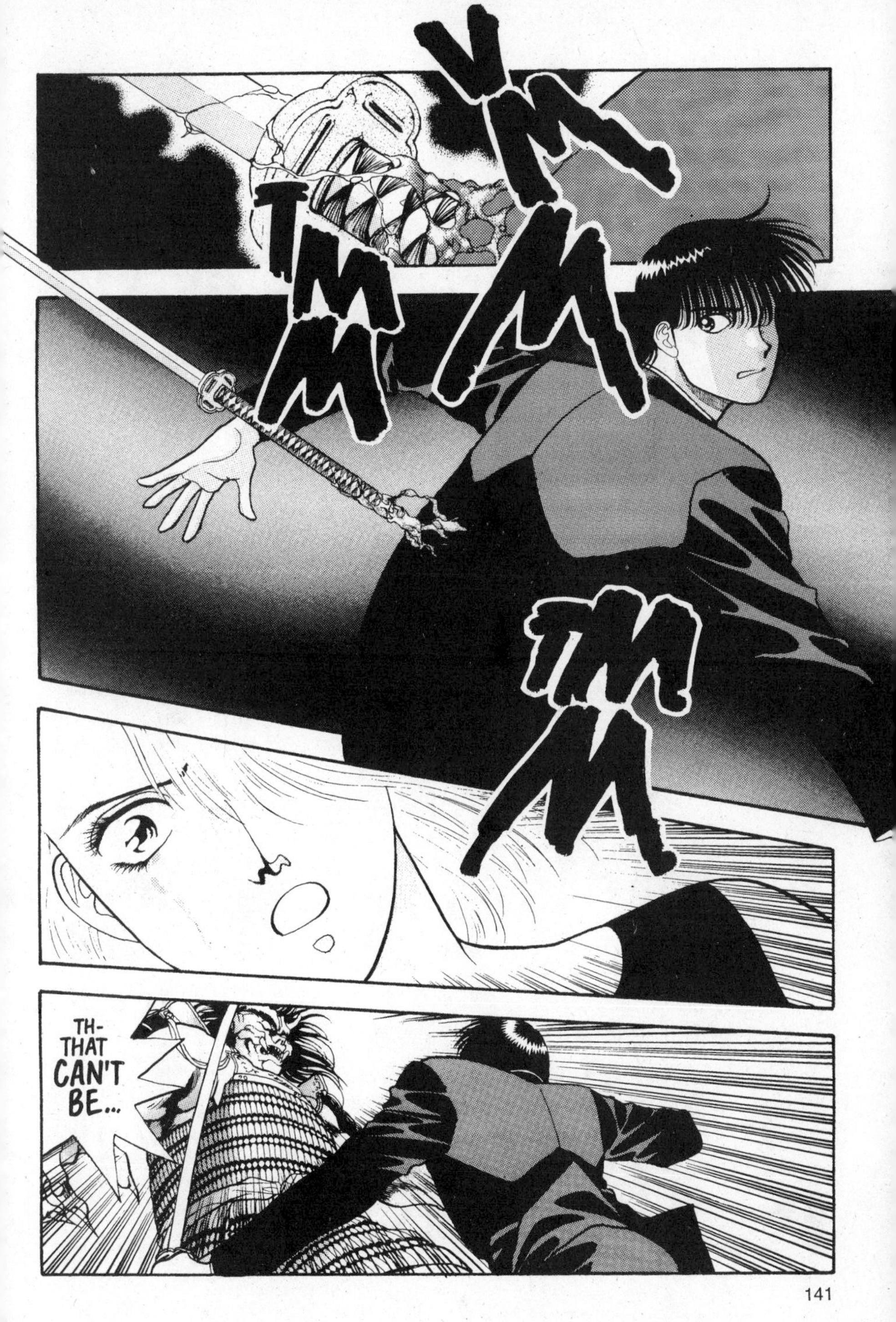
TMM
TMM
TH- THAT CAN'T BE...

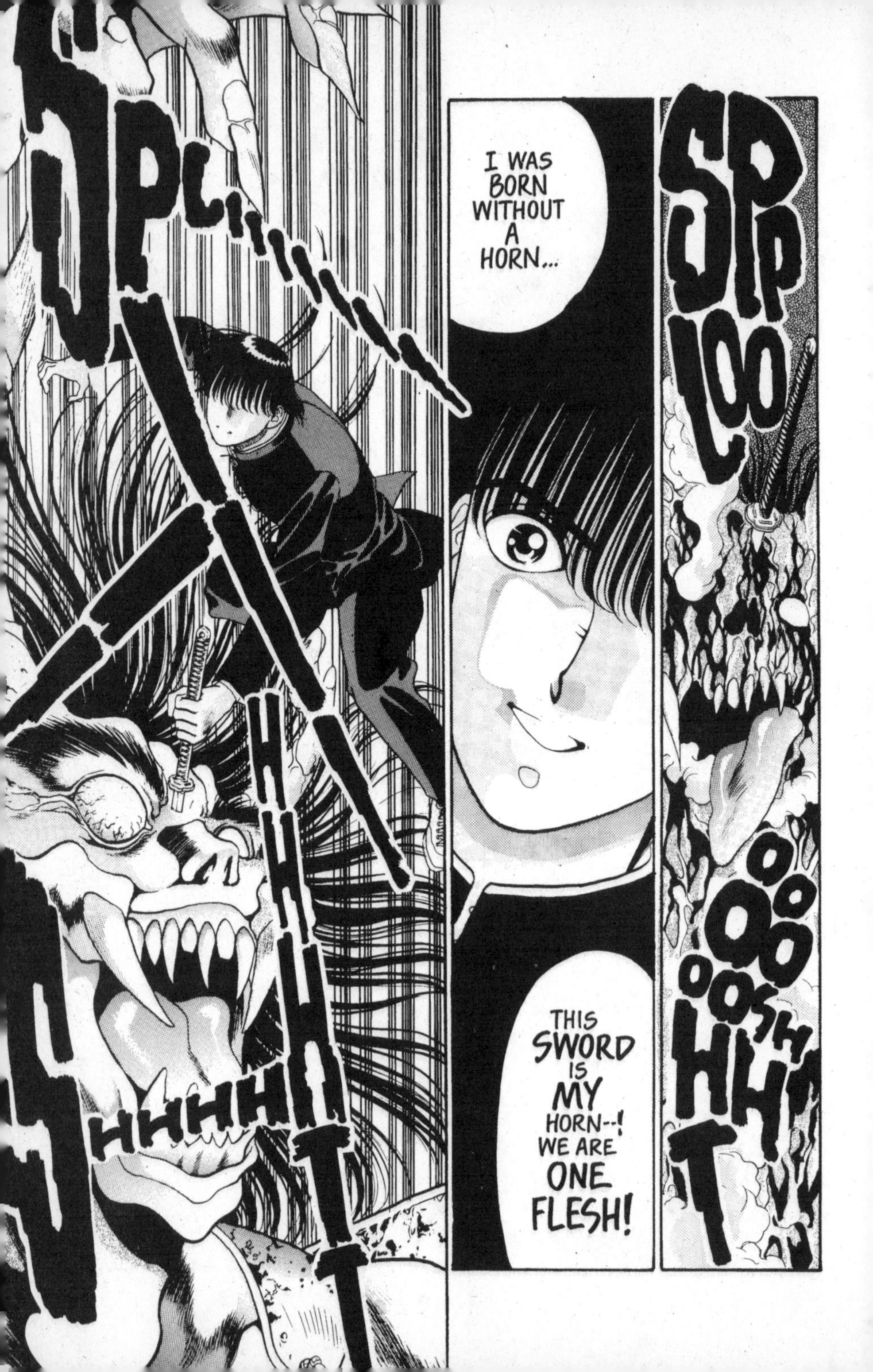
I WAS BORN WITHOUT A HORN...
THIS SWORD IS MY HORN--! WE ARE ONE FLESH!

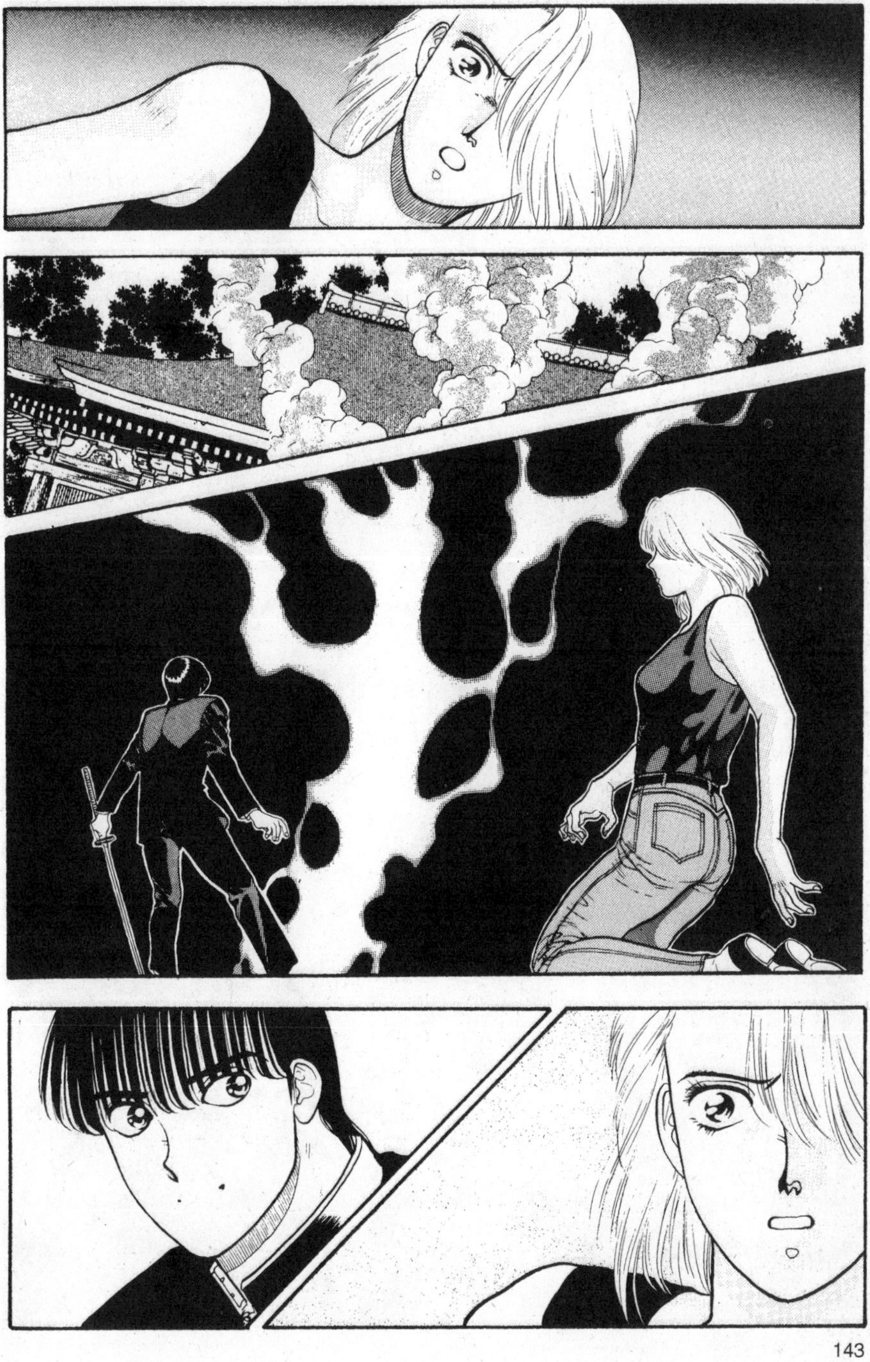

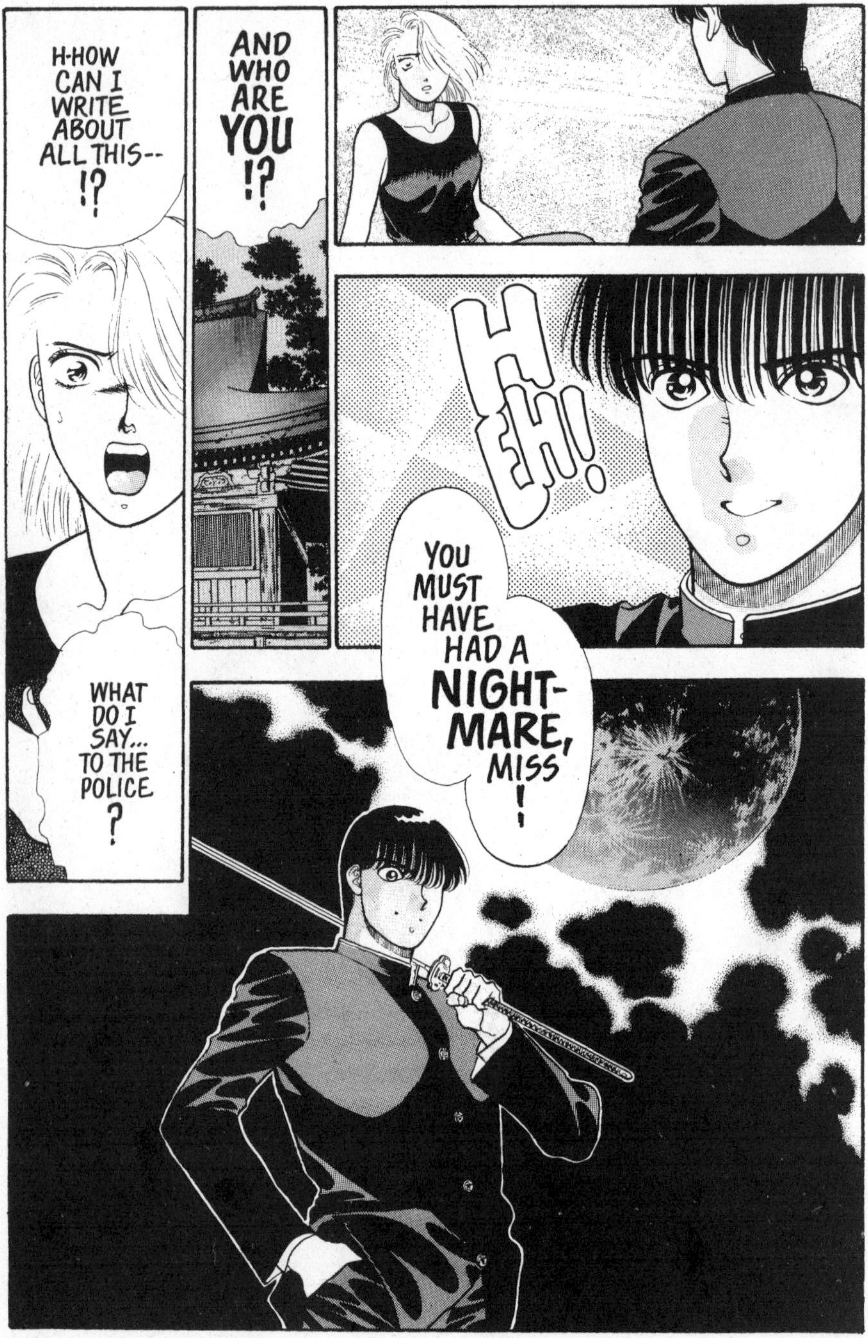
H-HOW CAN I WRITE ABOUT ALL THIS--!?
WHAT DO I SAY... TO THE POLICE?
AND WHO ARE YOU!?
HEH!
YOU MUST HAVE HAD A NIGHT-MARE, MISS!

HUNT FOUR
LOVE'S BITTER FRUIT

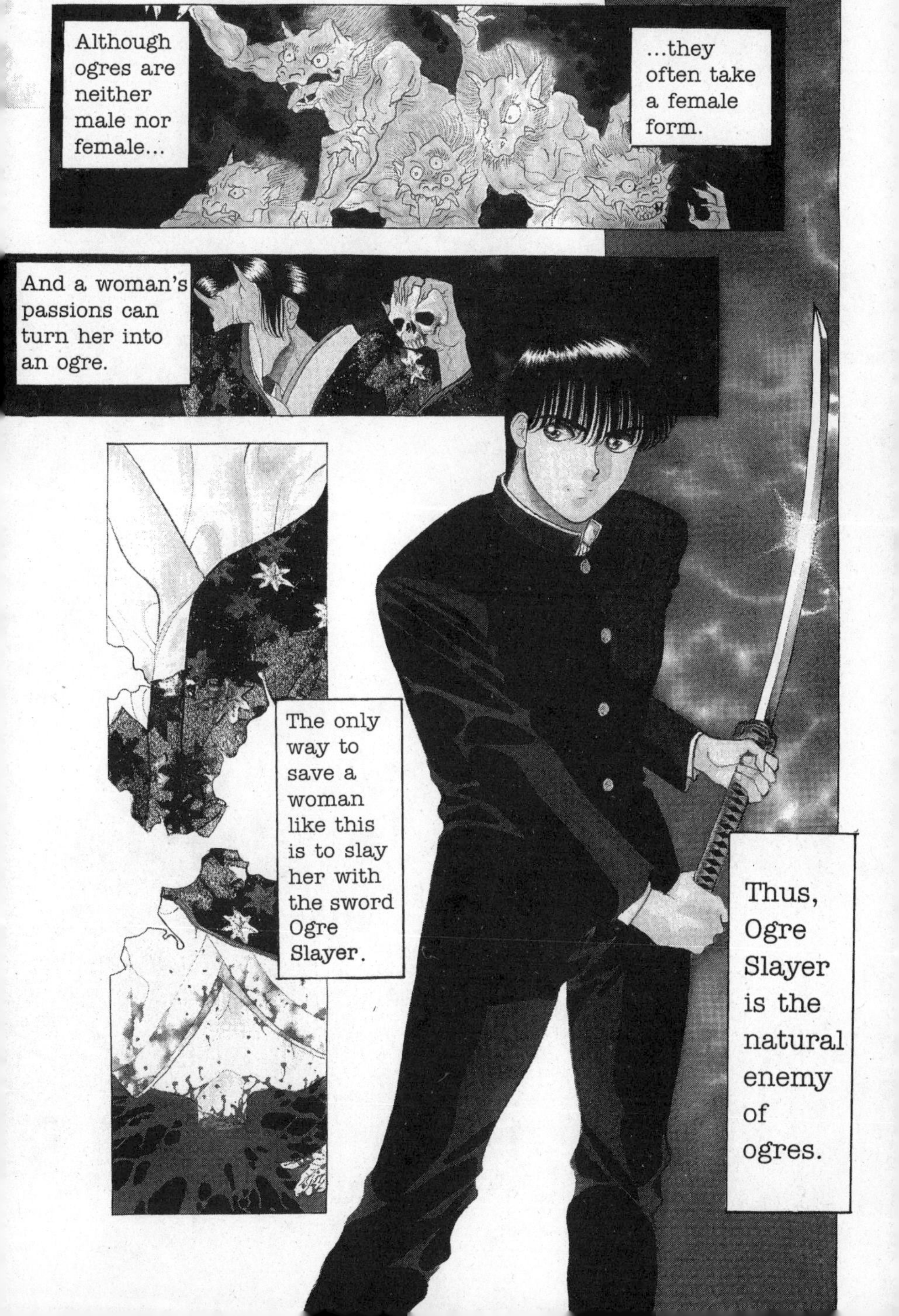

Although ogres are neither male nor female...
...they often take a female form.
And a woman's passions can turn her into an ogre.
The only way to save a woman like this is to slay her with the sword Ogre Slayer.
Thus, Ogre Slayer is the natural enemy of ogres.

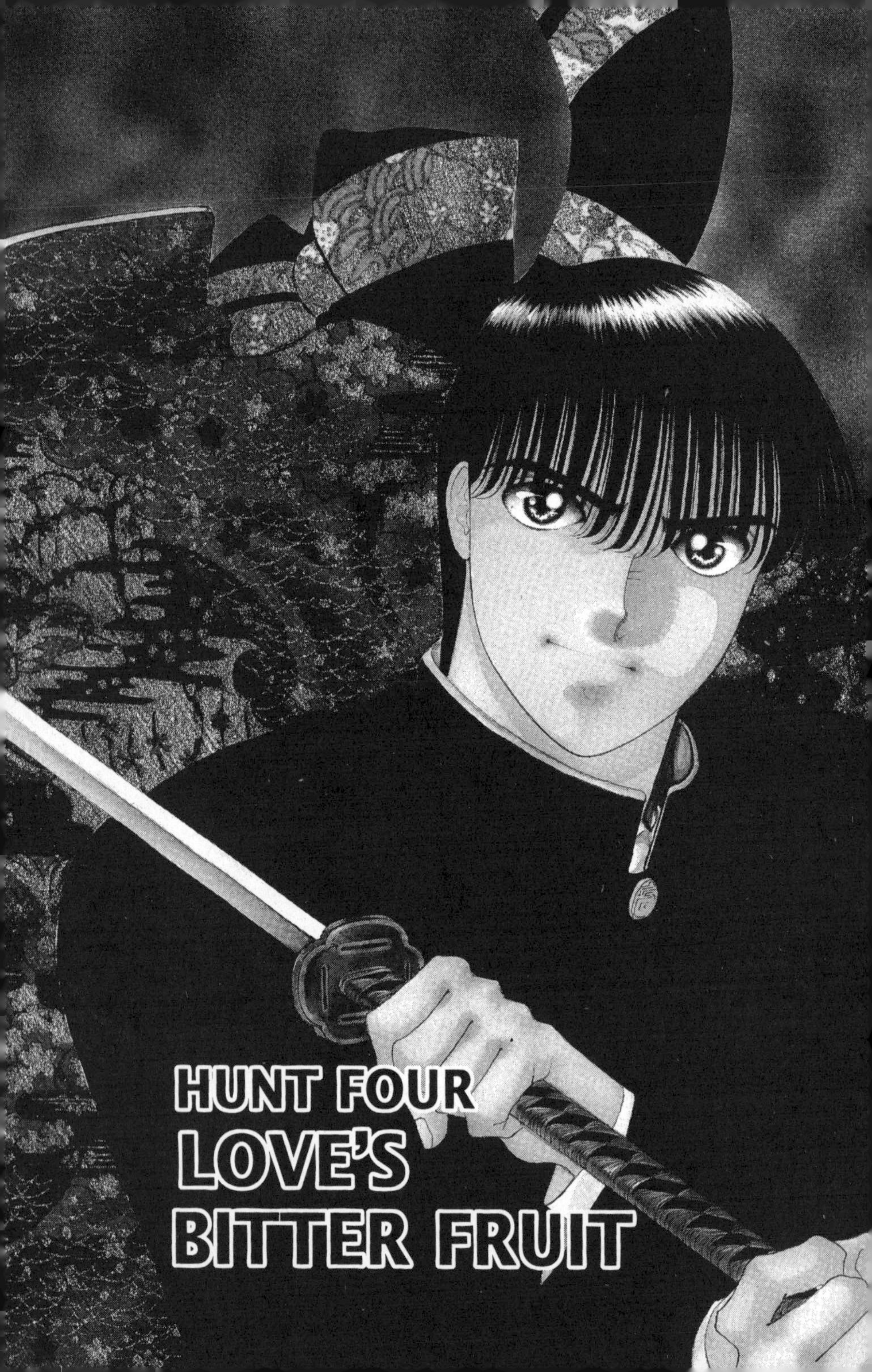
HUNT FOUR
LOVE'S
BITTER FRUIT

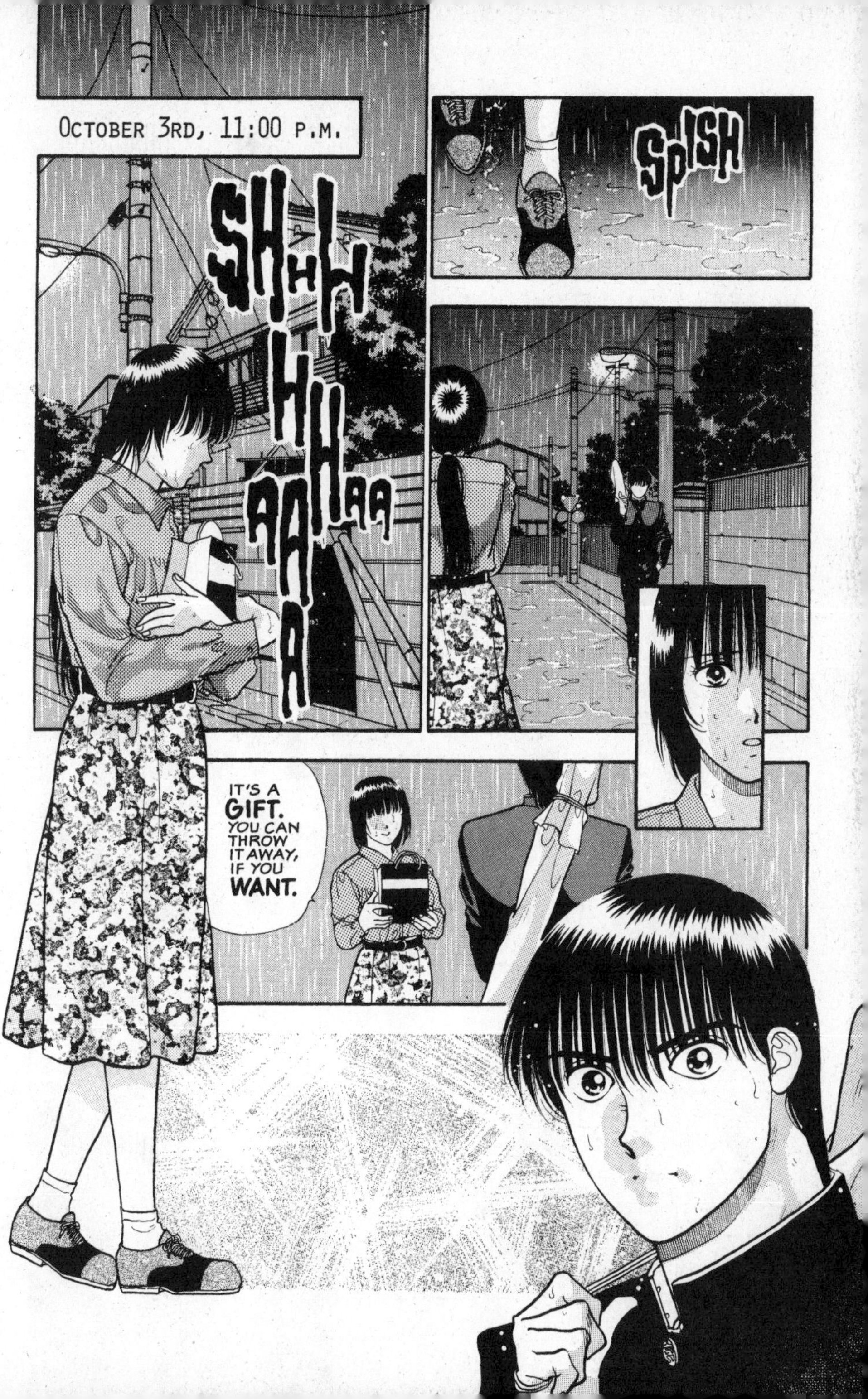
OCTOBER 3RD, 11:00 P.M.
SHHHHHAAAAAA
SPLISH
IT'S A GIFT. YOU CAN THROW IT AWAY, IF YOU WANT.

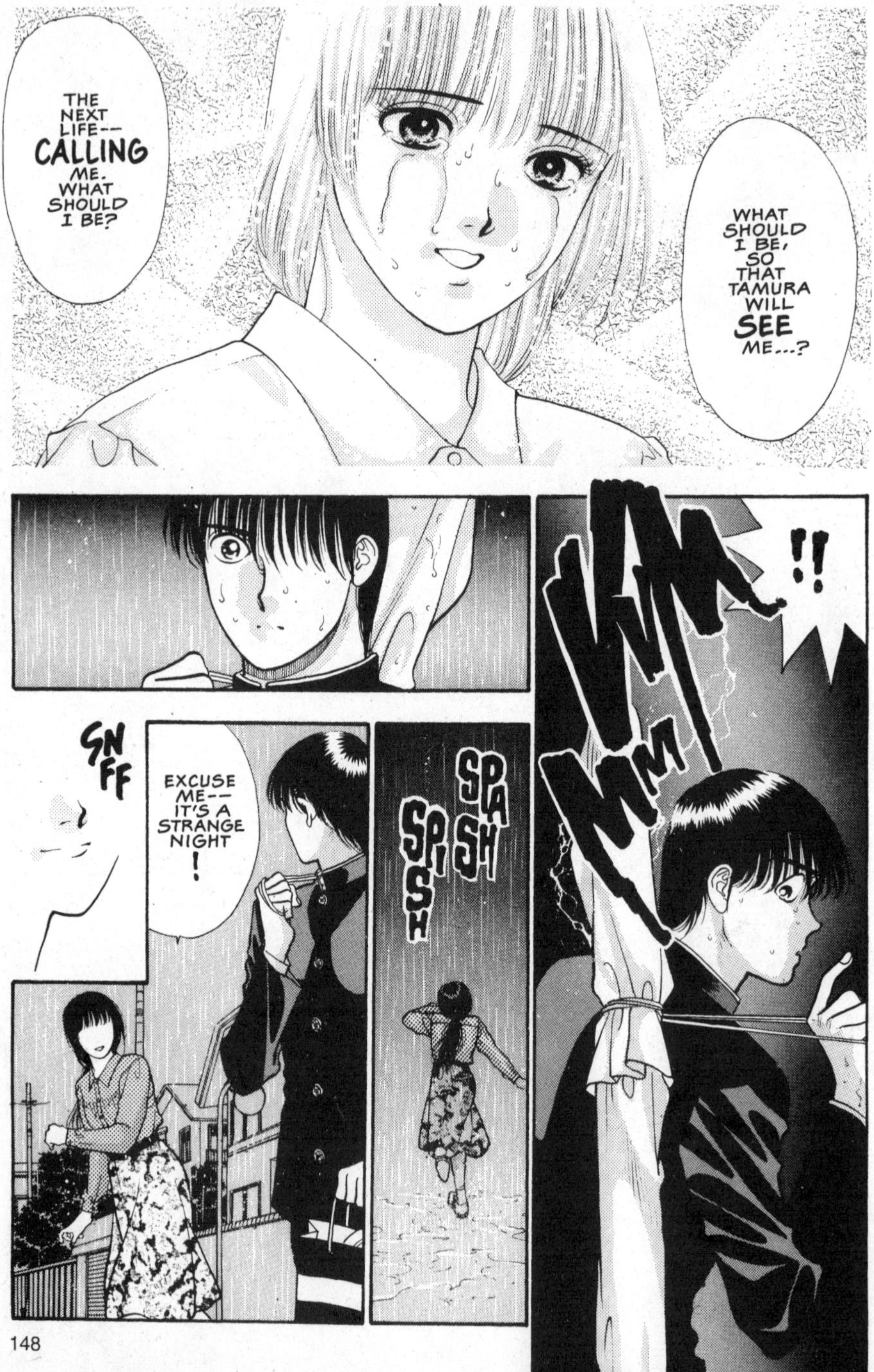
THE NEXT LIFE-- **CALLING** ME. WHAT SHOULD I BE?
WHAT SHOULD I BE, SO THAT TAMURA WILL **SEE** ME...?
SNFF
EXCUSE ME-- IT'S A STRANGE NIGHT!
SPLASH
SPISH
!!

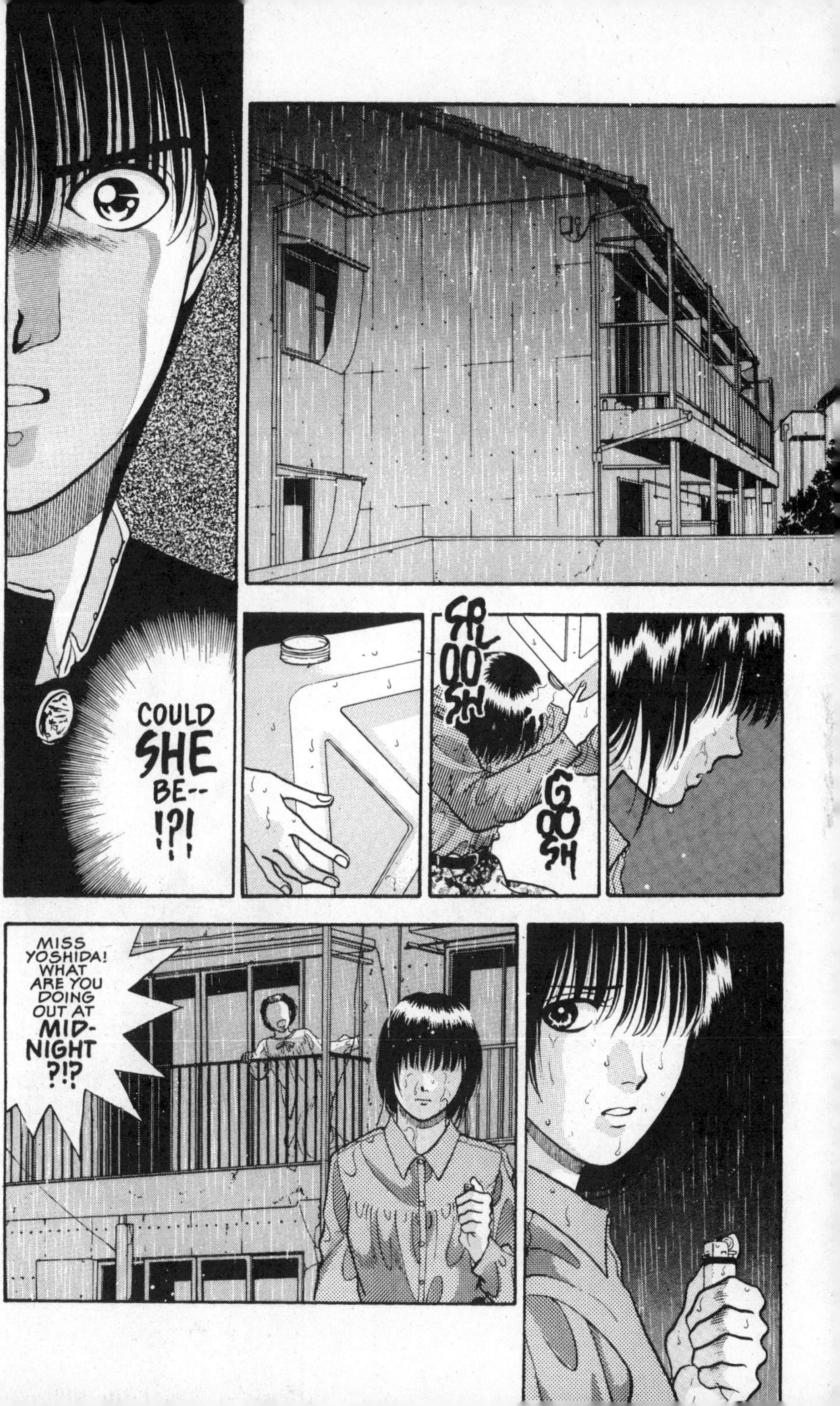
COULD SHE BE--!?!
SPLOOSH
GOOSH
MISS YOSHIDA! WHAT ARE YOU DOING OUT AT MIDNIGHT?!?

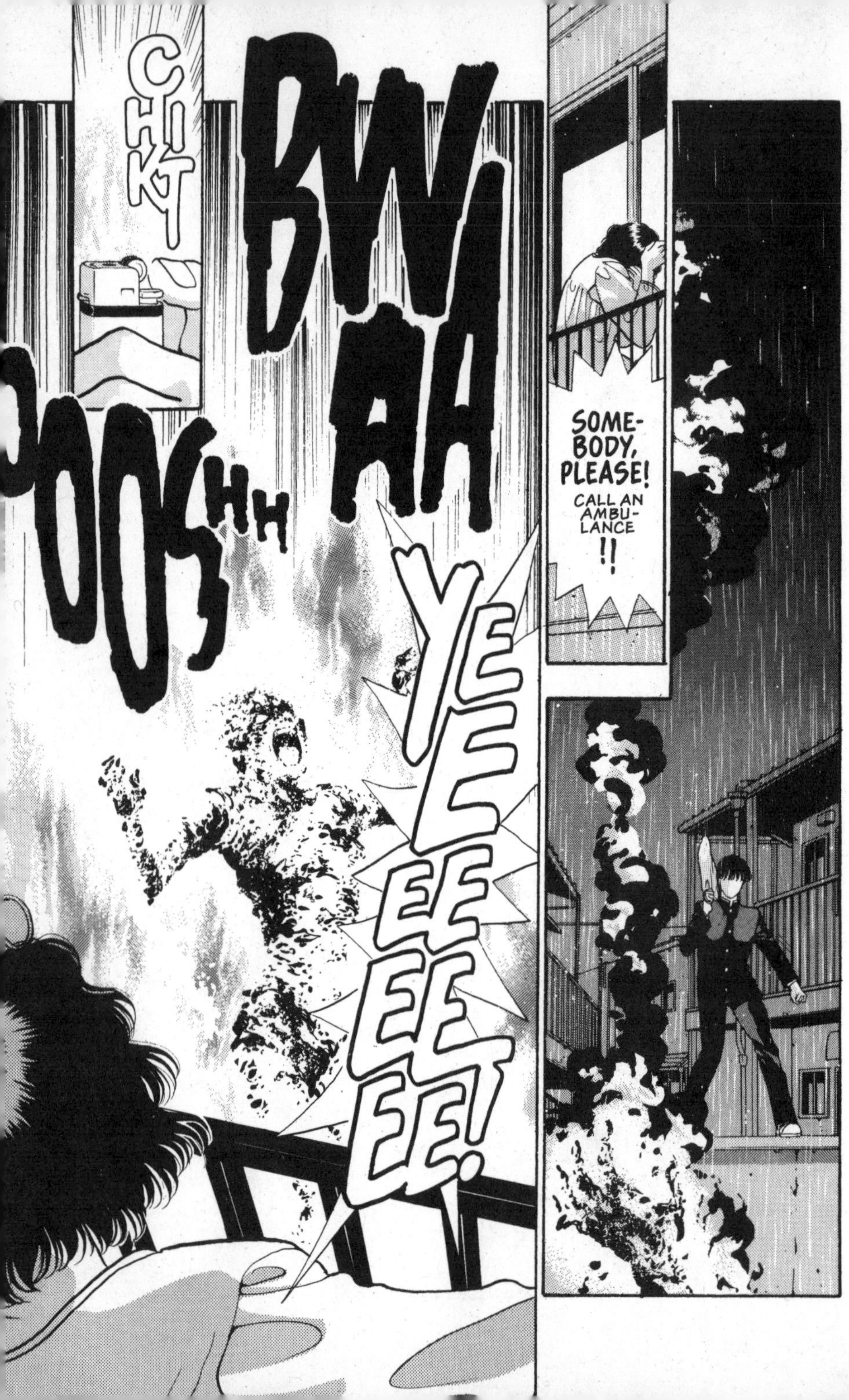
CHIKT
BWAA
OOSHH
YEEEEEEEEEE!
SOMEBODY, PLEASE!
CALL AN AMBULANCE!!

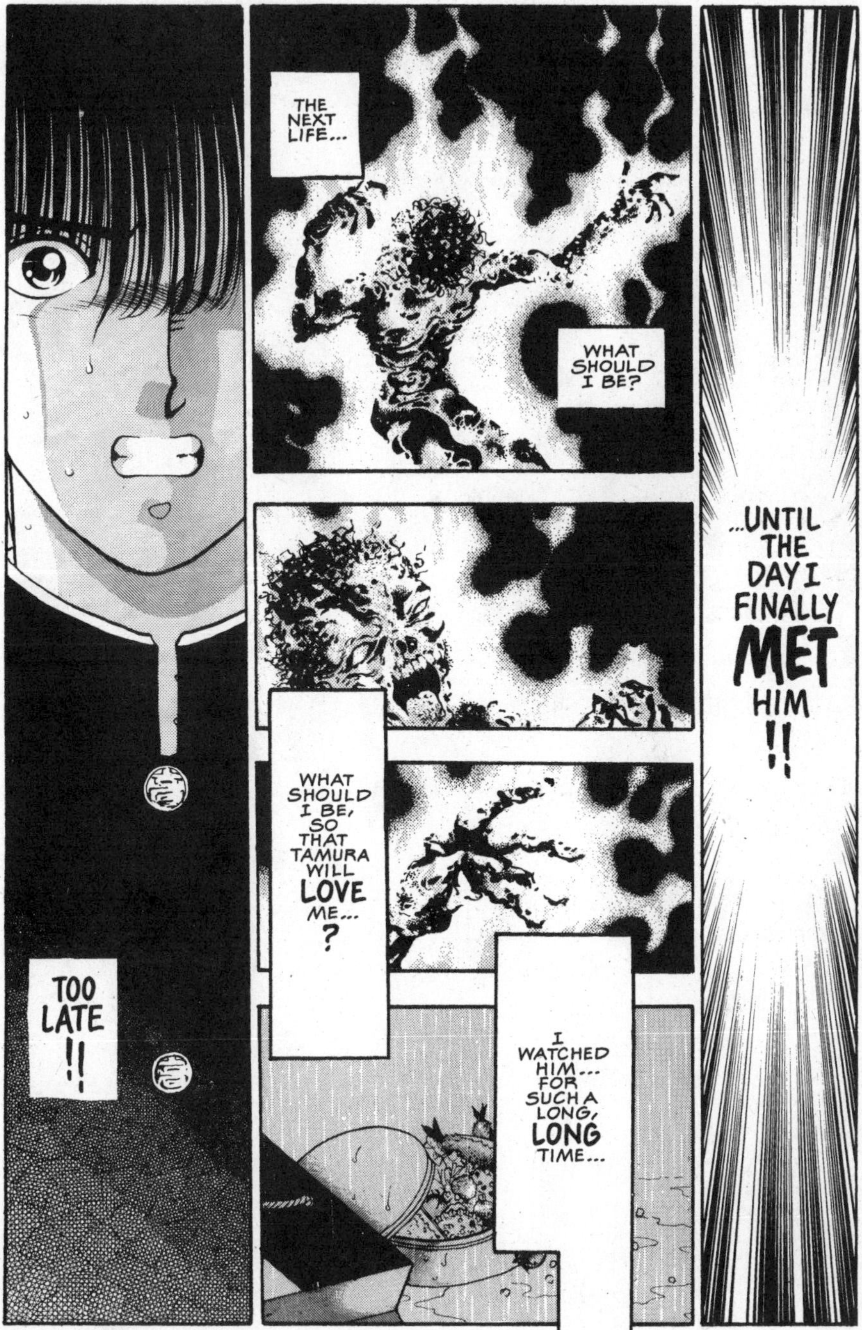
TOO LATE!!
THE NEXT LIFE...
WHAT SHOULD I BE?
WHAT SHOULD I BE, SO THAT TAMURA WILL LOVE ME...?
I WATCHED HIM... FOR SUCH A LONG, LONG TIME...
...UNTIL THE DAY I FINALLY MET HIM!!

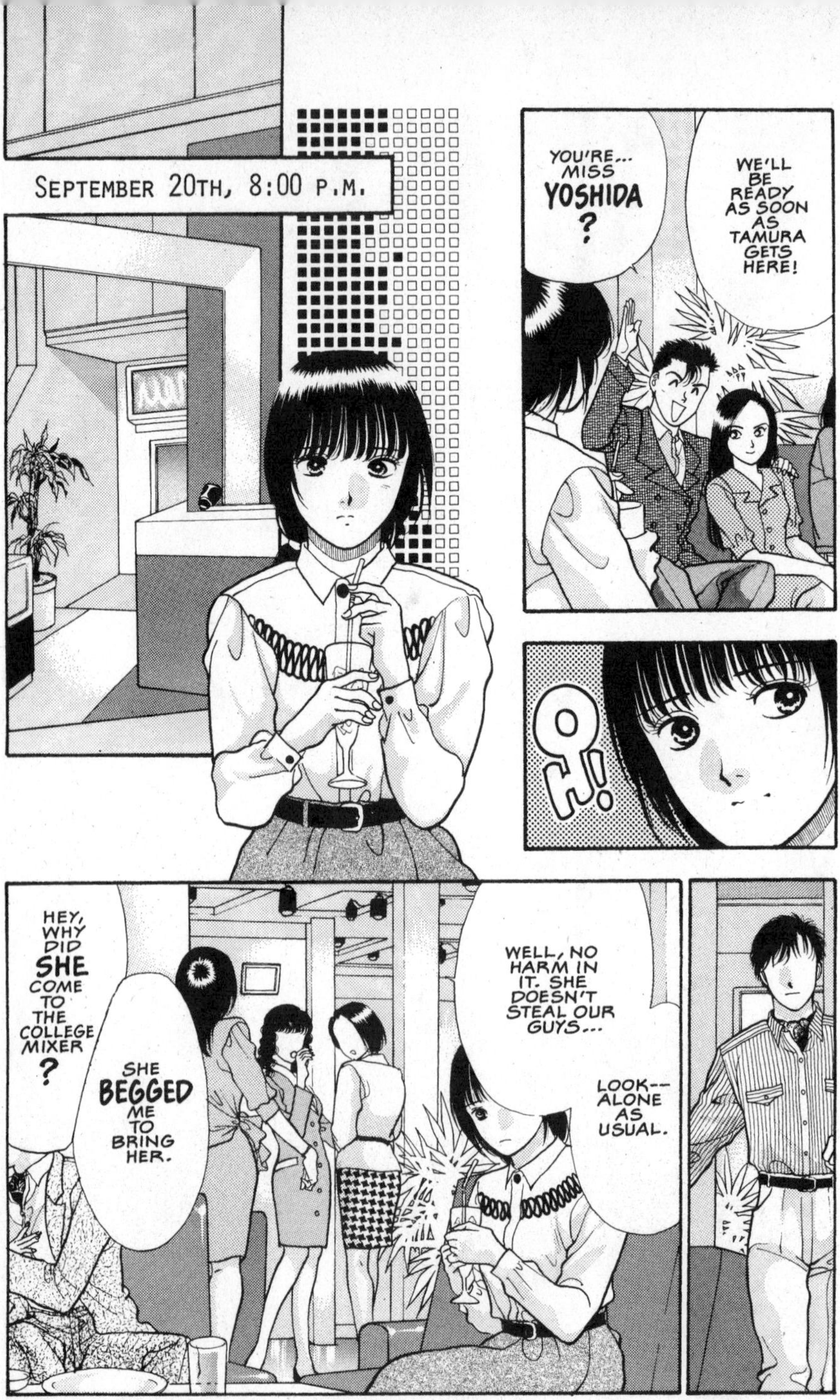
September 20th, 8:00 p.m.
You're... Miss Yoshida?
We'll be ready as soon as Tamura gets here!
Oh!
Hey, why did she come to the college mixer?
She begged me to bring her.
Well, no harm in it. She doesn't steal our guys...
Look-- alone as usual.

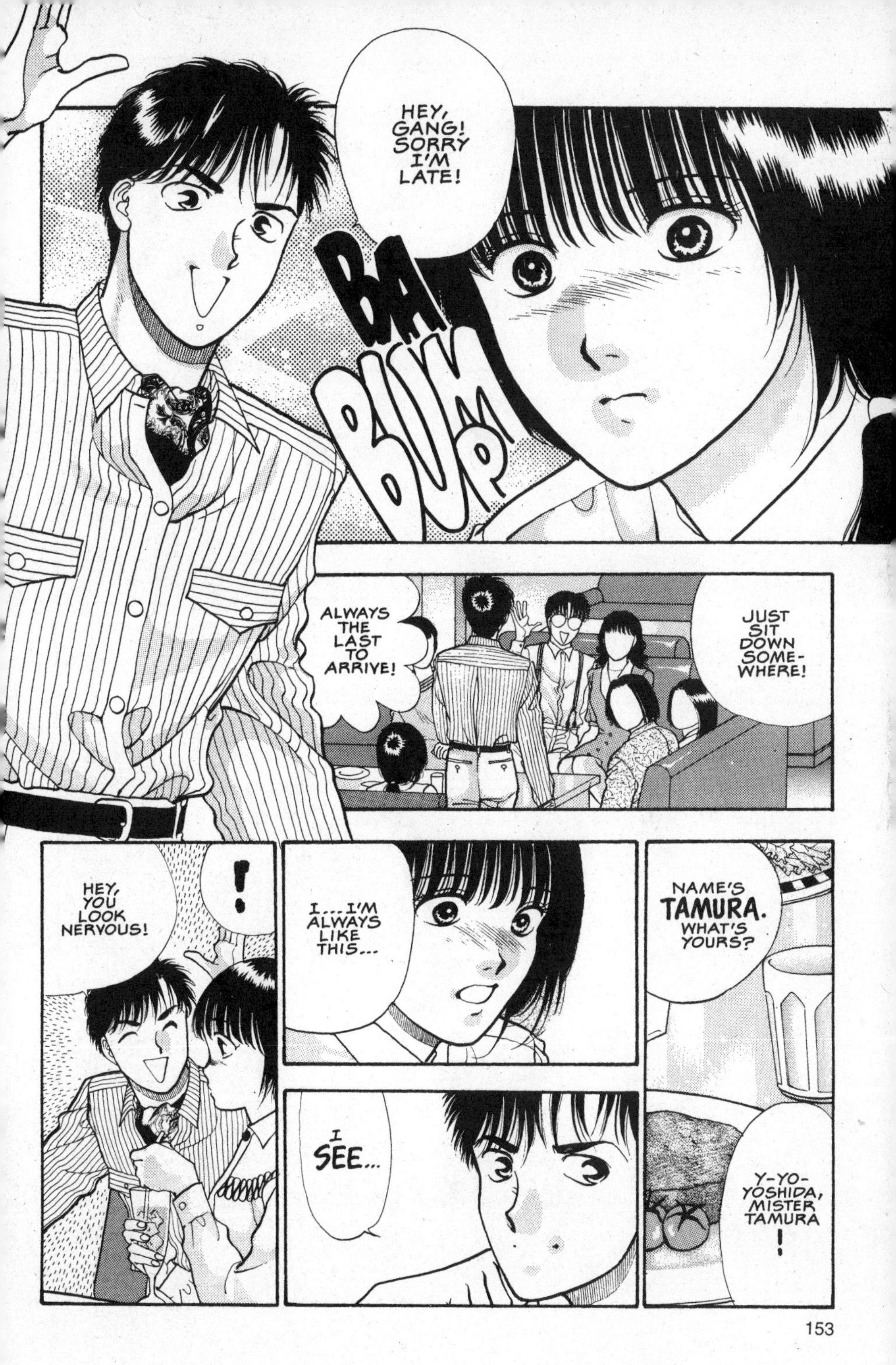
HEY, GANG! SORRY I'M LATE!
BA BUM BUMP
ALWAYS THE LAST TO ARRIVE!
JUST SIT DOWN SOME-WHERE!
HEY, YOU LOOK NERVOUS!
!
I... I'M ALWAYS LIKE THIS...
NAME'S TAMURA. WHAT'S YOURS?
I SEE...
Y-YO-YOSHIDA, MISTER TAMURA!

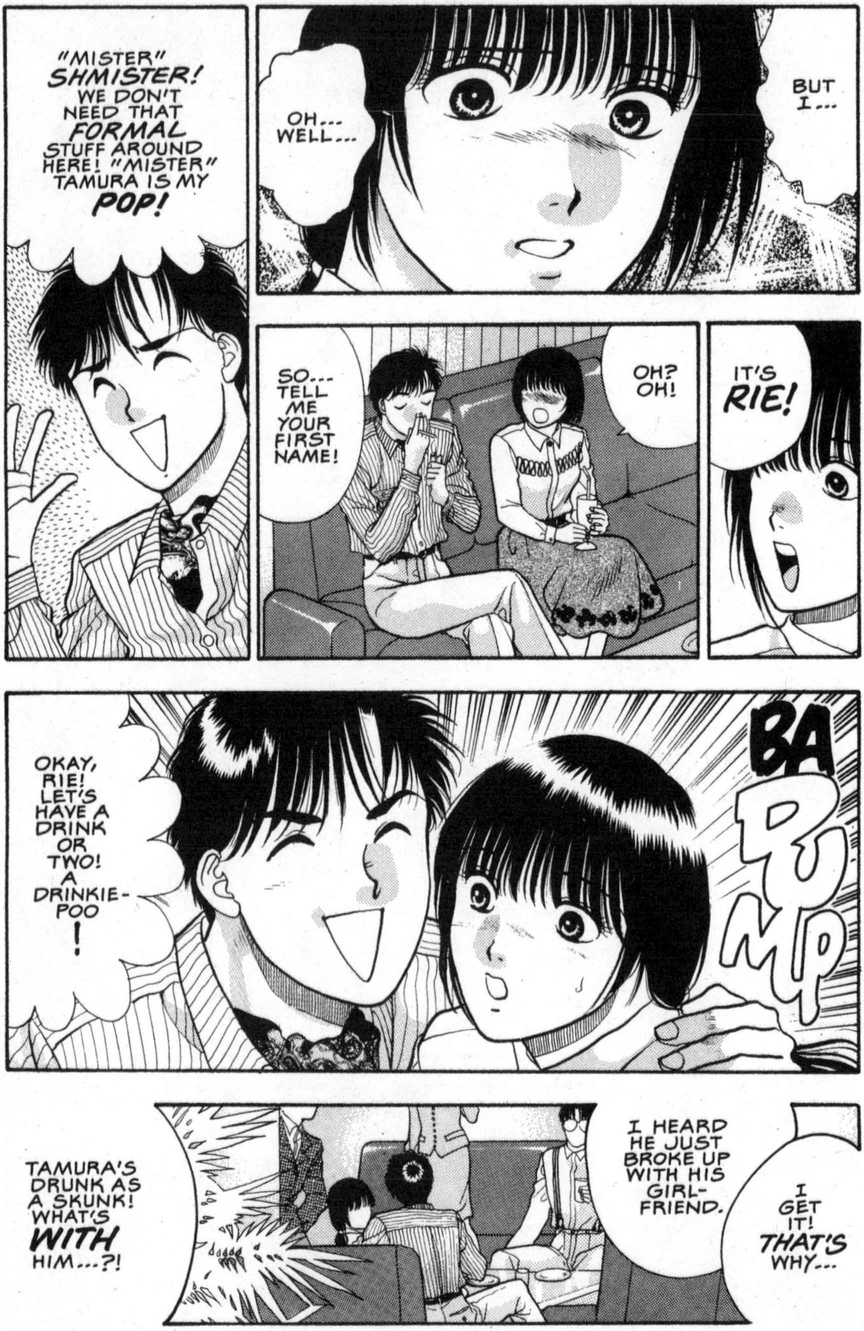
"MISTER" SHMISTER! WE DON'T NEED THAT FORMAL STUFF AROUND HERE! "MISTER" TAMURA IS MY POP!
OH... WELL...
BUT I...
SO... TELL ME YOUR FIRST NAME!
OH? OH!
IT'S RIE!
OKAY, RIE! LET'S HAVE A DRINK OR TWO! A DRINKIE-POO!
BA DUMP
TAMURA'S DRUNK AS A SKUNK! WHAT'S WITH HIM...?!
I HEARD HE JUST BROKE UP WITH HIS GIRLFRIEND.
I GET IT! THAT'S WHY...

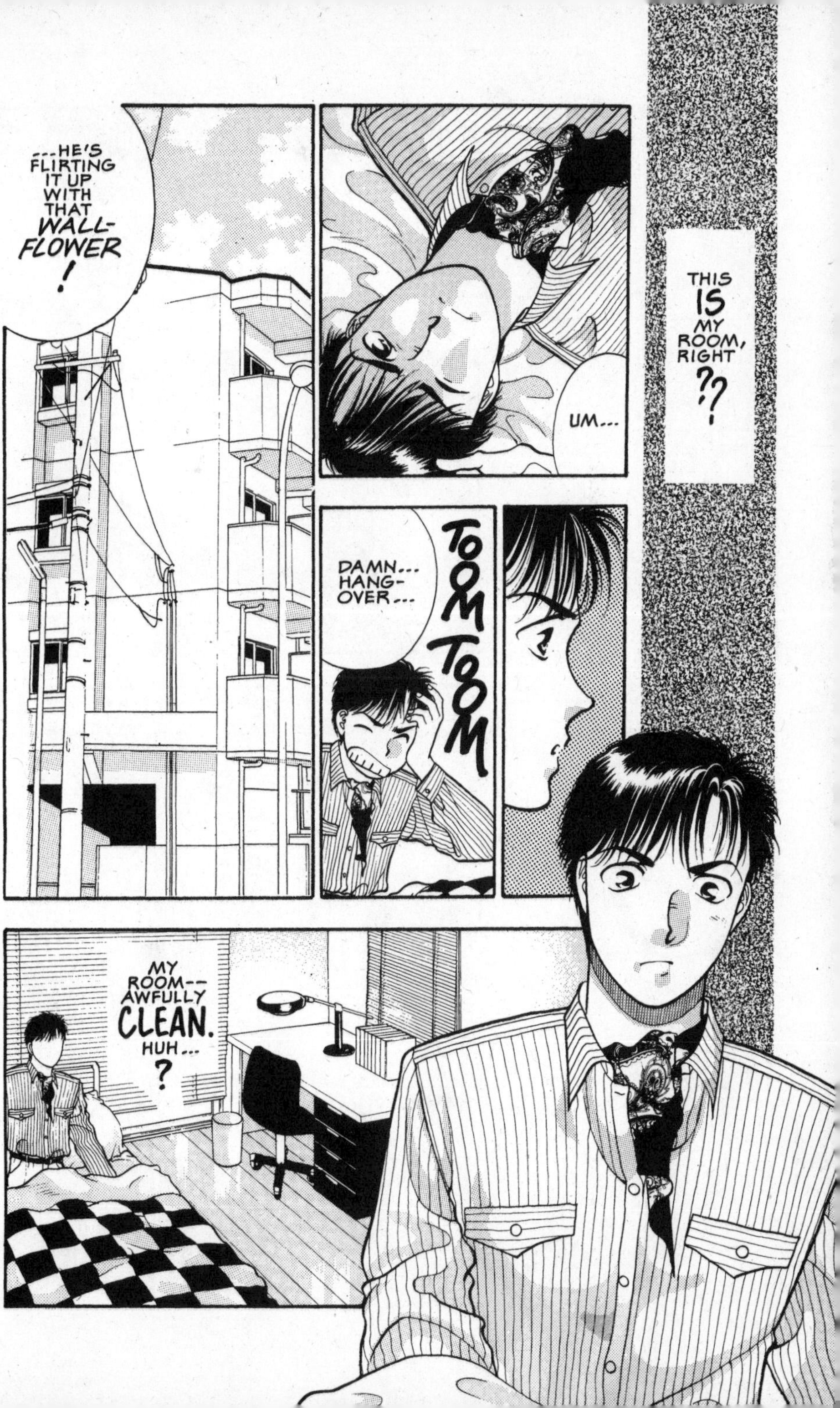
...HE'S FLIRTING IT UP WITH THAT WALL-FLOWER!
UM...
THIS IS MY ROOM, RIGHT??
DAMN... HANG-OVER...
TOOM TOOM
MY ROOM-- AWFULLY CLEAN.
HUH...?

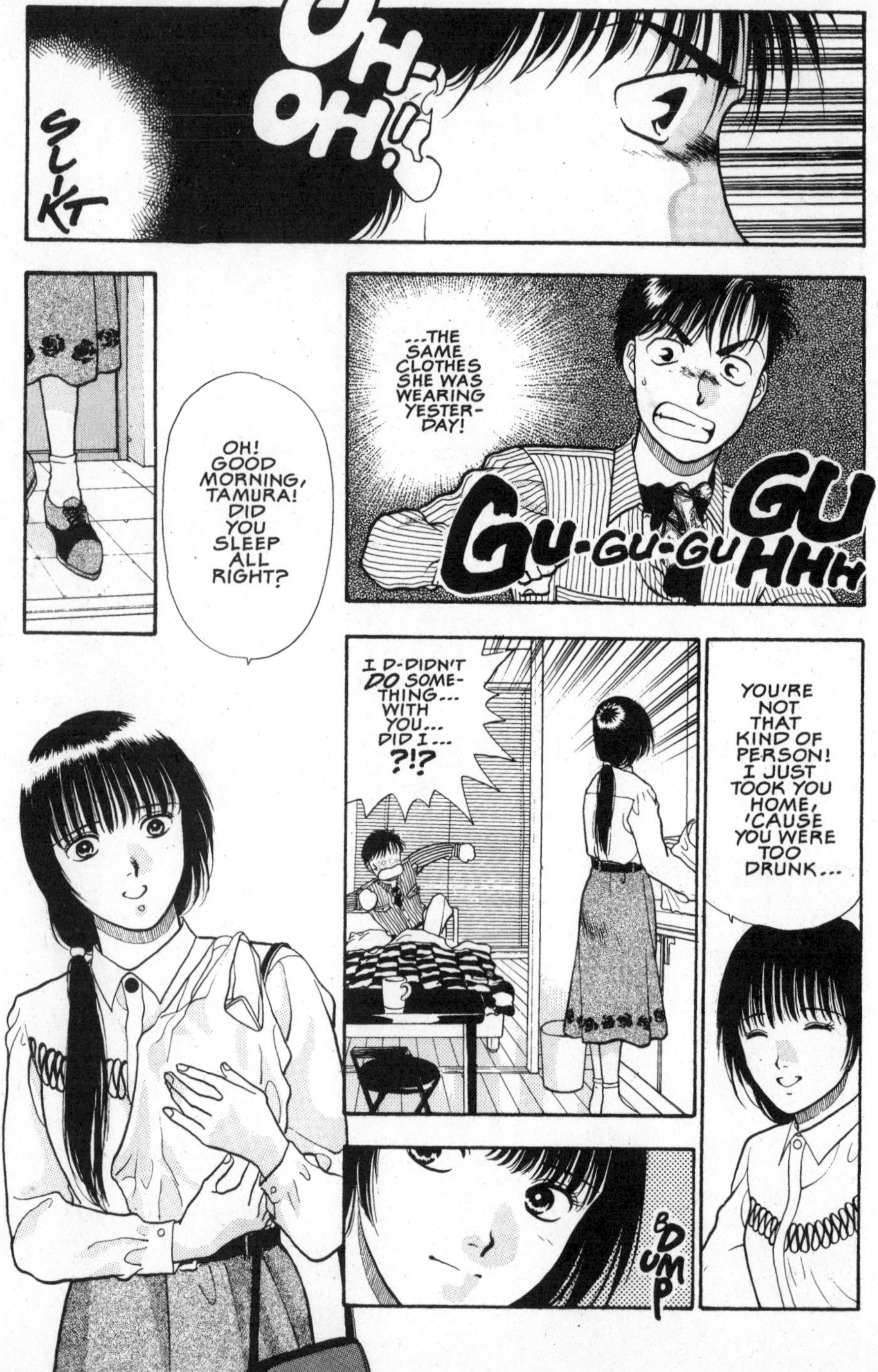
SLIKT
UH-OH!!
OH! GOOD MORNING, TAMURA! DID YOU SLEEP ALL RIGHT?
...THE SAME CLOTHES SHE WAS WEARING YESTER-DAY!
GU-GU-GU-GU GUHHH
I D-DIDN'T DO SOME-THING... WITH YOU... DID I... ?!?
YOU'RE NOT THAT KIND OF PERSON! I JUST TOOK YOU HOME, 'CAUSE YOU WERE TOO DRUNK...
B-DUMP

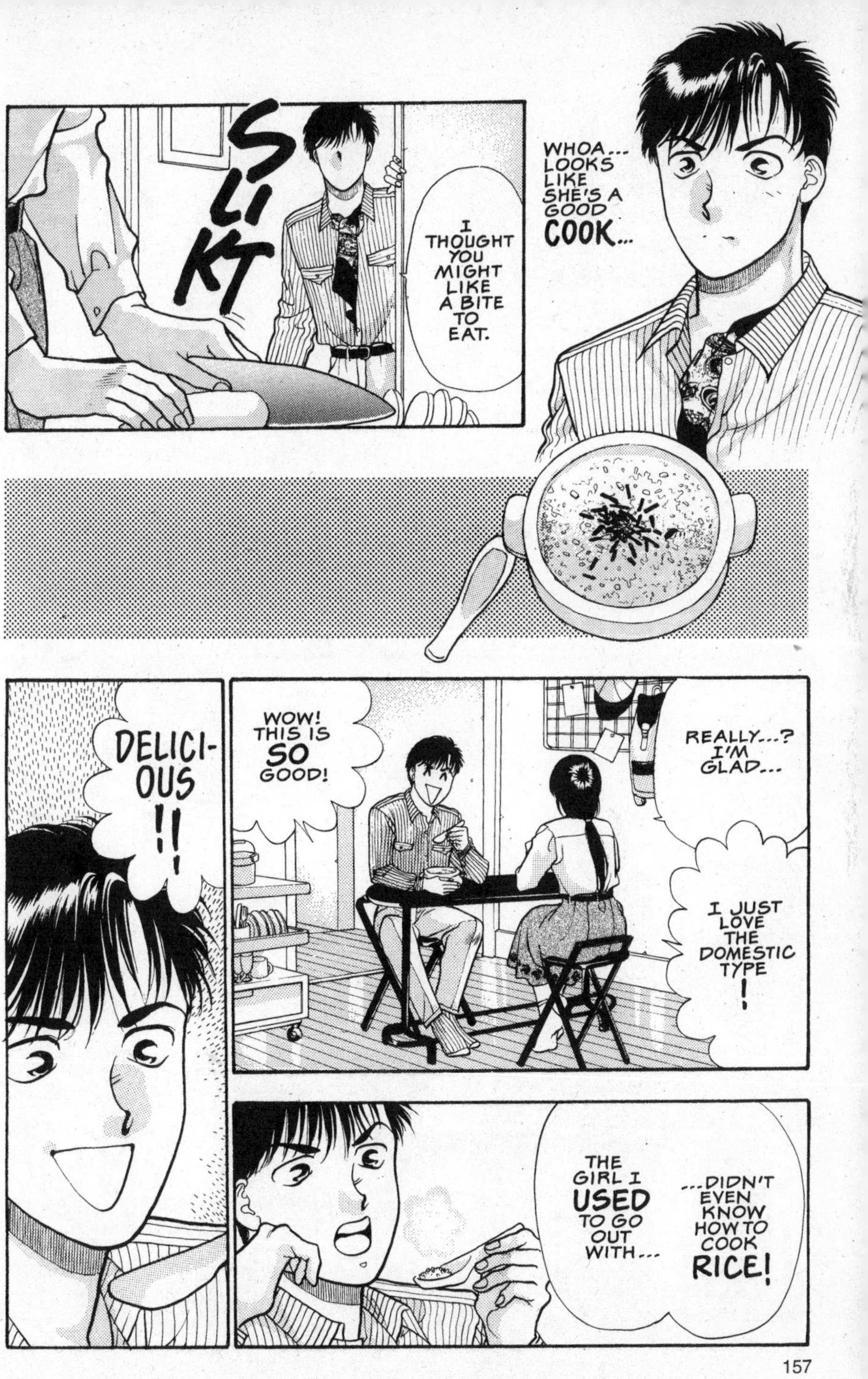
SLIKT
I THOUGHT YOU MIGHT LIKE A BITE TO EAT.
WHOA... LOOKS LIKE SHE'S A GOOD COOK...
DELICI-OUS!!
WOW! THIS IS SO GOOD!
REALLY...? I'M GLAD...
I JUST LOVE THE DOMESTIC TYPE!
THE GIRL I USED TO GO OUT WITH...
...DIDN'T EVEN KNOW HOW TO COOK RICE!

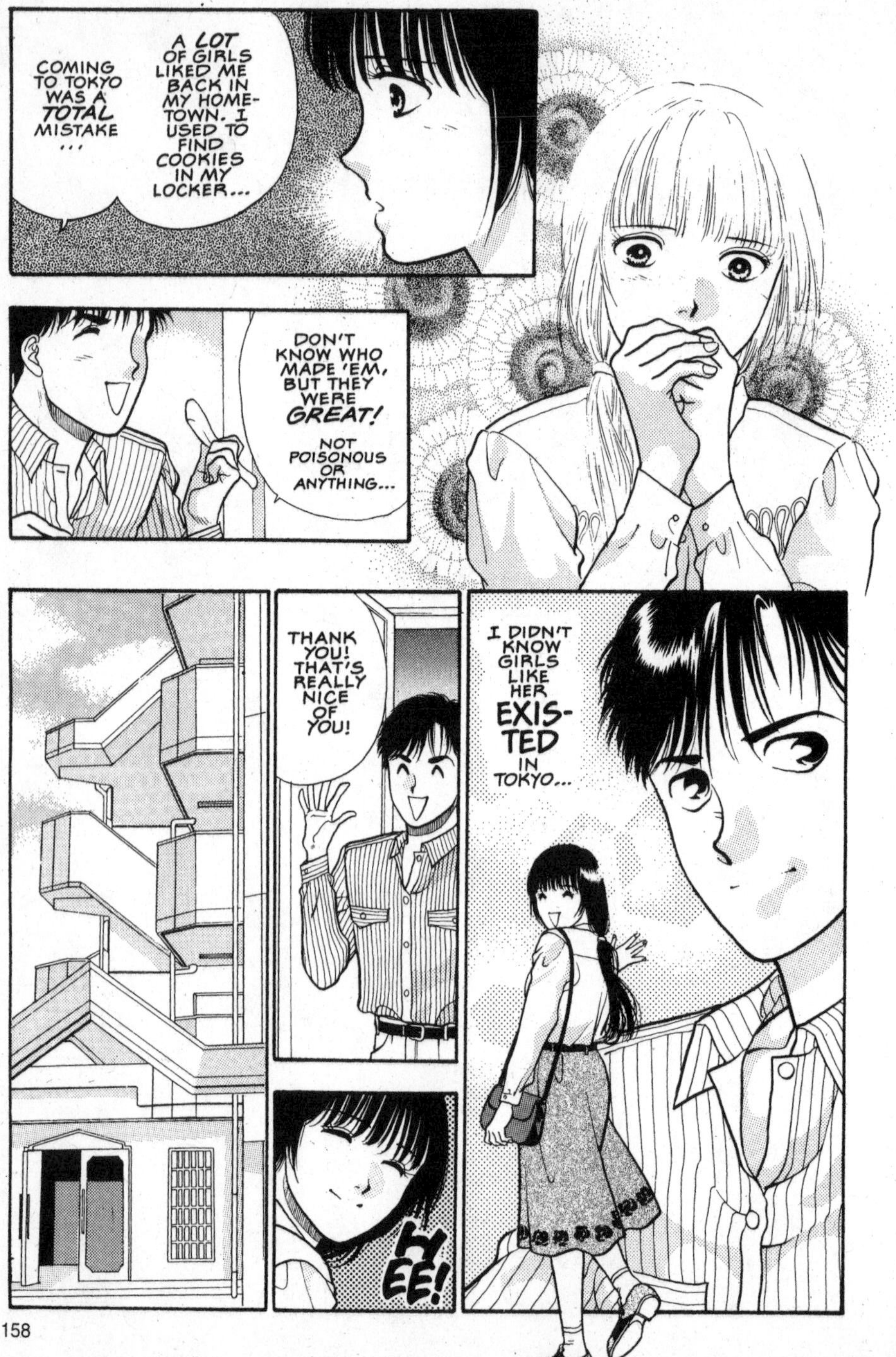
COMING TO TOKYO WAS A TOTAL MISTAKE...
A LOT OF GIRLS LIKED ME BACK IN MY HOME-TOWN. I USED TO FIND COOKIES IN MY LOCKER...
DON'T KNOW WHO MADE 'EM, BUT THEY WERE GREAT!
NOT POISONOUS OR ANYTHING...
THANK YOU! THAT'S REALLY NICE OF YOU!
HEE!
I DIDN'T KNOW GIRLS LIKE HER EXIS-TED IN TOKYO...

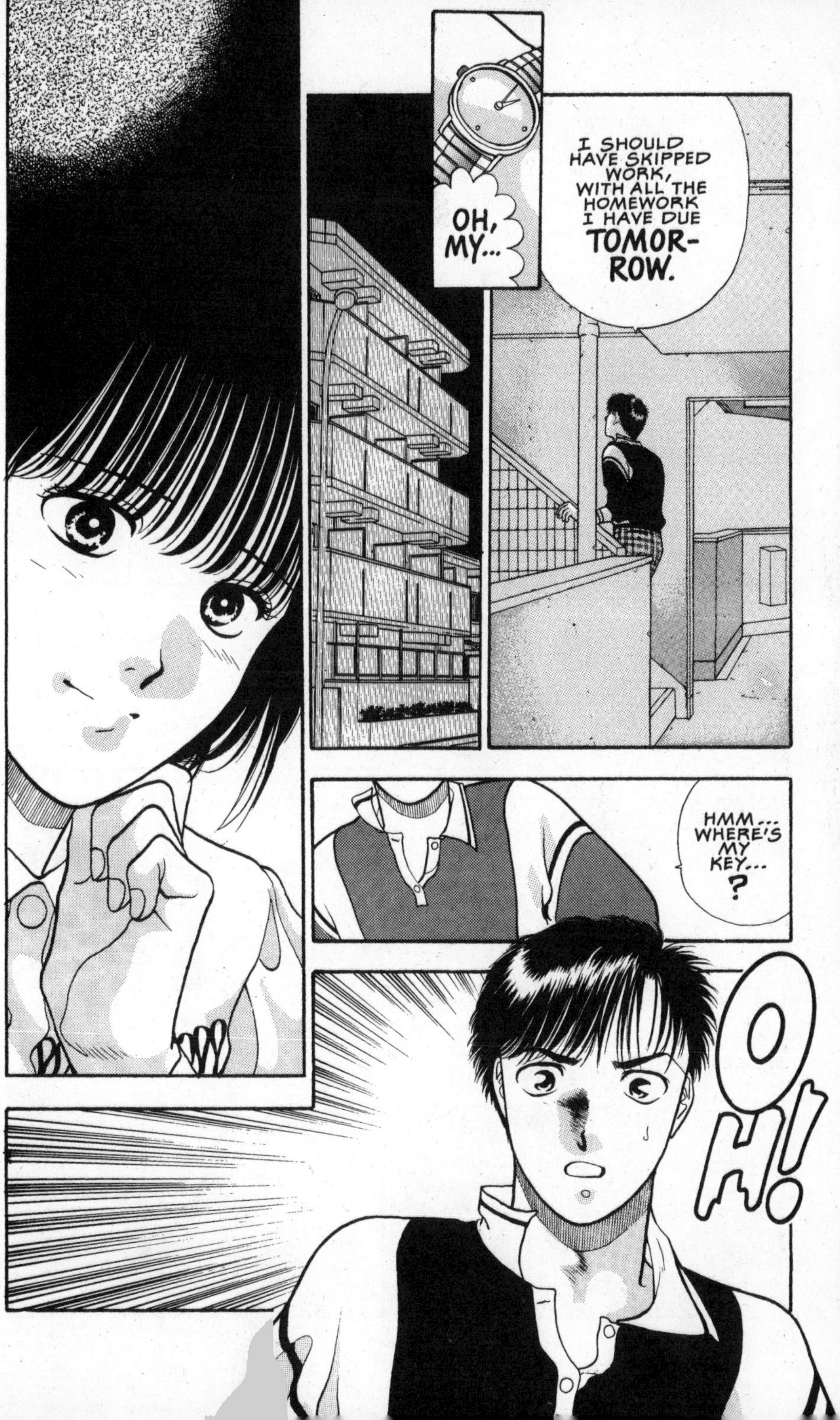
OH, MY...
I SHOULD HAVE SKIPPED WORK, WITH ALL THE HOMEWORK I HAVE DUE TOMOR-ROW.
HMM... WHERE'S MY KEY...?
OH!

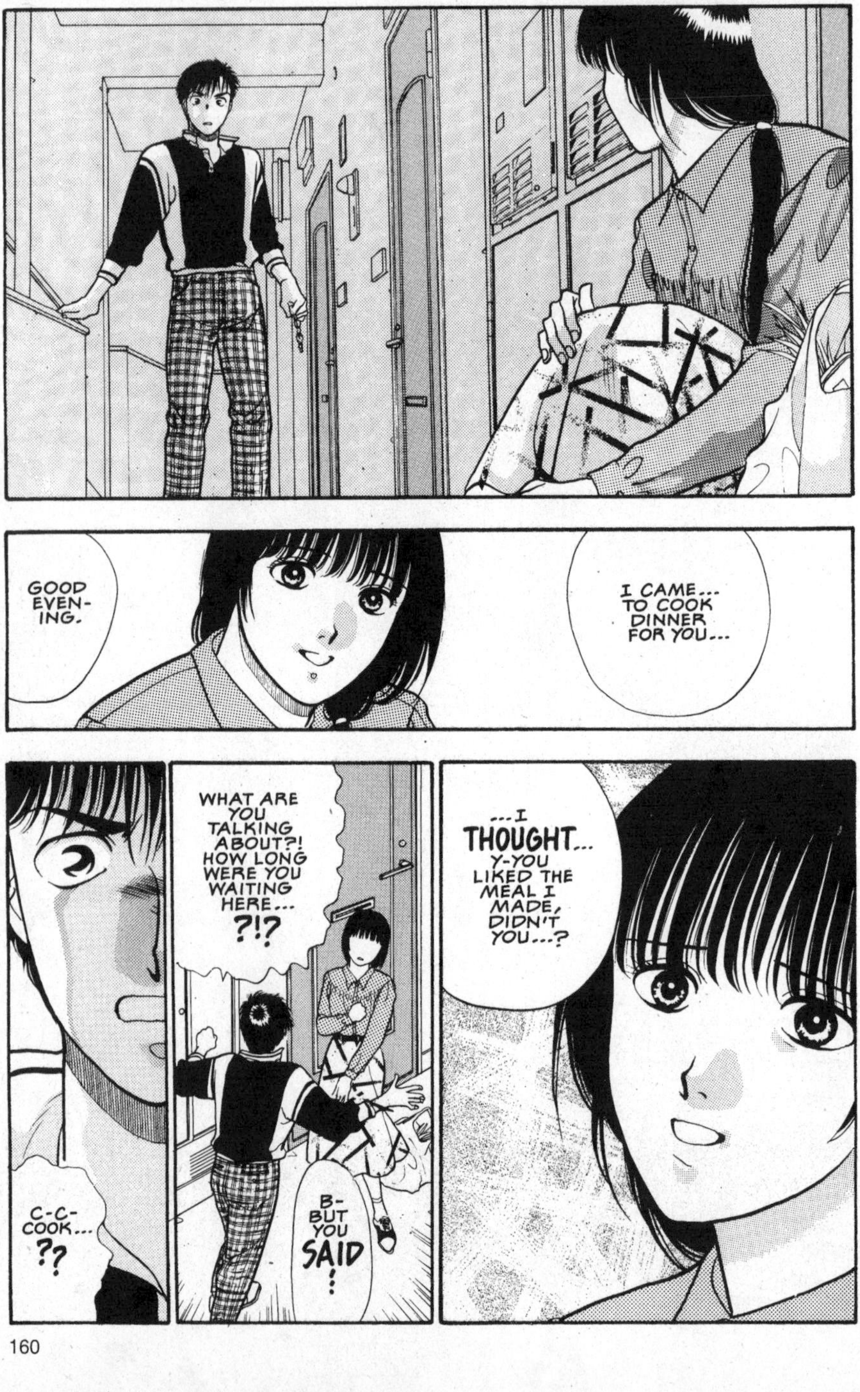
GOOD EVENING.
I CAME... TO COOK DINNER FOR YOU...
C-C-COOK... ??
WHAT ARE YOU TALKING ABOUT?! HOW LONG WERE YOU WAITING HERE... ?!?
B-BUT YOU SAID!
...I THOUGHT... Y-YOU LIKED THE MEAL I MADE, DIDN'T YOU...?

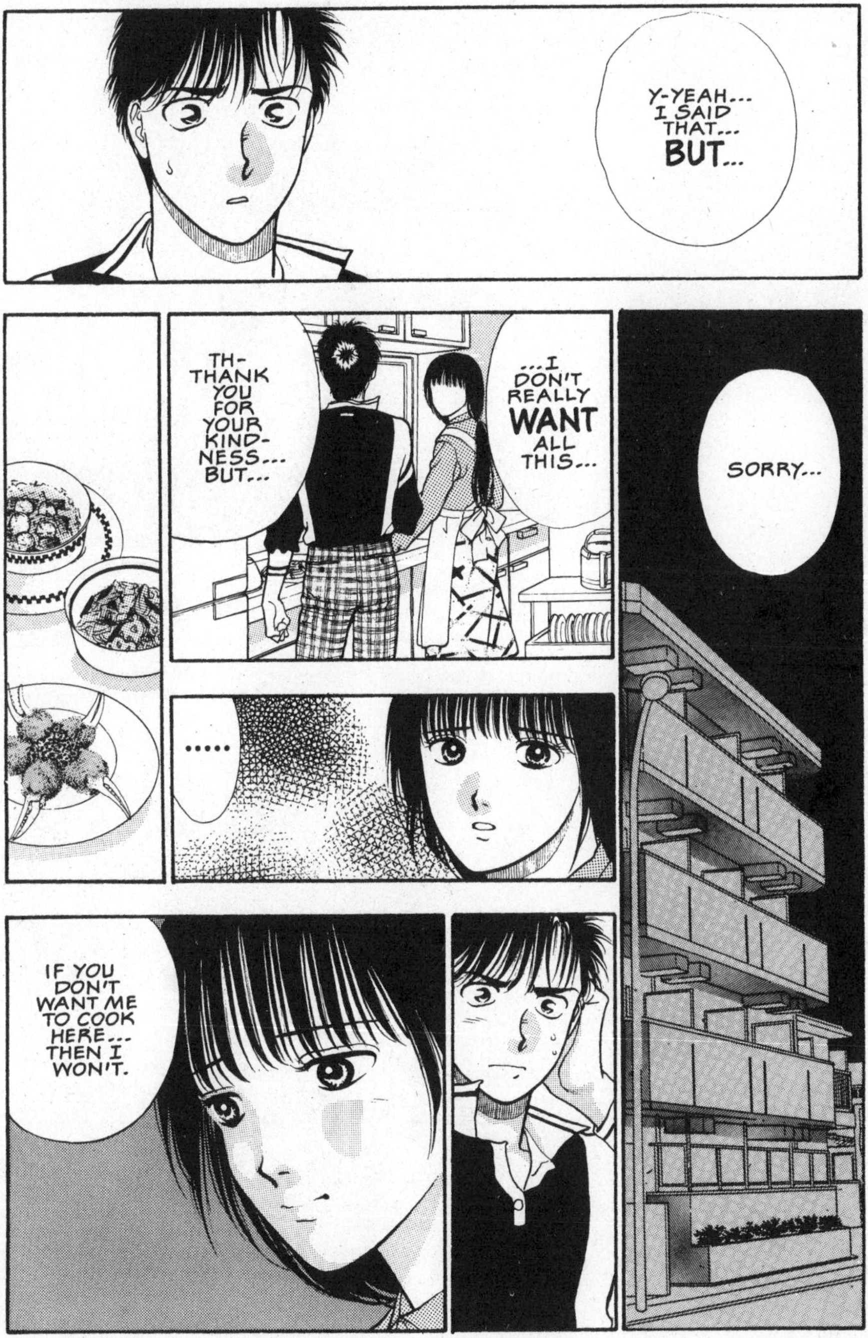
Y-YEAH... I SAID THAT... BUT...
TH- THANK YOU FOR YOUR KIND- NESS... BUT...
...I DON'T REALLY WANT ALL THIS...
.....
IF YOU DON'T WANT ME TO COOK HERE... THEN I WON'T.
SORRY...

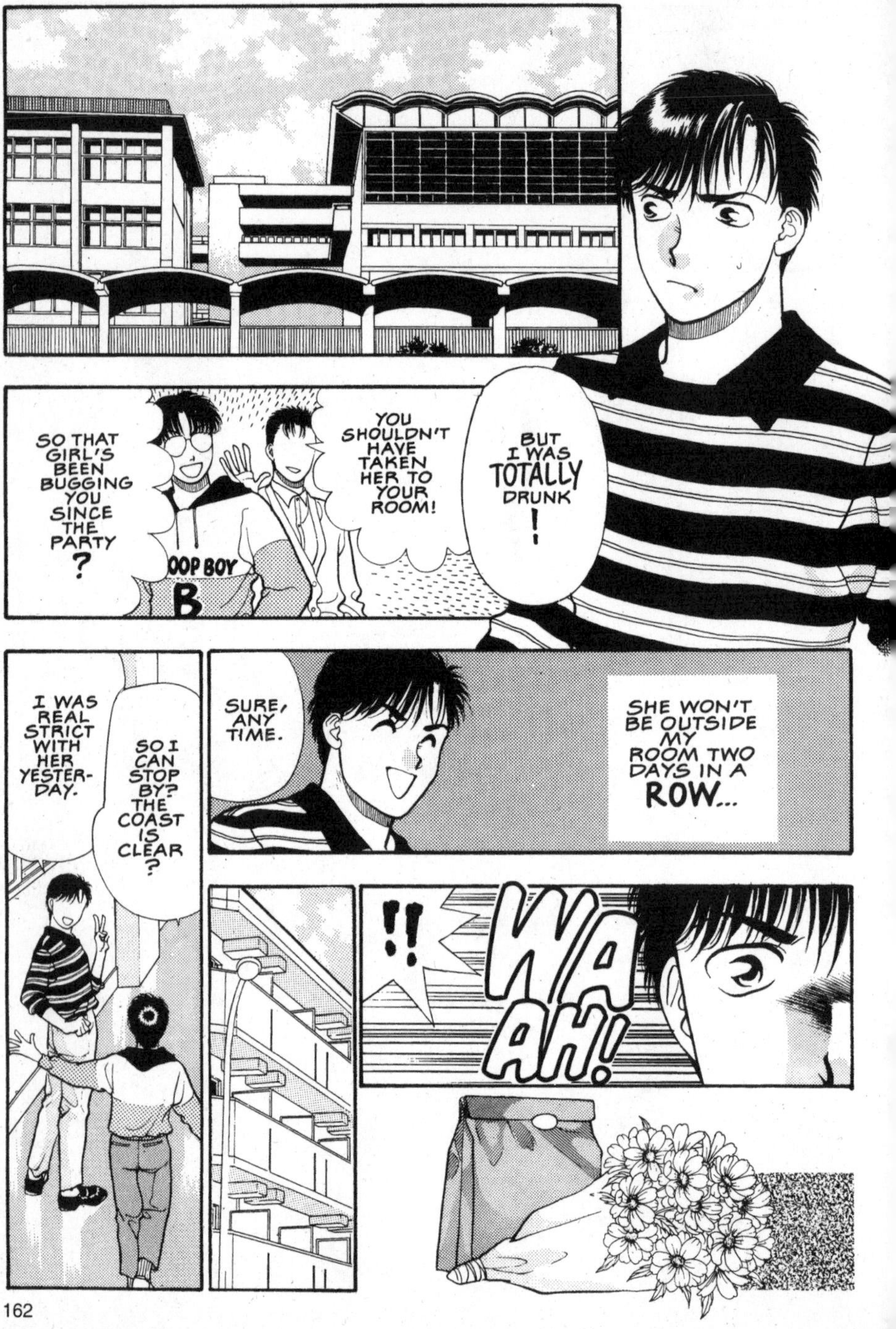

SO THAT GIRL'S BEEN BUGGING YOU SINCE THE PARTY?
OOP BOY
B
YOU SHOULDN'T HAVE TAKEN HER TO YOUR ROOM!
BUT I WAS TOTALLY DRUNK!
I WAS REAL STRICT WITH HER YESTER-DAY.
SO I CAN STOP BY? THE COAST IS CLEAR?
SURE, ANY TIME.
SHE WON'T BE OUTSIDE MY ROOM TWO DAYS IN A ROW...
!!
WAAH!

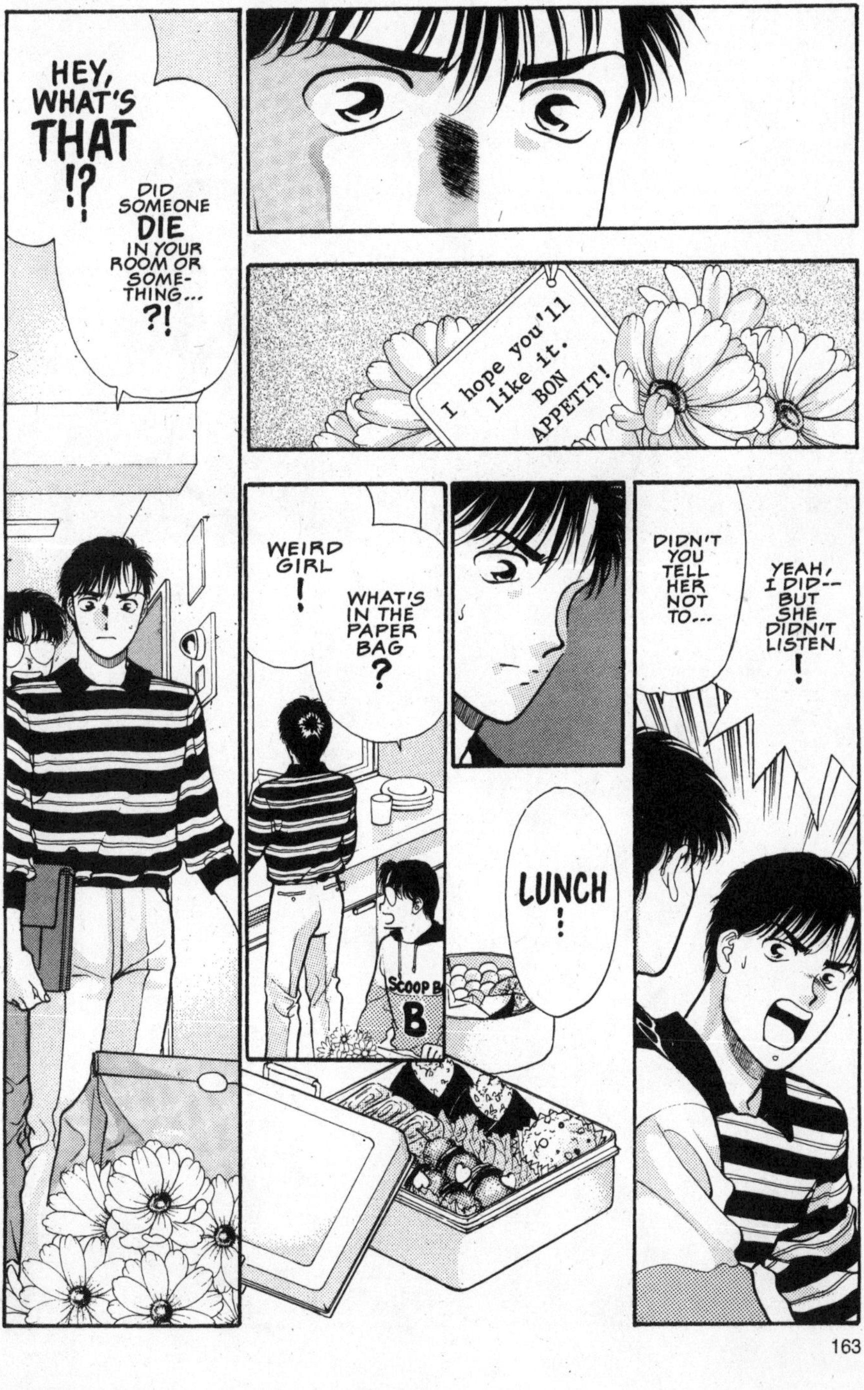
HEY, WHAT'S THAT !?
DID SOMEONE DIE IN YOUR ROOM OR SOME-THING... ?!
I hope you'll like it. BON APPETIT!
WEIRD GIRL !
WHAT'S IN THE PAPER BAG ?
SCOOP B
B
LUNCH !
DIDN'T YOU TELL HER NOT TO...
YEAH, I DID-- BUT SHE DIDN'T LISTEN !

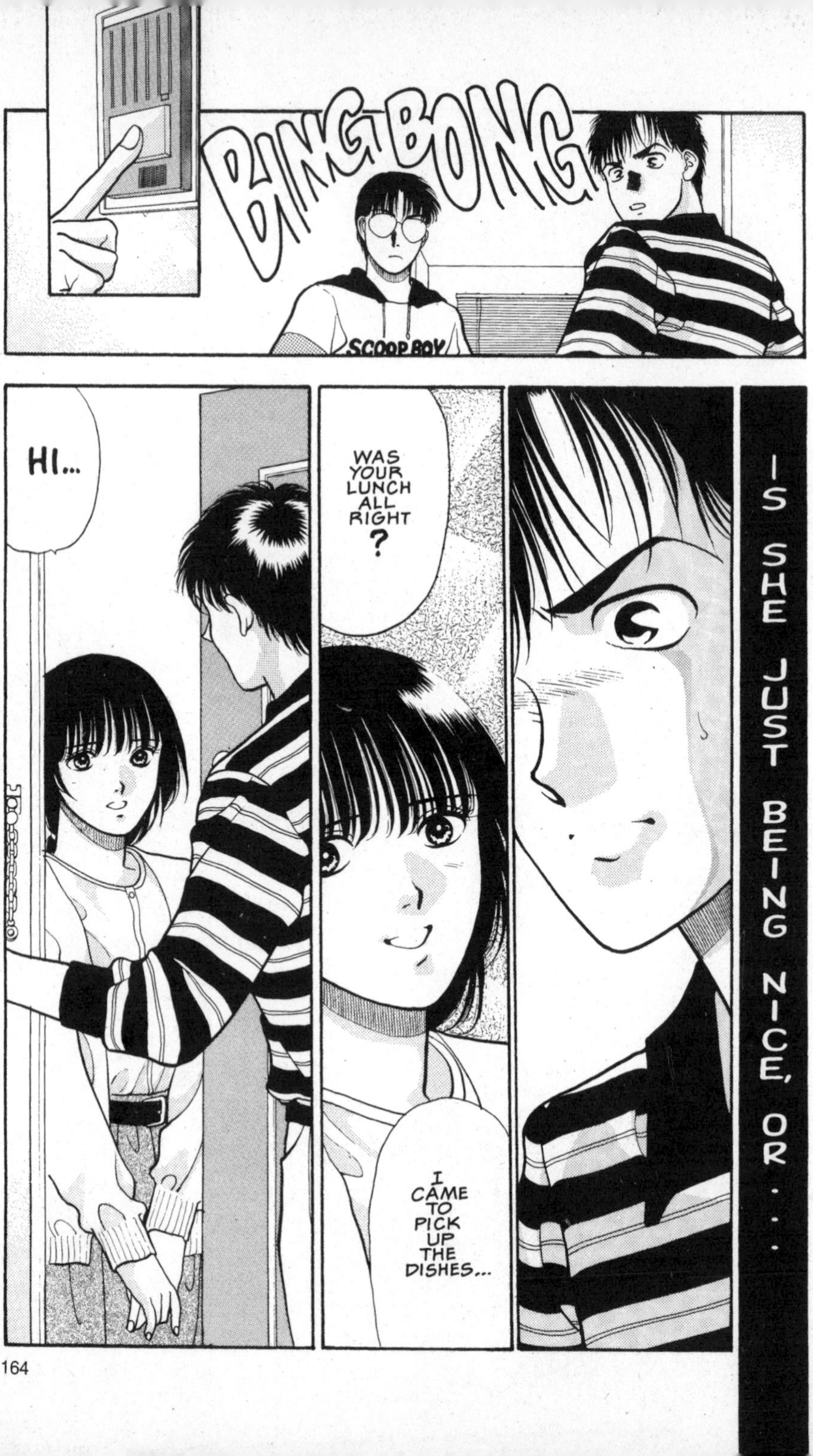
BING BONG
SCOOP BOY
HI...
WAS YOUR LUNCH ALL RIGHT?
I CAME TO PICK UP THE DISHES...
IS SHE JUST BEING NICE, OR . . .

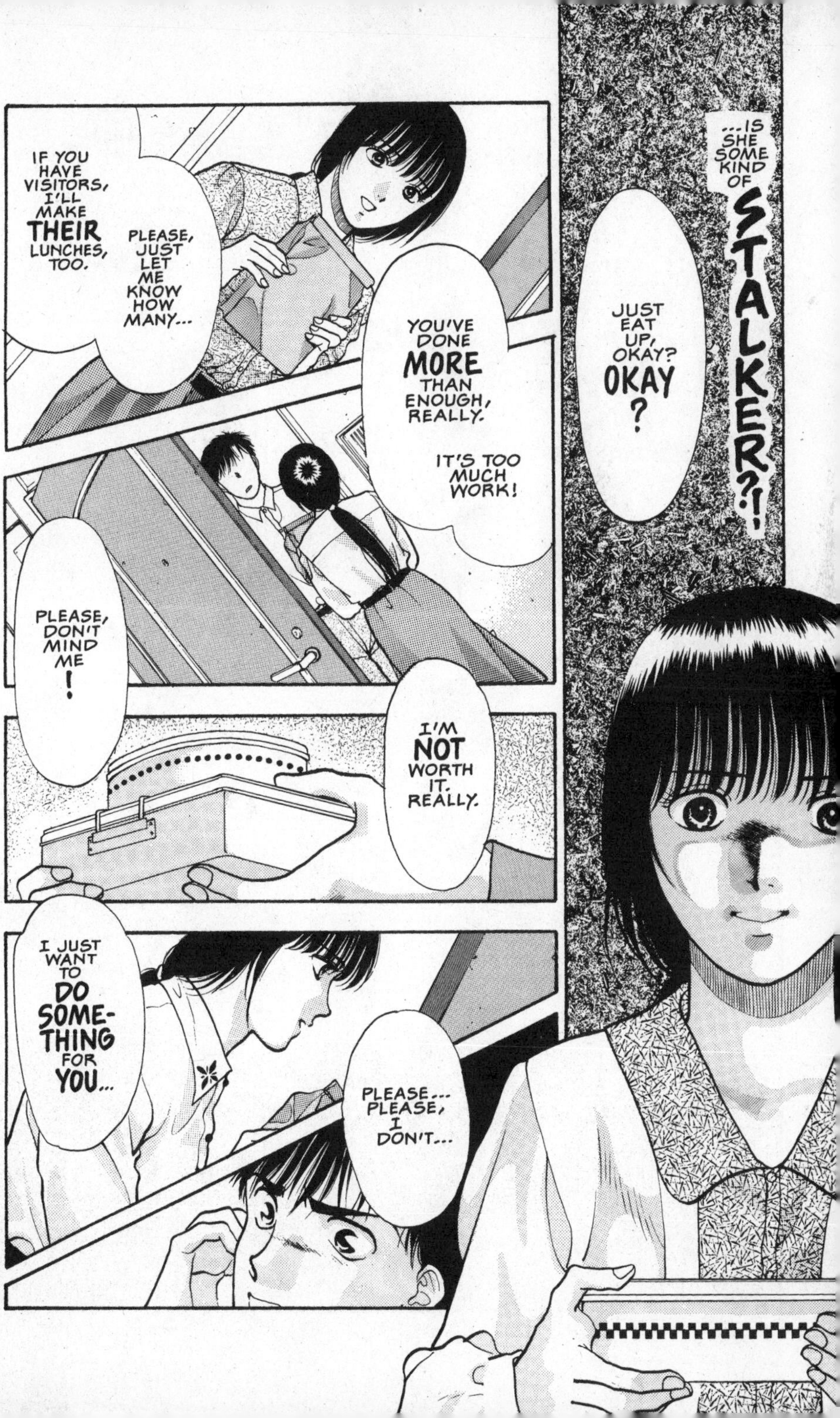
IF YOU HAVE VISITORS, I'LL MAKE THEIR LUNCHES, TOO.
PLEASE, JUST LET ME KNOW HOW MANY...
YOU'VE DONE MORE THAN ENOUGH, REALLY.
IT'S TOO MUCH WORK!
PLEASE, DON'T MIND ME!
I'M NOT WORTH IT. REALLY.
I JUST WANT TO DO SOME-THING FOR YOU...
PLEASE... PLEASE, I DON'T...
JUST EAT UP, OKAY? OKAY?
...IS SHE SOME KIND OF STALKER?!

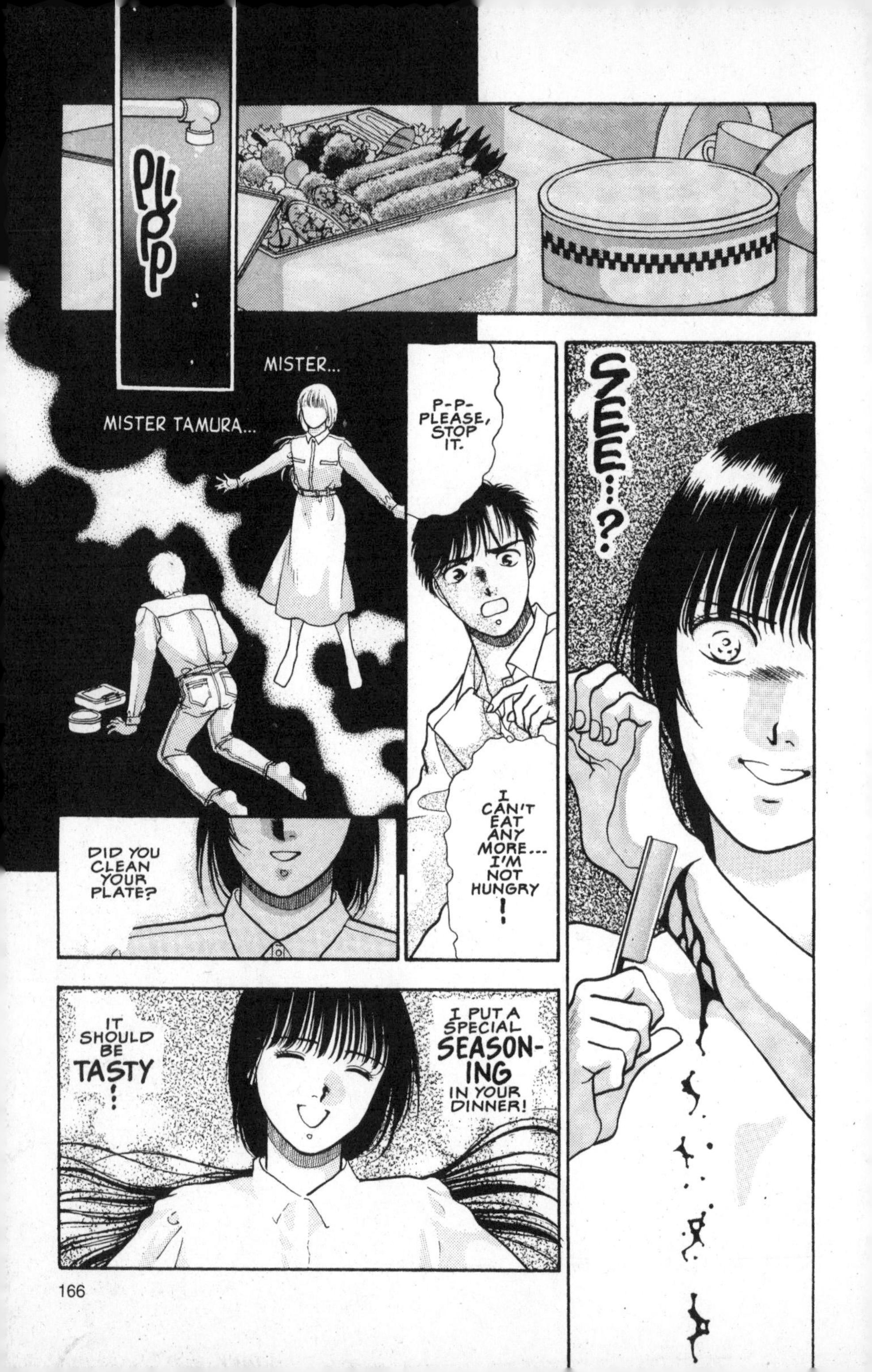
PLIPP
MISTER...
MISTER TAMURA...
P-P-PLEASE, STOP IT.
I CAN'T EAT ANY MORE... I'M NOT HUNGRY!
DID YOU CLEAN YOUR PLATE?
IT SHOULD BE TASTY!!
I PUT A SPECIAL SEASONING IN YOUR DINNER!
SEE...?

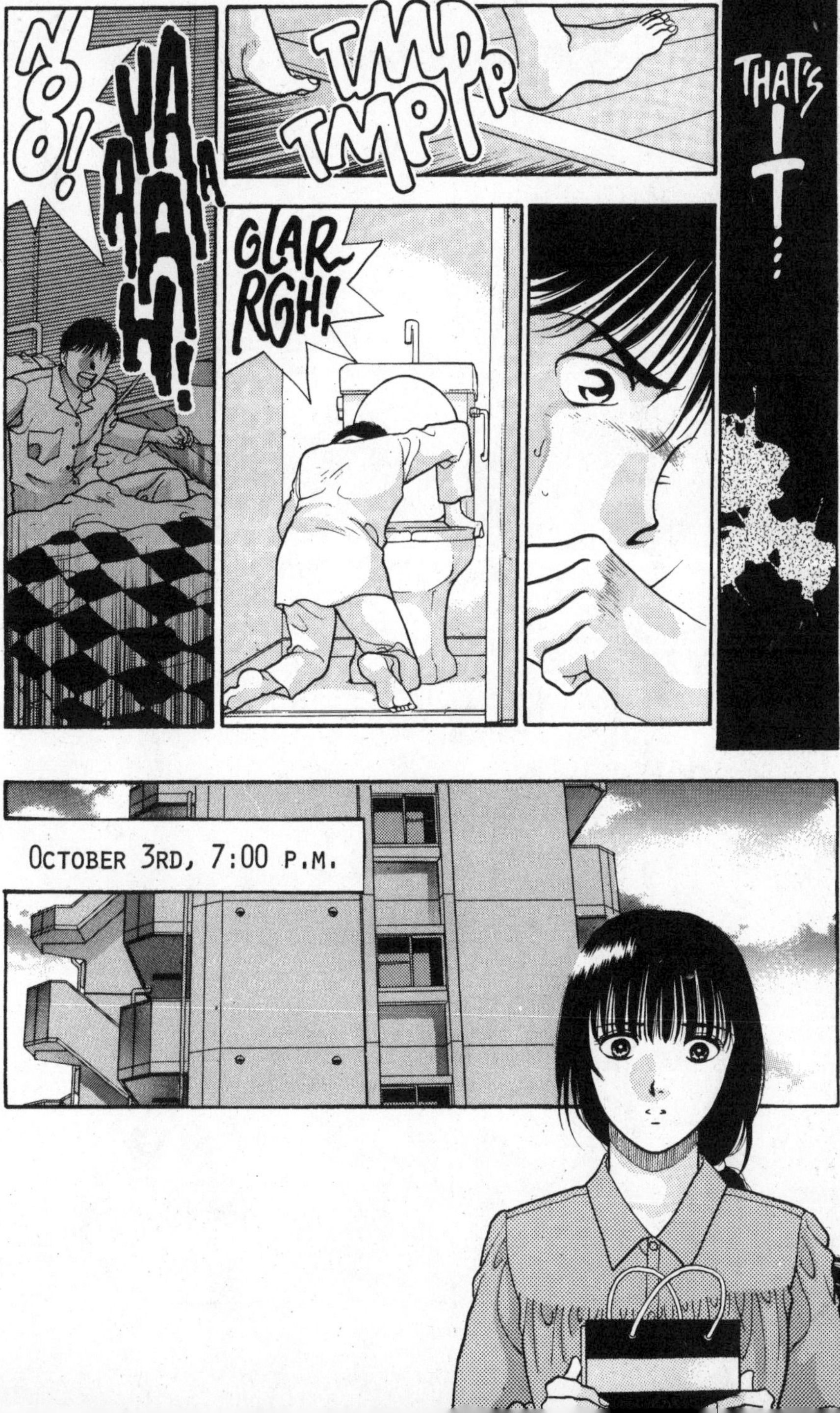
NOOO!
YAAAAAH!!
TMP TMP TMPP
GLAR-RGH!
THAT'S IT!...
OCTOBER 3RD, 7:00 P.M.

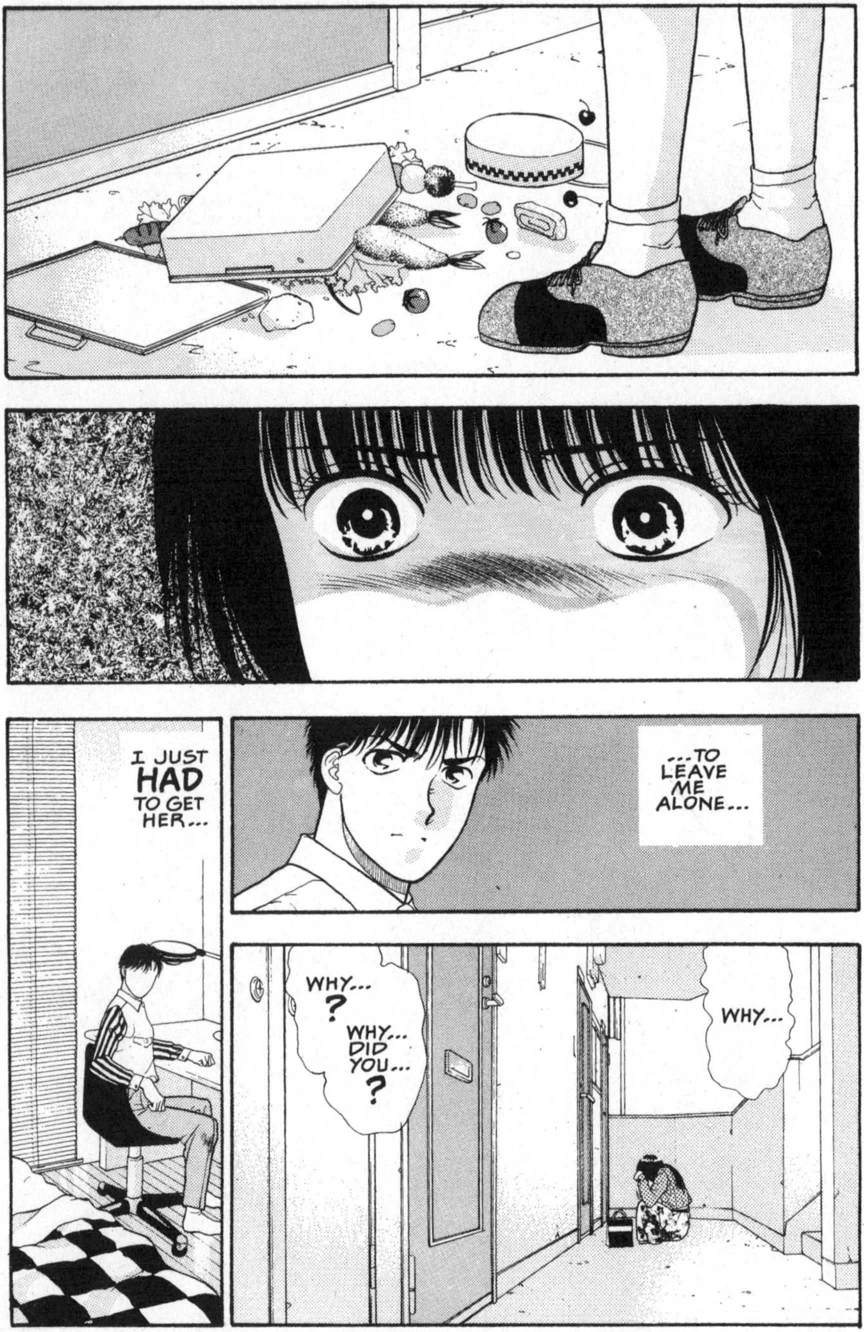
I JUST HAD TO GET HER...
...TO LEAVE ME ALONE...
WHY...?
WHY... DID YOU...?
WHY...

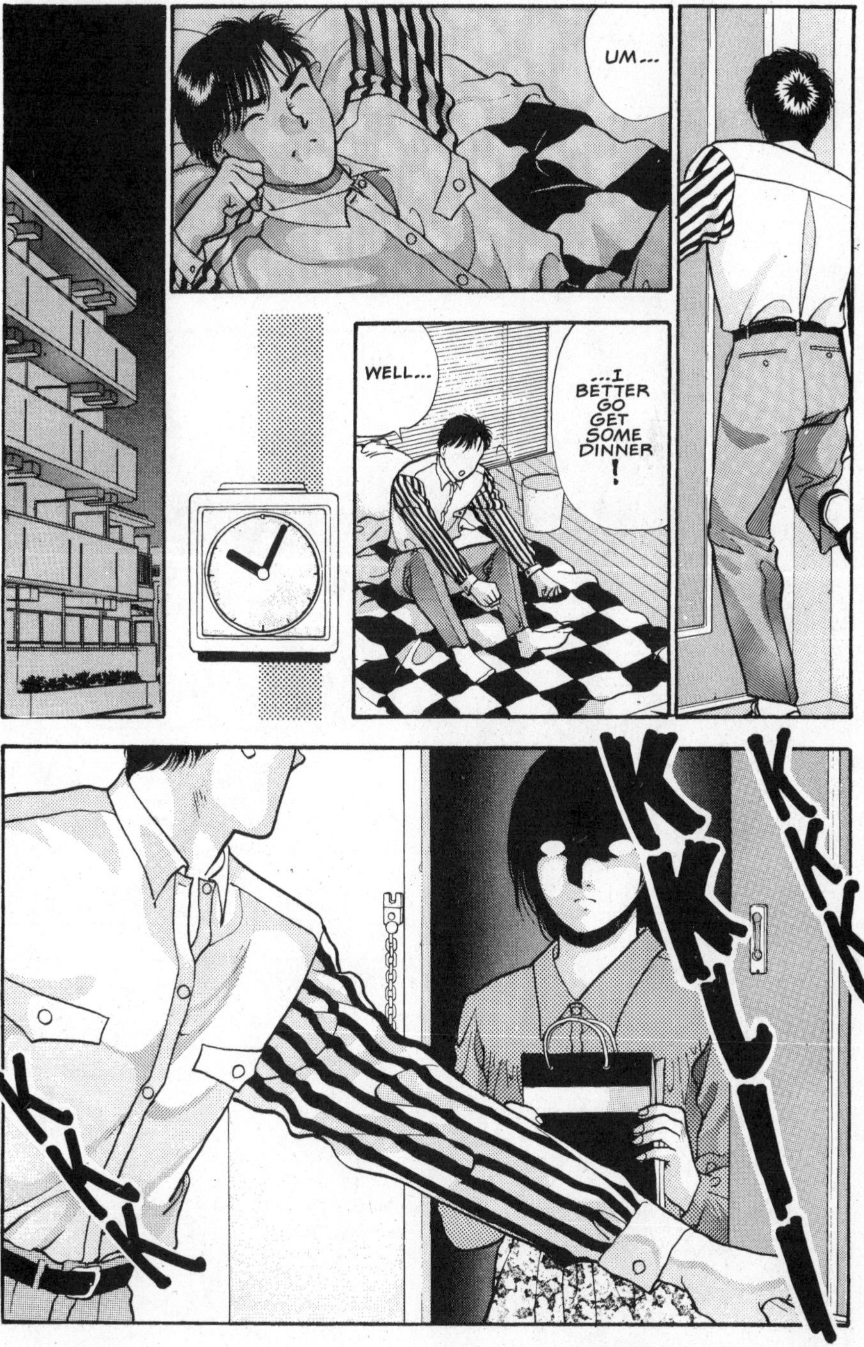
UM...
WELL...
...I BETTER GO GET SOME DINNER!
KKK
KKKK
KKKK

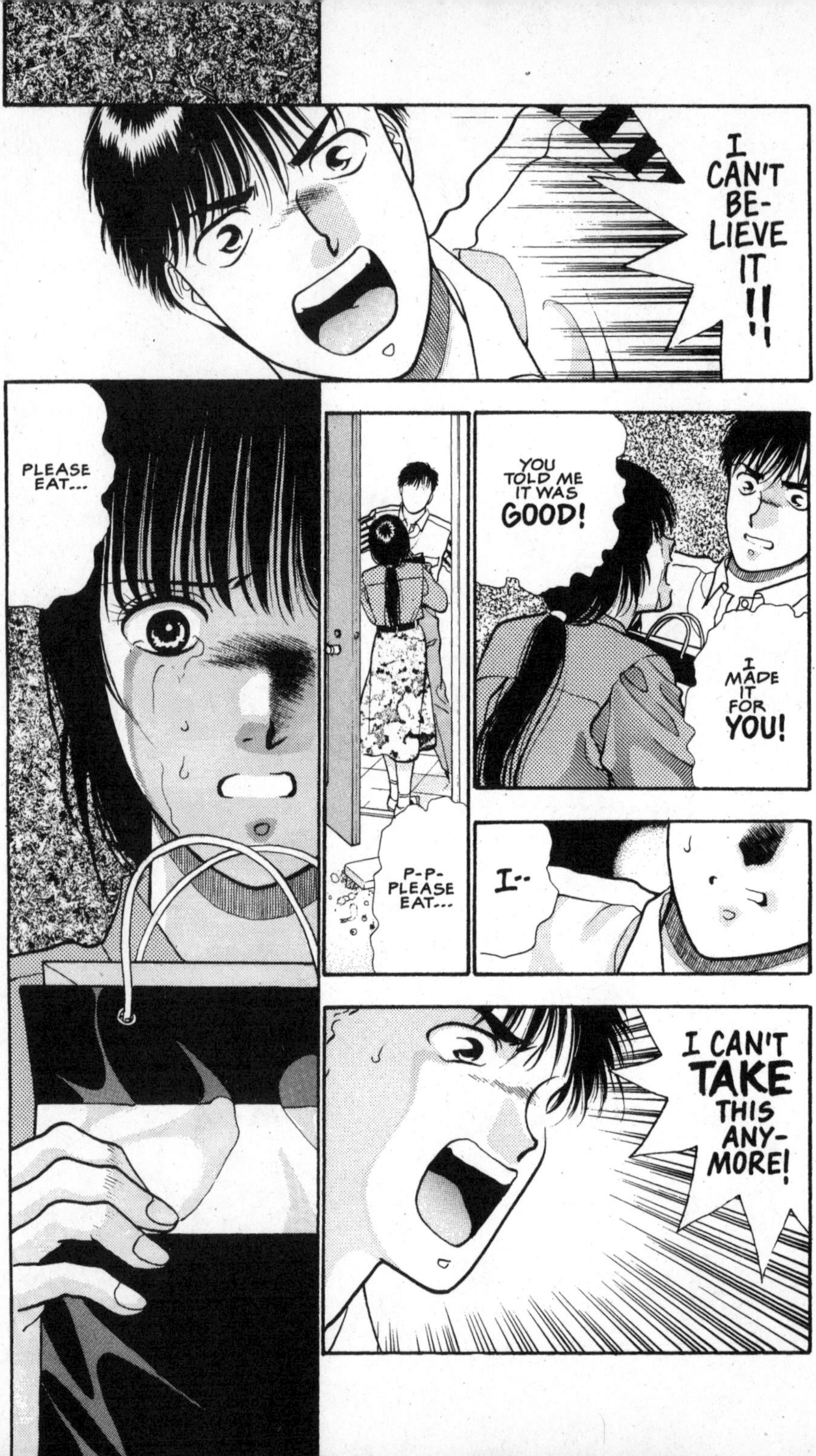
I CAN'T BE-LIEVE IT!!
PLEASE EAT...
P-P-PLEASE EAT...
YOU TOLD ME IT WAS GOOD!
I MADE IT FOR YOU!
I--
I CAN'T TAKE THIS ANYMORE!

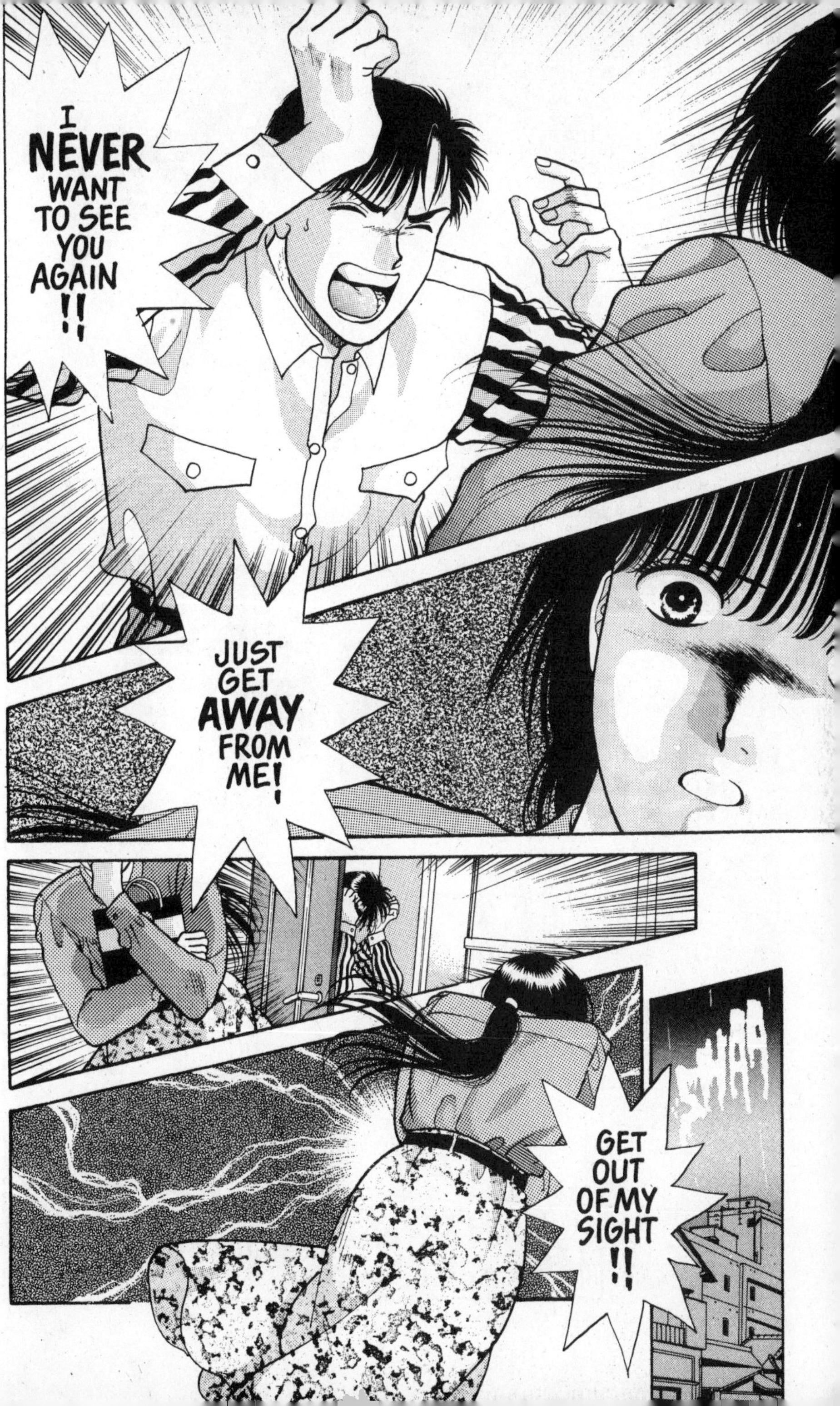
I NEVER WANT TO SEE YOU AGAIN!!
JUST GET AWAY FROM ME!
GET OUT OF MY SIGHT!!

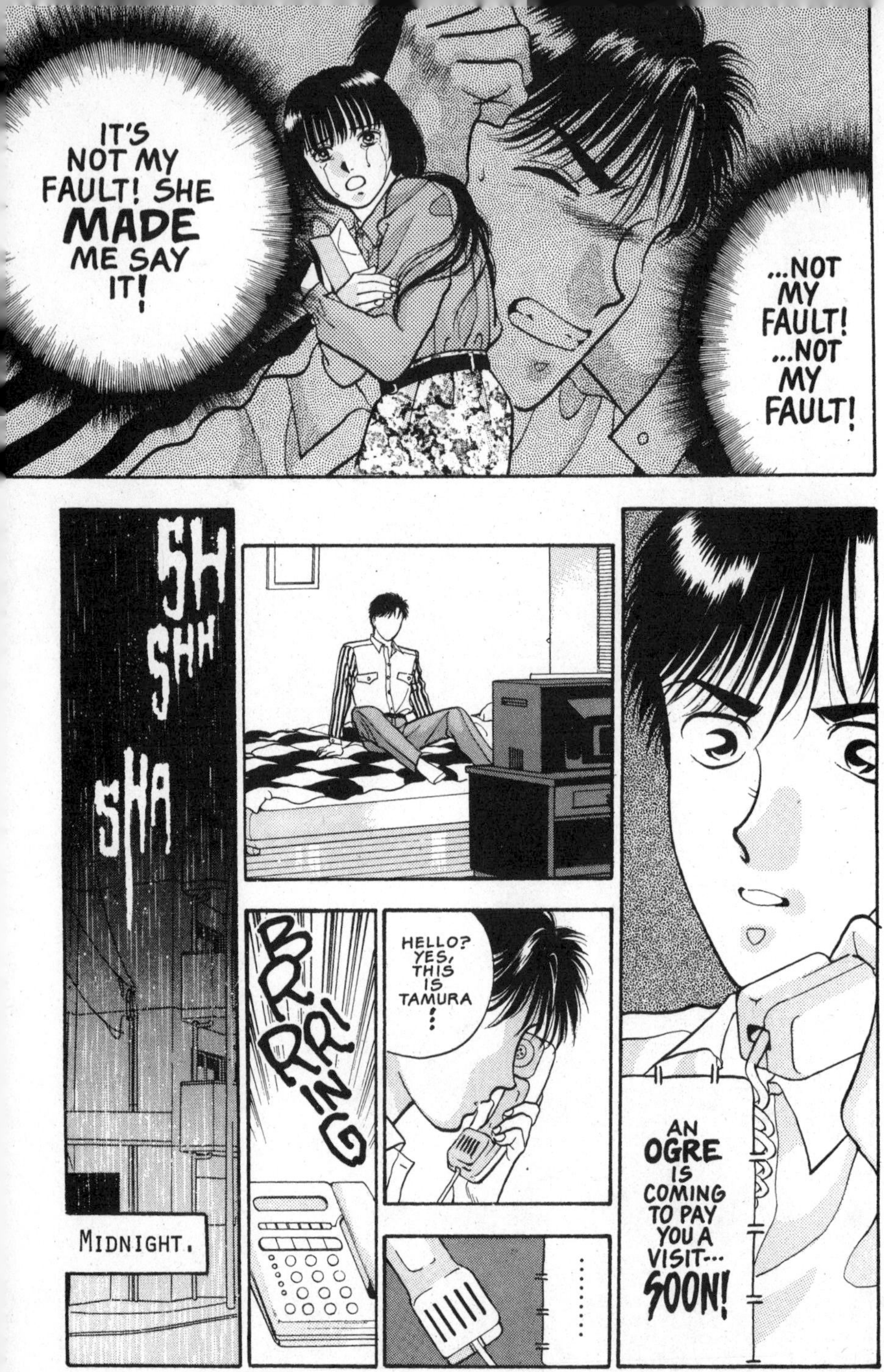
IT'S NOT MY FAULT! SHE **MADE** ME SAY IT!
...NOT MY FAULT! ...NOT MY FAULT!
SH SHH SHA
MIDNIGHT.
BRRRIING
HELLO? YES, THIS IS TAMURA...
......
AN **OGRE** IS COMING TO PAY YOU A VISIT... **SOON!**

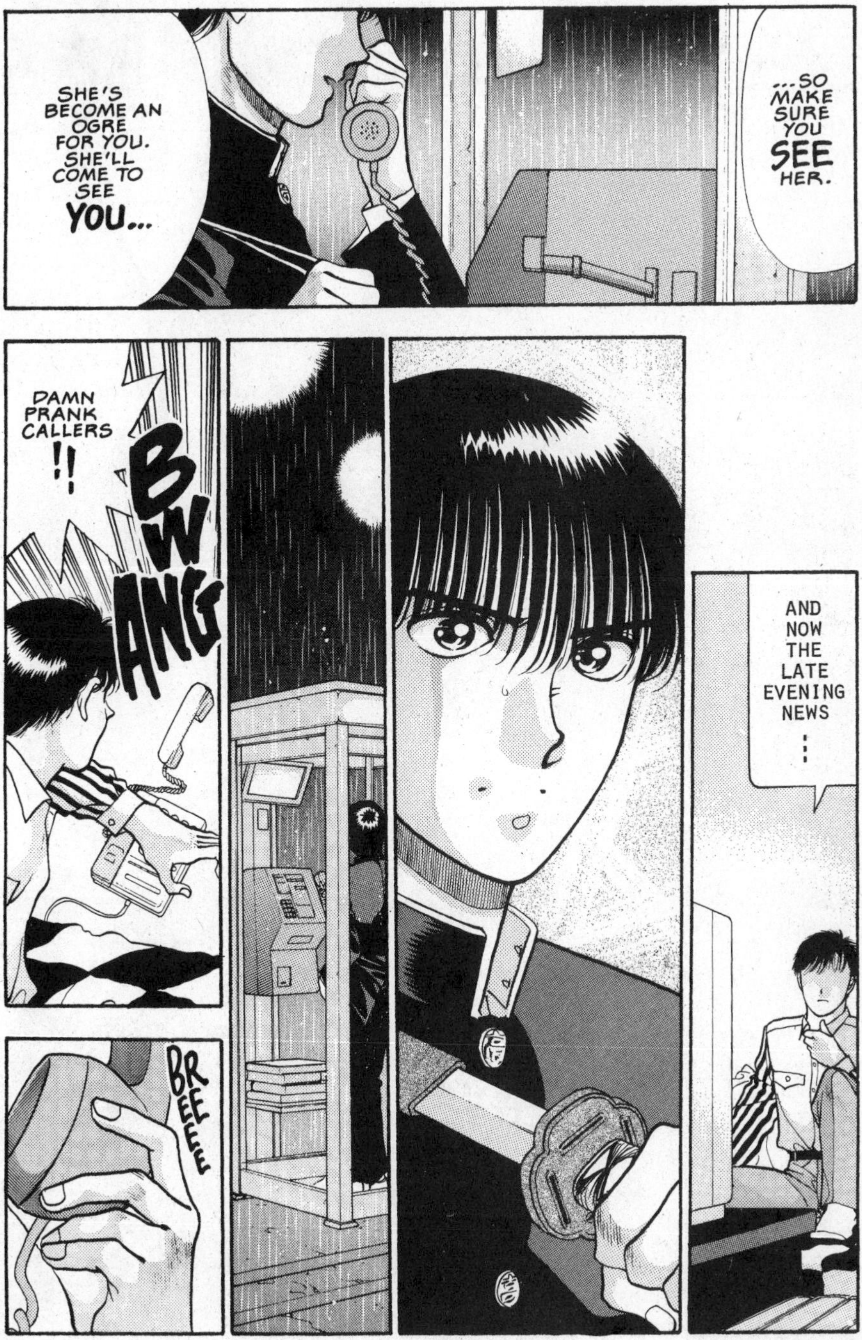
SHE'S BECOME AN OGRE FOR YOU. SHE'LL COME TO SEE YOU...
...SO MAKE SURE YOU SEE HER.
DAMN PRANK CALLERS!!
BWANG
BREEEE
AND NOW THE LATE EVENING NEWS ...

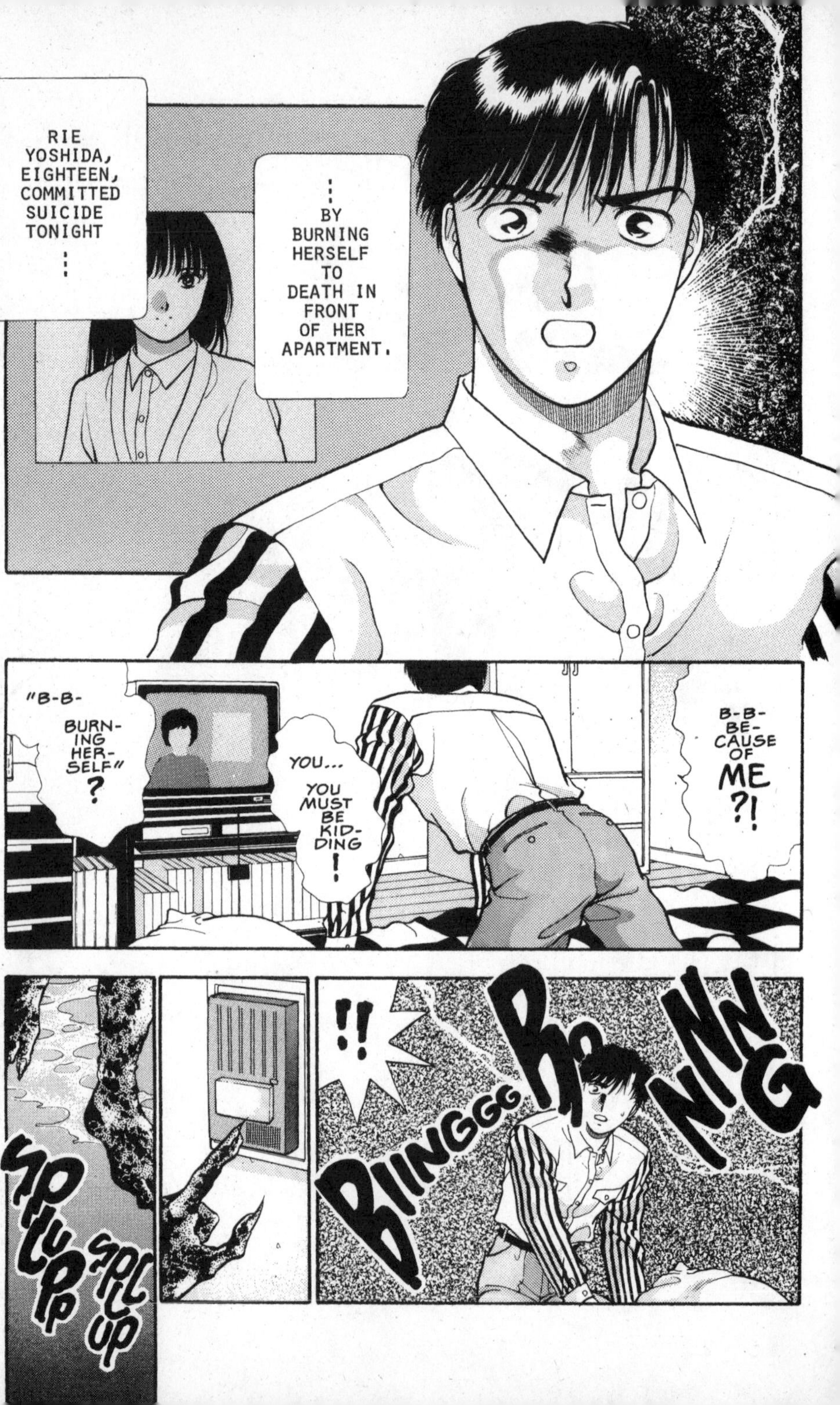
RIE YOSHIDA, EIGHTEEN, COMMITTED SUICIDE TONIGHT ...
... BY BURNING HERSELF TO DEATH IN FRONT OF HER APARTMENT.
"B-B-BURNING HERSELF"?
YOU... YOU MUST BE KIDDING!
B-B-BE-CAUSE OF ME?!
SPLUPP
SPLUP
!!
BIINGGG
RRNNNG

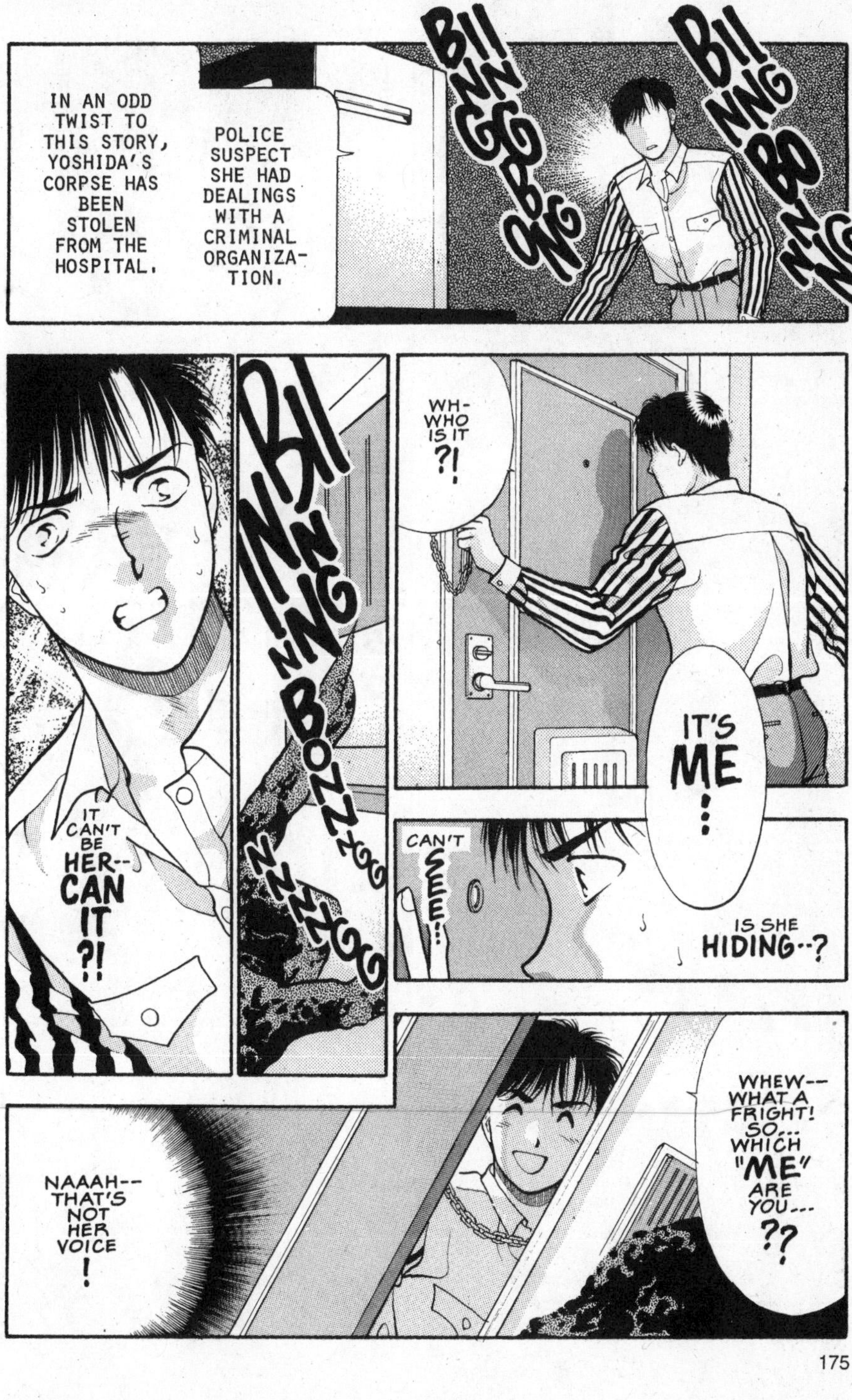

IN AN ODD TWIST TO THIS STORY, YOSHIDA'S CORPSE HAS BEEN STOLEN FROM THE HOSPITAL.
POLICE SUSPECT SHE HAD DEALINGS WITH A CRIMINAL ORGANIZA-TION.
BIINNGG BOONG
BIINNG BONNNG
IT CAN'T BE HER--CAN IT ?!
BIINNNNG BONZZOO
WH-WHO IS IT ?!
IT'S ME !!
CAN'T SEE!!
IS SHE HIDING--?
NAAAH--THAT'S NOT HER VOICE !
WHEW--WHAT A FRIGHT! SO... WHICH "ME" ARE YOU...??

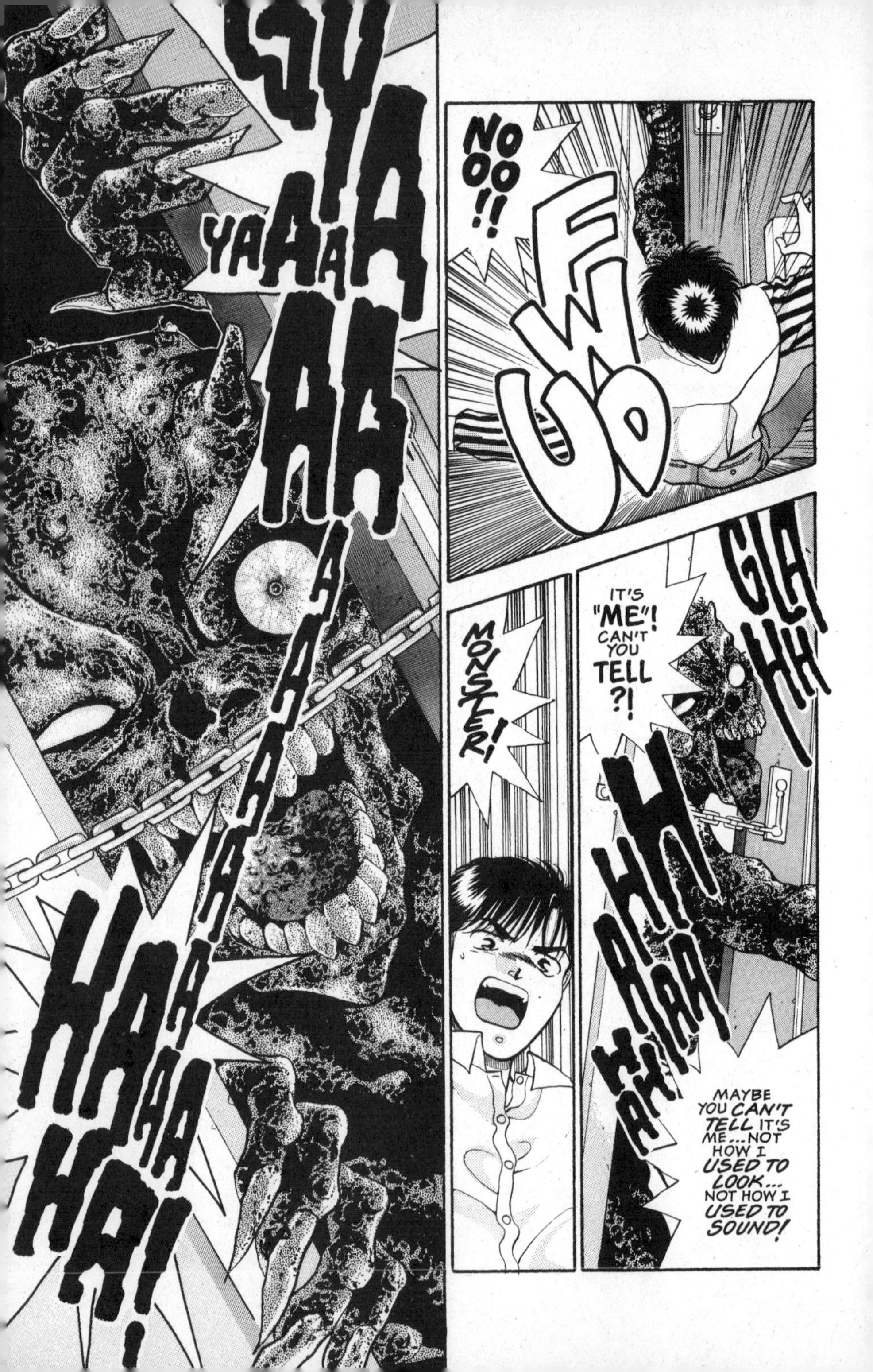

GUYAAAAA
YAAAA
HAAAAHA!
NOOOO!!
FWUD
MONSTER!
IT'S "ME"! CAN'T YOU TELL?!
GIAHH
AHHHHA
MAYBE YOU CAN'T TELL IT'S ME... NOT HOW I USED TO LOOK... NOT HOW I USED TO SOUND!

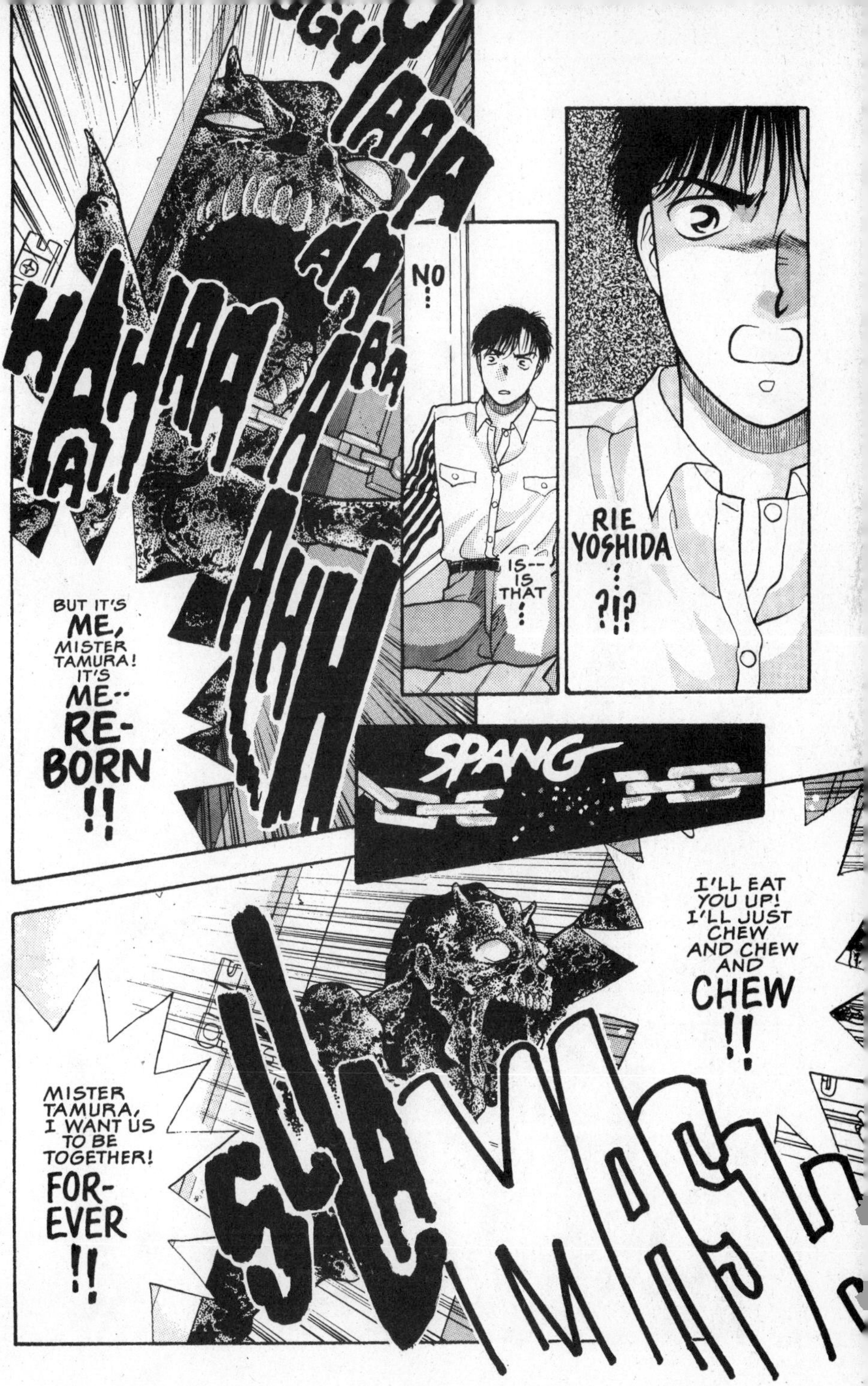
BUT IT'S ME, MISTER TAMURA! IT'S ME-- REBORN!!
NO...
IS-- IS THAT...
RIE YOSHIDA...?!?
SPANG
MISTER TAMURA, I WANT US TO BE TOGETHER! FOREVER!!
I'LL EAT YOU UP! I'LL JUST CHEW AND CHEW AND CHEW!!

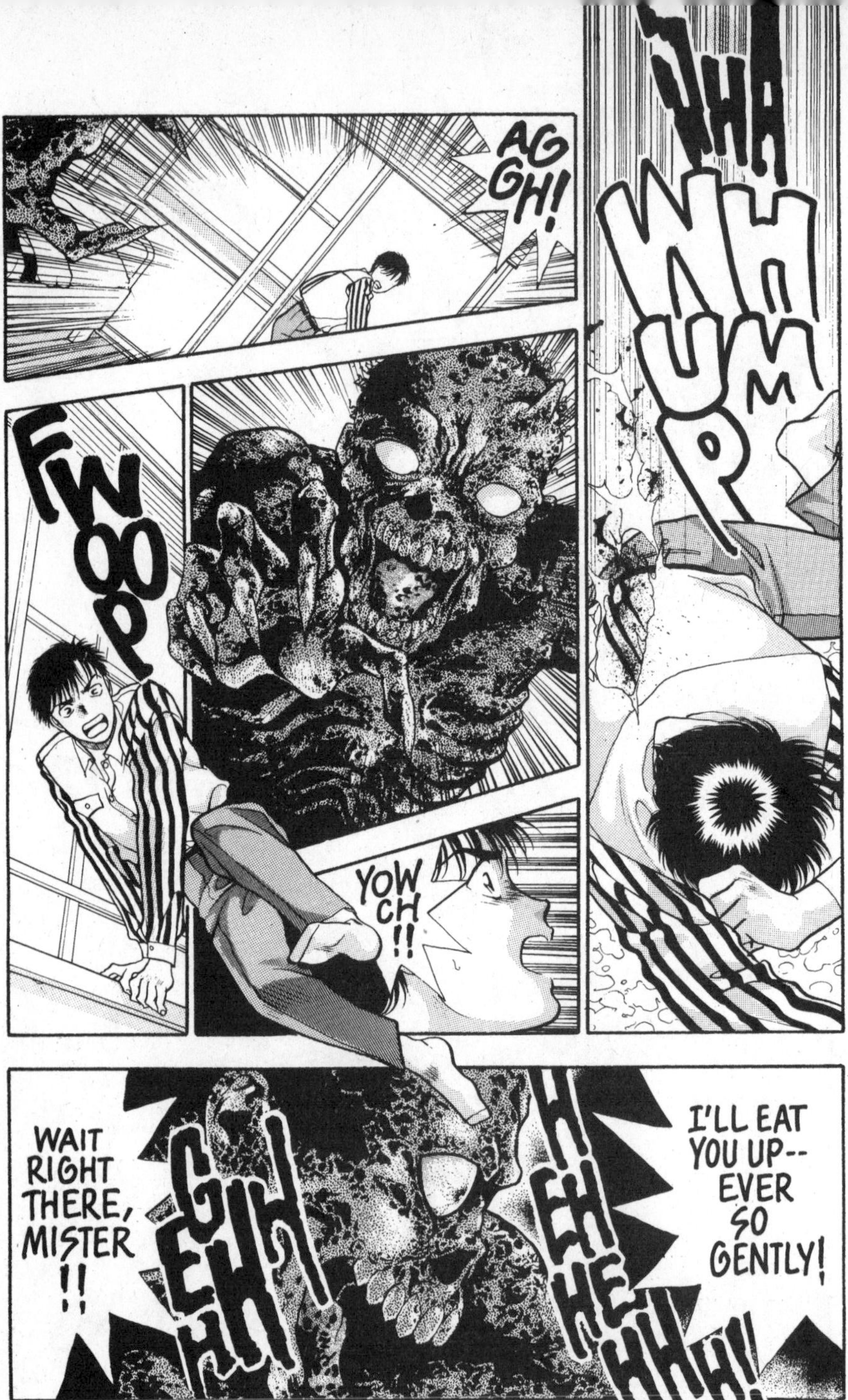
AGGH!
FWOOP!
YOWCH!!
WAIT RIGHT THERE, MISTER!!
I'LL EAT YOU UP-- EVER SO GENTLY!

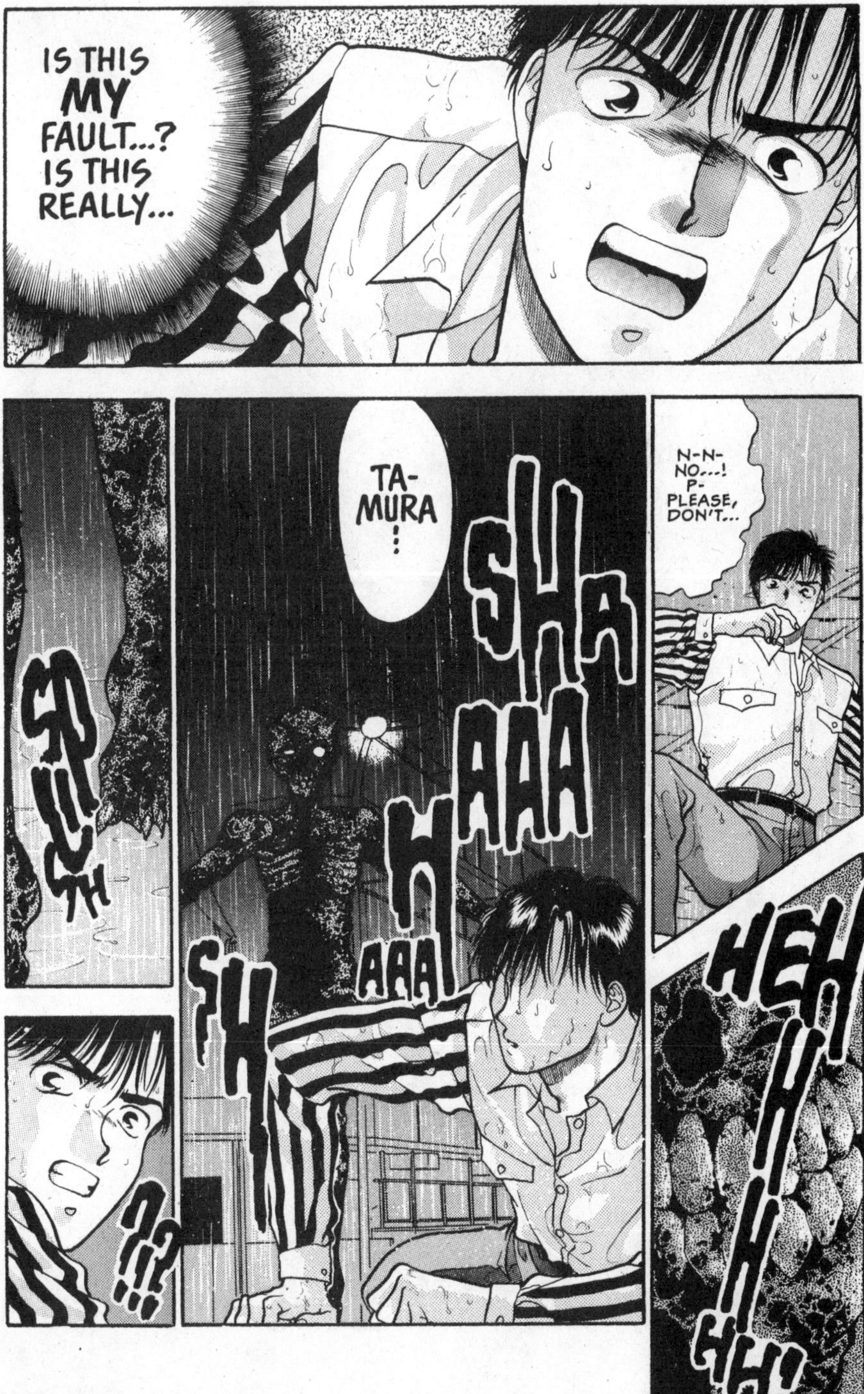
IS THIS MY FAULT...? IS THIS REALLY...
SPLUSH
?!!?
TA-MURA...!
SHAHAAAA
SHAAA
N-N-NO...! P-PLEASE, DON'T...
HEHHHHHGH!

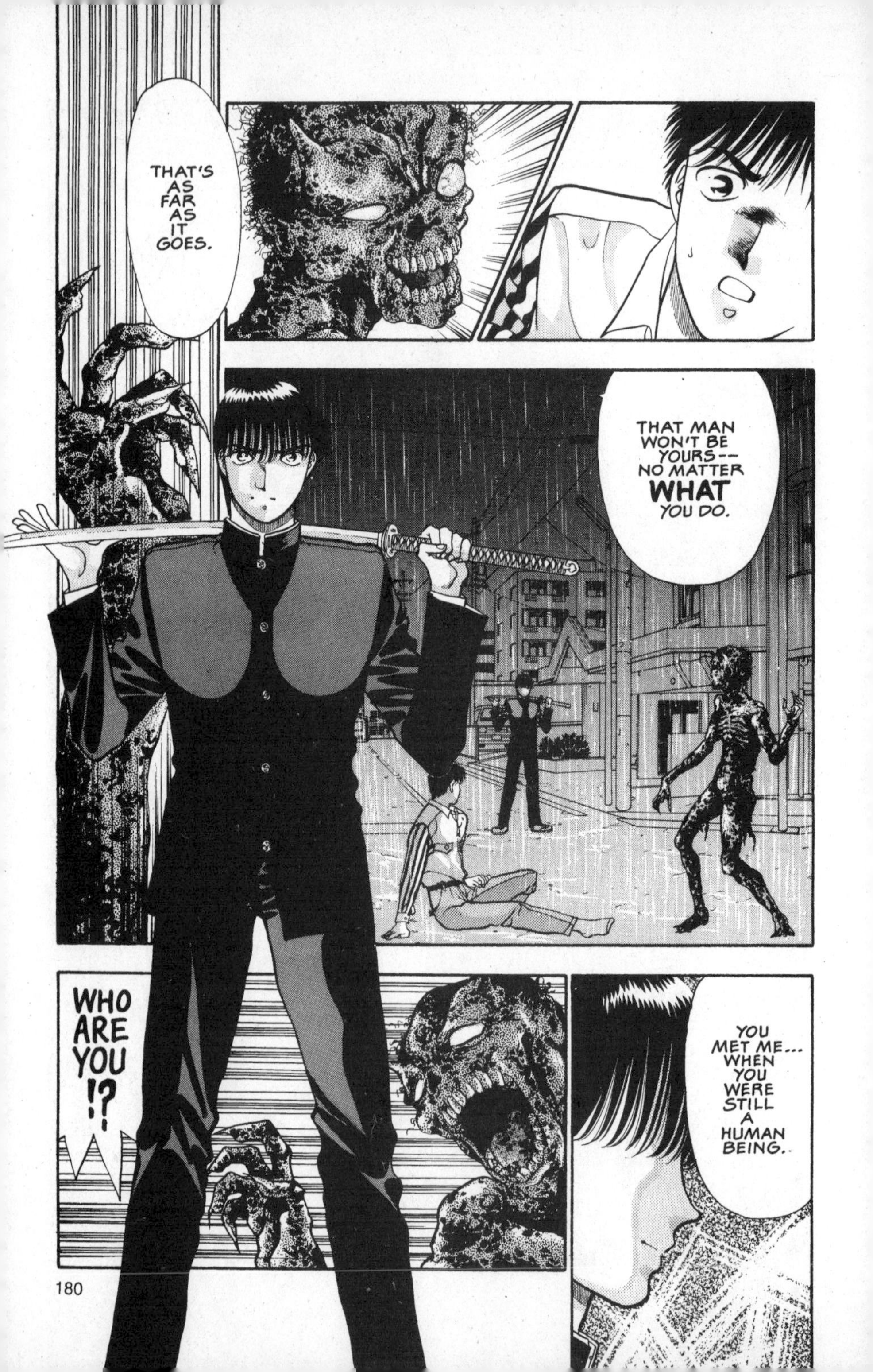
THAT'S AS FAR AS IT GOES.
THAT MAN WON'T BE YOURS-- NO MATTER WHAT YOU DO.
WHO ARE YOU !?
YOU MET ME... WHEN YOU WERE STILL A HUMAN BEING.

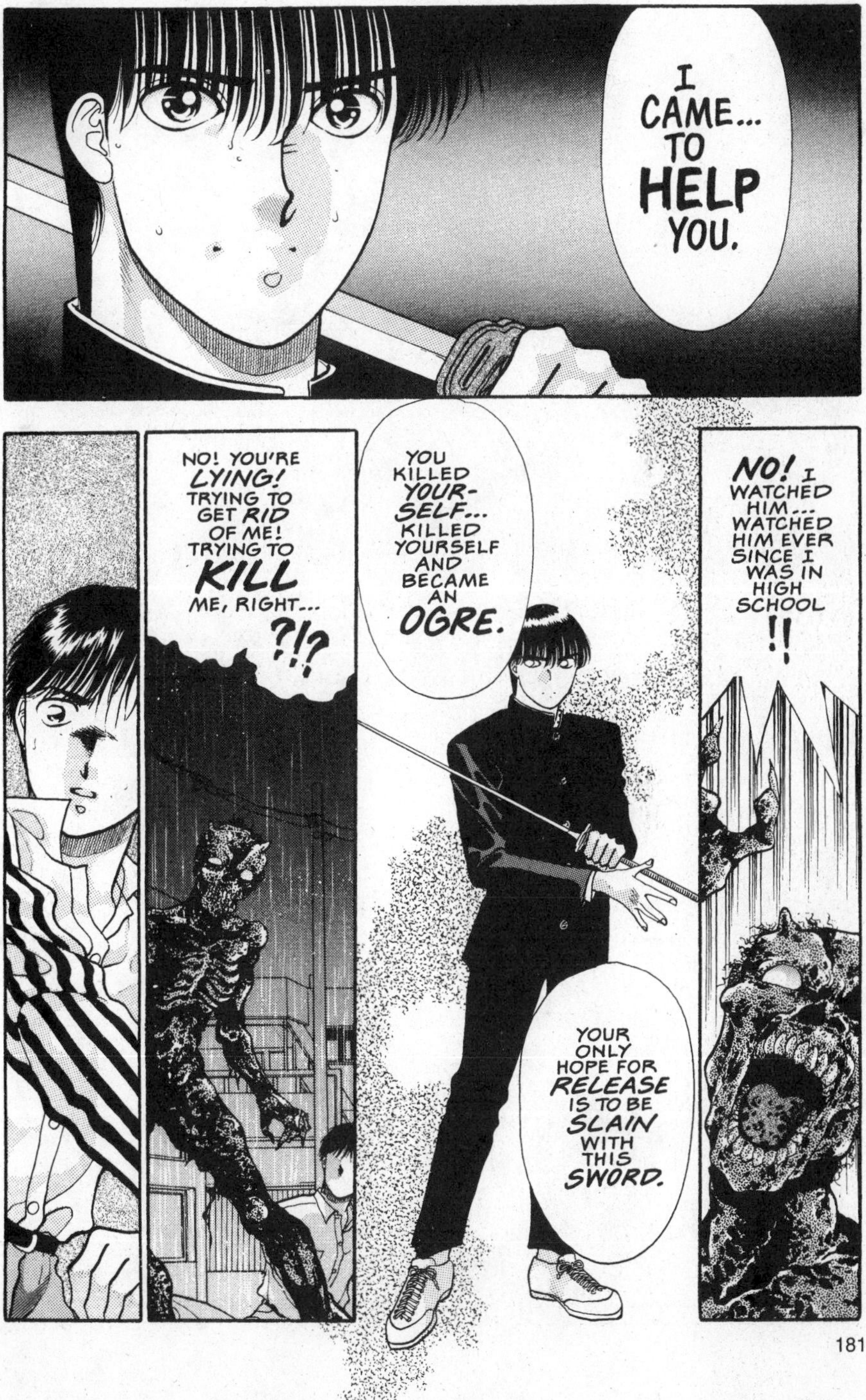
I CAME... TO HELP YOU.
NO! YOU'RE LYING! TRYING TO GET RID OF ME! TRYING TO KILL ME, RIGHT... ?!?
YOU KILLED YOURSELF... KILLED YOURSELF AND BECAME AN OGRE.
YOUR ONLY HOPE FOR RELEASE IS TO BE SLAIN WITH THIS SWORD.
NO! I WATCHED HIM... WATCHED HIM EVER SINCE I WAS IN HIGH SCHOOL !!

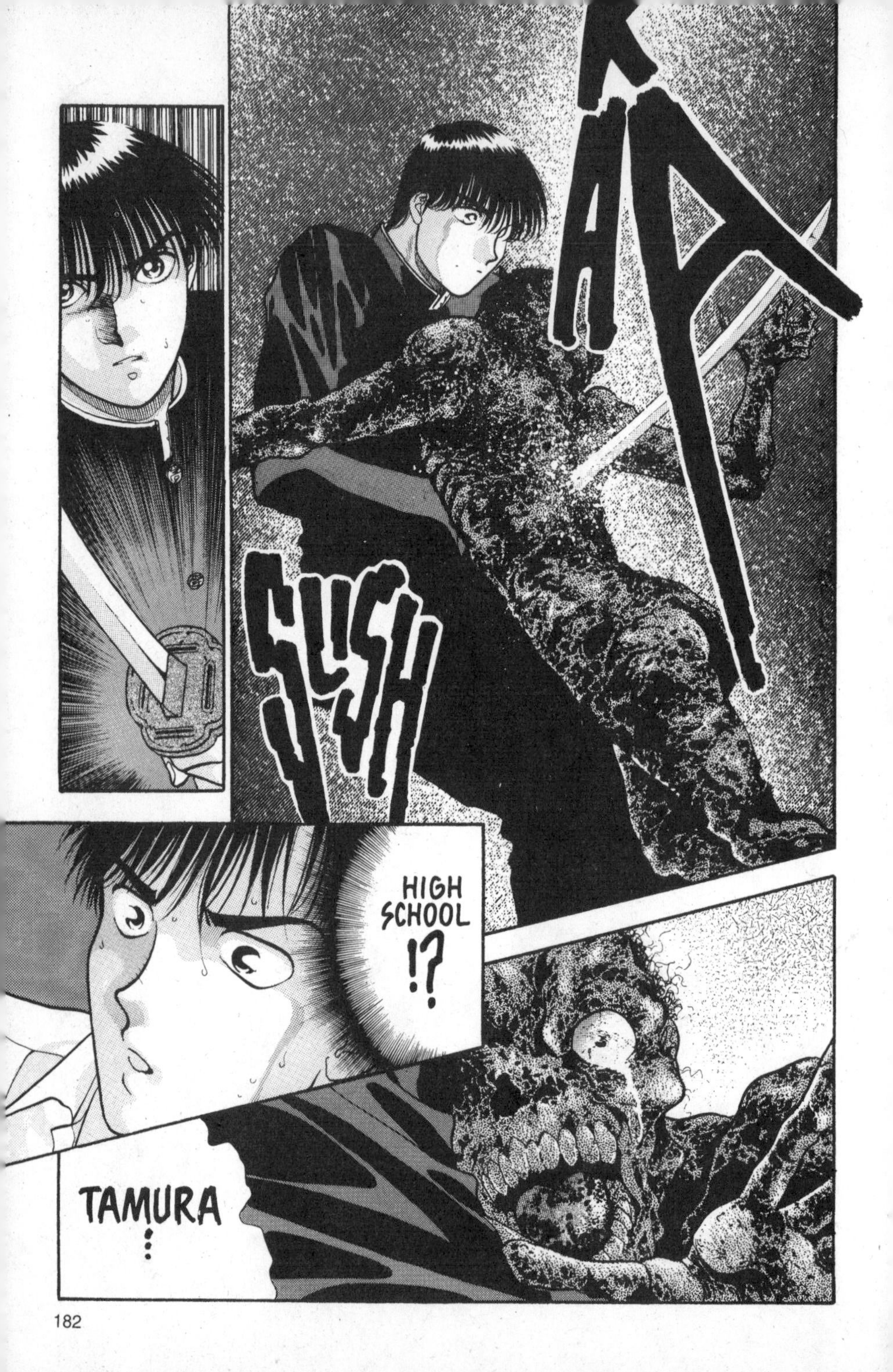
SLUSH
HIGH SCHOOL !?
TAMURA
...

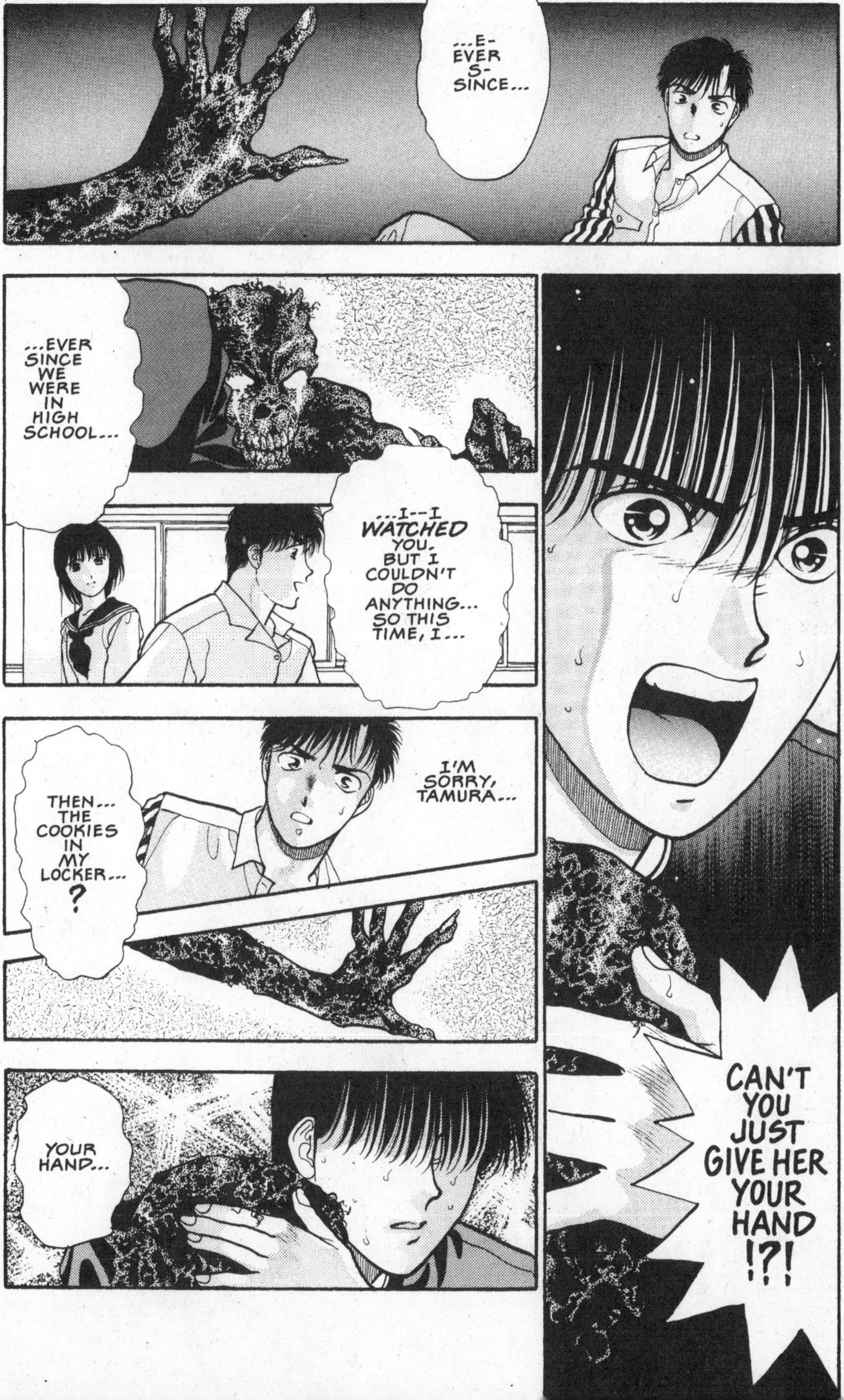
...E- EVER S- SINCE...
...EVER SINCE WE WERE IN HIGH SCHOOL...
...I--I WATCHED YOU. BUT I COULDN'T DO ANYTHING... SO THIS TIME, I...
THEN... THE COOKIES IN MY LOCKER...?
I'M SORRY, TAMURA...
YOUR HAND...
CAN'T YOU JUST GIVE HER YOUR HAND!?!

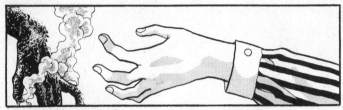

I
JUST
WANTED
TO
BE
CLOSE
TO
YOU...

SHE DIDN'T HAVE TO BECOME AN OGRE...

SHE DIDN'T HAVE TO...

SHHH AAH HH

SHHH HH

HOW?

HOW CAN THIS BE?

THIS... IS HOW A WOMAN BECOMES AN OGRE.

The End.